SINGULAR CONTINUITIES

SINGULAR CONTINUITIES

Tradition, Nostalgia, and Identity
in Modern British Culture

EDITED BY GEORGE K. BEHLMER
AND FRED M. LEVENTHAL

STANFORD UNIVERSITY PRESS

Stanford, California 2000

Stanford University Press
Stanford, California
©2000 by the Board of Trustees of the
Leland Stanford Junior University
Printed in the United States of America

Library of Congress Cataloging-in-Publication Data

Singular continuities : tradition, nostalgia, and identity in modern British culture /
edited by George K. Behlmer and Fred M. Leventhal.
    p. cm.
    Includes bibliographical references (p.) and index.
    ISBN 0-8047-3489-5 (alk. paper)
    1. Great Britain—Civilization—20th century.   2. Influence (Literary, artistic,
etc. 3. National characteristics—British.   4. Popular culture—Great Britain. 5.
Group identity—Great Britain. 6. Great Britain—Civilization.   7. Nostalgia—
Great Britain.   I. Behlmer, George K.   II. Leventhal, Fred M.

DA566.4.S474   2000
941.082—dc21   00-039487

This book is printed on acid-free, archival-quality paper.

Original printing 2000

Last figure below indicates year of this printing:
09 08 07 06 05 04 03 02 01 00

Typeset in 10/13 Galliard by John Feneron

To PETER STANSKY

exemplary scholar, inspiring mentor, beloved friend

in gratitude and tribute

Contents

Contributors

GEORGE BEHLMER received his Ph.D. from Stanford University in 1977. After holding postdoctoral positions at Stanford and Yale, he moved to the University of Washington, where he is now Professor of History. He is the author of *Child Abuse and Moral Reform in England, 1870–1908* (1982) and, more recently, *Friends of the Family: The English Home and Its Guardians, 1850–1940* (1998). He is currently at work on a study of "savage practices" in the British Empire.

SUSAN GROAG BELL is a Senior Scholar at the Institute for Research on Women and Gender at Stanford University. She specializes in the cultural history of British and American women. Among her publications are: *Women, the Family and Freedom: The Debate in Documents, 1750–1950* (2 vols., 1983), *Revealing Lives: Autobiography, Biography and Gender* (1991), and *Between Worlds in Czechoslovakia, England and America: A Memoir* (1991). At present she is working on a book about the lost tapestries of Christine de Pizan's "Book of the City of Ladies."

JAMIE BRONSTEIN, who completed her Ph.D. at Stanford in 1996, is Assistant Professor of History at New Mexico State University in Las Cruces. Her first book, *Land Reform and Working-Class Experience in Britain and the United States, 1800–1862*, appeared in 1999. She is currently researching workplace accidents and their social and cultural consequences in nineteenth-century Britain and the United States.

FRED LEVENTHAL, who received his Ph.D. at Harvard University in 1968, has taught at Harvard, the University of Kent, the University of Sydney, and, since 1969, at Boston University, where he is Professor of History. He is the author of *Respectable Radical: George Howell and Victorian Working Class Politics* (1971), *The Last Dissenter: H. N. Brailsford and His World* (1985), and *Arthur Henderson* (1989); he is also the editor of *Twentieth-Century Britain: An Encyclopedia* (1995) and co-editor of *Anglo-American Attitudes* (2000). He is a co-editor of the journal *Twentieth-Century British History* and past president of the North American Conference on British Studies. His present research is concerned with the projection of Britain in America during the 1930's and 1940's.

HOWARD MALCHOW is Professor of British History at Tufts University. After finishing his Ph.D. at Stanford in 1972, he published his dissertation on the politics of nineteenth-century emigration as *Population Pressures* (1979). Since then his research interests have included the social background of nineteenth-century reform movements (*Agitators and Promoters*, 1983), the cultural milieu of Victorian businessmen (*Gentlemen Capitalists*, 1991), and "race" relations and prejudice (*Gothic Images*, 1996). He is presently engaged in a study of "alternative" culture in London in the 1970's.

LAURA MAYHALL received her Ph.D. from Stanford in 1993 and is currently Assistant Professor of History at The Catholic University of America. She is completing a book on gender and citizenship in late Victorian and Edwardian Britain, and is co-editor (with Ian Fletcher and Philippa Levine) of *Women's Suffrage in the British Empire: Race, Citizenship, and National Identity, 1890–1930* (forthcoming).

JOHN OSBORNE is Associate Professor of History at Dickinson College, where he has taught since completing his Ph.D. at Stanford in 1979. He has written *The Voluntary Recruiting Movement in Britain, 1914–1916* (1982), as well as scholarly articles on social and sporting life in Britain during the First World War.

MICHAEL SALER, who received his Ph.D. at Stanford in 1992, is Associate Professor of History at the University of California, Davis. His first book, *The Avant-Garde in Interwar England*, was published in 1999.

PATTY SELESKI completed her Ph.D. at Stanford in 1989 and is currently Associate Professor and Chair in the Department of History at California State University, San Marcos. She is the author of several essays on the changing nature of domestic service in the lives of laboring women in late eighteenth-century London and is at work on a book about the relationship between middle-class mistresses and their servants.

REBA SOFFER, whose Ph.D. is from Harvard University (1962), is Professor of History at California State University, Northridge. Among her extensive publications on late nineteenth- and twentieth-century intellectual, social, and institutional history are *Ethics and Society in England: The Revolution in the Social Sciences* (1978), which was awarded the Pacific Coast Branch of the American Historical Association monograph prize, and *Discipline and Power: The University, History and the Making of an English Elite, 1870–1930* (1995). She is a former president of the North American Conference on British Studies and was a Guggenheim Fellow in 1995–96. She is currently studying British and American historiography in the twentieth century.

CHRIS WATERS received his Ph.D. at Harvard University in 1985 and was a Visiting Assistant Professor and Mellon postdoctoral fellow at Stanford before assuming a position at Williams College, where he is currently Associate Professor of History. He is the author of *British Socialists and the Politics of Popular Culture, 1884–1914* (1990) and co-editor of *Moments of Modernity: Reconstructing Britain 1945–1964* (1999). In 1996–97 he was a fellow at the National Humanities Center, where he worked on his forthcoming *History and Heritage: Collective Memory and the Working-Class Past in Twentieth-Century Britain*.

STEWART WEAVER completed his Ph.D. at Stanford in 1985 and is now Associate Professor of History at the University of Rochester. He has written *John Fielden and the Politics of Popular Radicalism* (1987) and *The Hammonds: A Marriage in History* (1997).

SINGULAR CONTINUITIES

GEORGE K. BEHLMER

Introduction

At millennium's end, the mass media would have us believe that Britain is suffering an identity crisis. If the pundits are right, we are witnessing a manipulation of the British past at the hands of those keen to project a new national image—or, in the language of commodification, to "rebrand" Britain. Although British republicanism is hardly a creation of the late twentieth century, its champions have been particularly outspoken in recent years, arguing that the monarchy is a cultural as well as an economic millstone encumbering the body politic. That body is presently governed by apostles of modernization. Prime Minister Tony Blair's "New Labour" party seems poised to vivisect an antique peerage before specifying what the House of Lords would become without Their Lordships. New Labour's surgery also calls for devolving power to the disparate entities that comprise the United Kingdom; not only Scotland and Wales, but Northern Ireland and possibly even regions of England itself would win a measure of autonomy in this operation. Sounding strangely like Mrs. Thatcher, Blair defends his party's fixation on newness in terms of the national good: "What I am bothered about is Britain's standing in the world, the strength of our economy and the prosperity of the British people." From such concern flows Blair's impatience with backward-looking institutions. "I want Britain to be seen as a vibrant, modern place," he explains, "for countries wrapped in nostalgia cannot build a strong future."[1] A young prime minister has set out to convince the world that Britain is a young country. After all, Blair declares: "Change is the blood and bones of the British people."[2]

Singular Continuities takes issue not with the content of New Labour's political agenda but, more broadly, with a current tendency to misrepresent the depiction of the past in modern British culture. The contributors to this volume hold a variety of political and intellectual allegiances. What they share, however, is a common interest in the uses to which history has been put in Britain over the last two centuries. Since the early 1980's, several scholars and social critics have heaped scorn on what they view as the dead weight of British tradition. A preoccupation with the nation's cultural heritage, they assert, has served to dampen the entrepreneurial spirit, reinforce class inequality, and sustain otherwise moribund patriarchal precepts. "Heritage-baiting," as Raphael Samuel terms this (unthatched) cottage industry, has prepared the ground for New Labour's promotion of a "new" Britain.[3] The heritage baiters merit close attention. But perhaps the best preface to their war on fossilized cultural forms is actually an afterword. For the rise and fall of the recent "Cool Britannia" campaign offers a review of the antiheritage discourse from which it evolved.

Blair himself denies ever having uttered the catchphrase "Cool Britannia." Yet for a year after his party came to power on May 1, 1997, Blair and his advisors certainly exploited this theme. If credit belongs to anyone for coining the expression, it probably should go to a group of student satirists who, in 1967, during the reign of Carnaby Street, Mary Quant, and the Beatles, recorded a "twist" version of "Rule Britannia": "Cool Britannia, / Britannia take a trip. / Britons ever, ever, ever shall be hip. . . ." Improbably enough, the catchphrase resurfaced in the spring of 1996 when an ice-cream maker launched a new flavor with this name. An American tax attorney then working in London not only suggested the name but, months later, also agreed to dress up as Britannia and ride a chariot around the Royal Albert Hall, dragging behind her a ten-foot inflatable ice-cream tub. Thereafter the chariot mutated into a bandwagon. "By 1997," *The Guardian* observed, "Cool Britannia meant rock bands and restaurants, football managers and fashion designers, Union Jacks on everything; by the beginning of this year [1998], it was shorthand for the Government's entire arts policy; this spring, it has virtually become shorthand for the Government itself."[4]

To be sure, most incoming British governments over the past half-century have sought to reconceive the nation in one way or another. Attlee proclaimed Labour's vision of a "new Jerusalem" in 1945. Churchill in 1953 tried to link his Tory administration with the queen's coronation, a linkage made explicit by Sir Winston's proclamation of a "new Elizabethan age." Harold Wilson in 1964 spoke of a new Britain "forged in the white heat of the technological revolution." Still, Blair's appropriation of "Cool Britannia" conveys a sense of urgency about the need for clever public relations to transform the national psyche — or, failing that, to spruce up the national profile. That the "cultural output of a country is like a large advertising campaign on behalf of that country" found expression in a 1995 position paper ("Nations for Sale") written by Anneke Elwes, then director of planning for a London marketing firm.[5] Two years later, Mark Leonard, a denizen of the New Labour–aligned think tank Demos, published the bible of rebranding, *Britain*™: *Renewing Our Identity*. Lamenting that Britain, despite eighteen years of Thatcherism, was still perceived abroad as strike-ridden and hostile to free enterprise, Leonard went on to suggest that the nation needed new "stories" to tell about itself. These stories should depict Britain as a global hub for the transfer of goods and services, as a "hybrid nation, mixing diverse elements into something new," and as a land full of "buccaneering entrepreneurs." Together, such narratives would provide "a toolkit for renewing Britain's identity." Anticipating flak from those mired in tradition, Leonard assured readers that forging a new national identity "does not imply casting off what has gone before," but instead finding "a better fit between our heritage and what we are becoming."[6]

Mark Leonard was of course correct to note that much of what is assumed to be characteristically "British" was the product of continuous creation throughout the eighteenth and nineteenth centuries. Yet his accompanying confidence that the accretions of generations could be deconstructed during the lifetime of one government—assuming, literally, that Britain could be made cool by committee—has raised hackles. Not that New Labour was shy about implementing Leonard's plan. On the contrary, when the membership of Blair's "Panel 2000" was announced in April 1998, this chic crew of TV personalities, former athletes, diplomats, and business people seemed all too ready to rebrand the land. The subsequent suspension of Panel 2000's work said less about New Labour's ambitions than about popular weariness with the politics of image.

As the backlash against "Cool Britannia" accelerated during 1998, New Labour reined in its rhetoric. Mark Leonard now concedes that "you can't market . . . a country like a product," although he continues to insist that a national image can be "managed." For his part, Prime Minister Blair now favors "Best of British" as code for an inclusive, modern national identity. Recent New Labour references to a Blairite "Third Way"—which is purportedly "about traditional values in a changed world"—are as bland as "Cool Britannia" was brash.[7] Beneath New Labour's new wooliness, however, lingers a conviction that to dwell on cultural continuity is to handcuff creativity. In no small part such conviction assumed its fin-de-siècle form during the 1980's.

Margaret Thatcher's electoral triumph in the spring of 1979 was not a precondition for the critiques of "heritage" and "nostalgia" that surfaced soon afterwards. Six years before Thatcher moved into 10 Downing Street, Raymond Williams had argued that ruralism—a cultural homage to pastoral values—was a cloak for "unconscious reaction."[8] Still, most of the subsequent assaults on ruralism and its associated veneration of "heritage" meshed closely with Thatcherism's vision of history. That part of the past which served to legitimate class conflict, particularly as reflected in labor militancy, was jettisoned. At the same time, Thatcher's depiction of Britain as a superior nation required the affirmation of certain historic traits. Most obvious perhaps was the "tradition" of a patriotic fighting spirit that had energized Britain's home front during the Second World War. Whether the new enemy were bellicose Argentines invading the Falkland Islands or troglodyte trade unionists seeking to sabotage the nation's economic recovery, Mrs. Thatcher vowed that "the sterling qualities which shine through our history" would once more carry the day.[9] Treating the past as a smorgasbord, Thatcher feasted on those historic "values" (often billed as "Victorian") that seemed supportive of her vaunted "enterprise society" even as she disdained those customs that appeared to buttress the much-maligned "entitlement society." Thus, when and where a reverence for Britain's past appeared likely to thwart the restoration of business to a place of honor in national life, the Thatcherite tendency was to mock such reverence as a symptom of moral decay.

This highly selective repackaging of time-honored "values" soon found expression in more systematic work. Martin Wiener's *English Culture and the Decline of the Industrial Spirit 1850–1980* (1982) did not so much bait heritage enthusiasts as indict them. And he charged the late-Victorian era with having allowed the moral rot to start:

> A shift from the use of the past to make innovation palatable to a preoccupation with the past for its own sake began to become visible in the eighteen-seventies and eighties. . . . The ruling-class style that was just taking shape was "to make big things seem small, exciting things boring, new things familiar." It was admirably suited to damp down social tension, and minimize the disruptive effects of change. It lowered the temperature of society. In doing so, however, it drained prestige from innovation to preservation, from novelty to antiquity, and from change to continuity.[10]

Preoccupations with the past, cast in these terms, are central to what Wiener saw as the modern tendency to equate Englishness with "holding back the flood" of social and economic progress.[11]

Later damned with quaint praise as a "brilliant squib,"[12] *English Culture* has drawn trenchant criticism on several fronts. Recent scholarship has cast doubt on Wiener's contention that national elites walled themselves off from the dynamic sectors of British society. We now know, for instance, that between 1870 and 1920 the highest-ranking history graduates of Oxford and Cambridge were far from indifferent to the commercial world.[13] Equally debatable is Wiener's portrait of scientific pursuits growing steadily more irrelevant to a dominant literary culture—one alleged result of which was a marked antimodern sensibility that could tolerate economic stagnation. As several scholars have noted, it was precisely a keen awareness of historical continuities that allowed late nineteenth- and early twentieth-century Britain to come to terms with the modern and the scientific.[14] Yet these correctives did not appear in time to blunt the impact of *English Culture*. Instead, Wiener's book became a foundational text for those who echoed his lament over a purported loss of national nerve after the heroic optimism of the mid-Victorian years, a dwindling self-confidence reflected in Britain's embrace of a nostalgic, anticommercial, rural ethos.[15]

Particularly sharp have been the attacks on Britain's heritage boom. Irked at the imprecision of "national heritage," and at the imagined "Deep England" often implicit in this phrase, Patrick Wright sought to lay bare the politics of preservation. *On Living in an Old Country* (1985) argued that beneath the vast diversity of preservationist concerns runs a view of history as "entropic decline." With the future presumed to be bleak, Wright reasoned, the British past tends to get reconstructed as irreplaceable heritage.[16] More partisan still have been the pronouncements of Robert Hewison, whose *The Heritage Industry: Britain in a Climate of Decline* (1987) lampooned nearly everything redolent of the preservationist impulse, from postage stamps and Laura Ashley catalogs to the National Trust and industrial museums. In fact, museums that aim to preserve a sense of vanishing lifestyles head Hewison's list of dubious heritage endeavors. Granted, he did not join those who blame British museums for helping to inculcate an uncritical patriotism in citizens, nor did he single out for abuse the "heritagization of space"—an ugly phrase for the transformation of the built environment into tourist zones.[17] Hewison nevertheless held that the remarkable proliferation of museums in Britain after the Second World War symbolizes the "imaginative death of this country." Too many museums, it seemed to him, confuse too many people by conflating history and heritage.[18]

Illustrations abound. Thus, with his radar scanning for the ironic,

Hewison located the Wigan Pier Heritage Centre. Here, amidst the derelict Lancashire townscape that George Orwell made infamous in 1937, a partnership of local government, the English Tourist Board, and the European Union has opened a tidy canalside exhibition of "The Way We Were." Curiously, the period mummified here is not Orwell's Depression-era Wigan but rather a comparatively prosperous 1900. The Brookers' squalid boardinghouse is nowhere to be seen. Instead, visitors can stroll from a display of late-Victorian family life to the Orwell Pub to the Pier Shop, where a wide range of Victorian simulacra—soaps, sweets, and model miners' lamps— compete for tourist attention with copies of *The Road to Wigan Pier*.[19] If this is what passes for heritage, growls Hewison, it has remarkably little to do with an authentic past. Indeed, if heritage consciousness actually means a collective willingness to be misled, then New Labour's quest to "rebrand" Britain would make perfect sense.

Yet "heritage," along with "continuity," "nostalgia," and "tradition," can also signify something genuinely popular. Even those most troubled by what they read as the antimodern subtext of heritage enthusiasm will concede that a fascination with the British past is far from an elite hobby. Although hereditary gentry may still own or inhabit many English country houses, the country house as *symbol*, Peter Mandler notes, has in an important sense been "nationalized."[20] The popular face of preservation shows even more clearly in Britain's love affair with the steam railway. It is easy enough to deride "the romance of steam." It is considerably more difficult to dismiss the fact that by 1991 steam railways accounted for 3 percent of the British commercial leisure market.[21] The triumph of diesel locomotives and the closing of many rural branch lines throughout Britain during the 1950's and 1960's helped fuel a passion for steam that now connects landscape and line. To those who realize that a century ago the champions of landscape preservation fought furiously against plans to lay track through the heart of the Lake District, the modern equation of steam engines and the pastoral can seem perplexing. But against this, as Raphael Samuel points out, we must place the broad appeal of steam's resurrection: "In its reliance upon volunteers, and its emphasis on shared experience, [this cause] prefigured the 'living history' movements of more recent times."[22] Samuel, in fact, has tried to resuscitate "heritage" as a progressive impulse. From Sir Thomas More's denunciation of enclosure in the early sixteenth century to the founding of the open-space lobby in the mid-nineteenth, Samuel insists that there has long been an affinity between rural preservation and radical politics. Nor, according to him, should we automatically privilege history over heritage. For heritage, imbued with an archaeological sensitivity, may be better positioned than academic history, encumbered as it has been by statistical quarrels, to make Britain's industrial past accessible to a mass audience.[23]

Notwithstanding the fact that Raphael Samuel was himself an accomplished academic historian, his bid to accentuate the democratic inclusiveness of heritage work invites reflection. After all, "heritage," whether an industry or a habit of mind, functions as a secular assurance of continuity.[24] Although postmodern theory may have rendered problematic all grand narratives, such concerns do not faze ordinary folk. As Adrian Mellor puts it: "You can't walk through a shopping mall, watch late-night TV, attend a seminar, buy a sweater, or spend the day out at Wigan Pier, without . . . meta-narratives dying at your feet." Yet when average people go shopping, "they stubbornly insist that they are buying something to wear, rather than constituting their subjectivity."[25] An everyday, narratable sense of the world is essential for most of the British population, with the result that an eagerness to embrace cultural continuities remains as palpable now as it has been at any time since the Second World War.

Similar observations may be offered about the role of nostalgia in fin-de-siècle British culture. As with critiques of heritage, it requires only modest mental effort to realize that people (and nations) are far too preoccupied with the way things never were. Rather more creativity has gone into the charge that nostalgia is a masculine retreat to the past in the face of modern feminist authority.[26] Actually, the term "nostalgia," coined in the late seventeenth century by a Swiss physician, derives from the Greek *nostos*, a return home, and *algos*, a painful condition—hence "homesickness." Over time, however, its meaning has gradually drifted from a label for the condition of certain Swiss mercenaries fighting abroad to a much less precise mix of sentiments.[27] To the extent that this word now conveys a widely understood meaning, it has to do with the juxtaposition of an idealized past with an unsatisfactory present. That the nostalgic bent can lapse into cloying sentimentality is obvious. No less evident is the potential for commercializing the fond backward gaze. Finally, it would be foolish to deny that, under some circumstances, nostalgia can serve to foreclose the future, to reject the possibility of productive change. Yet at the same time nostalgia can also be a strategy for coping with change, loss, or anomie. The nostalgic view, then, can provide an integrative service by reassuring individuals (and nations) that continuity—what one sociologist calls a "restitutive link"—exists between former and current conditions.[28]

It is mainly in this last sense that *Singular Continuities* will treat nostalgia. As for "tradition," readers will find that by no means all discussion of this necessarily vague word is framed in terms of "invention." A decade after he and Eric Hobsbawm edited *The Invention of Tradition* (1983), Terence Ranger confessed to misgivings about the accuracy of their famous title. An invention presupposes an inventor. But in Ranger's area of colonial African history, to assume an inventor is to obscure the fact that the production of colonial knowledge was not exclusively a top-down process. An "invention," moreover, conjures up a once-and-for-all event, rather as if the inventors, having perfected their device, need merely apply for a patent. Since the "invention" trope ill fits the finding that identities are constantly being reshaped, Ranger now prefers to speak of "imagined" traditions.[29] The contributors to this volume have noted his self-critique.

∽

Singular Continuities views the imagination of tradition from several angles and over a span of two centuries. It begins with three essays that analyze English identity through the lens of alien cultures. In "Identity, Immigration, and the State," Patty Seleski questions conventional wisdom about the nature of anti-Irish prejudice. Far from timeless, this prejudice, she argues, derived in part from questions of early nineteenth-century public policy, especially those hinging on access to poor relief. Another immigration crisis drove late-Victorian Jews to historicize their relationship with the dominant liberal culture. Jamie Bronstein's "Rethinking the 'Readmission'" makes it clear that the efforts of Jewish people during the 1880's to embellish their assimilation saga were inseparable from contemporary fears over the influx of poor Ashkenazim. No less creative was the narrative that aimed to reconfigure distant Boer farmers as the virtuous citizens of a pastoral commonwealth. In "The Pro-Boers," Stewart Weaver shows how rural nostalgia could draw upon veldt as well as vale for ideological inspiration.

Custom as an inspiration for future action receives further analysis in the essays on social casework, women's suffrage, and the administration of sport that follow. George Behlmer's "Character Building and the English Family" suggests that the alleged "professionalization" of English social work between 1870 and 1930 masked an enduring concern with the moral rehabilitation of poor homes. Laura Mayhall traces the roots of another progressive cause—votes for women—back to a "traditional" female activity: reading. In "The Making of a Suffragette," Mayhall demonstrates how "the higher development" of the self through books proved vital for the Scots activist Eunice Murray. Self-improvement on the playing fields, John Osborne holds, remained an obsession of the old amateur ethos. His "Continuity in British Sport" reminds us that the Great War was hardly a "deluge" where the nation's recreational habits were concerned.

The pressures of modernity, intensified by the First World War, compelled British artists and intellectuals to reconsider the world around them. Three essays depict this process at work during the interwar years. The visual haven that Bloomsbury's Vanessa Bell created at her Sussex farmhouse was both a reflection of and a stimulus to her painting. Susan Bell's "Vanessa's Garden" offers us an intimate example of how horticulture presumes a continuity that is at once botanical and spiritual. The surrealist history produced by the British filmmaker, poet, and painter Humphrey Jennings can certainly be seen as an attack on the bourgeois faith in eternal progress. But as Michael Saler contends in "Whigs and Surrealists," Jennings's *Pandaemonium* is actually suffused with a celebratory sense of the English past. The more transparently conservative historians that Reba Soffer studies were linked through temperament as well as subject with a long-standing effort to extract "object lessons" from the past to smooth the road ahead. In "The Long Nineteenth Century of Conservative Thought," Soffer reveals how F. J. C. Hearnshaw, Keith Feiling, and Arthur Bryant all contributed to a veneration of tradition that descended from Burke.

Recent considerations of nostalgia and national identity round out this collection. Examining the 1939 Royal Visit to the United States, Fred Leventhal notes that Britain's bid to rehabilitate Anglo-American relations on the eve of the Second World War called for a cautious "national projection." In "Essential Democracy," Leventhal explains how an inexperienced King George VI and his more astute minders sought to reassure Anglophiles that the glamor of royalty lived on while convincing the foes of special privilege that the monarchy had been modernized. Chris Waters turns to the 1970's and 1980's for his assessment of "Autobiography, Nostalgia, and the Changing Practices of Working-Class Selfhood." The stream of working-class memoirs produced during these years, he shows, typically invoked an "industrial nostalgia" that associated fading forms of sociability with an altered cityscape. Finally, Howard Malchow brings us back to Thatcher's Britain with his "Nostalgia, 'Heritage,' and the London Antiques Trade." Amidst Thatcherism's worship of entrepreneurial verve, observes Malchow, "heritage" all too easily came to signify history for sale.

Like "heritage," "continuity" is a protean notion whose perceived usefulness as an analytical category for historians ebbs and floods with scholarly fashion. When Stefan Collini sighed in 1995 that "at times it . . . [seems] as though we are all simply extras in a continuous performance staged by Sceptr'd Isle Productions,"[30] he was giving voice to an understandable impatience with Olde England, Ltd. As used in our collection, however, "continuity" refers not to static cultural forms but rather to enduring preoccupations which are nonetheless malleable. George Orwell's wartime ruminations on the future of his country captured this sense of change-within-continuity. England, observed Orwell at the height of the Nazi bombing, was "an everlasting animal stretching into the future and the past, and, like all living things, having the power to change out of recognition and yet remain the same."[31] It is the curiously elastic nature of British cultural continuity that prompts us to term it "singular."

Identity, Immigration, and the State: Irish Immigrants and English Settlement in London, 1790-1840

In the early hours of July 16, 1813, two London laborers stumbled across a grisly scene: Edward (Ned) Clifford, lying in a water-filled gravel pit at the bottom of Gray's Inn Lane, his skull shattered by a hammer. The gruesome murder attracted a good deal of notice.[1] In the days following his death, the public learned more about Ned Clifford and his circumstances. A stranger to London, Irish, born in County Tipperary, he had only recently arrived in the metropolis with his pregnant common-law wife, Mary Burke, and her four young children. The Clifford family had landed at Bristol and made their way to London, where Mary, who had lived there briefly as a child, still had relatives. They settled in the parish of St. Giles-in-the-Fields. The move to London solved none of the family's problems and created even more. Ned had no trade. A Gaelic speaker with little knowledge of English, he had trouble finding work and supporting his family. He talked openly of abandoning Mary Burke and going home until, befriended by a countryman, Clifford found work and postponed his return to Ireland.[2]

To those following the case during the summer of 1813, the reporting of it was familiar, playing upon assumptions about the metropolis and confirming St. Giles's reputation as a haven for criminals. Although the press took some notice of the Irish origins of the Cliffords, Irishness as a signifying identity played no role in the accounts. The Clifford story disappeared from public view until 1828, when Andrew Knapp and William Baldwin resurrected it in the *New Newgate Calendar*. There, Knapp and Baldwin changed the emphasis both of the earlier press coverage and of the original Old Bailey trial.[3] The difference? Knapp and Baldwin concluded that Ned

Clifford's murder justified their call to end Irish immigration into Britain. In their hands, the story transcended its eighteenth-century roots as a cautionary tale about the dangers of the metropolis and became a more threatening narrative about the peril of Irishness. An especially noteworthy change was the way Knapp and Baldwin transformed the story's most innocent victims, Mary Burke and her children, into objects of condemnation. What accounts for this narrative transformation? How did it happen that a tale of immigrant vulnerability and urban danger also became a story about Irish predation?

This essay seeks to explain the significance of Mary Burke's transformation in the minds of her English hosts and, more important, to explore how Irishness acquired meaning in Britain. Only in the last decade or so has it seemed necessary to address such issues at all. More than three-quarters of a century ago, Dorothy George summed up what has long been the prevailing view when she declared that the Irish "were a police problem, a sanitary problem, a poor-law problem and an industrial problem."[4] The problematic nature of the Irish, especially in relation to the English, has long seemed obvious, even natural, to historians, who have until quite recently been largely unconcerned with the question of national identity.[5] In the last decade, however, the question of how national identities are created and sustained has preoccupied scholars almost to the point of obsession. Since the late 1980's experts in many fields have paid much closer attention to the ongoing consolidation and construction of national identities, seeing them not as natural but as cultural phenomena, as ideological constructs, created and maintained to justify larger political or imperial projects.

These days, any exploration of the shifting meanings assigned to Ned Clifford's death or to Mary Burke's Irishness invites reference to what Linda Colley has called "nothing less than the redefinition" of the British nation in the years between Waterloo and the accession of Queen Victoria. Prior to 1815, Colley argues, British national identity was staunchly Protestant, defined by its century-long military struggle against Catholic France. But postwar Britain lacked an obvious military enemy; furthermore, the union with Ireland challenged Britain to rethink the Protestant nature of the constitution. British identity was, she implies, largely political and therefore proved flexible enough to withstand granting civil rights to propertied Catholics in 1829. Yet the record of cultural accommodation with Catholicism after political emancipation was another matter. Colley leaves the question largely unexplored, though Mary Poovey has argued that after

1829 anti-Catholicism quickly reconstructed itself as anti-Irishness. Britons' understanding of Irishness, she claims, encoded fears not only of Catholicism but of general social disorder, too, and gave British elites a new opponent against which to consolidate British national identity as both Protestant and middle-class.[6] Inventing Irishness meant that Britons could simultaneously congratulate themselves on their tolerance and their expansive notion of political liberty, while at the same time preserving the respectable, Protestant character of the nation and justifying the exclusion of others from national life.[7]

Although the reading of the Clifford murder underwent its metamorphosis concurrently with the changes that Colley and Poovey describe, neither account can adequately explain the particular history of the case. Indeed, Catholicism never played a part in any contemporary considerations of the Clifford story; rather, what concerned Knapp and Baldwin in 1828 was the mechanics of immigration, not Catholicism. What explains Mary Burke's transformation, especially its particularly gendered quality, is anxiety about how the Irish might *literally* be accommodated within Britain. This essay does not go so far as to argue that anti-Catholicism was not an ingredient in the construction of Irishness during this period, nor does it claim to be exhaustive in its discussion of how Irishness was understood in these years. It recognizes that the process was multifaceted and that it took place on multiple sites. Not the least important of these sites was Ireland itself, where O'Connell was mobilizing the Catholic peasantry.

What follows is designed to be suggestive. This essay grounds its discussion of identity formation not in ideology—the conflict between Protestantism and Catholicism—but in practice. It argues that English definitions of Irishness were shaped decisively by direct experience with the Irish. More important, it demonstrates that when the nature of that direct experience was altered, identities also changed to encompass newly salient differences that emerged in the reconstructed context of encounter: beneath what even historians often regard as the timeless and inveterate nature of the conflict between English and Irish identities, there lay concrete moments in which new identities were imagined and solidified. In the period after Waterloo, a specific public-policy concern shaped English understandings of Irishness: How would England cope with the unprecedented numbers of poor Irish immigrants who were making their way across the Irish Sea? The answer to this question explains the rather sudden shift in English attitudes toward Mary Burke's plight. Thus, rather than assume that ideology prompts the formation of identity, this essay will highlight as an overlooked factor in identity formation England's limited practical capacity to deal with and to adapt to changing circumstances.[8]

By the end of the eighteenth century the Irish were settling in British cities in unprecedented numbers. Neither Colley nor Poovey ignores this phenomenon, but both do fail to contextualize it or to appreciate its concrete significance. Indeed the years so pivotal to their accounts saw a steep rise in the numbers of all foreigners who settled in Britain. The century of war that ended in 1815 might have—to use Colley's term—forged a nation, but the global scale of Britain's eighteenth-century wars also brought with it an expansion of Britain's global economic empire. One major result of economic expansion and overseas military adventure was the movement of people across territorial boundaries. As the hub of an empire whose spokes extended to India, Asia, Africa, the Caribbean, and North America, London by 1800 was the world's most populous and most important city.[9]

Despite its new status as a global urban center, London was also a city just beginning to come to grips with how this changed reality might affect traditional practices and structures. Nowhere was this more apparent than in the realm of poor relief. London had always been a city of immigrants, with a long history of addressing their material needs when they fell into poverty. But London was unprepared for the likes of Ned Clifford and Mary Burke, or for the thousands of other Irish men and women who came to London during the early years of the nineteenth century. This essay argues that the mechanism available to Londoners to address poverty—the Poor Law—was at its core about identity. The successful administration of parochial poor relief depended on communities' being able to identify and to recognize their members. Belonging determined access to the community's, and ultimately the nation's, resources, making both the definition and the recognition of individual identity expressions of a larger, national, identity. Mary Burke and those like her did not become problematic for the English *just* because they were Irish. Irishness became problematic in the early nineteenth century because, as a result of economic transformation, Irishness in London was newly poor, female, and permanent. As such, Irishness could not be accommodated—either practically or mentally—within the traditional structures that defined belonging, structures that not only were narrowly English but predated both "Britain" and the British Empire.

There is no little irony in the fact that the English both embraced and resisted change as they reacted to the Irish among them. Britain eagerly sought its union with Ireland as well as its new global empire, but it also sought to mitigate the impact of these acquisitions on what was still a very English state. Driven by a desire to protect English parishes from financial ruin as a result of relieving Irish immigrant poverty, Parliament experimented with the Poor Laws and with Poor Law policy in ways designed to preserve traditional boundaries of belonging. In doing so, Parliament helped change the way the public saw Mary Burke and her children, as well as the way in which they understood Irishness.

↝

The large numbers of Irish already resident in Britain by the census of 1841 have been overshadowed historically by the tidal wave of Irish immigrants who entered Britain after 1845. To ignore the earlier group, however, would be a mistake. Although emigration had already been a fact of Irish life for at least a century, historians estimate that between 1780 and 1845 (especially after 1815), over 1.5 million people emigrated from Ireland. Most went to North America, but about 600,000 crossed the Irish Sea to Britain, where more than 400,000 subsequently settled.[10] Not only was the volume of this migration greater than any previous movement to Britain, but the characteristics of the migrants were also different, as George Cornewall Lewis observed to Parliament in 1836:

> The emigration from Ireland to England and Scotland is of a very remarkable character, and is perhaps unparalleled in the history of this world. It has usually happened that emigration has taken place from more civilized to less civilized nations. . . . But the Irish emigration into Britain is an example of a less civilized population spreading themselves, as a kind of substratum, beneath a more civilized community.[11]

What Cornewall Lewis was describing is precisely the kind of migration associated with the growth of world cities as relatively unskilled workers from the periphery encounter "modern" modes of economic production.[12] By the nineteenth century, the increasingly global nature of Britain's economic activity meant that London began to display characteristics of what modern political economists now call a "world city." Distinguished by their integration in the international economic system—often superseding in importance the nation-state in which they are located—world cities serve as sites where international capital is concentrated and accumulated. World cities have characteristic socioeconomic profiles, too. Like modern world cities, London increasingly became the destination for many international migrants displaced by the global market—migrants who brought the underdeveloped economy of the periphery with them to the developed core. A workforce arose that was both differentially skilled and culturally different in comparison with the workforce of the host city, a development that increased the degree of social isolation such newcomers experienced and exacerbated social polarities. Because they are very likely to be part of permanent, family-based movements, migrants to world cities generate social costs that often exceed the fiscal capacity of the host state to deal with them.[13] When Cornewall Lewis described the developing Irish substratum in London, he was describing this aspect of world-city growth.

In fact, Irish immigration to London in the period after Waterloo was part of a much larger movement of people to the metropolis that did not go unnoticed. Writing in 1838, one observer called London "a little world in itself," claiming it was inhabited by "men of all countries and climes."[14] Ample anecdotal evidence exists of numerous foreign communities already in the metropolis by the beginning of the nineteenth century. Dorothy George noted the growth of sizable colonies of Jews, lascars, Africans, Scots, and Irish during the eighteenth century, minority populations that joined already established Huguenot, Dutch, and Portuguese communities dating from the seventeenth century. In what the Mendicity Society considered an ominous development, by 1820 almost half of the two thousand beggars they assisted came from over seventeen countries or world regions other than England.[15]

The Mendicity Society assisted more Irish beggars than foreigners of any other description. This makes perfect sense, since by the end of the eighteenth century the Irish were the largest immigrant group in Britain. Before 1800, estimates suggest that no more than 100,000 lived in Britain.[16] After 1800, however, the rate of Irish immigration increased dramatically: the census of 1841 estimated that there were over 400,000 Irish natives then settled in Britain. This number, together with an estimated 100,000 children born after their parents' arrival, meant that even prior to the Great Famine over half a million Irish may have been permanently based in Britain.[17]

In fact, Irish settlements had existed in London since the seventeenth century, and throughout the eighteenth century a small but steady stream of migrants made the journey to the metropolis. Most of these migrants were men, seasonal workers who came to harvest crops in the counties surrounding London. Comparatively few of them actually settled in London, preferring instead to return to their families and their smallholdings in Ireland to harvest their own potato crops.[18] In addition to the few harvesters who stayed behind in the metropolis, the Irish residents of the capital also included contingents of discharged soldiers and sailors, veterans of Britain's successive military adventures in the eighteenth century. A floating population of Irish domestic servants also resided for some time each year in London, having accompanied affluent families over from Ireland. Although some of these servants stayed and became permanent residents, and although some of the seasonal or domestic workers were women, the permanent Irish immigrants to London before 1800 were almost all men and likely to be skilled workers. Indeed, far from being peasants, the vast majority of Irish men who settled permanently in London during most of the eighteenth century were town dwellers in Ireland, many of whom had served apprenticeships with skilled craftsmen and artisans.[19]

Beginning in the 1780's, however, the characteristics of emigrants from Ireland changed. The number of permanent emigrants greatly increased and began to outpace other movement out of Ireland.[20] The reasons behind such massive emigration lay with Ireland itself. Although landowners seemed to have prospered during the French wars, those who worked on the land saw their livelihoods deteriorate. The rapid transformation of Irish agriculture in order to supply the British market and the spread of cash wages in the years after the Act of Union (1801) heightened pressures on Irish cottiers. Furthermore, the post-Union integration of the Irish and British economies and the shift within England to a capital-based economy left Ireland exceedingly vulnerable to Britain's economic muscle. Irish industry also felt the pressure of Union: failing to keep pace with mechanized English competition, its most important sectors declined. Ireland became a market for English goods and a source of cheap agricultural produce. James Brownlow demonstrated his understanding of this relationship when he told his fellow M.P.'s: "The Irish send labour to this country in the shape of human beings; but the English sent labour back to Ireland, in the shape of boxes of manufactured goods."[21] When subsistence crises hit Ireland, as they did periodically from 1790 until the 1840's, Irish men and women had little choice but to leave.[22]

The permanent migrants, those with wives and families in tow, were the ones who alarmed George Cornewall Lewis. The Irish pushed off the land after 1800 had a much different profile than did those Irish whom the English had seen before. Most of them were still male, and many were still from Protestant and artisanal backgrounds. Although seasonal migrants came in greater numbers than ever before, the character of seasonal work also changed dramatically: it was far more likely to be merely a subsistence strategy. New populations of migrants took their places beside seasonal workers in rapidly growing numbers: more single women, more families, more Catholics, and more unskilled laborers joined the ranks. One study suggests that although overall emigration from Ireland was still predominantly by single men, these men more often preferred transatlantic relocation; thus the passage to Britain was more likely to involve higher numbers of single women and married men with families.[23] By the end of the 1830's, witnesses reckoned that there were more migrants from the western Irish-speaking province of Connaught in London than there were in Dublin. London seems to have been the preferred destination of the least skilled migrants, possibly because of its traditional prominence as a destination of unskilled harvest workers. Skilled migrants were much more likely, as in the case of Ulster spinners and weavers, to wind up working in the factories of northern cities.[24]

The increasingly desperate nature of Irish immigration can be seen in an 1803 study of London beggars: over 90 percent of the beggars were women, and almost a third of these women were Irish. More than a third of the children counted in the survey also were Irish.[25] Many of these women and children shared circumstances much like those reported by the Mendicity Society in describing one of their clients, "EH,"

> aged 36, a native of Cork, who through the hope of getting a livelihood in London, came over on the death of her husband (a master tailor), who left her with five children. On her arrival, she endeavoured to get into some way of providing for her family; but after repeated attempts, the only one left to her to embrace, was selling fruit, which she continued, till poverty compelled her to give up even that occupation, for want of the means wherewith to go to market. Thus reduced to the first stage of human misery, she applied to the overseers of the parish wherein she slept; but they would not relieve her *unless she was willing to be passed home.*[26]

Deprived of her husband's earnings, without skills herself, and with many mouths to feed, "EH" could not survive in Ireland and so came to London to improve her prospects. There, her lack of skills and the demands of her family left her with few ways to support her family other than street selling—a poorly paid occupation, but the alternatives to it were limited and no more lucrative. As she was a woman with children, the relative security of domestic service was denied "EH." Other alternatives such as laundry work or charring were, like street selling, unreliable and unlikely to produce a steady wage. Her options were few, and all involved cobbling together enough makeshift jobs to get by. Such work was already being done by thousands of other poor women, ensuring stiff competition and making survival uncertain. Without an accompanying male wage coming into the family, Irish women and their children were almost guaranteed to require relief of some sort. Had "EH" been an English woman in similar circumstances, she would have had a legal right to support from the community. As an Irish woman, however, she collided with an important, and harsh, administrative reality: although Ireland was now part of the Union and "EH" was a British subject, she was not—at least so far as the Poor Law was concerned—British. The only way the Poor Law could imagine dealing with "EH" was to get rid of her by sending her home to Ireland.

"EH," like Mary Burke and the other Irish men and women who came to London in the years following the Union, encountered a city which was only beginning to grasp the consequences of economic empire and the way in which imperial obligations could redefine and restructure the most basic social and political relationships. Although even domestic migration presented difficulties for those administering the Poor Laws, migration across territorial boundaries greatly complicated the matter. Under the Poor Laws, as under the Law of Settlement, local communities defined the boundaries of belonging when they recognized the right of an individual to relief in times of need. The Poor Law, described as "that holy national institution, by which the great fraternity of the English people insures the necessaries of life to individuals of its *own body*" (my emphasis), effectively fixed membership both in local communities and, by implication, in the nation. Those who fell outside the Poor Law's boundaries and its definition of belonging were not, and could not be, recognized as being part of the community.[27] They were, quite literally, different and something other than British.

⤳

When the characteristics of Irish migrants changed, so too did the likelihood that they would interact with the Poor Law. Although the Poor Law certainly reflected an inscribed ideology about identity and belonging, it is important to note that it was not consciously or deliberately anti-Irish.[28] Dating from the reign of Elizabeth I, the Poor Laws fixed the notion of community around the parish church, obligating parishes to assist their members in times of need and to levy rates for that purpose. The Poor Laws encoded an ideology about a particular kind of social order, based on the control of populations that were essentially stable and rooted in local communities. Even when people moved within England, they retained their rights to relief in their home parishes unless they earned settlement, and therefore membership, in their new location.

The Poor Law presumed a vision of England as a land of stable settlements and face-to-face relationships. It was never a vision well suited to cities, because it depended on the ability to identify and to recognize those who shared the same space: "The nature of the legislation of England is, that it always goes upon the idea of the whole, and not of a crowded metropolis; and it supposes the profligacy or industry of each individual be known."[29] Of course, this notion was always more ideal than real, and despite their assumptions about the nature of Englishness, the Poor Laws nevertheless proved adaptable enough throughout the seventeenth and eighteenth centuries to accommodate high internal migration rates and the growth of towns. This was true in part because those most apt to move—young, single individuals of both sexes—were those who were unlikely to require parish relief except in unusual or tragic circumstances. They were also those most likely to establish new settlements by the methods allowed by the law. Under the Law of Settlement, individuals were born with, or assumed, the settlement of their fathers or husbands. (Illegitimate children were a notable exception.) The law also made provision for internal movement by granting new settlement to those employed for over a year in the same job, or to those who became ratepayers. Even for those able-bodied individuals who failed to acquire new settlement when they moved, the Poor Laws were frequently applied benignly: though they were not legally obligated to provide it, parish officers often gave casual relief at their own discretion when they judged that an individual might soon work again and would no longer require assistance. Although this flexibility helped those who were in temporary need, for others, such as the old and infirm, the unemployable, or women with dependent children and without husbands, the Poor Law could prove oppressive. This was especially true for those who ventured too far from their home parish. Parishes met their obligations to care for their own poor, but they were much less enthusiastic about helping, or encouraging, strangers.

As unwieldy as the Poor Law and the Law of Settlement could be, Taylor asserts that both worked well in regulating internal migration.[30] Significantly however, the provisions of the English Poor Law did not cover most of the Irish in England, nor did they extend to Ireland. Theoretically, although any Irish person meeting the requirements for a settlement in England—time in work, marriage, ratepaying, and so on—could establish one, the vast majority of Irish immigrants had little chance of doing so. Furthermore, the growing numbers of subsistence migrants like "EH" were much more likely to fall into need and become dependent on their

English hosts. What complicated the situation further was that because Ireland had no Poor Law, the Irish had *no* settlement—no place to which they legally belonged—anywhere. Thus the remedy available to parishes in the case of poor English migrants—removal to the pauper's parish—did not apply to the Irish. Under the law, the Irish *could not* be removed to Ireland merely for being poor and falling on an English parish: only persons convicted under the Vagrancy Laws could be passed legally to Ireland, and then only after being whipped or after serving a week in the House of Corrections. Furthermore, English parishes that removed "vagrant" Irish immigrants had no home parish in Ireland to bill: the cost for removing an Irish "vagrant" was borne entirely by the English parish. It is no wonder, then, that when the number of poor Irish in an English parish was small, most English parishes chose to provide casual relief when dealing with these strangers. And it is equally unsurprising that the flood of poor Irish arriving in England after 1800 rendered this response inadequate.

By the early years of the nineteenth century parishes were actively searching for ways to reduce the growing costs associated with the influx of poor Irish immigrants. For example, in 1797, the joint vestry of St. Giles-in-the-Fields and St. George, Bloomsbury, reported spending more than £2,000 a year out of the poor rates for the casual relief of Irish newcomers. St. Giles had always been an area where large numbers of Irish settled, but by the late 1790's vestry officers felt swamped by the growing numbers of Irish in the parish. Vestrymen also were frustrated by and resentful of the Vagrancy Law, which required them to whip or to confine the Irish as vagrants before sending them back to Ireland.[31] Such a law, they argued, induced "an unwillingness in humane magistrates to carry it into effect," especially against the many new immigrants who were merely poor. Additionally, to the extent that they were able to remove Irish immigrants in this manner, they also felt overburdened by the cost. The vestrymen pressed Parliament for legislation that would relieve them of the financial responsibility for removing "vagrant" Irish. They argued that the costs "incurred by parishes in relieving either natives of Ireland or others who have no parochial settlement should, by orders of the Justices, be repaid out of the County Rate; in which case the charge would be more equally borne, and consequently be less a burthen on some particular parishes than it is at present."[32]

What was a problem at the end of the eighteenth century was, by 1818, a crisis. In the economic downturn that followed the end of the Napoleonic wars, observers noted a "sudden and alarming increase in the numbers of

Vagrants in the Metropolis." The situation in which London parishes found themselves during the postwar period was unrecognizable to a Poor Law system that still employed controlling definitions and practices dating from the sixteenth century. The Mendicity Society summed up the situation:

> But there can be no doubt of the faultiness of the present practice, and of the practicability of introducing improvements in some of its most essential particulars. The pressure of the Irish poor, especially on one or two of the London parishes; the facility of acquiring settlements in the Metropolis, the wretched condition of many Africans and persons of colour, as well as other classes of foreigners, who, having served this country, have lost their own without acquiring another; and the disinclination or inability of parishes to give relief by employment to the able-bodied; are evils calling aloud for remedy, and will, it is hoped, occupy the serious attention of Parliament during the present session.[33]

But reforming the Poor Laws did not appeal to all. The officers of St. Giles vehemently resisted comprehensive reform of the Poor Laws or the Law of Settlement. Though they continued to look for help with the Irish poor, they fought any attempts to reform the Law of Settlement for fear lest, as a result of reform, the Irish might gain legal settlement in the parish. Especially frightening was a radical proposal that sought to aid labor-starved northern cities by doing away with the principle of settlement altogether. Even William Sturges Bourne's compromise, which proposed to grant settlement based on mere residence and which allowed individuals to gain settlement after three years of relief-free residency in a parish, set off howls of protest.[34] St. Giles, whose magistrates had deported over six hundred Irish in the previous year, and where the annual cost of casual relief to the Irish was fast approaching £10,000, feared that people "who although they do not at present possess or claim a parochial settlement" would migrate to St. Giles just to get one. The vestry complained of the "heavy injustice" such a bill would lay on parishes that were charged already "with the support of thousands of idle, disorderly and profligate persons."[35] Only two years earlier they had testified before Parliament about the fraudulent practices engaged in by the Irish—who, claimed a former overseer of the parish, never worked when they could beg, and sent their children out to beg as well.[36] Like many other parishes, but particularly urban ones, St. Giles fought Bourne's settlement proposal and ensured the defeat of the clauses amending settlement regulations.

Rather than seek ways that the Irish might be accommodated within the larger national community, St. Giles supported measures to exclude them. At the same time that they were working against Bourne's poor-settlement amendment, St. Giles's parish officers were lobbying for another measure that made removal of the Irish easier.[37] Their efforts, both in opposing amendments to the Laws of Settlement and in facilitating removal of the Irish, bore fruit. Under the provisions of 59 Geo. III, cap. 12, Parliament gave magistrates new discretionary powers to remove Irish immigrants who were chargeable to the parish. Immigrants no longer needed to be charged and convicted as vagrants before finding themselves sent back across the Irish Sea. Even more helpful to the officers of St. Giles, Parliament stipulated that removal expenses would be paid out of the county rate, not by the parish. Buoyed by this success, St. Giles's officials remained implacably opposed to any settlement reform. Even minimal reform had to await the new Poor Law of 1834, and no residency-based approach was adopted until the 1860's.

Once it became easier and cheaper for them to pass the Irish poor, London parishes reduced the indiscriminate provision of relief by disposing of the Irish. The effect of equipping parishes with a weapon against the poor that previously could be used only against criminals was, as William Parnell complained to Parliament, "to consider Irishism a crime."[38] In some cases, Irish paupers who had resided in London parishes for upwards of twenty or thirty years were refused relief when they could no longer work or fell ill; instead, they were sent back to Ireland.[39] The parish officers of St. Andrew, Holborn, allegedly deported an Irish man receiving a government pension when he requested a small advance from them, arguing that it was cheaper to have the *county* pay to remove him than for the *parish* to advance the small sum. In another instance, an Irish man who had lived in St. Giles, Cripplegate, for twenty-two years was sent back to Ireland rather than being allowed casual relief to tide him over until his injured leg healed. Parish officers apparently avoided spending their own money whenever they could pass the cost on to the county rate.[40]

Despite the enthusiasm with which London parishes disposed of the Irish poor, the sense of crisis only deepened. Since conditions in Ireland had not improved, immigration continued unabated; and because life in the metropolis was no more economically secure, immigrants continued to need assistance. By 1828 the Mendicity Society was assisting over ten thousand Irish beggars a year; by 1831 the number had soared to over twenty thousand. Dealing with immigration puzzled everyone—the Mendicity Society recommended that all except a few long-term Irish residents "should be disposed of at once"—and increased conflicts between parishes and counties.[41] Officials in Middlesex, Surrey, and the other counties through which Irish paupers passed on their way to Bristol and Liverpool attacked the behavior of London parish officers in Parliament, which subsequently debated reinstating the old policy of holding the passing parishes financially responsible for removing paupers. Predictably, the affected parishes resisted. St. Giles's officials, who considered the 1819 reform a rousing success, saw no need for further tinkering. But though they successfully fended off further reform in the late 1820's, St. Giles's residents acknowledged the difficulty involved in reconciling the interests of counties and parishes, and suggested instead that the best solution might be to "dispossess" the Irish of their presence in the metropolis.[42]

Part of the difficulty in reforming the Poor Law as it affected the Irish was that Irish immigration had a differential impact in Britain as a whole. Although London parishes sought to expel large numbers of the Irish poor rather than relieve them, authorities and employers in northern cities like Manchester and Liverpool, whose manufacturers depended on Irish labor, frequently preferred to dispense casual relief in order to keep their workforce close at hand. Some northern parishes informally accepted the notion that long-term residency itself was tantamount to legal settlement when considering questions of relief. One Liverpool manufacturer declared, in direct contradiction to St. Giles's claims, that "the impotent and aged Irish do not come to this country in great numbers," but that Irish workers did. As a result, he believed the benefit to Liverpool from its Irish workers more than compensated "for any legal increase of poor rate, or sums spent relieving the poor."[43]

The complicated and often conflicting interests of English parishes forced Parliament to examine conditions in Ireland. If chronic poverty was the cause of emigration, then the creation of an Irish Poor Law might convince the Irish to stay home. Or so some M.P.'s thought. As one witness told Parliament: "Parish relief on one side of the Channel, and none on the other, holds out just the same inducement to the open importation of poverty as the difference in the duty on spirits does to the smuggling of whiskey."[44]

Thus in the early 1830's, some Irish and English M.P.'s urged that the Elizabethan Poor Law be extended to Ireland. Frightened by the findings of a committee of inquiry that revealed how expensive such a system would be, Lord John Russell authorized another inquiry of the Irish poor, to be headed by George Nicholls. In 1838, Nicholls recommended introducing

England's new Poor Law, absent the principle of settlement, into Ireland. The conflict in Britain between Poor Law reformers and traditionalists was heated enough, but the debates over extending the Poor Laws to Ireland show the united unwillingness of Britain to accommodate the Irish poor. Regardless of political persuasion, British politicians were adamant in their belief that, despite the political fact of Union, Ireland and the Irish could not be part of Britain. They argued that in much the same way as Irish immigration threatened to overwhelm London parishes, the fiscal implications of Union would overwhelm British prosperity if Britain were obligated to care for the Irish poor. One M.P. argued that the English Poor Law represented England's "security" against the Irish and that extending the Poor Law to Ireland would be disastrous. Another pointed out that to create an Irish Poor Law would hinder English parishes in new ways:

> If the poor laws were introduced into Ireland, the practice of sending the Irish out of England in a summary manner could not then be acted on. Before any man was sent home, an inquiry must be introduced, litigation would follow on inquiry, the disputes that now existed between parishes in England would be extended to Ireland.[45]

The question that M.P.'s did not want to consider, let alone answer, was put to them directly by William Cobbett. He insisted that he could "see no reason why a person born in Ireland should, by the mere circumstance of a six hours' sail, be placed in a different position as to his claims on society; or why his means of support should be so greatly altered." Cobbett reminded his colleagues bluntly of the implications of Britain's position as an economic empire when he pointed out that since "Ireland sent much of her subsistence to England, . . . great consideration was due to those who came to England in search of food."[46] Nevertheless, Fergus O'Connor's insistence that the "poor law was not an Irish question merely, but a *national* question" (my emphasis), went unheeded.[47]

When the Irish Poor Law was finally introduced in 1838, it authorized transferring the costs of relief for the Irish poor to the landowners and ratepayers of Ireland, believing that costs could be kept low by importing the innovations of the new Poor Law. Other than sharing common ideological foundations, however, the English and Irish Poor Laws remained separate and distinct. Furthermore, the introduction of an Irish Poor Law did not bestow any settlement rights on Irish men and women. English parishes could still pass Irish immigrants summarily back to Ireland. Reformers hoped that if the Irish poor were offered the workhouse as an alternative to emigration, they would stay in Ireland. But as Cobbett had pointed out, the more dynamic English economy, along with continued poverty, over-population, and agricultural restructuring in Ireland, guaranteed that the ships steaming between Irish and English ports were filled with migrant passengers well into the 1840's.[48]

⌐⌐

By the time Knapp and Baldwin retold the story of Ned Clifford's murder in 1828, Irishness was a much more troubling identity in English cities than it had been in 1813. In part, this resulted from the fact that most forms of poverty had been reinterpreted as moral failure during these years. How-ever, Irishness was rendered especially problematic by the Poor Law. Le-gally, Irish poverty might remain unrecognized and unrelieved. As more and more Irish men and women streamed into Britain to find work, they overwhelmed the capacity of the Poor Law to cope with Irish need. Irish poverty was seen as having much less to do with being poor than with be-ing Irish. When Knapp and Baldwin rewrote the Clifford murder, they in-corporated this new understanding of Irishness and the Irish menace into their story.

Thus Knapp and Baldwin declared that anyone who left Ireland was ei-ther a criminal, "obliged to fly from the violated laws of their country," or a traitor, willing to "desert" Ireland in vain hopes of a better life. Whichever category Irish emigrants fell into, they were seen as morally flawed. Thus, Knapp and Baldwin argued, "it can no longer be surprising that the la-bouring Irish in London are brutal, drunken and vicious."[49]

But Mary Burke, Clifford's common-law wife, also came in for strong condemnation in the retold story. She stood condemned not only for her union with Clifford, but also for what Knapp and Baldwin saw as her im-position on the charitable citizens and Poor Law officers of London. With Clifford dead, the only hope Burke and her children had for support was the parish. And the parish's choice—to relieve her or to pass her back to Ireland—was one that either way imposed on the pocketbooks and the good will of parish ratepayers.[50] For Knapp and Baldwin, the problem that Mary Burke presented to the parish was emblematic of the new face of Irish poverty in London. In their opinion, it would have been better if neither Burke nor her compatriots had ever come to London.

It is tempting to conclude that Knapp and Baldwin were as frightened of Mary Burke as they were of Ned Clifford's real killer, his friend James Leary, and to suggest that English society felt more threatened by the armies of the Irish poor than it did by a murderer. That conclusion, however, reads more into their retelling of the Clifford murder than is warranted. There is another conclusion worth considering here: that the limited ability of the English Poor Law to cope with Irish poverty combined with the magnitude of Irish immigrant poverty in the years 1800–1840 to demonize both the Irish poor and Irishness itself.

What difference, then, did it make to Mary Burke that she, her partner, and her children were Irish? This essay has suggested that Irishness had little meaning as an identity in eighteenth- and early nineteenth-century London until it interacted with the English state. The history of Irishness as an identity defined by the English must be understood both by analyzing those structures, such as the Poor Law, within which the English and Irish interacted on a daily basis and by exploring the context in which those interactions took place. Like the rest of the laboring poor, the Irish lived precariously close to the line between survival and starvation. When the poor crossed that line, they became enmeshed in wider discourses of power, and their identity became subject to different definitions. The Poor Law structured the ways society understood and treated the poor: it helped codify the manner in which the nation defined its obligations and its boundaries. For the growing numbers of Irish poor who were helping to create London as a world city in the early nineteenth century, their anomalous status under the Poor Law, especially regarding settlement, positioned them outside the nation. The failure of Parliament to turn poor relief into a truly national question played a role in making the Irish in Britain permanent "others." Thus Mary Burke's Irishness was constructed and controlled by the wider English society, and her identity changed with prevailing practices to address poverty and migration.

Rethinking the "Readmission": Anglo-Jewish History and the Immigration Crisis

From April to July of 1887, impressive examples of Jewish ritual artwork hung on display in the Royal Albert Hall. Spice boxes, torah covers, kiddush cups, and shofars crowded up against crumbling parchment documents tracing the Jewish contribution to humanity back to biblical times.[1] The organizers of the exhibition—including historian Lucien Wolf, Frederic Mocatta, Sir Isidore Spielman, and other prominent English Jews—displayed the history of the Jews in England as a Whiggish progression. Derogatory caricatures of Jews drawn in the early part of the nineteenth century were included in the exhibition to educate young people about the social position of Jews before the inevitable march of civilization had resulted in their inclusion in the political state. Standing before monuments to Jewish art and learning, former opponents of Jewish emancipation could repent of their sins but, more important, rejoice in having become proponents of liberal toleration:

> The Gentile visitor will be ashamed of these misrepresentations, and his shame will be to his credit. . . . The Exhibition is a remarkable record of prejudices outlived by dint of honourable conduct, a record of which not only Jews may be proud, but of which England has reason also to be proud. England has to be proud of her treatment of Jews, and Jews have to be grateful to the great country that has held up the beacon of tolerance through so many years of misrepresentation and ill-will. From this point of view the Exhibition is truly Anglo-Jewish, and in the best sense of the word, national.[2]

Yet even as a parade of notables attended this celebration of the contributions of the Jewish community, readers flooded the *Jewish Chronicle* with letters and editorials debating the future of the "destitute alien" Jews who crowded the streets of East London.[3]

That moment in 1887 illustrates an irony: at the same time that the question of Jewish immigration to England had become a divisive issue, threatening some of the gains Jews had made in preceding decades, prominent members of the Jewish community began to investigate—even to celebrate—the history of England's Jews. The timing of their investigation is significant. For their antiquarian probings coincided both with the beginnings of Zionism and with the entry of modern history into English school curricula.[4] England's Jews wanted to stay in England; to do so comfortably, their history as well as their conduct had to erase the picture of the Jewish community as a "wandering race" incapable of true patriotism. It was important for the Jewish version of English history to emphasize the long and respectable pedigree of the Jews in England—a pedigree which could be traced back to the intentional "readmission" of the Jewish community to England in 1656.

The discovery and publicity of the "facts" of the readmission coincided with, and may have been intended to defuse, the furor over Jewish immigration and the potential of that furor to ignite latent English anti-Semitism. Part of the unspoken bargain between urban Jews and the English middle classes was the Jews' willingness to maintain liberal standards. To be accepted fully into English society, they deemphasized their religious observances and contained the poverty associated with new Eastern European immigration by privately funding their own social services and by discouraging immigration.[5] As Bill Williams has noted, they also headed off xenophobia by generating a "Whig Anglo-Jewish historiography in which the policies of the elite are seen as a proud, courageous and altruistic contribution to the inexorable progress of Anglo-Jewry in British society."[6] Thus, the "story" of the reintroduction of Jews to England, published for the first time shortly after the controversial and long-sought political emancipation of the Jews, brought them into the "master narrative" of English life in an acceptable way. Furthermore, the readmission story was crafted just at the moment when the English themselves were beginning to understand and propagate the importance of a distinctive English history and linguistic tradition. While the historical record concerning the influx of Jews to England during the Cromwellian period is more complex and disheartening than early Anglo-Jewish historians claimed, the narrative which they generated illustrates the pressures to find a place in English history that late nineteenth-century English Jews desired. The narrative of the readmission served a dual purpose: it wove the Jews into the fabric of the gradually liberalizing British state, but it also emphasized the degree to which religious toleration was—and therefore should continue to be—inseparable from the meaning of "Englishness."

The Readmission Narrative

According to the narrative as it was constructed in the late nineteenth century, Amsterdam Rabbi Menasseh ben Israel approached Oliver Cromwell three and a half centuries after the official expulsion of the Jews from England in 1290, purportedly at the behest of a constituency of prosperous Amsterdam Jews. He sought to secure recognition of their lawful settlement in England. Menasseh's overtures to Cromwell resulted in the convening of a conference at Whitehall to discuss the Jewish question in November and December of 1655. The Whitehall Conference ended in indecision, and no charter granting such liberties as the petition requested survives from the Cromwellian period. The first official government decree regarding the status of the Jews was not issued until 1663. Nonetheless, late nineteenth-century historians, primarily Lucien Wolf, interpreted ensuing events as evidence that some sort of legally binding "readmission," impelled by a combination of religious and political factors, had occurred.[7]

Lucien Wolf made very imaginative use of scanty materials when he presented Oliver Cromwell as the main proponent of readmission at the Whitehall Conference and claimed that Cromwell even called an end to the conference through fears of a negative result. In his groundbreaking 1901 study of the readmission, Wolf "reconstructed" an impassioned Cromwellian speech on toleration from sources that do not support such an unambiguous claim.[8] It is just as likely that Oliver Cromwell prorogued the Whitehall Conference after taking no action not because he was a champion of toleration in the abstract, but rather because he remained unconvinced that a legally recognized readmission would bring benefit, given the strong opposition to readmission which was expressed at the conference. This is certainly the sense which seems to emerge from Henry Jessey's contemporary account of the conference. Cromwell "had no engagement to Jews, but only what the Scripture holds forth. . . . He had hoped by these Preachers to have had some [in] clearing the case, as to conscience. But seeing these agreed not, but were of two or three opinions, it was left the more doubtfull to him and the Councel."[9] Although Cromwell did informally allow a small community of Jews to enter the country after 1656, it is most likely that his motivations were financial.[10]

There was nothing personally appealing about Cromwell for English

Jews. Rather, Cromwell became a central figure in the narrative because the Whitehall Conference could be portrayed as a liberal, democratic body which had been duly constituted to discuss the benefits that a readmission of the Jews could bring to England. It is particularly notable that, within his history of the readmission, Wolf reprinted a tract written by Menasseh ben Israel which outlined all the benefits wealthy Jews might bring to England, in terms similar to those used to argue for the removal of Jewish political disabilities in the 1850's. Yet Wolf omitted from his narrative the rest of the discourse about Jews which surrounded the Whitehall Conference — tirades which do not suggest that Jewish readmission was being contemplated in the spirit of religious toleration, as Wolf suggests. Rather, Jews were characterized as blasphemers and excoriated as economic competitors by the merchants of London.[11] One document, which may be an agenda from the Whitehall Conference, notes that its members were willing to see the Jews readmitted only under a series of conditions, the most obnoxious being that they were not to discourage anyone who pressed them to convert to Christianity.[12]

A second element of readmission which late nineteenth-century Jews would celebrate concerned the recognition of public worship at the time of the readmission. In 1656, Menasseh ben Israel participated in getting up a petition on behalf of a small group of Iberian traders of Jewish ancestry who were living and trading in London. The petition requested recognition of the Jews' right to public worship.[13] Late nineteenth-century Anglo-Jewish historians would overlook the fact that this community petitioned for recognition as Jews not so that they might enjoy religious toleration, but rather for financial reasons. As citizens of Spain, they were liable to have their goods confiscated because of Anglo-Spanish hostilities; as Jews, perhaps they would be spared. This group had been so well disguised as Spaniards before the Whitehall Conference that there was speculation "whether they be Jews. . . . Some of them have made but little conscience of their own principles."[14] No reply to the petition for the right of public worship has been found.[15] Nonetheless, 1656 was taken to mark the date of the readmission of the Jews and their religious customs to England.

According to Wolf's official history, then, the readmission of the Jews was an intentional act. The English turned to the Jews not for the anticipated financial contribution that Jews might make, but rather to express their farsightedness and beneficence. Such a positive interpretation of the Whitehall Conference — making the Jews and the English appear to have harmonious interests — required Anglo-Jewish historians to deemphasize the fact that those who did favor readmission of the Jews to England did so because they hoped to convert them to Christianity and hasten the millennium.[16] The voices of other Cromwellian Englishmen, who had been quite antagonistic to the idea of readmission because they thought the Jews would be a subversive influence, were dropped from the narrative.[17] The peaceful readmission story set the tone for the rest of the tale. While historians writing between 1880 and the early twentieth century admitted that the post-readmission history of the Jews in England had encompassed moments of struggle, they portrayed the movement from readmission to emancipation as a natural progression, aided by the willingness of the Jewish community to conform to English expectations.[18] Through the codification of this official history—which has proved surprisingly durable—Anglo-Jews ensured that their inclusion in the English nation would be predicated on a continued willingness to conform to "English" standards of behavior on a number of levels.[19]

The Story Behind the Story

Why did the official history of the Anglo-Jews appear in the 1880's? The attempt to reach out to both the Jewish and the non-Jewish communities through an Anglo-Jewish Historical Exhibition and the generation of a particularly English Jewish history were related ways of attempting to overcome the persistent portrayal of Jews as Semitic foreigners incapable of true patriotism.[20] The history that late nineteenth-century English Jews wrote would contain an assimilationist perspective both consciously, in order to avert harsh racial feelings toward England's Jews, and unconsciously, since English Jews had been raised within a society whose culture promoted the superiority of Europeans over Eastern peoples. The crisis over the immigration of Jews from Eastern Europe was only the catalyst for the Jews' scholarly action against a centuries-long discourse of inferiority.

English Jews were unable to make a claim for English nationality by celebrating the uniqueness of their contribution (as, for example, late nineteenth-century conservators of Gypsy culture managed to do). The drawbacks of asserting racial difference were evident for late nineteenth-century English Jews even before Zionism; Anglo-Jews had seen them worked out in the career of Benjamin Disraeli.[21] Despite his early conversion to Anglicanism, Disraeli clearly considered himself a racial "Jew" throughout his life. Disraeli conjured up thoughts of the East in the observer, not only through his sallow skin, brown eyes, and curling brown hair, large nose, and goatee, but also through the somewhat flashy style of dressing he affected in his youth.[22] Disraeli's "racial Judaism" was always evident to his countrymen and fellow politicians, and observers hinted that he had not laid aside all his childhood beliefs upon his conversion to Christianity. As the *Illustrated London News* noted upon the occasion of Baron Rothschild's becoming the first Jewish M.P.:

> The faint tinge of colour that came over the pallid cheeks of Mr. Disraeli as he grasped the hand of the first Judaic member of the Parliament, and the momentary gleam of his eye, indicated a sense of the triumph of race; and perhaps at that moment there may have been a deeper feeling still in his heart—one of regret that he was not leading the House of Commons without having been compelled to use those hitherto cabalistic words, "upon the true faith of a Christian."[23]

Whether they liked him or not, Anglo-Jews were forced to accept Disraeli as a symbol for their own community.

Once Disraeli had managed to enter Parliament he made little attempt to distance himself from his background. At the time that the question of allowing Jews to participate fully in political life as Jews was debated in Parliament, in the late 1840's and early 1850's, despite the danger to his political position, Disraeli supported Jewish emancipation:

> Sir, when I remember for how much we are indebted to that people [the Jews], of what ineffable blessings they have been the human agents—when I remember that by their history, their poetry, their laws, our lives are instructed, solaced and regulated—when I recall other considerations and memories more solemn and reverential, I confess that I cannot as a Christian oppose the claims of those to whom Christianity is under so great obligations.[24]

Although Disraeli was nominally a Christian, his English countrymen looked for signs of Jewish biases, especially in his foreign policy—and claimed to find them in his treatment of the Bulgarian atrocities.[25] During the summer of 1876, the *Daily News* and the American consul in Turkey reported that the Turks in Bulgaria had in May begun an incredible persecution, including rape, torture, murder, looting, and burning, of the Bulgarian Christians, in response to local rebellion. As reports trickled in, Disraeli dismissed Parliament. He was evidently confident enough that what he had on his hands was only a minor incident and that public interest in the issue would be fleeting.[26]

Although Disraeli was sanguine on the subject of the massacre, public opinion immediately and violently censured him on racial grounds. Disraeli's evident lack of concern about the original press reports of the atrocities gave his opposition something to grasp at. William E. Gladstone returned from self-imposed political exile with a scathing condemnation of governmental policy which asserted doubts about Disraeli's commitment to the freedom of Bulgarian Christians.[27] "Dizzy's crypto-Judaism has had to do with his policy," he mused to the Duke of Argyll.[28] Gladstone was compassionate compared with Liberal journalist E. A. Freeman, who noted: "I am sure we are a large enough part of the English people to make even the Jew in his drunken insolence think twice before he goes to war in our teeth."[29] England's Jews would have noticed this reception of Disraeli's foreign policy, especially if, as Anne Pottinger Saab claims, his attitude toward the atrocities reflected his solicitousness toward the English Jews' policy goals.[30] Disraeli's eventual foreign-policy victory could not erase the fact that Jews became a racial "other" to the English in times of national crisis.[31]

Even as allegations surrounding the crisis in Bulgaria died down, the mass immigration of purportedly destitute Jewish aliens loomed, again threatening to divide Anglo-Jews from their adopted home on racial grounds.[32] Mass Jewish migration to England from Russia and other Eastern European states began between 1880 and 1882, in response to pogroms, and continued in waves until after 1900 at rates of between 2,500 and 7,000 immigrants per year. Although influential members of the English Jewish community attempted to stem some of this immigration by redirecting poorer immigrants to the United States, when all else failed they did provide social services for those who chose to stay. With these needs taken care of, immigrant Jews did not become an issue for public concern until they were transformed into one by the press and by Members of Parliament who represented working-class sections of London and other industrial towns.[33] The working-class Englishmen represented by these M.P.'s saw the Eastern European Jews as economic competitors, rivals whose supposed "lower standard of comfort" allowed them to work for a smaller wage.[34]

In March 1888, in response to sustained public outcry against the foreign Jews, the government agreed to appoint a select committee to investigate the impact of immigration. The select committee met for fifteen months, during which awareness of, and partisanship about, the immigration issue increased. Although at the end of the fifteen months the committee did not recommend legislative action, it did urge two measures which would keep immigration in the public eye: systematic collection of data about immigration, and contemplation of future legislation against immigration should the immigrants have measurable effects on the standards of living of England's native working poor. Nor was the House of Commons alone in attending to the supposed Jewish problem—the House of Lords also appointed a committee to study the impact of the sweatshop system, a mode of labor which was particularly associated with immigrant Jews.[35]

In this politically charged atmosphere, Lucien Wolf, a prominent publicist for the established Anglo-Jewish community and the first to examine the relevant archives systematically at the end of the nineteenth century, began to codify the Jewish readmission narrative. In scholarly papers and eventually in a book prepared for the edification of English Jews, Wolf not only described a deliberate readmission of the Jews, but also identified this readmission as the beginning of a liberal evolution that had started with the Jews' readmission and culminated in their emancipation.[36] The readmission narrative could not be separated from its culmination, the removal of the bar against Jewish participation in Parliament. According to Wolf, like the readmission of the Jews, "Jewish emancipation in England was . . . the work of the English democracy. . . . The gradual emancipation of the English Jews, first socially and then in the municipalities, enabled them to show that their civic qualities entitled them to the fullest rights of citizenship; and it was the realisation of this fact—not by statesmen or philosophers, but by their neighbors and fellow-citizens themselves—that eventually gave them the position they now enjoy."[37] The history that Wolf constructed was seamless and teleological.

Wolf had a personal investment in using history to promote the acceptance of Anglo-Jewry.[38] The compiler of a *Dictionary of Anglo-Jewish Biography*, and the author of the article on anti-Semitism for the eleventh edition of the *Encyclopedia Britannica*, Wolf knew that Jews in England were relatively lucky to have found a secure footing.[39] He actively discouraged further Jewish immigration to England in order not to awaken the sleeping giant of intolerance.[40] Nor was Wolf alone in seeking historical legitimization. As the *Jewish Chronicle* proclaimed:

> No longer an alien, the English Jew is now an integral part of the nation, as closely identified with its interests as any other Englishman. And all this has happened in spite of adverse influences abroad. . . . Happily we have shown that we are not unworthy of the liberties which we have claimed as our right. The outward progress of the community has been matched by an advance from within.[41]

Another editorial in the *Chronicle*, entitled "Englishmen and Jews," argued that being one did not preclude being the other, and suggested that it was the responsibility of Jews to help Anglicize new Jewish immigrants as thoroughly as possible.[42]

Anti-Zionism was a related impulse that helped to unite the first generation of Anglo-Jewish historians in their search for historical legitimacy. Wolf and another founding father of the Jewish Historical Society of England, Israel Abrahams, were prominent opponents of Theodore Herzl's plans for a Jewish state in Palestine. Although Zionism appeared to contemporaries to be based on racial claims for self-determination, English anti-Zionists, who wanted to remain in England, went to great lengths to argue that Judaism was a religion. To do otherwise might have cast doubt on English Jews' complete commitment to the citizenship and participation that they had fought so hard to win. One way to prove that Jews were not racially distinct was to emphasize their success at social assimilation over time — to establish for the Jewish community in England an impeccable historical pedigree.[43]

Wolf's contemporary concerns can be seen to have shaped his historical narrative about the readmission of the Jews to England. As Stuart Cohen points out, Wolf argued that England's first Jews had "won social respectability before they had attained full political equality; in fact, they had made use of their individual acceptability in order to obtain that communal right."[44] Wolf emphasized that those Jews who had been "readmitted" to England in 1656 were socially acceptable, wealthy Jews of Sephardic heritage. His historical research thus helped to heighten the distinction between pedigreed, well-assimilated Sephardic Jews and the refugees flooding into England from Eastern Europe at the end of Victoria's reign.

Wolf was able to employ the difficulties of conducting historical research to support his cause. As he constructed his work on the "readmission," the one document he could never find was the outcome of the Whitehall Conference — any Cromwellian legal document stating that the Jews had been legally readmitted. The lack of such a document in fact enhanced Wolf's narrative. He argued that the absence of a decree granting readmission not only had enabled Jews to escape unscathed from their dealings with Cromwell when the Restoration overturned Interregnum laws, but also had kept out the more religious Ashkenazi undesirables.[45] Because the Cromwellian readmission was only de facto, Anglo-Jewry continued to consist of forty or fifty wealthy merchant families of Sephardic origin throughout the 1650's.[46] Had the English government in fact decided to issue a decree expressly recognizing the Jews' right to public worship, "London would have been overrun by destitute Polish and Bohemian Jews driven westward by persecution, some fanaticised by their sufferings, others plying the parasitic trades into which commercial and industrial disabilities had driven the denizens of the Central European Jewries."[47]

Wolf's language, while purportedly referring to the events of the 1660's, reveals the connection of this history to the contemporary debate over immigration, in which the Eastern European immigrants were constructed as Yiddish-speaking, low-trade-practicing Jews whose unrestrained religiosity verged on the embarrassing.[48] For more assimilated Anglo-Jews, the presence of the Ashkenazi immigrants posed an identity problem, since, despite the persistent attempts of the wealthy Sephardic Jews to assimilate to English custom, anti-Semites and average Englishmen alike had long remained unable to differentiate between them and the long-bearded Ashkenazi peddlers. The Anglo-Jews' historical emphasis on the multiple origins of England's Jews helped counter the assertion that all Jews were "Asiatic," the opposite of civilized Westerners.[49]

In his eagerness to differentiate the Anglo-Sephardic from the Anglo-Ashkenazic heritage, Wolf ignored the fact that the people of Sephardic descent who were living in England in the 1650's were not Jews who outwardly practiced their religion but rather were "New Christians." These former Jews, sometimes referred to as "crypto-Jews," had at least nominally converted to Christianity under the pressure of the Spanish Inquisition. "New Christians" could live in the England of the 1650's precisely because they did not mind living outside Jewish social circles, without access to synagogues.[50] It is ironic, but somehow apt, that it was this completely assimilated, outwardly non-Jewish group which Wolf identified as the progenitors of England's nineteenth-century Jews. At one point Wolf even censured Menasseh ben Israel for his too-noisy, too-disruptive attempt to gain the right of public worship for this small settlement of crypto-Jews. Wolf also celebrated one of the crypto-Jews, who had been able to pass as a Christian so well that he had been granted a patent of endenization (the first step on the road to citizenship), as "the real founder of the Anglo-Jewish community."[51]

Wolf became the publicist for a group of like-minded, well-off Jews who were able to use their resources to disseminate the new history in several ways. His first presentation of the readmission story, in front of an audience of scholars at the Jews' College, coincided with one of these vehicles for dissemination—the first celebration of the Jews' historic contribution in England, the Anglo-Jewish Historical Exhibition in 1887, Victoria's Jubilee year. The exhibition, which was also the forum for lectures on the Jewish contribution to English history, echoed the comment that one reporter had made about the displayed portraits of the Goldsmid family: "distinctly Jewish, yet characteristically English."[52] The exhibition also brought together a group of influential Jews interested enough in the potential of Anglo-Jewish history to found the Jewish Historical Society of England, centered in London but with an infrastructure intended to support the formation of related societies in the provinces.[53] In this forum — the social-assimilationist alternative to the new Zionist movement — the readmission story would find its fullest expression.

As Todd Endelman has noted, until 1970, most books and articles on English Jewish history were written by amateur historians affiliated with the Society,

> in part, to defend Jews through research that emphasized their rootedness in England and their positive role in its development. These historians approached their subject in a spirit of uncritical admiration. Their work focused on the establishment of synagogues and charities, the founding of provincial communities, the rise of great merchant and banking claims, the triumph of toleration, and the "contributions" of talented Jews to the larger society.[54]

Endelman notes that their version of history was apologetic and Whiggish, emphasizing the harmony between Jewishness and Englishness while ignoring the discordant aspects of the assimilation process. It is not surprising, then, that when Lucien Wolf addressed the first meeting of the Society in 1893, he took the readmission of the Jews as his subject, noting that "the reciprocal movement of the English people to welcome [the Jews] to their shores" was the outcome of an evolution in the public consciousness, from complete intolerance in 1290 to appreciation in 1656.[55]

Controversy about Jewish immigration and its possible impact on the English willingness to tolerate the Jewish community continued into the 1890's and 1900's. Despite the best efforts of assimilated Jews, the East End became virtually a foreign country, filled with new immigrant Jews whose political affiliations, mother tongues, and religious practices were different from their own.[56] In his study of poverty in London, Charles Booth accused immigrant Jews of blind competition, "unrestricted by the personal dignity of a definite standard of life, and unchecked by the social feelings of class loyalty and trade integrity."[57] In addition to this bad press, the rise of violent anti-Semitism on the European continent made English Jews, especially those in the assimilated middle classes, more aware than ever of the tenuousness of their English identities. "A large area of East London is a foreign town, with its whirl of sewing machines, with its babel in a foreign tongue, with its separate markets, and even in its daily alien press," H. H. Gordon complained to the *Jewish Chronicle*. Like many others, he blamed the Jews rather than the English for intolerance by noting that these things "incidentally serve as a first-class hothouse forcing establishment for Anti-Semitism."[58] As David Cesarani points out, the years between the early 1880's and the passage of the Aliens Act in 1905 saw major figures, including the editors of the *Jewish Chronicle*, vacillate between paternalistic concern for their immigrant coreligionists and the desire to see them redirected to other countries.[59]

Under these circumstances, the immigrants had few champions. Opponents of Jewish immigration—particularly Conservative backbenchers—called for government control of immigration.[60] Lord Salisbury introduced an Aliens Bill in 1894 which was read twice before it died, and the Trade Union Congress passed anti-alien resolutions in 1894 and 1895 despite indignant opposition from Jewish trade unionists. Although anti-alienism was derailed by other nationalistic concerns during the period of the Boer War, sentiment in favor of regulation surged again soon after. In 1902, in response to agitation out of doors, the government set up a seven-member royal commission to investigate the impact of alien immigration. The royal commission entertained a wide variety of testimony—much of which supported the view that immigrants were particularly criminal practitioners of vice who lived in overcrowded housing, menaced the public health, and threatened to compromise the strength of the Anglo-Saxon race.[61]

As the agitation over the immigration question intensified, so also did the attempts of the Anglo-Jewish historians to lay claim to their place in their country and its history. Wolf's glowing account of the events of 1656 continued to serve particular political purposes. In the spring of 1901, Henry Straus Quixano Henriques gave a paper on Jews and the English law before the Historical Society. In reference to the readmission, he made the distinction which Wolf refused to make, noting that while the 1656 Whitehall Conference had reemphasized that Jewish converts to Christianity were free to enter England, it was still not legal in Cromwell's time "to practice Jewish rites in a Christian land." Moses Gaster, a pro-Zionist and the principal rabbi of the Bevis Marks synagogue, joined Henriques in questioning Wolf's interpretation of the readmission story. In a long article in the *Jewish Chronicle*, he specifically promoted the idea of solidarity

among the Spanish, Portuguese, and Eastern European Jews which extended back to the foundation of the original Sephardic synagogue.[62] Even
as Gaster opposed in print Wolf's use of history to support a separate history for English Jewry, Gaster's interpretation supported the notion that
Zionism and Sephardic acceptance of Eastern European Jews were not
alien ideas but deep-rooted ones. This dissent from Lucien Wolf's official
narrative was discouraged by the Chief Rabbi of England, Hermann Adler,
then an anti-Zionist.[63]

The attempts to celebrate the Jewish community in England also continued.[64] The Jewish Historical Society of England therefore invented a
new tradition—the celebration of "Resettlement Day" each February.[65] On
Resettlement Day in 1894, Dr. Adler, the Chief Rabbi of England, delivered a "Homage" to Menasseh ben Israel, who was increasingly lionized as
the hero of the readmission story. Although Adler admitted that Menasseh's mission to Cromwell had not been completely successful on Menasseh's own terms, he celebrated Menasseh's attempts to free the Jews from
the calumnies heaped upon them by seventeenth-century anti-Semites such
as William Prynne. The occasion of Adler's speech was thought to merit the
reprinting of all known documents relating to the readmission—the state
papers, newsletters, and private correspondence relating to the Whitehall
Conference. Finally, Adler called for a fitting celebration of the tercentenary
of Menasseh's birth to take place in 1904.[66]

This tercentenary dinner—held in the same year that the government
successfully shepherded through the Aliens Bill—brought together some of
England's most influential Jews to cement the political meaning of the readmission as a chapter in the narratives of both Christian toleration and
Anglo-Jewish assimilation. Expanding on his idea that the Whitehall Conference had produced an ambiguous legal result, Lucien Wolf gave public
thanks that its failure to prescribe particular limitations on Jewish readmission had saved English Jews from the ghetto system:

> We consequently owe to it, too, the solid foundations in which our rights as
> British citizens rest, for in a very large measure, the fact that our social assimila-
> tion with our non-Jewish fellow-citizens is, and always has been, far more
> complete in this country than in any other country, and that, as a result, the
> baleful wave of anti-Semitism which has swept across the Continent, has
> dashed impotently against our shores.[67]

The Earl of Crewe, one of the invited guests, testified to the potential of social assimilation by boasting of having a Jewish great-great-grandmother

and celebrated the Anglican convert Benjamin Disraeli as "the most distinguished Englishman of the Jewish race who has lived since the Whitehall Conference."[68] Although at the dinner concern was expressed for Russian Jews, who did not enjoy the same civil liberties as the lucky English, the specter of persecution in Russia only increased the fervor with which the Anglo-Jewish community celebrated itself.[69]

The Long-Term Impact

Through festive dinners, exhibitions, and scholarly papers and articles, Anglo-Jewish notables and historians constructed their history—including the myth of the readmission, and various anniversaries of Jewish emancipation—to promote Jewish assimilation and non-Jewish toleration, to keep British anti-Semitism latent rather than apparent, and to ward off accusations that the Jews were an alien element in British society. The history which they affirmed for political purposes during a period of crisis in English life would outlive the crisis and shape the development of Anglo-Jewish history well into the twentieth century, even after Anglo-Jewry had come to terms with the impact of the Russian Jewish immigration. By 1953, Redcliffe N. Salaman, giving the Lucien Wolf Memorial Lecture, could admit that the Russian Jews had had some salutary influence, bringing a new vibrancy and love of learning to the existing Anglo-Jewish community, while also proving to be easily assimilated to English political customs.[70] Yet the scant attention paid to Russian emigrants by the historical establishment did not reflect this new respect.

Even as the reasons for the initiation of Anglo-Jewish historical research were being forgotten or papered over, the celebration of a particular version of Anglo-Jewish history endured. During events to commemorate the tercentenary of the resettlement in May and June of 1956, Jews and non-Jews alike entertained the idea that the resettlement testified to the power of British "toleration." Like Lucien Wolf, twentieth-century Anglo-Jewish historian Cecil Roth thought that Jewish history should serve the concerns of contemporary Jews:[71] "To the Jew, Jewish history should be more important by far than to anyone else. It is for him not merely a record, it is at once an inspiration and an apologia."[72] Bringing new life to an often retold story, at one of the official lectures commemorating the tercentenary event, Roth revealed that he had made a miraculous historical discovery. Although Lucien Wolf had never been able to find Oliver Cromwell's answer to the Jews' petition for the right of public worship, Roth said he had found evidence that key minutes from the Council of State were missing. These minutes, Roth claimed, must have contained Oliver Cromwell's long-sought positive answer to the Jews' 1656 petition for the right of public worship: "To my own amazement . . . I stumbled across new and exciting information, as a result of which the climate of my story now emerges in a substantially new light and with a hitherto-unsuspected dramatic—or even melodramatic—quality."[73] No one else has been able to verify Roth's discovery. Perhaps the momentum of the readmission narrative proved so strong, and its ability to satisfy Anglo-Jewish needs for acceptance so complete, that Roth was impelled to find the historical "facts" to fit the myth.

The tercentenary of the readmission was followed in the recently minted tradition of Anglo-Jewish self-celebration with a Guildhall Banquet and an Exhibition of Anglo-Jewish Art and History at the Victoria and Albert Museum. As Arthur Balfour had done at the celebration held fifty years before, the Duke of Edinburgh congratulated the Jewish community on its achievements. As had Balfour, the Duke of Edinburgh took a page from the Anglo-Jews themselves when he thought to congratulate the Jewish community above all on its success both in assimilating and in evoking Christian toleration. Prince Philip referred to the Jewish community's "success in fitting itself into the life of its adopted country, and yet, at the same time, retaining a strong sense of common interest and reverence for all the best traditions of Jewish tradition and culture."[74]

In the context of a celebration of Jewish contributions to English culture, three hundred years after the much-vaunted "readmission," one of the most visible figures in English society congratulated the Jewish community on its ability to achieve relative invisibility. Anglo-Jews had written their own history, but frequently omitted the point that toleration had always been contingent on social assimilation, whether during the Cromwellian period or the period of nineteenth-century emancipation. The relative security that British Jews had enjoyed in contrast with some of their counterparts on the European Continent has often been chalked up to English exceptionalism rather than to the changes the Jewish community itself has made—to fit in, in advance of feeling pressure.[75] Well after the immigration crisis had passed and a Jewish state had been created, the Jews' own version of history continued to teach them the importance of being English.[76]

The Pro-Boers: War, Empire, and the Uses of Nostalgia in Turn-of-the-Century England

On Saturday, August 16, 1902, one week after the coronation of Edward VII and scarcely ten weeks after the signing of the Treaty of Vereeniging formally ended the Anglo-Boer War, three prominent Boer generals—Louis Botha, Christian De Wet, and Jean De la Rey—arrived in England to plead for amnesty for the Cape and Natal rebels and to raise money for the rebuilding of Boer farms. Declining to attend the coronation naval review in Southampton—they were in no mood to suffer a display of England's imperial might—the generals made their way directly to London, where to their equal surprise and discomfiture they found themselves the objects of near-riotous acclaim. Just two years earlier, news of the relief of Mafeking had roused London to a crazed fit of public celebration, and now the arrival of the besieger himself (Botha) had something of the same effect, first at Waterloo Station, where the crowd yelled itself hoarse with admiring welcome, and then at Horrex's Hotel, Norfolk Street, where the generals were effectively besieged in turn for the duration of their stay. Leader-writers were at a loss, content, for the most part, to attribute the uproar to unthinking curiosity, to the metropolitan public's simple love of spectacle. *The Times* imagined that it was all ironic: that in cheering Botha and de Wet as they might have cheered Roberts and Kitchener, the crowds "merely manifested all unwittingly their satisfaction with British arms." But Botha himself was not so sure. "I am now convinced that in this country . . . all are in sympathy with us," he reported to Jan Smuts in September. "While visiting we meet thousands of people, but I hope they will back their sympathy with their pockets."[1]

In this hope Botha was to be disappointed: his "General Boer Relief Fund" raised less than £125,000 in Great Britain and on the Continent combined.[2] Amnesty, too, was a lost cause. On this point Chamberlain and Milner were immovable, and the generals returned to Pretoria in December with nothing tangible to show for their time away. The impression of English affection lingered, however, and helped reconcile Botha at least to colonial dependence. Did he imagine it then? And if not, what precisely was its basis? What was the sum and substance of this English regard? Usually, when contemporaries spoke derisively of "pro-Boers," they had a specific political type in mind: the Cobdenite pacifist, or the Gladstonian nationalist, or the Marxist socialist, each of whom in varying degrees opposed empire and thus, by often reluctant extension, supported the territorial claims of the Boers.[3] But Botha was detecting something different: admiration, affinity, a keen delight in the idea of a Boer that often exceeded any precise political purpose. "Such a Saturday," wrote a young Barbara Hammond to her mother after meeting the Boer generals:

> fancy seeing De la Rey and De Wet face to face and clasping their hands! L. [J. L. Hammond, Barbara's husband] and I can't get over it. They are magnificent, like great masses of rock with a patriarchal simplicity. . . . De Wet is marvellous to look at, a tremendous man, towering and broad and stout and rough hewn, with an air of extraordinary simple dignity. De la Rey has a most beautiful face; neither of us could think of anything else for a long time. He told L. how he longed to be back on his farm (only it is all destroyed), and how there was no life so delightful, "You are like a little king."[4]

Here again, as with the crowds at Waterloo, we have in part the simple thrill of a brush with celebrity. But the particular qualities that thrill—patriarchal simplicity, roughness of shape, a longing to be back on the farm—are revealing and speak to an often overlooked logic to this pro-Boer attraction. Like her husband, Barbara Hammond was a prominent Liberal, radically forward-looking in her commitment to social democracy. At the same time, however, like her husband (and like many an Edwardian Liberal), she felt an aversion to the modern age, to progress and all its works, and sought a kind of mental solace in imaginings of simpler times. Thomas Metcalf has written in another context of how late Victorian distaste for the liberal industrial order, its individualism, competitiveness, and ugliness, encouraged a vision of India as "a land of abiding traditions and enduring artisanal crafts." So too, I would add, it encouraged a vision of the Boer republics as pastoral commonwealths splendidly isolated, until of late, from the degrading forces of modern commerce. To what extent the crowds gathered to welcome the Boer generals shared that nostalgic vision, we cannot say. But if the Boer War was, as L. T. Hobhouse claimed, the "test issue" of his generation, it was in part because it seemed to pit not just Britons against Boers, not just war against peace, not just tyranny against freedom, but modernity against antiquity, innovation against tradition, and change against continuity.[5]

❧

It was an illusion, of course, this changeless Arcadia, this "little farming commonwealth," as G. K. Chesterton romantically styled the Transvaal Republic.[6] Since the mineral revolution of the 1880's, both the Transvaal and (to a lesser extent) the Orange Free State had rushed headlong into the industrial age, and while the Boers reaped relatively few of the profits, it was not for want of their trying. The president of the Transvaal, Paul Kruger, may have looked and sounded like he just stepped out of the Book of Isaiah, but he was deeply implicated, personally and politically, in the speculative frenzy on the Witwatersrand. Boer society generally was far less homogeneous at the turn of the century than its republican image let on. A small, corrupt oligarchy of notable families was getting rich in Johannesburg while an unhappy combination of circumstances—the closing of the frontiers, a run of droughts, the massive land-grab of the mining companies—drove more and more farmers off the land and into the ranks of a distinctly unrepublican class of urban hirelings. Arcadia was gone, paradise lost, and the Boers themselves knew it. All recent scholarship suggests that Kruger and his oligarchs went to war in 1899 not to arrest the modernization of the republic, but to further it within the local confines of a political system that they, and not the British, controlled.[7]

Boer intention was one thing, though, and the Boer image quite another; in British minds the latter rested on conveniently little direct acquaintance. True, British settlers had been at the Cape in significant numbers since the 1820's, but by then the Boers were already wandering north, and after 1836 they removed altogether to establish their nebulous republics beyond the Orange River. From Cape Town and from London, the British had watched the exodus with bemused indifference: they did almost nothing to stop it. A few evangelicals protested the incursion of "a horde of plundering and sanguinary banditti" into the African interior, but if "the natives should choose to slaughter each other and the Boers and Missionaries should choose to assist them, we can't prevent their doing so," wrote Sir William Molesworth, the Colonial Secretary, in a cabinet minute of 1854.[8] And with that, the perfect expression, really, of midcentury public sentiment, relative obscurity settled on the Boers for the better part of a generation.[9]

The diamonds were their undoing, or, if not just the diamonds, the whole mineral revolution that the discovery of diamonds in 1867 presaged. A backward community of slaving farmers to the north of Cape Colony was one thing; a backward community of slaving farmers in possession of the richest mineral deposits known to man was quite another, and it is no wonder that the 1870's saw the quickening in England of the annexationist urge. Along with it, though, came a novel and strikingly preservationist interest in the Boer. We have made more than we should, in recent years, of a late-century decline of England's industrial spirit. I myself remain unpersuaded of Martin Wiener's ironic and influential view that the very nation that gave birth to the Industrial Revolution quickly became so "ill at ease" with its prodigal progeny as to "deny its legitimacy by adopting a conception of Englishness that virtually excluded industrialism."[10] Still, deep disquiet at the dizzying pace of industrial change was indisputably a part of "the Victorian frame of mind," especially after 1870, when the fact of a permanent underclass of industrial indigents became undeniable. The Commons Preservation Society, the Society for the Protection of Ancient Buildings, the "back to the land" movement, the arts and crafts movement, Ruskin's Guild of St. George, Morris's Socialist League, Toynbee Hall—all date from the late 1860's to the early 1880's; all reflect the widening appeal of a pastoral impulse hitherto reserved to a few disgruntled cranks. Coming when it did, then, the "rediscovery" of a passably pastoral community of white farmers on the South African frontier was bound to evoke sympathetic interest. It was bound to encourage the regressive fantasies of those for whom the march of progress no longer held much promise.[11]

A prominent case in point, here, was James Anthony Froude, the historian and essayist turned amateur diplomat who at the request of Lord Carnarvon, the Colonial Secretary, went to South Africa in 1874 to promote the idea of an Anglo-Boer confederation. Froude was an imperialist, "a passionate believer," his first biographer said, "in the expansion of England, in the energy, resources, and prospects of the Queen's dominions beyond the seas."[12] But he was also a loyal disciple of Thomas Carlyle, and though that accorded perfectly well with one form of imperialism—both Froude and Carlyle looked to colonial emigration as the key to the rejuvenation of the Anglo-Saxon race—it first assumed naked hostility to commerce, equality, political economy, and all other forward-looking philosophies that assured mankind of health, wealth, and happiness. South Africa presented Froude with a real dilemma, then. Politically, he supported the case for English sovereignty; he had none of that liberal fondness for freedom that led others (Gladstone most especially) to respect the territorial claims of the Boers. Yet once on the scene he could not help but admire the Boers as "the worthiest people in the Colony." They "are precisely what their ancestors were two hundred years ago," he wrote to his daughter Margaret:

> The young ladies look as if they had stepped down out of van Eyck's pictures. The sons might have sat to Teniers. The big solemn old family Bible lies on the hall table with the family register in it of half a dozen generations. Long graces precede and follow supper, said seriously, however, and listened to seriously, not yet by any means a humbug or a form.[13]

How could this not have appealed to Froude? How could this not have appealed to one who lamented no less than Carlyle himself the loss of the old, unquestioned faith? And more appealing still was the depth of Boer attachment and commitment to the land. Like many a Tory Radical before him—Bolingbroke, Burke, Cobbett, Oastler, and Carlyle come at once to mind—Froude looked to the land as the only basis of true patriotism and public spirit. His great life's work, *The History of England from the Fall of Wolsey to the Defeat of the Spanish Armada* (1856–70), is from one point of view the classic invocation of a late medieval smallholders' paradise. That it "nevertheless approves Tudor England's break with the past, appears to endorse progress, and celebrates the origins of England's commercial empire" speaks more to "the adhesiveness and resilience of basic Whig ideas," as John Burrow puts it, than to Froude's own predilections, which were decidedly regressive.[14] He profoundly distrusted all forms of mobile wealth, even to the point of imagining a time "when the giddy whirl of industry and progress" would "cease among us," the great estates dissolve, and the soil "again be divided among unambitious agricultural freeholders." England itself was lost, of course; there a peasant proprietary was "a dream," Froude conceded. But in the unlimited expanse of Greater Britain, far from the brick lanes and chimneys of Manchester, "the fable of Midas is reversed," he imagined; "food does not turn to gold, but the gold with which the earth is teeming converts itself into farms and vineyards [and] children grow who seem once more to understand what was meant by 'merry England.'"[15]

They were Dutch children, though. The unhappy tendency of the English abroad, Froude to his own dismay discovered, was to reproduce brick lanes and chimneys. In South Africa they were merchants, shopkeepers, and businessmen; "they made railways, managed ostrich farms, dug diamonds and copper" while the Boers "almost alone were cultivating the soil." The Boers, then, were "the only true colonists." They alone made South Africa their home. In his South African diary, Froude recorded approvingly the "characteristic story" of a Boer farmer who sold an estate adjoining the diamond fields for a tenth of its value and moved off impatiently into the wilderness rather than suffer the intrusion of the diggers on his solitude. "Which was the wisest man?" he then asks: "The Dutch farmer or the Yankee Englishman who was laughing at him?" The "whole talk" among the English was of diamond fields and gold fields, but "diamonds and gold never made the material of a nation," Froude observed, "and never will." One rightly detects in such entries as these the voice of republican foreboding. For Froude, as for so many nineteenth-century Englishmen, the fall of Rome was history's great cautionary tale. No less than the Pax Romana, the Pax Britannica was doomed by its own commercial success to corruption and spiritual decay, unless the English could learn something from the humble example of the Boers, "the Boers of South Africa," who "of all human beings now on this planet," Froude wrote, "correspond nearest to Horace's description of the Roman peasant soldiers who defeated Pyrrhus and Hannibal."[16]

Lord Carnarvon, the Colonial Secretary, might have done well to heed such ancient analogies before attempting the annexation of the Transvaal in 1877. Expecting gratitude, he got defiance instead, defiance so violent that it culminated, in February 1881, in the greatest reversal to British arms since the Charge of the Light Brigade. At home, meanwhile, the immediate effect of annexation was to awaken an interest in South African affairs in Leonard Courtney, the Liberal M.P. for Liskeard who over time was to prove the most prominent and consistent of pro-Boers. Courtney was no romantic; he was a banker, lawyer, and economist whose hostility to empire reflected Gladstonian loyalties. Yet owing in part to Froude's influence, he felt a genuine and sometimes uncritical admiration for the Boers. "They are honest, healthy men," he said in Parliament, "—simple in manner and simple in their mode of life—resolved to go forth into the wilderness, if they must go, in defence of their rights." Against Earl Granville's claim that the Boers' policy toward the Zulu had been "without intermission" one of "violence, cruelty and fraud," Courtney pleaded that they not be judged by European standards. The notion "that all the characteristics of European States should be found among rude farmers, severed from European thought and influence," was, he maintained, "an extravagant one." Neither history nor the knowledge of human nature justified a demand for highly civilized qualities in the Boers, and therefore, Courtney concluded, "we had no ground for the annexation of [their] territory." The outbreak of the Transvaal War in December 1880 found Courtney in office as colonial undersecretary, and thus inhibited from speaking his mind in Parliament. He kept busy in private, however, reminding his chief of "the error of annexation," and urging him to abandon "the impossible task of coercing the Boers."[17]

Froude, meanwhile, in order to keep his own distance from the "wild annexation dance," threw himself into the work of the Transvaal Independence Committee, a public association formed in early 1881 for the purpose of promoting "by all legitimate means the re-establishment of the independence of the Transvaal."[18] Other prominent members included George Russell, a writer and radical M.P., Sir Charles Trevelyan, the former governor of Madras (and grandfather of the historian), Sir David Wedderburn, M.P., Karl Blind, the German émigré, and William Morris, the poet and socialist who, though never a leading member of the committee, suggests by his very presence some romantic inclination. In letters to the press, members praised "the courage, perseverance, and determination of the Boers." In pamphlets they depicted them as "men of simple faith, who were to be admired because they were largely self-taught." Morally, they were "men of quiet, virtuous lives and their women were respected and virtuous," said E. H. Verney when on the stump for the committee in Sheffield: "They were men whose habit it was and is to gather around them night and morning their labourers and their families to hear the word of God read." J. Ewing Ritchie struck an even more pastoral note in *Imperialism in South Africa* (1881): "They are simple Republican farmers, anxious mainly to increase their flocks, and to live on the soil they and their fathers have cultivated and reclaimed." Whether such sentiments influenced Gladstone in his decision to let the Transvaal go is unclear. Privately, he thought the Boers "a dirty lot" who throughout the peace negotiations had "taken their stand on £.s.d." But in Parliament he likened them to the Pilgrim Fathers and thus appeased, evidently, his evangelical and abolitionist conscience. The Boers won their qualified independence from Great Britain in August 1881.[19]

The discovery of gold on the Witwatersrand five years later found Gladstone and his ministers too absorbed in the Irish question to care. The initial pressure to reannex the Transvaal came not from London but from Cape Town, where Cecil Rhodes, the king of Kimberley, having made one fortune in diamonds, was keen to make another in gold. He found willing accomplices in London only from the moment of Chamberlain's ascendancy in June 1895. In the Transvaal, meanwhile, the effects of the gold discoveries were nothing short of revolutionary, as in the space of a few years, a vast and impoverished pastoral wilderness became home to the most capital-intensive mining operations in the world. Johannesburg rose mushroomlike almost overnight. Foreign speculators poured in, tripling the white population of the Transvaal in under four years. The Boers themselves were not slow to take advantage of all this, either by selling their farms to the mining companies at great profit, or by converting from subsistence to market-oriented farming.[20] But from the distance of Europe the impression was of the sixteenth century in stark collision with the twentieth. More than two peoples, two ages were in conflict. "The old, obstinate religious political fanaticism," as Theodore Mommsen described it, was struggling with "modern civilization, based on a not less fanatical desire of exploiting the whole world."[21]

Among the more influential purveyors of this apocalyptic view of the Anglo-Boer conflict was the novelist Olive Schreiner. Born on a mission farm in South Africa in 1855, Schreiner's upbringing, as she frequently pointed out, was "exclusively and strongly English." She started out in life "with as much insular prejudice and racial pride as it is given to any citizen who has never left the little Northern Island to possess," she once confessed, and some of each surfaced in her unflattering portrayal of Tant' Sannie, the grotesquely traditional Boer woman of *The Story of an African Farm* (1883).[22] Schreiner's later renderings of the Boers, however, are deeply reverential, reflecting both her own misgivings about progress and the influence of Edward Carpenter, the freethinking, communitarian socialist who from 1886 was to be her mentor in the gospel of the simple life. "The Boer" (1896), for instance, envies the Afrikaners their isolation from the Enlightenment and their consequent immunity to the European addiction to commerce. "The Wanderings of the Boer" (1896) continues in the same vein, recalling "the days of hard living and hard fighting" when the Boer, having resolved to quit the Cape, made the inhospitable interior over in the image of the Promised Land. "The Boer Woman and the Modern Woman's Question" (1898) envies the possibility of sexual equality in a society as yet unburdened by modern conceptions of femininity. "The Boer and His Republics" describes the district gatherings, the central assemblies, the local militias, and all those other "true old Teutonic institutions" that the Boers, in Schreiner's rendering, proudly established wherever they went as if by ancient instinct. And finally, "The Psychology of the Boer" offers an awk-

ward apologia for the treatment of African peoples that along with a biblical sense of special election was soon to lend itself to a virulent form of Af-
rikaner nationalism. Taken together, the essays constitute a long polemic
sustained, as Schreiner's biographers have said, both by close personal observation of the Boers and by "fiercely protective, almost Jesuitical argument in their defence." Implicit throughout was an attack on the "Company Directors, Capitalists, and Speculators," who in the name of freedom
and progress were threatening to inflict proletarian blight on a fragile, rural
commonwealth.[23]

Unpublished in book form until after her death, Schreiner's essays on
the Boers appeared singly in a variety of English journals between 1891 and
1899, just as the crisis in South Africa reached its violent culmination.[24] One
important effect of the Jameson Raid—Cecil Rhodes's ill-fated attempt to
overthrow the Transvaal by force of private invasion—was to confirm
Schreiner in her worst anticapitalist suspicions and considerably augment
her capacity for public influence. Not that others were not already thinking
along similar lines. In *South Africa As It Is*, a vigorous polemic of 1897, F. R.
Statham denounced the "intrusion of the millionaire, of the living incarnation of the spirit of Mammon," into a republican polity blissfully unaccus-
tomed to both. In a less partisan spirit, James Bryce described the Jameson
Raid as the assault of "men bent on gain" and full of a "fondness for temporary pleasure" on a solitary pastoral people with an aversion to commerce
and an absolute incapacity for industrial occupations.[25] But Schreiner had
seen it all coming before most, and she brought to the pastoral case for the
Boers the considerable weight of her literary celebrity. Edward Carpenter's
Boer and Briton, with its dramatic juxtaposition of a simple, religious people
who "only asked to be left alone in their own country" and a gang of covet-
ous thieves, adventurers, and bankers in Johannesburg, was almost a
straight paraphrase of Schreiner. Keir Hardie's weekly deprecations of "a
capitalists' war, begotten by capitalists' money, [and] lied into being by a
perjured mercenary capitalist press" similarly betray her influence. "As a
pastoral people," Hardie wrote, "the Boers doubtless have all the failings of
the fine qualities which pertain to that mode of life; but whatever these
failings might have been they are virtues compared to the turbid pollution
and refined cruelty which is inseparable from the operation of capitalism."[26]

Of course Carpenter and Hardie were socialists (albeit of a peculiarly
English, backward-looking sort); one would expect them to sympathize
with republican farmers, however racist, against the "gold-greedy ghouls"
of Cape Town and Johannesburg. The real measure of the strength of the

pastoral ideal at the turn of the century lies in the degree to which it influenced even those liberals who despite their anti-imperialism might have been expected to side with the party of progress in South Africa. J. A. Hobson was an economist, after all, and an underconsumptionist one at that. He had little patience for the traditional, primitive virtues of self-help and thrift. He felt none of that sentimental fondness for the soil that routinely disposed others to look kindly on the Boers. And more clearly than most Englishmen, he appreciated the extent to which the Boers' much-vaunted independence rested on the virtual enslavement of Africans. When he went to South Africa as special correspondent for the *Manchester Guardian* in the summer of 1899, however, Hobson was suddenly struck by "the whole dramatic antithesis of the situation." The old seventeenth-century countryman, "with his crude, belated politics and his stern Old Testament direction," had, he discovered, been brought all of a sudden face to face with "a culminating type of modern capitalist civilisation in the luxurious, speculative, cosmopolitan life of Johannesburg." The war, he famously decided, was an elaborate conspiracy got up by a "small confederacy of international mineowners and speculators," and the thing to note about this, besides its latent anti-Semitism, is that it necessarily involved Hobson in a rhetorical reevaluation of the Boers, those "sons of the country," as he now called them, whose only connection with Johannesburg, "the treasure-center of their land," was an occasional early-morning visit to the market to sell farm produce to a "horde of foreigners" living in gold-besotted luxury. The bucolic effect here may not be intended, and in any case it should be set against Hobson's frequent strictures against Boer backwardness. Still, Hobson knew and admired Olive Schreiner. Insofar as his classically republican critique of luxury complements her primitivist socialism, it is not unreasonable, I think, to see his *War in South Africa*, the most influential of all pro-Boer manifestos, and her *Thoughts on South Africa* in a comparable light. If not a full-blown pastoral peroration, it does put the case for those "simple-mannered, plain-living farmers" whose only wish, as Hobson saw it, was "to be left alone and to lead a leisurely and somewhat lazy life upon [the] farm."27

⌒

When war broke out in October 1899, pro-Boer voices of every sort were lost in the patriotic din. For the better part of the preceding decade, Cecil Rhodes and Lord Milner, together with their well-placed friends in Westminster and on Fleet Street, had orchestrated a masterful campaign of concern for British subjects in Johannesburg (the Uitlanders), and now, as Elie

Halévy long ago put it, "the British were practically unanimous in the belief that they were waging a just war to liberate their fellow countrymen, oppressed by an oligarchy of corrupt and stupid peasants."[28] True, the Liberal party still sheltered a few Gladstonian skeptics, but they were not in the leadership, and with the ouster of H. W. Massingham from the editorship of the *Daily Chronicle* in November, they had no effective public voice in London.[29] Outside London, C. P. Scott's *Manchester Guardian* courageously maintained an oppositional stance and saw its circulation suffer accordingly.[30] Elsewhere, the daily press was, as J. L. Hammond's *Speaker* observed, "virtually unanimous on the side of Mr. Rhodes." Even radical newspapers like the *Reynolds News* spoke of the "ignorant, grasping and superstitious Boers" and supported the alleged war of liberation. The pro-Boers were truly, as Bernard Porter has concluded, a "tiny eccentric minority."[31]

The longer the war continued, however, the more difficult it became not to admire "the pluck," as Hammond put it, "the fatal pluck of this little band of Dutch conservatives" who for all their faults evidently took quite seriously amongst themselves the ancient obligations of republican citizenship.[32] "The Boers are, man for man, our superiors in dignity, devotion and capacity—yes, *in capacity*," Beatrice Webb confided to her diary at the war's low ebb in January 1900, and though subsequent British advances in the field led her to qualify this view, it proved impossible entirely to contradict, especially when victory still proved so maddeningly elusive.[33] The relief of Mafeking in May gave famous excuse for national celebration, but with that, public interest in the war began to wane, and the sordid business of counterinsurgency that followed—the barbed wire, the farm burnings, the forced resettlement of Boer women and children in concentration camps— gave the pro-Boers all the opening they needed. By the end of the year, several pro-Boer committees, ranging from W. T. Stead's sensationalist Stop the War Committee to Leonard Courtney's more self-consciously respectable South Africa Conciliation Committee, had found their niche in the propaganda war. John Burns, David Lloyd George, and Sir Henry Campbell-Bannerman were beginning to speak their pro-Boer minds in the House of Commons. J. L. Hammond's *Speaker* was weekly collecting instances of farm burning in South Africa and publicizing Emily Hobhouse's lonely investigation into conditions in the concentration camps. Most heartening of all, in January 1901 Lloyd George (revealing, as Stephen Koss says, that "genius for tactics that were later to be synonymous with his name") engineered a takeover of the *Daily News* and turned it around edito-

rially, giving the pro-Boers a much-needed platform in London, and helping to embolden the hitherto supine National Liberal Federation into a
strongly worded condemnation of the government's policy of uncondi-
tional surrender.[34] The war was still overwhelmingly popular, and would be
to the end. But the "tiny eccentric minority" was growing in confidence
and in strength.

   In what, then, did their more confident eccentricity consist? The pro-
Boer case was not a fixed creed; it did not spring from any consistent or coherent political philosophy. Still, trawling through the considerable body
of pro-Boer propaganda, one encounters continually the same overworked
themes: the war was unnecessary and unjust; it had been forced on the Boer
republics by British aggression; the Uitlanders' grievances were real and to
be deplored, but they were also a convenient pretext; in truth, the war was
about gold—gold and the regular supply of cheap, submissive African labor; and now it was being carried on by "methods of barbarism" that were
a disgrace to a "civilized" nation. I simplify, to be sure. More painstaking
studies of the pro-Boers have rightly identified many variations on these
themes that usually correspond to identifiable tendencies in Liberalism. For
surviving stalwarts of Cobdenite orthodoxy (Francis Hirst and John Morley) the war represented a violation of both fiscal and pacifist imperatives.
For surviving stalwarts of Gladstonian orthodoxy (Scott, Courtney, Hammond, Morley again) it represented a violation of national and moral
imperatives. For forward-looking "new liberal" progressives (Hobhouse,
Hobson, Hammond again) it represented a conspiracy to "place a small
international oligarchy of mine-owners and speculators in power at Pretoria."[35] These distinctions were real and important. But they ought not to
obscure the often purely visceral quality of response to this war. "I em-
phatically was a Pro-Boer," G. K. Chesterton confessed in his autobiography: "My point was that the Boers were right in fighting," that they were
"perfectly entitled to take to horse and rifle in defence of their farms, and
their little farming commonwealth, when it was invaded by a more cosmopolitan empire at the command of very cosmopolitan financiers."[36] Again,
the level of romantic self-delusion here is high. But these were still romantic
times, and though more nostalgic and bombastic than most, Chesterton
was not alone in seeing the war as essentially one between farmers and capitalists. On the surface, pro-Boer could mean a lot of precise political things,
but at bottom it signified an imprecise, even unconscious, aversion to the
modern age.

   Take the more ambiguous case of John Morley, the most clear-sighted and unsentimental of pro-Boers, one for whom, indeed, the epithet itself was a positive misnomer. "I have no love of Boers," Morley assured Lord Curzon in November 1900, "and I am not for peace at any price."[37] What to A. M. S. Methuen, like Froude before him, looked like the Boers' "high and splendid faith" looked to Morley like bigotry and racial arrogance, and he regretted the twist of fortune that for the moment put him on the side of those whom he indelicately called "the worst nigger-drivers now left."[38] Yet the (to his mind) unprovoked annexation of the Orange Free State in May 1900 moved even him to a pastoral eulogy over this once proud yeoman republic.[39] And the even greater offense of farm burning, deplorable mainly on simple grounds of humanity, likewise stirred a deeper regret over the loss of a rural way of life. "I do not believe there can be greater difference in temperament, in pursuits, in taste, in beliefs, than there are between the Boers and [myself]," Morley once insisted to his constituents at Arbroath. That he, too, in spite of himself occasionally indulged what Preben Kaarsholm has called this "unctuous Boer idyll" speaks more persuasively than anything, perhaps, to its irresistible appeal.[40]

Not that everyone succumbed to it, by any means. "The knocking over of a Krugerite theocracy by a Milnerite plutocracy leaves me as cool as the extinction of the stage coach by the locomotive," wrote G. B. Shaw with a perfectly Fabian equanimity.[41] H. M. Hyndman strenuously opposed the war, to be sure, but more out of contempt for "Jew capitalists and Christian financiers" than sympathy with the Boers, who had, after all, he persistently pointed out, stolen the country from Africans.[42] Hobson was not insensitive to this racial snag. "Boer treatment of natives in the Transvaal has never been enlightened or humane," he knew. But he doubted whether British treatment had ever been much better, and Hammond, for his part, refused even to enter into "the revolting hypocrisy," as he put it, "with which a chivalrous protection for the weak is claimed as the object for this war by the organs and the admirers of the men who exhausted the resources without recognising the restraints of civilization in annihilating Mashonas, Matabeles, and Bechuanas." Between the old tyranny of the Boer farmer and the new tyranny of the mining capitalist, there was, in other words, little room to choose, and in many an anxious Liberal mind, this cleared the way for positive appraisal of these citizen farmers who now stood on the frontier of the British Empire, plowshare and rifle in hand, ready to fight rather than submit to the commercial spirit of the age.[43]

That they lost in the end, these citizen farmers, only added to their charm for those of an incurably nostalgic turn of mind. To have put up a surprisingly stubborn and courageous fight, and then lost, was much the best thing the Boers could have done, from the point of view of attracting British sympathy. The Boer triumphant, after all, would no doubt soon have revealed his unsavory, perhaps even commercial side; the Boer defeated could live in the memory as a pastoral relic, a worthy remnant of a simpler, more faithful time whose only wish, as Barbara Hammond reported of De la Rey, was to be back on his little farm. And so it was that the pro-Boers, lonely and isolated for most of the war, finally came into their own afterwards, when constraints on criticism of the war were lifted, and empire (at least of the aggressively forward, Milnerite sort) began its long, slow fall from public grace. This is not the place to enter into consideration of the Liberal revival that culminated in the dramatic electoral victory of January 1906.[44] Many things made for it, including the resurgence of social and domestic as against imperial priorities. But the pro-Boer coloration of the cabinet from Campbell-Bannerman on down—Asquith at the Exchequer notwithstanding—was surely no accident. Nor was the immediate restoration of self-government to the Transvaal, which Campbell-Bannerman proudly regarded "the finest & noblest work of the British power in modern times."[45] Whether the pastoral impulse we have been tracing influenced this devolutionist policy decision in any way is hard to say. But surely it strains nothing to imagine that the same disenchantment with modern commerce that informed the new government's interventionist emphasis on social welfare also informed its commitment to Boer autonomy. In both instances, radical political innovation served the ironic purpose of cultural preservation.

And served it badly, for just as the exigencies of the People's Budget failed ultimately to stem the socially corrosive influence of modern industrialism at home, so too federal autonomy failed to preserve a "little farming commonwealth" in South Africa. Once secure in their self-governing Union, the Boers disappointed their friends, first by refusing to entertain proposals for a native franchise, and thus effectively (if not as yet officially) prescribing white supremacy, and then by unleashing the forces of economic growth no less enthusiastically than the British themselves had done. The simple-mannered, plain-living patriot, so dear to the imagination of British radicals, turned out to be, if not an "utter imposture," as Milner put it, at least a partial one.[46]

It would be easy, then, in conclusion, to speak of pro-Boer credulity, of the unthinking innocence with which a group of nostalgic intellectuals embraced a people whose true purposes they little, or only partially, understood. But if this ideal Boer was in any degree a contrivance, a rhetorical invention designed to serve an anti-imperial purpose, this would be to underestimate them. The pro-Boers were romantics, yes; the Chestertons among them dabbled too freely in a pure politics of nostalgia. But they were also astute social critics who understood the usefulness of arguing from tradition to achieve political change. The Boer who beguiled them, that is to say, was a Boer of their own making, an artful blend of historical fact and pastoral fancy whose brief it was to recall the English to a sense of their own agrarian roots and diminish if not defeat their imperial resolve. Mafeking night showed the enormity of the task, but that "crazed and rather unlovely carnival," as R. C. K. Ensor (himself an old pro-Boer) once described it, was never to be repeated, not even for the Peace of Vereeniging, and by the time the Boer generals arrived in the summer of 1902, a cultural tide had palpably turned.[47] "Such a Saturday," the crowd itself now seemed to say; "fancy seeing De la Rey and De Wet face to face and clasping their hands!"

Character Building and the English Family: Continuities in Social Casework, ca. 1870-1930

In 1891, Octavia Hill, England's leading advocate of "scientific" benevolence, curled her lip at "the old plan of district visiting with a shilling or half-crown ticket in one hand and a tract in the other."[1] By "scientific" benevolence Hill meant a calculated rationing of charitable aid—in stark contrast to what she saw as the traditional philanthropic chaos unleashed by slumming Lady Bountifuls. Miss Hill surely underestimated the degree of personal commitment that district visiting entailed.[2] But for her, and for a growing number of middle-class activists who shared her views, the defining weakness of previous charitable effort was its woeful failure to build working-class character. "Character" was a protean notion. At its core, however, good character signified firm impulse control, with the key corollary that private habits ultimately shape public virtue.[3] Since family life reigned supreme as the forge of character, it followed that "scientific" charity should devote special care to remoralizing humble homes.

This late Victorian campaign to fortify the family produced a style of investigation later labeled "social casework," a practice often associated with the Charity Organisation Society. The founding of the COS in 1869 was not the first expression of frustration with benevolence that supposedly taught the English poor "to lean upon others."[4] Nor could one maintain that the COS appeared when it did because previous decades had witnessed comparatively meager levels of private giving. Writing in 1842, Dickens was probably right to describe the outpouring of early Victorian charity as "unexampled in the history of the earth."[5] What mattered most about the COS's advocacy of casework principles was rather the publicity its views could command. The leading figures within the COS during its late Victorian heyday—Octavia Hill, Charles Loch, Bernard and Helen Bosanquet—

were highly literate and well-connected people, and their voices, heard through a formidable array of essays and books, carried far, particularly westward across the Atlantic. Whether the COS invented social casework or sent the first true social workers into the field will not be discussed here.[6] Of greater interest is how this group and its philanthropic rivals approached their character-mending mission.

In the beginning, the COS used volunteer visitors to evaluate the "home circumstances" of those who sought charity. To keep inexperienced helpers from being duped by a London population that had "extensively graduated in the arts of mendicancy," all visitors were obliged to report their findings to a district committee, which alone possessed the authority to grant an application for relief.[7] The COS Council adopted this system at the urging of two veterans of the war on pauperism, Sir Charles Trevelyan and Octavia Hill.

Trevelyan demanded a "systematic" style of benevolence. From his Malthusian supervision of relief projects during the Irish famine to his stern tenure as governor of Madras, Sir Charles had long preferred combat to compromise. In 1870 Trevelyan trained his rhetorical guns on what he deemed to be "a spreading decay of the spirit of independence among our metropolitan poor, and a demoralisation which threatens grave moral consequences."[8] Such an alarming loss of self-reliance among the urban masses was, in turn, largely attributable to a corruption of the gift relationship. "By passing through official hands," Trevelyan held, "the gift loses the redeeming influence of personal kindness and the recipient regards it, not as charity but as a largesse to which he has a right."[9] The "official hands" belonged not only to Poor Law personnel but also to the agents of private philanthropy: any administrative separation of donor and recipient was apt to erase the sense of obligation in the latter from which a character-mending bond might be cemented. The COS very soon found that it was impossible to coordinate the work of local charities with the Poor Law. Thus the society turned to refining the old practice of "house-to-house visitation." Its emissaries, like conventional district visitors, would strive to "befriend, aim, and elevate the suffering and struggling poor," although COS visitors would do so while recording all pertinent family data in "uniform notebooks" supplied by their district committees. Trevelyan and his allies among London's urban gentry were confident that they could create a new sort of visitor who would combine the virtues of the "gentle doer" and the "wise thinker."[10]

Their confidence seemed justified in light of what another middle-class activist had achieved almost single-handedly. Where Sir Charles Trevelyan spoke expansively about the war on pauperism, Octavia Hill preferred to cite chapter and verse when explaining how the housing of the "destructive classes" could be made to pay. Of all the strategies devised during the 1860's and 1870's to deal with London's severe overcrowding, none was more celebrated than Miss Hill's scheme for training tenants in habits of respectability, and hers was certainly the first to touch the unskilled poor.[11] Like Trevelyan, Hill was deeply concerned about the perversion of charity that seemed to be corrupting the lower orders. As she wrote to Florence Davenport Hill (no relation) in early 1867:

> I think that when gifts are given and received by the same person, they are ennobling. It is the greediness of the recipient that is the awful result [of impersonal charity] at present; and the helpless indolence of expectant selfishness. . . . All presents, too, should depend to some degree on character; we do not . . . select those calculated to deepen any tendency we disapprove, rather to awake fresh admiration of what is noble.[12]

The "gift" that Miss Hill had begun giving to the poor of Marylebone, West London, in 1861 was accommodation in clean, well-managed buildings—buildings purchased and repaired as investments. In return for shelter she could demand much, since "the great want of rooms gives the possessors of such property immense power over their lodgers." What she demanded above all else was the punctual payment of rents. Both to insure that her backers did indeed receive a minimum 5 percent return on their investments and to impress upon her tenants the importance of self-discipline, Hill used "lady" rent collectors to guard against arrears. Having discovered to her surprise "the docility of the people" and their "gratitude for small things," Miss Hill urged rent collectors to treat tenants as she herself had always done, with "perfect strictness in our business relations, perfect respectfulness in our personal relations."[13] Hill wished her collectors to "take the position of *queens* as well as *friends*, each in her own domain." By assuming "complete" control over her tenants, the lady collector became responsible for everything from keeping drains clear to repairing locks, from arranging Christmas festivities for an entire building to insisting on regular school attendance for a particular child. The work of a collector was "one of detail," of constant, quiet concern for the "small things" in the physical and emotional environment of her building. Her loving vigilance over practical matters would be appreciated, Hill declared, and would make possible the sort of trusting relationship that was obviously lacking between landlord and tenant in most model dwelling blocks.[14]

Octavia Hill's famous variation on "5 percent philanthropy"[15] was flawed in both theory and practice. Her refusal to permit irregular rent payments ignored the structural reality that London's poor were often hostages of an unstable market for casual labor. So too, her professed concern with the "want of delicacy felt, and courtesy shown, towards" common folk rings hollow in view of the energy she devoted to refashioning the private lives of her tenants. *Justice*, the voice of the Social Democratic Federation, proclaimed her "inquisitrix-general into the homes of the poor."[16] Yet however suspect Hill's brand of caring capitalism, the tasks she set her rent collectors provided a widely noted example of family intervention—as well as training for the future professionalization of female philanthropy.[17] Deeply suspicious of any attempt to reduce social work to a series of "plans," Hill nevertheless gave great weight to the weaving of a personal tie between collector and tenant. Mary Richmond, the first American theoretician of social work, recognized in Hill's experiment the essence of sound "friendly visiting": an "intimate and continuous knowledge of and sympathy with a poor family's . . . life."[18]

Octavia Hill's faith in her approach to moralizing the working-class home proved infectious. Under the able guidance of Charles Bosanquet, the COS had established thirty-two district committees around London by the end of 1871. As of 1879, seventeen provincial committees were affiliated with metropolitan headquarters, while in America by the same date Buffalo, New Haven, Philadelphia, and Cincinnati had all founded their own charity organization societies.[19] Of course, the history of the original COS has been anything but a tale of unqualified admiration. Contemporary critics as well as many latter-day scholars have depicted the COS prior to the First World War as the embodiment of heartless individualism, an agency whose initials sometimes seemed to proclaim "cringe or starve."[20] For a brief period in the mid-1880's, Beatrice Webb later confessed, the COS appeared to her as "an honest though short-circuited attempt to apply the scientific method of observation and experiment, reasoning and verification, to the task of delivering the poor from their miseries by the personal service and pecuniary assistance of their leisured and wealthy fellow-citizens." Once she had seen the light of Fabian socialism, though, Webb grew distinctly less forgiving, emphasizing instead how members of the urban middle classes had, as COS visitors, "found themselves transformed into a body of amateur detectives, in some cases initiating prosecutions of persons they thought to be imposters, and arousing more suspicion and hatred than the recognized officers of the law."[21] To George Lansbury, future leader of the Labour party, the conduct of the COS in late Victorian Whitechapel seemed "perfectly brutal." Canon Samuel Barnett, dean of the East London settlement-house movement, rebuked COS workers for "refusing to do anything except to clothe themselves in the dirty rags of their own rightness." This was a stinging critique, coming as it did from a lifelong member of the society who had married one of Octavia Hill's rent collectors.[22]

The thrust of historical opinion has been to regard the COS as a discredited experiment in social control, although a useful laboratory for the refining of family-casework techniques. If the society did not go so far as to perform a "cultural lobotomy" on the masses, we are told, it did seek to administer a "social sedative" by rearticulating the mutual responsibilities of rich and poor. Yet out of its mission to resuscitate "character" in the demoralized individual there emerged, happily enough for future generations, a form of home visiting that stressed full understanding of the individual's social predicament.[23] Gareth Stedman Jones was the first scholar to challenge this interpretive tendency to separate the society's social philosophy from its casework methods. The leaders of the early COS, Stedman Jones pointed out, were members of an urban elite whose prestige rested not on wealth or birth but rather on education and the possession of professional credentials. Small wonder, then, that such mainstays of the society as C. S. Loch and the Bosanquets would promote a form of charitable intervention that prized social knowledge over the unthinking distribution of money.[24]

Since the appearance of Stedman Jones's *Outcast London*, the image of the COS has undergone further revision. The traditional view of this body as a bastion of extreme laissez-faire individualism, for example, ill fits the fact that the society had long advocated greater state intervention in such areas as municipal sanitation and training for the "feeble-minded," or that by the Edwardian years its leaders could urge the creation of public-works projects as one antidote to mass unemployment.[25] We have learned, moreover, that any assessment of the society must recognize that its status in many provincial towns was much lower than in London, and that, especially in the northeast, there existed a notable *lack* of cooperation between Poor Law officials and local COS leaders.[26] Yet the practice of COS family intervention has not received equivalent scrutiny. To what extent did its "new technology of professionalized social casework"[27] actually produce an intensified examination of private lives? And how "new" was its casework "technology"?

The first leaders of the COS allegedly understood the "dangers of over-visitation" and recognized, in principle, the right of the poor "to freedom from unasked for intrusion."[28] Helen Bosanquet, who offered this assurance, was herself a keen believer in the sanctity of domestic privacy. In *The Family*, her last major book, she made clear her sympathy with the Victorian notion of home-as-haven:

> It is an essential feature of the House . . . that it can be closed against outsiders. If it is nothing more than a gipsy's van, or the shelter of cave or tree, so long as its limits are respected by the rest of the community, the privacy and consecutiveness of family life can be preserved. . . . And this power of exclusion is not of merely negative value, exercised *against* the outsider; it gives rise to the whole range of virtues and rights and duties which gather around the conceptions of hospitality and guest and host. To hold the balance true between the duties of the house towards the outside world, in the exercise of hospitality, and the duties of the house towards the Family in preserving its privacy, is no small part in the problem of its management; the family life may as easily become swamped in a multiplicity of guests, as it may become selfish in its exclusiveness.[29]

Helen Bosanquet's image of "the House" here is obviously class-bound, for few "houses" belonging to the very poor — that is, one- or two-room dwellings — could have endured a "multiplicity of guests" for very long. All the same, she was both temperamentally and intellectually committed to a view of the nuclear family as requiring its own private space, a space wherein parents wielded a "necessary autocracy."[30]

Just as autocracy can sometimes degenerate into tyranny, however, so the privacy of the home might occasionally need to be breached in order to save its dwellers from self-defeating habits. In such cases what Mrs. Bosanquet termed "thorough charity"[31] should be undertaken. "Thorough charity" required the COS visitor to compile an inventory of individual family characteristics as well as financial resources, and assumed that a short-term invasion of the inner sanctum could produce behavioral changes which would allow a home to regain its "family feeling" and so also its efficiency as a character factory. "Character," in the Bosanquets' Idealist sense of the word, was that aspect of mind which enabled the individual to impose order on social circumstances. A father addicted to drink, clearly, remained a disorderly person.[32] Hence, an essential part of the COS visitor's task was to distinguish among varieties of disorder. The social and economic circumstances weighing upon a poor family mattered. "I do not . . . belittle material conditions," Bernard Bosanquet explained, "or deny that insuperable misfortune may destroy the industrial qualities and drag a man down among the invertebrate Residuum."[33] But COS visitors and their district committees were nonetheless warned against conceding primacy to environmental factors, a concession that could encourage parents "to think that the world is a lottery." As Octavia Hill's work had shown, it was safer to improve homes and the habits of their occupants simultaneously.[34]

In theory, a social-work protocol to implement this mission had taken shape by the mid-1880's. The COS district committees might learn about cases of family distress from several sources: concerned citizens, the police, other charitable agencies, COS visitors, or the distressed families themselves. If, as often happened, a parent approached the district committee directly, he or she received the society's "form no. 28" ("Notice to Persons Applying for Assistance"). This notice left would-be clients in no doubt about COS precepts. Its first sentence announced: "The Society desires to help those persons who are doing all they can to help themselves, and to whom temporary assistance is likely to prove a lasting benefit."[35] Whatever the source of information about a family allegedly in need, district committees would dispatch one of their visitors, usually female, to investigate the home. The most useful visitors were those who had studied their assigned districts and as a result were familiar with the neighborhood's major occupations, its range of household incomes, its provident organizations, and its Poor Law services. Already accustomed to viewing the district as "an organic whole" rather than as "a chaotic agglomeration of atoms," such visitors could conduct an informed interview with family members.[36] A skilled interviewer was at once a "friend" and an interrogator. She should bring the working-class home moral refreshment, although while refreshing the weary, she might ask to see the rent books and any pawn tickets. In 1886 the harsh designation "undeserving" may have been replaced in COS reports with "not likely to benefit" (a phrase replaced two years later with the neutral "not assisted"), but visitors continued to judge "whether, granted the facts, the distress can be stayed and self-support attained."[37] Data gathered during home visits would be added to the "casepaper" that a district committee compiled for each applicant. These family records grew so detailed—and the society's demand for uniformity in their preparation so strong—that by the 1890's COS leaders were calling for trained persons to manage them.[38]

In practice, however, this imposing social-work protocol functioned spasmodically, even in London, the society's stronghold. By 1886 COS visitors there were trying to cope with twenty-five thousand cases per year.[39] Since the great majority of visitors were still unpaid volunteers at this time, the inevitable turnover in their ranks made recruiting able replacements a headache for COS leaders and, more important, weakened the bond between visitor and visited, a bond best maintained through years of "friendship." Adding to these difficulties was the society's principled objection to relieving worthy cases out of a general fund. Because every case approved for relief presented both COS volunteers and the English public with an opportunity for further "education in charity organisation," according to C. S. Loch, the society's secretary from 1875 to 1914, a letter-writing campaign for each case should be mounted.[40] The labor demanded by "scientific" benevolence grew more arduous still on those occasions when churches, hospitals, and other charities refused to help COS officials find resources for "deserving" families.[41]

Outside London, the chasm between COS theory and casework practice yawned wider. In some provincial societies the systematic assessment of family needs was virtually nonexistent.[42] At least during March 1889, for example, the Bournemouth COS performed charitable triage during the weekly meetings of its executive committee. This was a small, all-male club of retired army officers, Nonconformist ministers, a doctor, and several "resident gentry." They placed great faith in their ability to judge a supplicant by his or her appearance. Thus, when "an oldish, shambly man clad in a once fashionable black cut-away coat" came before them asking for financial aid so that he could return to his family, the COS sages observed that "his puffy white face and fat white hands" did not resemble those of a professed pipe fitter. His application was swiftly dismissed. Faring better was the bricklayer who wished for support so that he and his family might emigrate to Argentina. He had already secured passage to Buenos Aires; now he needed money to buy clothes and tools. Fortunately for him, this applicant "appeared in his workman's dress and answered questions freely." What won over the committee, however, was this ex-soldier's vague recollection of an officer with whom two of the COS watchdogs had once served. A gift of £3, to be dispensed through a minister, was the man's reward for apparent honesty.[43]

Thanks to the preservation of some thirteen hundred case records, we know considerably more about the operations of the Leamington COS. Established in 1875, this body sought to smother what it saw as haphazard benevolence in a town down on its luck. The first half of the nineteenth century had brought both prosperity and people to Leamington as the comfortable classes discovered its rejuvenating "spa" waters. When changing leisure fashions began sending the wealthy abroad or to seaside resorts, however, population growth slowed in this East Midlands town, its building boom ceased, and hard times arrived for the wide range of tradesmen dependent upon the patronage of the rich.[44] By the mid-1870's, local newspapers were filled with bitter comment about the alleged indifference of town leaders to the plight of the underemployed. Yet Leamington's COS did not respond to this criticism in ways that would have won praise from the parent society in London. Between 1876 and 1900, the Leamington COS received roughly 23,500 applications for aid. During the twenty-one years for which reliable statistics exist, only 13.2 percent of the applicants received no help. This figure implies a noteworthy lack of selectivity, since, by comparison, in London 22.7 percent of all applicants were judged to be either "ineligible" or "undeserving" in 1872. Equally telling was the type of charity offered in Leamington. By far the most common kind of relief was the emergency grant of money or food, with tickets for treatment at Warneford Hospital or at local convalescent homes constituting the next most frequent form.[45] The majority of those who received charity, moreover, did so repeatedly, over a period of years. Loans designed to push industrious families along the road of self-reliance were rare. Much more common were loans (secured by interested middle-class citizens) to erase arrears in rent or to help poor parents avoid the stigma of a pauper's burial for their children.[46] Taken together, these charitable practices depict the Leamington COS as a dispenser of doles rather than an instrument of "scientific" benevolence.

Further analysis of its surviving case records confirms this impression. The methodical investigation of family circumstances to which the London COS was theoretically committed found few echoes in the Leamington society's work. Only two sins consistently alienated its officials: imposture and sexual nonconformity. Jane Kelly, 46, met swift disapproval when she applied for a "little help" in 1889. Mrs. Kelly's husband had deserted her three years earlier, and since then she had struggled to make ends meet by selling firewood and taking in laundry. Hers was a sad story, as the COS had recognized by its five previous grants of cash, coal, or food. Nevertheless her sixth application for relief was "not entertained" after the enquiry officer found that Mrs. Kelly was living with a street sweeper.[47] The enquiry officer, it should be noted, learned of Kelly's indiscretion through rumor, not through sustained visitation. For as time went on the Leamington COS came to rely less on its visitors' reports and more on testimonials from employers and newspaper accounts of "problem" families. This outpost of the charity organization movement had neither the resources nor, apparently, the will needed to police the private lives of the poor. In Leamington it was visible poverty, especially beggars on the streets, that worried the local elite, not the manufacture of moral weakness in poor homes.

This is not to say that social casework failed to mature elsewhere in England. Given Octavia Hill's insistence on training for her lady rent collectors, it was logical that London COS officials would take the lead in social-work education, requiring their volunteers to serve apprenticeships "and so endo[w] emotion with strength and purpose." Their emphasis on training gained institutional support when in 1903 the School of Sociology was established in London and, one year later, the School of Social Sciences in Liverpool.[48] Yet by the early years of the twentieth century mere mention of "charity organisation" often conjured up an image of skinflint philanthropy. However unfair this association, the fact remained that in many communities, as a spokeswoman for the Newcastle COS confessed, the name alone "brings us a good deal of unpopularity." There was still a role for the "systematic method" to play in regulating the giving of gifts, Teresa Merz allowed in 1911, "but possibly the idea of citizenship—the idea that each of us has a responsibility towards our fellows—had come more to the fore."[49] Merz cited as an illustration of this "newer spirit" in social work the guilds of help that had appeared in several industrial centers, starting with Bradford in 1904. On one hand, the guilds closely resembled most charity-organization societies insofar as both dealt with the prevention of benevolent "overlapping" and the detection of "imposture." More self-consciously than any COS, on the other hand, these new agencies sought to make a concern for the poor part of "municipal patriotism" rather than a recapitulation of class differences.[50] Home visiting was a defining feature of both the old and the new social work. But the guild "helpers" were supposedly less interested in assessing character than in providing "the steady pressure of friendly influence and moral support" for working-class families in need.[51] Did these contrasting social-work styles actually produce a different form of domestic intervention?

By 1911, seventy guilds of help were at work in England, two-thirds of them concentrated in the north. The largest of these bodies, based in Birmingham, Manchester, and Sheffield, each supervised more than five hundred "helpers," while the smallest oversaw fewer than fifty. Bradford, where the guild movement began amidst deep depression in the worsted textile trade, claimed to have between four hundred and five hundred helpers dealing with five hundred to a thousand cases annually during the first two decades of the twentieth century.[52] Since the Bradford District Archives hold 5,682 guild casebooks, it is to this branch that historians must turn for evidence of shifting casework practice. Above all, what distinguished the guild of help from other local charities was its esprit de corps. The Bradford Town Mission had long since lapsed into obscurity, its few paid agents too preoccupied with spiritual salvation to analyze most temporal causes of family distress. Equally irrelevant to local needs was the Bradford COS, which remained fixated on the suppression of "mendicity." Taking inspiration from the volunteer relief system operating in the German textile town of Elberfeld, those who planned the new venture in 1903–4 were determined that their helpers would get to know a very few families (preferably no more than three) very well—precisely what Octavia Hill had been urging for a generation.[53] Out of such intimate knowledge, the details of which were to be entered in a casebook following each home visit, guild helpers and their district-committee supervisors would devise practical solutions for individual family problems.

Prominent among the Bradford guild's "Instructions to Helpers" was a caution against rash action: "A strong Helper must have the courage not to act until he understands the family. You must be prepared to see suffering and wrong-doing that you cannot prevent, and be willing to wait till you know what the difficulties and troubles arise from."[54] This warning proved much easier to issue than to honor. Dorothy Keeling, who would go on to establish Liverpool's Personal Service Society, started her social work career in 1907 as a part-time supervisor in one of the Bradford guild's poorest districts. Here she "always" instructed her helpers "to buy necessary food, and then to make enquiries" if a family appeared hungry. Keeling quickly learned through her own home visits that helpers often could not afford to watch "wrong-doing" from a distance. When, for example, she found that a mother had locked her adult daughter in an upstairs room for several days, Keeling felt fully justified in arranging the young woman's escape to a place of safety.[55]

All too often, though, the guild's agents had no choice but to look on in anguish as a family fell apart. A case supervised by Miss Keeling revealed the emotional rigors of such social work. On September 24, 1909, Mrs. Jackson paid her first visit as a guild helper to the home of Charles and Sarah Field. Mrs. Jackson did not record in her casebook how she happened to call on the Fields, or bother to comment on the conditions of their home. What most worried Mrs. Jackson was the welfare of thirteen-year-old Gladys, a troubled girl with a "stump" instead of a left arm. "Family in itself apparently quite alright," Jackson wrote: the parents and the eight children who remained at home seemed to find a weekly income of £2 10s adequate. Unfortunately, if Mrs. Field scolded Gladys "in any way," the girl would stay out all night whatever the weather. A former neighbor was sure that Mrs. Field did not mistreat her children. Mrs. Jackson reasoned, therefore, that the solution to this mother-daughter conflict lay in fitting Gladys with an artificial arm. The district committee to which Jackson reported agreed that the girl needed a prosthesis of some sort, but wondered how much of the estimated £5 to £10 cost the Fields would be willing to bear. So, over a period of several weeks the guild's helper tried to sell Mrs. Field on the idea of surgery for her difficult child, while convincing Gladys not to defy her mother.

In mid-March 1910 the Field case took several turns for the worse. First, the family moved to cheaper rooms without alerting Mrs. Jackson. On locating them again, she found an adult daughter presiding over the household while Mrs. Field was in hospital recovering from an attempted suicide. After her release, Mrs. Field "complained bitterly" about how her three grown children had returned home and "helped themselves" to their father's recently activated pension. Gladys's defiance had been hard enough, but now the distraught woman was facing an even more direct challenge to her domestic sovereignty. Mrs. Jackson contacted the Discharged Prisoners Aid Society, hoping that it might find temporary peace for Mrs. Field in a convalescent home. Mr. Field was prepared to pay five shillings per week— over half his pension—to make this possible, but no opening could be found.

By early August, with Mrs. Field threatening to jump into the canal again, the guild's helper was losing faith in the redemptive power of friendship: "Cannot write all I heard [during her most recent visit], but I feel very unfit for the case." Mrs. Jackson's morale suffered further damage when, over the next few weeks, three large children's charities declined to help Gladys: Dr. Barnardo's Homes refused to get involved because "the girl cannot be described as destitute," the National Children's Home because Gladys seemed to be suffering from "considerable mental disturbance," and the National Society for the Prevention of Cruelty to Children (NSPCC) because both house and young appeared "fairly clean." On September 19 Mrs. Jackson confessed: "It feels an impossible case for me." Six days later she severed her ties to the family. The helper who took over from Jackson learned on her first visit that although Gladys seemed less troubled now that she was working at a local laundry, Mr. Field had begun to beat his wife. The guild's district committee concurred with this agent's last evaluation: "It seems we are not able to do any more." In late April 1911, the case was marked "closed for the present."[56]

Admittedly, not all the Bradford guild's cases proved so vexing, although in roughly two-thirds of them the decision to cease visiting was a tacit admission of failure. As early as February 1905, the executive committee registered its frustration with cases involving husbands who deserted their homes.[57] The guild likewise found it very hard to persuade families in economic peril to "take the house"—that is, to accept relief inside a Poor Law workhouse. In mid-1911, for example, one helper began visiting a family of four who had recently sheltered the mother's parents. What made this arrangement dangerous was that sixty-year-old Allen Edmondson, now wracked by consumption, slept in the same room as the eldest child. Despite the helper's plea that Mr. and Mrs. Edmondson be moved to a Poor Law facility, their daughter could not bear to turn out her parents. Therefore, the file notes concede, "it seems of no avail to go on visiting the case."[58] Where the guild's interventions were deemed successful, that success frequently sprang from a helper's spontaneous (and technically improper) provision of money, clothing, food, or even part-time work. Less often, it appears, were happy endings attributable to a helper's "friendly" influence alone, as when a landlord was induced to repair an offending chimney or prosperous folk were persuaded to support their destitute kin.[59] Such remonstration was hardly new. Thus, scholars who wish to view the guilds of help as somehow more "democratic" and "progressive" than the COS, or as creating, in effect, a voluntary "welfare state" in several localities, need to appreciate how hit-and-miss guild social work actually was.[60]

Indeed, at no time prior to the Second World War did English social casework offer anything resembling a coherent "programme"[61] for disciplining the working-class family. It has been asserted that during the first third of the twentieth century American social workers "saw themselves as doctors to a sick society."[62] A similarly sweeping claim has been made for French social work during the same era, emphasizing its "promotion of a boundless educative solicitude" as a cover for its real project: the refining of "techniques" for manipulating poor homes.[63] Late Victorian and Edwardian England also witnessed the application of more systematic strategies for dealing with urban poverty, as well as new sites for their deployment (as, for example, in hospitals, where the COS began stationing "almoners" to prevent the abuse of medical charity).[64] But England proved remarkably resistant to the idea that casework could or should become a social technology.

This is all the more striking because America's Mary Richmond, often described as the founder of professional social work, gratefully acknowledged the influence of certain London COS figures on her thinking about the science of "differential casework." As we have already seen, Octavia Hill's "intimate and continuous" contact with her tenants helped shape how Richmond conceived of "friendly visiting." Similarly, Miss Richmond noted her "heavy debt" to C. S. Loch and his case-by-case approach to the rationing of benevolence.[65] Richmond, who began her social-work career as assistant treasurer of the Baltimore COS in 1889 and ended it as director of the Russell Sage Foundation's Charity Organization Department, is usually seen as the central figure in a revolt against nineteenth-century social work and its middle-class mission to revitalize the character of the poor. Her key contribution, we are told, was the articulation of a "diagnostic" approach to social work in which each "client" was to be treated as an individual, in accordance with the complex particulars surrounding the case, rather than as a member of a preconceived social category.[66] Richmond's casework classic *Social Diagnosis* (1917) is an exhaustive study of the collection and interpretation of "social evidence": "all items which, however trifling or apparently irrelevant when regarded as isolated facts, may, when taken together, throw light upon the question [of how to] place [a] client in his right relation to society." Every aspect of the caseworker's job was considered. Richmond devoted special care to dissecting the home interview, during which "leading questions" should be shunned, the caseworker relying instead on "slow, steady, gentle pressure" to extract information from the client.[67] In *What Is Social Case Work?* (1922), Richmond sounded even more un-Victorian when she cautioned against romanticizing family life. The home as "an institution for its own sake" deserved no special reverence from the trained caseworker.[68] One wonders, nevertheless, how far Mary Richmond moved beyond certain eminently Victorian notions about the goals of social casework. Tellingly, in *Social Diagnosis* she describes the accumulation of social evidence as essential to developing an "intimate understanding of character." Successful social work, in fact, demanded a grasp of what she termed "characterology."[69]

Across the Atlantic, Miss Richmond's writings found an interested but skeptical audience. Although her pronouncements on the meaning of casework soon penetrated the social-studies curriculum offered at Liverpool University and the London School of Economics, her practical influence was quite limited. As a comparison of case records compiled in 1924 and 1934 observed:

> One's first impression in pondering eighty case records is that there is no accepted discipline of social casework; that apart from certain administrative routines typical of different services, the whole process is largely determined by the immediate situation and the caseworker's common sense impressions and intuitive responses. The enthusiastic reader of Mary Richmond's *Social Diagnosis*, the student who comes expecting to find "all the reason of science" clearly marshalled for the solution of human problems will come away sadly disillusioned.[70]

Throughout the interwar years even professional, university-trained social workers continued to personify Sidney and Beatrice Webbs' prewar ideal of the voluntary agent: one who could, "if desired, lavish a wholly disproportionate amount of care on a difficult case or a difficult class of cases."[71] The social worker, wrote Clement Attlee in 1920, "is one who feels the claims of society upon him [*sic*] more than others."[72] Attlee's gender confusion aside, his definition epitomized the prevailing belief that social workers were necessarily creatures of conscience. To the champions of social casework as a respected profession for women, the implications of this view were troubling. Prior to the Second World War, declared one such champion, a caseworker would all but "apologize for her activities, conscious that she was . . . taking money for performing vicariously one of the normal and pleasurable duties of every . . . Christian—the duty to help one's neighbour."[73] No less an expert than Elizabeth Macadam, interwar England's most forceful advocate of academic preparation for social work, accepted that "inborn personal qualities" were the "essential qualification" for intervening in private lives. Macadam wished that her students would give American casework principles the benefit of the doubt. Yet she readily understood why English women might find "repellent" the prospect of sitting in a classroom "with typewritten records of . . . an 'unmarried mother' in their hands discussing minutely the diagnosis and treatment of an unfortunate example of 'social maladjustment.'"[74]

Well into the 1960's, many English voices could still be heard praising "neighbourliness," "goodwill," and "common sense" in casework.[75] Such resistance to the notion of social work as an aggregation of "techniques" reflected, in part, the fragmented state of the profession. For within both private charity and the expanding realm of local government, "social work" had always been a loosely linked assortment of specialized missions dealing with the elderly, the sick, the mentally ill, the physically disabled, children in need of care, and delinquents of all ages. The impact of the "psychiatric deluge" that allegedly swept over England after 1920 has been exaggerated. But the emergence of a unified theory of deviance, and its conceptual companion, the "problem family," *did* prompt traditionally inclined social workers to reassert the primacy of "friendship" in their duties.[76] Whatever may be said about the "bureau-professionalism" of English social work after 1970,[77] during much of the twentieth century this form of family intervention has been chaotically pursued despite—and occasionally because of—repeated claims that charity could be "organized."

Local social-work agencies proliferated during the interwar years, inspired by the example of the guilds of help. We know from scattered casepapers that their agents sometimes demonstrated crass insensitivity in dealing with working-class families. The records of these agencies also show, however, that the ideal of community responsibility for the distressed was often more than a pious pretext for meddling with the domestic habits of the poor. The first casepaper compiled by Newcastle's Citizens' Service Society dates from late 1923. Its many entries tell the story of a thirty-two-year effort to help the troubled family of Mark Cross, a Scots miner given to binge drinking and beating his wife and five children. The society could do only so much to end his reign of terror: an inspector from the NSPCC was summoned to warn Cross about the legal consequences of child abuse, and the aid of a health inspector was enlisted to remove the dog that had been allowed to defecate throughout the house. But something had to be done for the children, particularly for Mary Ann, seventeen, whose partial paralysis of the face testified to her father's brutal temper. One of the society's volunteers therefore saw to it that Mary Ann received training as a domestic servant. From the mid-1920's until her death in 1953, she stayed in touch, mostly by letter, with her "friends" at the society. It would take an ingenious reading of this correspondence to see Mary Ann as the victim of a bourgeois assault on her home.[78]

Nor could one argue that such sustained and highly personal contact represented a new style of family regulation. Hazel Newton, an American social worker, explained in 1930 that "going scientific" meant not "putting too much of one's own prejudices, sentiments, loves and hates, into one's job."[79] In England, at least, Newton's definition had faint resonance for her professional counterparts. Although helpers had become "caseworkers" and families in need had become "clients," the character-building impulse of late Victorian philanthropy remained fundamental. Thus, to speak of an evolution "from charity to social work" — let alone "from character building to social treatment"[80] — distorts lived experience. Octavia Hill would have shuddered to learn that Depression-era home visitors were now paid, sometimes with state funds, but she would have blessed the purpose for their visits.

LAURA E. NYM MAYHALL

The Making of a Suffragette: The Uses of Reading and the Legacy of Radicalism, 1890-1918

In her study of the reading practices of women in nineteenth- and twenti-eth-century Britain, critic Kate Flint argues that reading provided a means of "becoming part of a broader community," one in which readers shared "horizons of experience which have to a significant extent been built up through their common reading material."[1] The practice of common read-ing, Flint suggests, was of particular significance within the Edwardian phase of the campaign for women's parliamentary enfranchisement. Her examination of the representation of reading in women's autobiographies and in the suffragette newspaper *Votes for Women* makes a strong case that reading played a vital role in creating and sustaining suffragist allegiances.

Drawing upon Flint's belief that reading created bridges "between the consciousness and experience of many women," this essay argues that suf-fragettes used reading not only to communicate with each other about a contemporary agitation, but also to confirm links to a shared past.[2] In pub-lished accounts of their movement, late Victorian women activists identi-fied themselves as part of a tradition of reform beginning in the nineteenth century. They did this, historians have argued, in order to stake claim to participation in the political nation.[3] Suffragettes, in particular, viewed themselves as acting within a framework of radical causes, extending back in time from male working-class franchise agitation of the 1860's, through abolitionism in the early to mid-nineteenth century, and to the reform of Parliament itself, in 1832. Suffragettes wrote histories and made public, in such venues as the courtroom, narratives casting themselves as logical in-heritors of the radical tradition in British politics.[4]

This essay examines the uses of reading and the legacy of radicalism in the formation of one individual's political consciousness, by following her engagement in suffrage politics from an initial interest in the 1890's to her active participation as a militant during the Edwardian campaign. The Scots woman Eunice Murray, who would become a member of the National Executive Committee of the militant suffrage organization the Women's Freedom League, kept a journal from the 1890's until just after the First World War in which she commented upon her reading life.[5] A reconstruction of Murray's reading practices suggests some of the ways suffragists in Britain at the turn of this century utilized a rich heritage of radical protest in the creation of a modern political movement, drawing upon and yet transforming liberal discourses of citizenship in the process.

Born 21 January 1877, Eunice Guthrie Murray was the third child and youngest daughter of David and Frances Stoddard Murray, who had settled at Moore Park, Cardross, outside Glasgow following their marriage in 1872. Murray's father was an attorney in Glasgow, and her mother, whose parents on both sides were American, published in a variety of genres, including poetry and travel, and lectured locally on Scottish music and customs.[6] Murray's parents shared an interest in all aspects of what Victorians called "the woman question." In the years immediately following her marriage, Murray's mother took classes offered under the auspices of the Glasgow Association for the Higher Education of Women, which would become Queen Margaret College in 1882. The family tradition of higher education for women continued with Eunice's two elder sisters, Dorothy and Sylvia, who completed an M.A. at Glasgow University and a B.A. at Girton College, Cambridge University, respectively.[7] Eunice, however, did not attend university. She published more than ten works in a number of genres, including suffrage pamphlets, local histories of church and village, novels, and a memoir of her mother.[8]

Like many unmarried upper-middle-class women of the late Victorian period, Murray entered the public sphere through her philanthropic work. She was active in the local branch of the League of Pity, volunteered regularly at a local settlement, and pursued the cause of temperance.[9] Her voluntary efforts in the realm of social reform pushed her toward more explicitly political agitation. She circulated a petition on behalf of women's suffrage in her neighborhood in May 1897, and participated regularly in local and national suffrage organizing. Yet she criticized those who limited their political activism to work for women's political rights.[10] She professed a wide interest in politics and belonged to a local peace and arbitration society during the South African War.[11] And while she explored socialism through reading, and understood the relationship between poverty and other social problems, such as slum housing, she shared with other women of her class a discomfort at the political alliances necessary to bring about political and social change.[12]

While Murray described most of her neighbors in Cardross as opposed to any measure of women's suffrage, opinion in her own family tended toward support. With the exception of her brother, Anthony, and one of her sisters, Dorothy, who opposed women's suffrage, Murray's wider familial circle espoused a range of support for a parliamentary measure.[13] The primary point of disagreement within her family arose over the means women ought to use to attain political rights. Murray's sister Sylvia belonged first to the nonmilitant National Union of Women's Suffrage Societies, and later to the militant Women's Freedom League, while her cousin Elsa and aunt Alice were members of the Women's Social and Political Union.[14] Murray's mother had demonstrated early interest in "the woman question," although she exhibited considerably more doubt than would her daughters about the efficacy of political solutions. On a trip to the United States in 1867, Frances Stoddard Murray wrote to her own mother: "If you have a strong mind and force of character it is a misfortune to be a woman, and no voting papers, or removal of disabilities will compensate for the mistake."[15] Frances Murray later participated in various suffrage processions and demonstrations as a member of the Women's Freedom League, and frequently noted her support for her daughters' activism.[16]

Eunice Murray was proud of her family's history of involvement in radical movements. Her maternal grandfather, Stoddard, who had relocated his family from the United States to Scotland in 1844, supported the Union during the American Civil War and spoke publicly against the Confederacy from Scotland. The Stoddard family held strong connections to the American abolitionist movement. In the 1860's, William Lloyd Garrison visited Murray's grandparents at Broadfield, and her mother socialized with the family of Harriet Beecher Stowe while visiting relatives in the United States. From childhood, Murray understood herself to be enacting principles handed down to her by preceding generations. In a memoir of her mother published in 1920, she recounted a conversation held with her maternal grandfather at the tender age of four, during which he "instilled into [Eunice] an undying hatred for slavery and oppression," and urged her to adhere to her principles regardless of others' opinions.[17] In earlier, unpublished writings, Murray elaborated upon the beliefs inherited from her family: "I am more interested in causes than individuals . . . such as free speech, freedom for the slaves, wider education for the masses, rights for women, Jacobitism—anything like that has always made an instant appeal to me. In mind I have stood beside Grandfather Stoddard in demanding the abolition of slavery, beside Grandfather Murray in working for the repeal of the Corn Laws." To the list of radical and reforming family members, she added her mother and aunt, for women's rights, and her granduncles, for temperance.[18]

Murray inherited from her mother a love of reading and a belief in its capacity for transforming the self. Essential to that process was a period of reflection and writing. Murray described how, throughout her life, her mother took great pains to record her impressions of a book upon completing it:

> At no time in her life when she received a book or pamphlet did she acknowledge it in conventional words, such as "I have received the book which looks delightful and I am sure it will prove very nice reading"; of such ways my mother had supreme contempt; no matter how little the subject interested her, she read it faithfully and criticised it fully. Her criticisms of books were always good, and many a dull book has appeared quite brilliant when reviewed by her able pen. Even when inundated with work or feeling tired, her rule was put in practice, "read the book carefully, and then sit down and write your appreciation of it."[19]

Thus Murray learned that reading and conversation, in tandem with self-reflection, were necessary for what her mother termed "the higher development."[20]

Murray pursued "the higher development" of the self through the practice of keeping a journal, three volumes of which have survived. In these she recorded an array of impressions, anecdotes, and experiences—of life at home, and eventually, on the road as a suffrage organizer and prominent member of the Women's Freedom League. These volumes span the years from 1890 to 1918, chronicling Murray's life from roughly age fourteen to forty-one. They document not only the transformation of a reformer and suffragist into a suffragette, but also the uses of reading in shaping an individual's political subjectivity. Murray's journal reveals a political identity formed between the legacy of family values and history and an active engagement with the printed word. Murray's sense of self developed from her family's history of adherence to radical causes; her engagements with a variety of texts reveal the vitality of that connection, and its renewed expression. Murray's journal attests to the complex alchemy by which nineteenth-century radicalism became suffragism in the decades following the 1890's. Historian Sandra Stanley Holton has argued that "sexual politics and the power play within families, between husbands and wives, mothers and daughters" motivated middle-class women in nineteenth-century Britain to risk public ridicule by campaigning for women's suffrage.[21] Certainly, numerous autobiographies of former suffragettes attest to the connection between suffragettes' personal lives and political commitments. Such an understanding of the psychosocial formation of political consciousness, however, underestimates the matrix of ideas suffragettes inherited and reworked from nineteenth-century radicalism. Murray's journal suggests that not only family dynamics, but also systematic reading within the radical tradition, shaped suffragettes' political ideas.[22]

Reconstructing Murray's reading practices from the journal suggests that she, in fact, seldom implemented her mother's maxim that all texts be critiqued fully. At least in the writing she did privately, Murray rarely wrote extensively about the books, poetry, speeches, and newspapers she read (and in the case of certain texts, reread).[23] She occasionally commented briefly upon her reading, but more often, she wove references to it in and out of her narration. Murray used reading to several ends: for purposes of illustration, to substantiate her arguments, or as a foil against which to argue. Reading was integral to her understanding of herself in contrast to others, particularly her neighbors in Cardross, with whom she frequently disagreed on political issues. As she noted in August 1908: "I have read a great deal this week & feel mentally invigorated. Most people overfeed their bodies & starve their minds & souls."[24]

Murray's transformation from radical to suffragette accompanied a change in the uses to which she put reading. As she became more involved in campaigning for women's suffrage between 1896 and 1906, her journal documents a movement from reading and reflection to reading and action. Reading and its pleasures increasingly became a luxury of illness, as Murray's most intense bouts of reading coincided with periods of enforced inactivity. In 1909, 1912, and again in 1914, Murray used a week's bed rest to catch up on her reading and to revisit old favorites. "I have consoled myself with reading," she wrote after one such convalescence in 1909.[25] Suffrage campaigning, with its demands of constant travel and public speaking, changed the emphasis of her reading practices: what had acted originally as a goad to action became a comfort and consolation when action was no longer possible.

Murray's reading traversed disciplines and genres, but the great majority of what she read fell under the rubrics of romance, religion, and radicalism. These categories are slippery, because the observations she made about certain books suggest that what she took from her reading defied any simple understanding of genre. For example, upon reading William James's *The Varieties of Religious Experience*, she emphasized freedom of expression over what she might have gleaned about religious practices. She noted of her position on the book in discussion: "I stood for his freedom of thought."[26] Nor did she respond to canonical texts in expected ways. Her comment, upon rereading Thomas Carlyle's *The French Revolution* at age twenty-six, contradicts a recent historical interpretation of that work as a text significant to suffragette political formation. She noted that while she enjoyed reading the book, she was "not as thrilled as when [she] first read it when [she] was 11 years old."[27] However, for several reasons it remains difficult to reconstruct with accuracy a full list of what Murray read. She wrote infrequently in her journal and consequently did not record or comment upon all that she read. Additionally, she often made cultural references that would have been familiar to one of her class background, but it does not necessarily follow that she had, in fact, read the text to which she alluded. Furthermore, reconstructing her unabridged bookshelf, as it were, is of secondary significance to making sense of her reactions to the constellation of printed material in whose orbit she placed herself. For what becomes clear from compiling a reading list from Murray's journal entries is the predominance of texts important within the British radical tradition.

For a suffragist, Murray recorded reading remarkably few contemporary polemics on the condition of women. In an 1897 journal entry, she referred to a text by then canonical, John Stuart Mill's *The Subjection of Women*.[28] Surprisingly absent from her journal are the numerous pamphlets and books chronicling the legal, political, and economic status of women so central to the educational and fund-raising apparatus of the major suffrage organizations.[29] If women and women's suffrage were not the ostensible focus of what she read, her interpretations of texts nevertheless assumed the centrality of women's political status to major social issues. This was true of the reading she did in every genre. She read William Booth's *In Darkest England* as an argument for women's suffrage. "Booth's is depressing reading," she wrote:

> The great underworld of our cities, driven there through diverse means, bad health, drink, lack of means, lack of a helping hand. Surely if we made a deliberate effort we in our own lifetime could achieve much. Ibsen shows the rise of a feminine point of view, Booth shows the failure of civilisation as envisioned

by men, is it too much to hope that women will once they become citizens do much to improve social conditions.[30]

Murray also interpreted fiction politically. She liked the "rebellious spirit" of *Wuthering Heights*, and the author's depiction of characters "fighting and struggling against conventions."[31] Reading *Uncle Tom's Cabin* and *Alton Locke* in 1904 led her to "wonder if woman suffrage will be won without some sort of revolt and agitation." She explicitly connected these novels with political action: calling them "novels of purpose," she noted the extent to which Stowe's novel had "advanced the cause of freedom," and Kingsley's had helped to bring about the People's Charter.[32] If reading could inspire political action, it could also spur reflection on matters of a spiritual nature. In an entry from March 1914, Murray laid out, in stream-of-consciousness style, the process that led her from reading Mrs. Humphry Ward's antisuffrage writing, through Ward's novels, to novels by Hardy, Dostoyevsky, and Tolstoy, and back to Ward again. Her observations on the contributions of Dostoyevsky strikingly mirror her own political development. "Doestoyevsky struggles," she wrote, "torn between Faith & Doubt, battered but rising again, yearning for peace but torn by travail."[33] These remarks, and her seamless movement from politics to religion and back to politics again, suggest the degree to which inner struggle animated her own political activism and illuminate the connections she made between matters spiritual and political.

A passion for poetry rivaled her interest in novels. She was especially fond of the work of Shelley, Goethe, and Alice Meynell.[34] During the Great War, however, poetry became virtually all she recorded reading, aside from press accounts of the war's progress, letters from her brother, Anthony, at the Western Front, and the occasional novel she had read before. The war affected her reading much as her bouts of illness had earlier. "The war and the sorrows of war," she explained, "produce such a feeling of restlessness in me that nothing soothes like a certified favorite in the reading line or a game of patience."[35] When sick in mind or body, consolation, not inspiration, became reading's purpose.

Murray's prodigious nonfiction reading encompassed biography, history, and political theory.[36] In 1896, she recording drawing inspiration from an essay on Josephine Butler: "A good cause is an inspiration, and a woman like [Josephine Butler] inspires others to fight the good fight. So many people are content with things as they are—this is one of the hazards of life."[37] Murray also read political speeches and pamphlets from earlier political struggles. In 1912 she noted from her reading of the speeches of William Pitt the elder a number of parallels between the political situation of his time and that of her own. Impressed by Pitt's repression and subsequent loss of the American colonies, she adroitly drew an analogy to the long battle for women's political rights in Britain.[38]

Murray also read widely in the periodical press; it served for her as a critical source of information about women's political involvements.[39] On 9 November 1896, she noted that she was "reading carefully the report of the conference held in Birmingham in October," in which the women's societies working exclusively for women's suffrage on nonparty lines had formed the National Union of Women's Suffrage Societies. Her comment, "I should like to join such a society for the question of the emancipation of my sex is a stirring one and leads to vital matters," marked her first recorded interest in participating in the agitation for women's suffrage.[40] By May of the following year, she had begun circulating a petition on behalf of women's suffrage in her local village, Cardross, but encountered only "apathy and hostility."[41] Her journals record her continued interest in women's suffrage over the following decade.

Regardless of genre or discipline, Murray's reading invigorated her belief in the political necessity of women's suffrage, and it allowed her to draw upon exciting stories in the creation of a political identity. Murray's reading emphasized texts with radical lineages, such as *Alton Locke*, *Uncle Tom's Cabin*, and *The Subjection of Women*, and she interpreted these texts, as had many radicals earlier in the century, as clarion calls for action. In this respect, Murray drew upon one of radicalism's legacies: a belief that the people's role in the nation gave them the moral right to exercise force in the acquisition of their political rights.[42] But Murray, like so many radicals, also read religious materials, and romantic histories and novels, such as *The French Revolution* and *Wuthering Heights*. Her reading brought together the nineteenth-century history of radicalism, specifically the tradition of anti–Corn Law agitation and abolitionism, with a romantic tradition of rebellion and revolt, creating that peculiar combination of beliefs comprising suffragette militancy—all of which was underwritten by a sense of moral urgency and religious calling. Murray understood politics "as a massive drama of struggle, movement, and hope," and sought in her reading confirmation of that belief.[43]

Throughout her journals, Murray attested to the significance of struggle and movement in her conception of politics. She wrote of a disagreement with a friend:

she holds that contentment is a great gift, and I hold that discontent is a greater. There are so many things wrong with the world, why should [*sic*] be contented? Sex inequality, sweated workers, underfed men and women, sickly children, overcrowded areas, drunken homes to mention but a few of the evils. I for one never want to sit still while a wrong remains unrighted. I wish I were Prime Minister.[44]

Murray's litany of social ills would have been familiar to women reformers of the nineteenth century. But her conclusion, "I wish I were Prime Minister," with its desire for participation in the realm of parliamentary politics, reached far beyond what many Victorian feminist reformers would have desired for themselves, or even imagined. Nineteenth-century feminists directed their energies toward social reform, which had political implications, but which nonetheless rested upon different assumptions about women's domain.[45] One may be tempted to see in Murray's statement merely a parallel to her conscious choice of action over reflection, as when she wrote: "Fight the good fight is more my line than 'abide with me.'"[46] Nevertheless, that articulation, "I wish I were Prime Minister," attests to the primacy suffragettes attached to the realm of the political, traditionally conceived. No longer content to work toward the alleviation of overcrowdedness, poverty, hunger, and drink through work deemed "social," Murray desired to enter a realm traditionally defined as masculine—that of politics.

A Liberal from birth and by conviction, Murray experienced disillusionment with party politics—as did many other suffragettes in the early years of the twentieth century.[47] In June 1906 she noted, "politically I am a Liberal. I was born one and shall I hope remain one unless Liberalism ceases to exist." But she also observed that the Liberals courted disaster when they refused to put the principles of the party into practice. This she reiterated in 1908, when she observed that Winston Churchill and Lloyd George "dishonour the noble flag of liberalism." Murray distinguished between leaders and the rank and file of the party when she wrote: "It is Liberalism and its attitude of mind divorced from officialdom that appeals to me and the Cabinet are killing Liberalism by their folly." Throughout, however, Murray's grievance was with those Liberals not adhering to what she understood to be the underlying principle of the party, freedom. Her sense of betrayal by the Liberal party fueled an anger soon channeled in the direction of suffrage militancy.[48]

A sense of betrayal alone, however, did not transform Murray from radicalism to militancy. Murray's reading in the 1890's, and into the first years of the twentieth century, points to a wider process of transformation occurring across a spectrum of politically active and socially conscious women in Britain, who had come to believe that new strategies were necessary if women were to acquire the parliamentary franchise. Historian David Rubinstein has observed that in the 1890's the campaign for women's suffrage began to change. "There was, however," he writes, "no easy or universal movement from the constitutional methods of the 1890s to the militancy adopted by some suffragists several years after the start of the new century."[49] A variety of explanations have been offered to explain the origins of suffragette militancy. In an influential assessment published in the mid-1980's, Martha Vicinus suggested the role played by religious conviction, and particularly the power of the conversion experience, in stimulating suffragists toward more radical approaches. More recently, Sandra Stanley Holton has argued that "family life and sexual relations, not simply the franchise, became the ground over which Radical suffragists waged the battle for the citizenship of women."[50] Examination of Eunice Murray's reading practices as revealed in her journal suggests yet a third strand leading to militancy: the legacy of radicalism and the power of convictions formed through reading.

Murray formed her initial impressions of militancy from reading press accounts of the disruption of a Liberal party meeting by members of the Women's Social and Political Union (WSPU) at the Manchester Free Trade Hall in October 1905, an event viewed by many historians as the first militant protest. Murray admired the women's attempt to force the candidate, Sir Edward Grey, to respond to their question, "Will the Liberal Government give women the vote?"[51] She believed that the women were courageous to raise the question in public, and wondered "if the scenes were disgraceful was not the disgrace upon the part of the stewards who hustled them out, instead of allowing them to ask their questions." Murray's analysis of the arrests of the two women, Christabel Pankhurst and Annie Kenney, as they attempted to hold a political meeting outside the hall once ejected, located her assessment of the women's protest at the end of a trajectory of radical protest with roots in the eighteenth century. She lamented, "Oh for a Wilkes to proclaim the right of freedom of speech." And she laughingly relegated those women of her acquaintance who were "duly and profoundly shocked" by the protest to what she saw as the comparatively quiescent nineteenth century. The women's cause, rooted in a radical heritage, nevertheless pointed the way forward, toward "progress, justice, and equality." Murray would extend her lament for the death of liberty still further after the June 1906 arrests of WSPU members in London. "Oh for a

Wilkes to shout aloud not the liberty of the Press," she wrote, "but the liberty of the subject."[52]

Murray's embrace of militancy was not unqualified, however. A key to her thinking can be found as early as 1901, when upon reading a life of St. Augustine she reflected that it was harder to live a Christian life than die a martyr.[53] That observation accurately described the sentiments of many members of the Women's Freedom League (WFL), whose ranks Murray would join in 1908. Members of the WFL must have longed frequently for the conviction of martyrdom. The WFL, formed in October 1907, by a group of women dissatisfied with the authoritarian leadership of Christabel and Emmeline Pankhurst, found itself awkwardly situated between the more established National Union of Women's Suffrage Societies and the newly insurgent WSPU. Committed to democratic decision-making, and eventually, to nonviolent militancy and passive resistance, the WFL struggled to carve out a distinct place for itself within the Edwardian suffrage movement. Membership in the WFL, and work as an organizer for the organization in Scotland, brought Murray into contact with a wide range of suffrage activists in the years leading up to the Great War. By 1908, she had articulated a belief in the necessity of militancy, asserting that "somehow or other [opponents of women's suffrage] have to be won over whether by militancy or argument, for we intend to have the vote." And by 1911, she credited militancy with the ultimate success of the movement of which she was a part. Women's suffrage, she wrote, would be attained in her lifetime, "largely due to the courage & devotion of the militants."[54]

Murray came to question the WSPU's use of violence. Her analysis of the organization's tactics after 1912 was characteristic of WFL members; she disagreed with the WSPU's use of arson and other forms of violence, but refused to criticize the organization publicly.[55] Her journal accounts of meetings in London, Glasgow, and Edinburgh indicate that WFL and WSPU members attended and participated in each other's public events and demonstrations as late as 1913.[56] Murray consistently emphasized her identification with the WSPU's moral outrage even as she disagreed with its escalating violence. In 1914, she wrote a passionate avowal of their contribution to the movement:

> To many the W.S.P.U. tactics has [*sic*] been the dynamic fever that has achieved the feat of making these people think—of making them disapprove[,] of making them hostile, of making them enthusiastic supporters by making them ready to fight women's battles for them, that has made them eager to share women's triumphs with them. So believing this I cannot afford to watch

the W.S.P.U. without going with them, for my type of mind could never do the things they do, but saying this does not mean that I blame them for doing what they do. No—I blame the Government.[57]

Reading played a central role in shaping Murray's relationship to militancy, for reading strengthened and transformed beliefs she had inherited from her family. Much of the reading she pursued between 1890 and 1918 grappled with issues central to radicalism's nineteenth-century commitments: human freedom, agency, and will. From Mary Wollstonecraft to John Stuart Mill, from Arthur Balfour's *Foundations of Belief* to William James's *Varieties of Religious Experience*, from *Wuthering Heights* to *Alton Locke*, freedom—of body, mind, speech, and belief—structured her thinking. Indeed, freedom, and its opposite, could be characterized as an obsession of the age in which Murray lived.[58] Murray's invocation of the dyad of freedom and slavery was inflected by the battles her family had fought, and by those with which she chose to engage. Her professed liberalism inclined her toward disaffection with the Liberal party for failing to fulfill its mandate; and her feminism, toward analogies between the political status of women and that of slaves.

A number of historians have argued for the centrality of slavery in the thinking of late nineteenth- and early twentieth-century British feminists. The legacy of abolitionism, and the links between that movement and the international campaign to eradicate the Contagious Diseases Acts, ensured that the rhetorical uses of slavery would continue to feature in British suffragist discourse well into the twentieth century.[59] Murray invoked the very maxims most suffragettes used to describe their political status. From John Stuart Mill she noted: "There remain no legal slaves except the mistress of every house." From Byron she wrote: "Who would be free must himself strike the first blow." And from Shelley she borrowed: "Can man be free if woman is a slave?"[60] Yet her use of the idiom of slavery differed from that of an earlier generation of feminists, particularly those involved in the international campaign to eradicate the Contagious Diseases Acts (a campaign known to its adherents, in fact, as the abolitionist movement).[61] Conspicuously absent from Murray's invocation of slavery to describe women's political condition was the sexualized and sentimentalized language of slavery seen in the private correspondence and public writing of feminists like Josephine Butler. As Murray's use of quotations by Shelley, Byron, and Mill would suggest, an analysis of the sexual and familial roots of women's subjection underlay her invocation of slavery, but she used the analogy to encompass a wide range of meanings. Freedom, for Murray, encompassed the bodily integrity of women, but operated metaphorically as well as physically. The body politic subjected to the will of another such body featured frequently in her assessments. Murray's use of the analogy of slavery connected struggles for national liberation with the women's battle for political rights in Britain. In April 1900, in the thick of British prosecution of war in the Transvaal, she wrote: "I see now that Ireland should have Home Rule, the Boers should have been left alone, and women should have a say in all these burning questions."[62] Freedom, for Murray and numerous other nineteenth-century radicals, resonated across a spectrum of coercive relations.[63] And while Murray's preoccupation with freedom paralleled that of liberal suffragists who rejected militancy, like Millicent Garrett Fawcett and Catherine Marshall, it differed from theirs in one crucial respect. Casting themselves as inheritors of the radical tradition, suffragettes emphasized less the gradual progress of political reform than they did the sovereignty of the people, and the legitimacy of using force in making that claim.[64]

Murray's inheritance of freedom as a principle of radicalism is made nowhere more clear than in her June 1914 musings on the significance of Charlotte Brontë's *Jane Eyre*. At a family gathering, Murray responded passionately to another guest's dismissal of the novel as "one of the poorest books ever to obtain fame." Murray's rendering of this exchange in the pages of her journal began as an account of a conversation taking place between herself and a fellow partygoer; it quickly became a position paper on the novel and its meaning. Murray's ideas about the significance of reading *Jane Eyre* demonstrate how she chose and then interpreted texts on the basis of what they contributed to her understanding of freedom. She characterized the novel as concerned with "spiritual and intellectual revolt," and its protagonist as "a woman fighting against injustice." Murray's emphasis throughout was on the individual's self-assertion against domination by others. The novel was concerned above all, she insisted, with "the right of the individual to stand against convention . . . the right of man or woman to be able to say 'I am the captain of my soul / I am the master of my fate.'"[65]

Murray's interpretation of *Jane Eyre* as a political struggle would have been shared by her companions in the Edwardian women's suffrage movement. For these women, the novel carried a set of associations resonant with the struggle for freedom against tyrannical authority. Literary critics Sandra Gilbert and Susan Gubar have observed that when the novel was first published, in 1847, contemporaries commented most frequently upon its anger, and "its 'anti-Christian' refusal to accept the forms, customs, and standards of society—in short, its rebellious feminism." One critic, writing in the *Quarterly Review* in 1848, noted that *"Jane Eyre* is throughout the personification of an unregenerate and undisciplined spirit." Of the novel's author, the same critic went on to urge: "The tone of mind and thought which has fostered Chartism and rebellion is the same which has written *Jane Eyre*."[66] It would appear that the sixty-odd years between the novel's publication and Murray's musings vindicated these assessments. The desire to speak for oneself, and for representation in the political arena, connected Murray both to the articulated goal of emancipation in Brontë's fictional autobiography, and to the earlier agitation resulting in the People's Charter. Freedom, with its implied opposites slavery and tyranny, linked her struggle with those of earlier generations.

As Murray's engagement with *Jane Eyre* suggests, reading for her, and her compatriots in the women's suffrage movement, became a form of authoring the self. Murray read to legitimate the positions she held, and perhaps had acquired from her family, and she read as part of the process of self-creation, in order to form a political identity. A number of critics have argued recently that suffragettes used published autobiographical representations of militancy as a means of constituting community.[67] While this undoubtedly was true for many, it was also the case that suffragettes' reading encompassed genres aside from autobiography, as the entries in Eunice Murray's journal attest. For her, and doubtless for others, reading in a variety of genres resonated with family history and life experience to create political consciousness. In Murray's case, the interplay between reading and a legacy of family political activism was complex, and the strands never may be disentangled fully. At times, Murray herself emphasized the significance of reading. In 1910, following a bout of illness and reading, she wrote: "I have been reading a lot & feel mentally refreshed. I am now sure that my spiritual nature needs solitude in which to develop, but I know my mental mind needs to feed on the thoughts spoken or written by others for I have nothing in myself to keep me going."[68] But Murray's own accounting, both in her journal and in her published writings, suggests that reading never operated for her simply as a process of taking on the thoughts and beliefs of others; rather, reading integrated the past and the present in an active struggle to create political meaning.

JOHN MORTON OSBORNE

Continuity in British Sport: The Experience of the First World War

For some time now, social historians have been engaged in a lively reassessment of the effect of the First World War on life in Britain. Simplistic views of the war as "destroyer of worlds" have given way to a deeper awareness of the fundamental resilience of British society during wartime, as well as the successful rearguard actions that entrenched interests sometimes fought in order to maintain the status quo. One phenomenon now drawing the attention of social historians is the nation's sporting and recreational pursuits. How the British played and watched and wagered reflected the self-interest, the ambition, and the passion of a vibrant British community before, during, and especially immediately after the Great War. Evidence from the social arena, at least, supports the argument that many of the conventions thought "lost" in the "deluge" survived the leap from the prewar to the postwar world.

In the very week that Europe lurched toward the conflict, much of Britain was at play. As Continental leaders made fateful choices, ordinary Britons were preparing for what had become the most popular and traditional week of recreation on their calendar. The August Bank Holiday, one of the public holidays added in 1871, topped off the week with a welcome respite from the pressures of modern life. More than this, the holiday and the week that led up to it were the most significant in the calendar of British recreational sport. A casual observer would see men and women engaged in exercise and contest everywhere in mid-1914. This may have been the most ubiquitous communal activity in the culture, exceeding even work or the public house, and providing recreation and excitement across class, gender, and region. Sport had in the previous three decades become unmistakably national in scope and, as such, was beginning to join other representations of a unified and centralizing nation. It was also a vast "professional" under-taking for the thousands of men who earned their livings as players in a dozen sports played before large crowds. But this was also true of the disci-plined and organized ways in which the hundreds of new national govern-ing bodies, many with local chapters staffed by hardworking volunteers, oversaw games throughout Britain on the eve of war. Sport was also in-tensely commercial in a more modern sense. Players drew wages, spectators paid, shares were sold, and dividends were earned in the professional sports, of course. But there was as well a small army of contractors, book-makers, caterers, manufacturers and retailers of sporting goods, not to mention the sporting press, which, taken together, testified to the British fixation on sport. Within the sporting sphere, one could find all the com-plications of exploitation, boardroom complacency, and competition en-demic to the wider world of British commerce.

Though games of physical skill had developed both across and within social classes, preconceptions about sport were shaped largely by the upper-middle class. The leisured elite had done much to foster the idea that with-out high purpose games were merely decadent. As sports extended to the wider culture, this ideology opened massive fissures between the well-heeled amateur and the proletarian professional, and between the partici-pant and the "mere" spectator. The criticism of men like Lord Baden-Powell, who saw "spectatorism" as another sign of decay that only peace-time conscription could reverse, intensified this division between the "true sportsman" and the rest. Wider condemnation by those who deplored the barbarian grip of the athlete on schools and universities, and who wrote, like Kipling, of "flanneled fools and muddied oafs," ensured that any de-bate would be both rancorous and long-lived.[1]

The large sums of money that flowed to building contractors and others connected to the boom in sports indicated a burgeoning "sports industry." Sporting paraphernalia was also selling at record levels, with British manu-facturers expanding as never before on the Continent. Most visible, per-haps, was the accompanying boom in newsprint reporting the outcome of contests up and down the kingdom. Almost all the 223 daily newspapers in Britain, despite arguments about what was "fitting," carried reports and routine discussions of sports events. There were also three specialist sports papers, two daily and one weekly, and more than 150 weekly and monthly periodicals catering to sporting interests across gender, class, and locale, from *Billiard Monthly* to *Ladies Golf*, from *Football Spectator* to *Horse and Hound*.[2] Sports editors and reporters were the new specialists of the "new journalism." This growing fraternity included men such as Theodore Cook, editor of the upper-middle-class journal *The Field*, who was an Oxford Blue, a finalist for the post of tutor to Prince Arthur, and who was to be knighted in 1916. Further down the social scale was J. A. H. Catton, a career sports reporter who had risen to the editor's desk at Manchester's *Athletic News*. At the opposite end of the spectrum worked the anonymous army of "casuals" who were paid by the line to provide up-to-the-moment "winners and halftimes," without which the public would have considered the sports pages in most newspapers useless.

⌇

Into this deep enthusiasm for sport the deadly seriousness of the Great War intruded. As Britain mobilized morally and materially, organized sport seemed to join the patriotic throng. Although some had accused professional sports in particular of endangering the nation's fitness for struggle, belief in the positive worth of British sport prevailed at first. The Marylebone Cricket Club, organizer of the county championship, preempted the anticipated climax to the competition by declaring Middlesex, the leaders, as winners for 1914. General Friedrich von Bernhardi, in his *Germany and the Next War*, suggested that their fascination with games "by becoming exaggerated and by usurping the place of serious work . . . has seriously damaged the English."[3] Now came the opportunity for moral justification. The Germans' brutality in Belgium, noted F. S. Jackson, the former England cricket captain turned politician, could be traced to their not being sportsmen.[4] The number of sportsmen enlisting was announced daily, along with their particular suitability to the hardships and danger of modern warfare. The conflict itself was described as a "great game." One recruiting handbill, distributed in Hull, advertised the "grand International Tours of the British Empire Football Club" under its president, King George, its trainer, Lord Kitchener, and its captain, Sir John French. The handbill went on to explain: "The full team is not yet complete. The directors are prepared at once to sign on all eligible players" for "the preliminary rounds to be played in France and Belgium."[5]

British sport offered an easy target for a counterattack against such self-satisfaction. The war had become a "crusade" in which anything that was not geared to victory over Germany was to be set aside. At the same time, a parallel semiofficial determination to maintain "business as usual" further confused matters. This curious combination of high patriotism and commercial self-interest helped generate a storm over professional sport during

1914 and 1915. Certainly, such a complicated segment of the national life could not in all cases be subsumed into a simple definition of patriotism that demanded uncritical support for the war. Many asserted the equal demands of "business as usual," especially when their business seemed to provide fleeting moments of diversion for a population laboring under the pressures of war. Professional football came in for particular opprobrium when it started its season throughout Britain, "as usual," in late August 1914. Amateur sportsmen did not hesitate to attack the professionals with the cudgel they had been handed. Upper-middle-class opinion, in general, was condemnatory, even though little was mentioned about the continuation of horse racing or the theater. The responses of the press reflect this controversy. The "respectable" London newspapers imposed restrictions on themselves as far as the reporting of the "unpatriotic" professional sports of association football and rugby league were concerned. Since these organs had never targeted readers interested in such competitions anyway, they could afford such a harmless, if hypocritical, display of patriotism. Among the newspapers catering to the enthusiasm for football among the working class and lower-middle class, especially in the urban industrial areas, such gestures could spell financial disaster. One provincial editor defended his publication of the Saturday "football special" edition on the grounds that since "football takes up a large share of local public attention, even in war-time, we are justified in publishing adequate reports."[6]

The grip of sports on the national imagination hardly loosened in wartime. While many amateur sports folded their tents for the duration, almost every professional sport maintained some kind of presence during the first year of the war. At the end of the unhappy 1914–15 season in the football leagues, this professional sport was reduced to less contentious organized exhibitions in which, despite the sale of tickets, players received only "expenses." County cricket did not return, but northern league cricket did, scheduled as before on the weekend, and employing the added attraction of famous players from the county game—such as Jack Hobbs and Frank Woolley. The ambivalence of such young men, torn between their fleeting careers and their obligations to family and to their country, can only be imagined. Many continued, even while enlisting and training in England, to earn "expenses" money in the many "exhibition" contests up and down the country. The crowds that were drawn to "friendly" matches involving football's leading teams, the Sunday cricket leagues, and even the works sports competitions that thrived in factory centers like Birmingham, were clear evidence that the British affinity with sport was still vibrant. So too was the coverage in the sporting press, even after Germany's submarine campaign rendered newsprint scarce and more expensive. Despite the destructiveness of the war, the nation's preoccupation with sport was for many still an important antidote to "modern struggles." When the government, in 1916, levied a tax on ticket prices for all entertainment, it found the measure lucrative but unpopular. Indeed, the army itself took advantage of this interest in the physical training of troops. Games moved from the important but peripheral place they had long enjoyed in professional army life to the center of physical and morale training. There was not an infantry battalion without a unit football team in France, and the results of interbattalion matches were as keenly followed as those of the hometown professional clubs engaged in their shadowy "friendly" competitions.[7]

By late 1916, however, Britons had been forced to conclude that the Great War would not end soon. Many of the central ruling bodies of amateur sports simply closed up shop, leaving arrangements that remained for small contests in local hands. Professional concerns, especially those such as Birmingham's Aston Villa with significant investments to protect, struggled on. Little wonder, then, that from the beginning of 1917 the subject of postwar society, however distant, preoccupied many people. This was especially true of those who considered the role sport should play in British culture. Only by a determination to build anew, whenever the war did end, could the nation justify the enormous toll of the present. So, more and more, thoughts turned to what virtually everyone called "reconstruction."

Powerful among these currents was the symbolism of "cleansing" that the war had engendered. Images of sacrifice as purification had appeared immediately in 1914. Had not Isaac Rosenberg, one of the brilliant talents soon to be lost, called in his "On Receiving News of the War" for the conflict to "Corrode, consume, / Give back this universe / Its pristine bloom"?[8] As one would expect in regard to sport, enthusiasm for renewal did not imply a simple solution. Much elite opinion took Rosenberg at his word and dictated not the road forward but a road back. Many increasingly feared the consequences of the redistribution of power plainly evident before 1914 and clearly gathering pace under the influence of total war. For anxious Britons, it was imperative that reconstruction should preserve as well as reform, that the cleansing fire should rescue as well as sweep away.

For those concerned about the further "decay" in British sporting ideals, from the increase of spectators to the behavior of young cricket professionals, sport needed the "cleansing fire" urgently. As we have seen, vocal patriotism had largely hounded the professional sports industry from its place on center stage. In its stead came a widespread celebration of amateur sporting values as having produced the hundreds of thousands of young Britons who had brought fitness, adventure, and "pluck" from the playing fields to the battlefields. But by 1917, the demands for men to fill the gaps in the ranks had grown inexorably, and the physical standards of the new young recruits were declining alarmingly. This only intensified the feeling that British manhood would need to be "reconstructed," too.

The combination of elite pride and fear dominated the debate about what sort of nation should emerge from the war. How could the "physical deterioration" of the past be overcome? How could the preference for wholesome participation over decadent spectatorism be instilled in the people? How could character-building competition replace the commercial struggle that placed the purity of sport at dire risk? Men such as Theodore Cook, the influential editor of *The Field*, remained convinced long after the end of the war that the "flanneled fools and muddied oafs" had saved Britain. Cook wrote, eight years after the Armistice, that without sport

> we should never have lasted through the Great War at all. Nor merely had we, on the whole, the healthiest thousands in the world from which to pick our officers and men, we had throughout the community of the British Empire a spirit which every member recognized as common to other members, almost as hallmark of our blood, the spirit of fair play, the spirit that will never surrender while the last breath animates the fainting body, the spirit in which the cause is everything and the individual of nothing worth.[9]

The best of sport, in the estimation of the public school–nurtured amateur elite, had endured the sternest competition of all. Further, the values of the sportsman had faced down not only a foreign foe, but also domestic critics skeptical of their moral force. For people like Cook, sport in war had confirmed and strengthened their view of British values. The Great War had provided a timely opportunity to display, on the fields of France, the ultimate proof of the importance of sport in the life of the nation.

Motives in 1917 and 1918, however, went beyond vindication. Wishful thinking among those dedicated to the Edwardian amateur sporting ethos led to the belief that the war had offered perhaps a final chance to rescue their code from the shipwreck of modernizing society. The men of Cook's class seemed to sense at last the turning of the tide back to a more familiar world. For them, sport, or rather the ideal of fair play, the "hallmark of our blood," encompassed their upbringing, their education, and their lives, and provided for most of them the last best hope for the kind of society to which they aspired.

Propagandists for the amateur ideal equated good sportsmen with a moral and disciplined citizenry. The war experience seemed to promise that the civilizing qualities of the public-school sporting ideal could at last be extended to the entire nation. Cook, writing in *The Field*, defined reconstruction as "an organizing of the people for the propagation of citizenship," and went on to say:

> It is necessary at all costs, to turn the people into players rather than watchers. . . . We want good citizens now, if ever we did. But loyalty cannot be learned from lectures, nor patriotism from pulpits; these are things a man needs to experience, and in playing a game like Rugby football he does experience them: the team spirit gives him them all.[10]

The value of participatory sports to the renewed nation would be both material and moral.

For the moment, the war shrouded many of the obstacles to the realization of a nation imbued with the ideals of participatory amateurism. The conflict had seemed to arrest the main agents of decay—spectatorism, commercialism, professionalism, and the commitment to "success" rather than sportsmanship. For many of the elite, the moment seemed to hold the promise of bringing the classes together in an organic society under the umbrella of the public-school spirit. Clearly, the atmosphere of unreality that pervaded segments of the reconstruction effort infiltrated sports reform also.

Some saw increased discipline and order as vital tools for this reconstruction of sport. For them, the war had proven that prewar agitation for conscription had been justified. The organization of the nation for war after 1915 had inculcated the value of method. One letter-to-the-editor writer was convinced that collective action could reform sport. He wrote that, after the war,

> we shall find ourselves converted into a much more methodical and organized nation than we were hitherto, and the result will be that everybody will be able to devote the correct amount of time both to sport and business. In the future we are going to do things with more precision, to the elimination of that haphazardness which was so predominant in pre-war days. . . .The great lessons of the war have been to teach us the value of organization, and also what discipline and routine means. . . . The advent of more system, together with more social reforms, will enable the working classes to take work and play more evenly.[11]

∽

Such ideas obviously would concern government, as would the specific discipline that some advocated to "re-amateurize" their beloved pastimes. In the atmosphere of unreality, confidence was high. "Professionalism, we may take it for granted, will not for many years reach anything like its prewar dimensions," opined the *Sports Trade Journal*, whose readers naturally had much to gain from the fullest development of participation in games. A letter to the editor in *The Field*, signed "Corpore Sano," spoke directly about what should be done if this were not in fact to be the case. "Youth must be encouraged to play games," the correspondent insisted, "so professional games must be prohibited for a time till more room can be found for youth." F. Davidson Currie, a leading analyst of sports, echoed "Corpore Sano" in his desires to protect the nation's youth, declaring that "in plain words, if professional football bars progress of our youth in development of industry and moral training, the sooner the better professionalism is swept away." Cook's own cricket writer soon thereafter made the radical suggestion of doing "away entirely with county championship and return[ing] to the old methods when county met county in friendly rivalry without any thought at all about points."[12]

Though in less heretical fashion, some leaders in sports associations also took up the cause of "re-amateurization," even if they had no idea how to guard against creeping professionalism. The chairman of the first annual general meeting of the Warwickshire County Cricket Club after the Armistice, for example, hoped that cricket would cease to be a business and "that there would be no return to the dull monotony of professional cricket." And, on the day after the cease-fire took effect, Lord Kinnaird opened the gathering of the most influential sports institution of them all, the Football Association, with the injunction that the meeting's purpose was "to remedy certain evils connected with the game." When the transfer system of buying and selling player contracts then came under bitter attack, the association's vice president, J. C. Clegg, ended the meeting with a motion "that it is desirable that players, in addition to playing the game, should continue their trade." This notion, of course, was anathema to professional sportsmen, since it suggested that the professional club could more easily hold down wages when a player worked at football only "part-time." It was clear that even the untrammeled professionalism of league football had become a target for those who wished to exploit the war to renew British sport in harmony with elite values.[13] To save a valued past for a storied future took on the mantle of a crusade. One leading amateur footballer told a journalist friend that his own sport must be renewed: "It is up to us to do our best, for somehow in this way we shall be carrying out the wishes of those clean white men who have crossed the Great Divide."[14] Any method to achieve this, including government action, seemed warranted.

Inside government, especially among the enthusiastic would-be reformers of the Ministry of Reconstruction, there were indeed those who would use the power of the state to save the body and soul of the people. This was especially evident after a disturbing Ministry of National Service report in 1918 revealed that only 36 percent of men of all ages were fit for front-line service. Such concern was, of course, not new. An Inter-Department Committee on Physical Deterioration had raised similar fears in 1904 after recruitment for the Boer War had faltered. But nothing much had been done. The historian J. L. Hammond, working for the ministry in 1918, dismissed "intermittent and spasmodic fits of concern" and asked whether this time a greater impression of the vital need for a healthy populace had not been produced.[15]

For a time it seemed that lessons had been learned. Sir George Newman, chief medical officer in the new Ministry of Health, noted the "overwhelming success" of games behind the lines in France. To him, this suggested "that we have made far too little use of our national aptitude and love for games in the education and training of the young and as a means of wholesome recreation for the adult."[16] The new president of the Board of Education, H. A. L. Fisher, hoped some of his own reforms would encompass the "education of the whole man," adding: "Our standard of physique as a nation is deplorably below the standard which a great people should set before them. Our common taste in amusement, though greatly improved, is still, in the main, rude and uncultured."[17]

While government departments competed in their planning for a new world of physical fitness, others demanded still more. Accordingly, in keeping with the tenor of reconstruction discussions, an extragovernmental agitation arose to suggest ways in which the state should act to help build a truly new sports world. This agitation illustrated again that although the reconstruction movement was unified in its commitment to new futures, within it lay what Paul Barton Johnson has called a "kaleidoscope of shifting, converging, separating ideas and attitudes"[18] born of the prejudices, fears, and self-interests of those who held them.

Leaving aside the glacial development of games in state-provided schools, government involvement in sports and recreation had been non-existent in Britain before 1914. The simplest and most fundamental explanation for this is twofold. First, modern sports developed in Britain at the height of mid-Victorian liberalism, when state intervention in most social endeavors beyond sewage treatment and the workhouse was minimal. Second, those who developed sports, the educated and well-to-do middle and upper-middle classes, did so for their own participation and enjoyment. They had soon built corporate organizations such as the Football Association and the Amateur Rowing Association or elite gatherings such as the All England Tennis Club or the Marylebone Cricket Club. In such a climate, even the periodic scares over national deterioration, such as that after the Boer War, did not materially advance government intrusion into the nation's patterns of leisure. Although by the Edwardian period politicians had discovered the electoral value of being seen at crowded football grounds,[19] the ideal remained one of mid-Victorian liberalism: the state should not be involved with sport. To be sure, this attitude had allowed the massive laissez-faire growth of commercialized games that tended to subvert liberal values. But the impulse to promote "correct" sporting values continued to be moral rather than legislative.

The experience of government control in wartime, not to mention rampant self-interest, softened some long-cherished prejudices against officialdom. Where elite groups had once clamored for compulsory military service, they now spoke up for other types of compulsion in the national interest. An early voice for a wider state involvement in the leisure of the people was George Sullivan, influential editor of the *Sports Trader*, who first raised the matter in a 1916 editorial advocating a Ministry of Sport that "could foster and encourage all forms of manly exercise . . . [and] remove the reproach of those who have bewailed our devotion to sport and sportsmen." If such a ministry were to materialize, Sullivan concluded, it would "command the sympathetic interest not only of sports lovers, or of the members of the Sporting and Athletic Goods industry, but also of all those who have the future welfare of the country at heart."[20]

Sudden victory in November 1918 meant not only a time to rejoice but also the moment to embark on the building of this better Britain. And government was called upon to act. Leading voices urged sportsmen to use their united vote to elect M.P.'s who recognized the importance of proper recreation. Alfred Martin, a recent president of the National Union of Journalists, typified many writers who advised their readers to attend political meetings during the 1918 general election campaign and to question local parliamentary candidates. It would be advantageous, Martin reasoned, "for all good sportsmen who have votes to ascertain [the candidates'] views upon the subject of the State and healthy recreation for all, even if it has to receive some sort of subsidy from the country's revenue."[21]

The record of the Parliament elected in 1918 shows that the political effects of such appeals were limited. But pressure-group politics to promote government involvement in sport continued well into 1919. Early in that year, sports associations moved to unify their efforts by calling together a "Conference of National Bodies Governing Sports." Continuing the familiar trend of alliance that the war had accelerated, its membership was indeed impressive, and perhaps unprecedented in the history of British sport. Representation came from dozens of sports bodies, from the Marylebone Cricket Club to the Football Association, from the giant Amateur Swimming Association with its half-million members to the sixty-four clubs of the National Amateur Wrestling Association. All, of course, spoke for nonprofessional sport.

Alfred Martin noted the development with satisfaction: "Sport has proved itself a national benefactor and it is time that Whitehall recognized the fact. . . . If only sportsmen in the country would present a united front there is no reason why the authorities should not be made to move."[22] And a memorial sent to the prime minister from an early meeting of the conference stated flatly that the reconstruction of sport along the correct lines "cannot be done by private enterprise." The *Sports Trader* spoke for many at the gathering when it branded as "unadulterated nonsense" the alleged impossibility of finding facilities to meet the demand that full participation would create and predicted that the "organized effort by the State will quickly surmount any difficulties."[23]

↬

But the flexing of what the world of amateur sport presumed to be its muscle brought almost no response from the government. Whitehall was preoccupied with demobilization, continued food rationing, and deteriorating industrial relations.[24] Simultaneously, many, especially among the industrial employers now so well represented in the new Parliament, and particularly in the ranks of the Conservative party, were cooling to the idea of collectivist reconstruction and reasserting the primacy of laissez-faire attitudes in British economy and society. This sensibility grew as the chaos of early 1919 was briefly transformed into prosperity born of pent-up demand. Arthur Marwick has observed, rightly, that as "the war receded behind the golden horizon of the postwar boom, the anti-collectivist sentiment of the employing classes hardened."[25]

This meant retrenchment. The Ministry of Reconstruction was wound up as early as January 1919, and almost all the new programs planned, together with many of the programs already in place, succumbed to the "ax" that Sir Eric Geddes wielded in his attack on government spending. One can see that "retrenchment" also expressed itself in the thinking of the sporting elite in peacetime. For many of these men, the wartime flirtation with state involvement in sport had been a passing fancy. The demands for state sponsorship of sport had always had feet of clay, based as they so often were on blind self-interest. After all, despite sporadic conservative demands, the tradition of hostility to state involvement was long-standing. J. A. H. Catton, responding to the propaganda for a Ministry of Recreation published in his *Athletic News*, warned that too deep a centralizing could very well take sports and "destroy their intrinsic character and convert them into lessons for boys and girls and duties for men and women."[26] Catton had earlier complained of government's leap from "the one extreme of positive indifference to the other of exaggerated interference."[27] In the end, the state could not be trusted to uphold the amateur ideal.

Moreover, when the administrators of sport resumed the full running of their associations, they were immediately concerned with restoring their games and their own control over them. They soon concluded that more government direction would mean less independence of action. As time went on, they tended to concentrate on enlisting state aid in reversing legislation harmful to sport rather than to court state regulation—launching, for example, a strong but unsuccessful effort to repeal the entertainment tax. C. E. Sutcliffe, chairman of the Football League, saw no need to add in March 1919 "to the vast array of paid officials in Government service in this country." Two months later, J. C. Clegg, now the tyrannical chairman of the Football Association, attended a luncheon at which Lord Henry Bentinck toasted the benefits of a Ministry of Sport. Clegg responded tactfully with the advice that those who ran sport at present knew "what was desirable and necessary better than some gentleman who might be appointed."[28] And, by 1927, in one of his several volumes of memoirs, Sir Theodore Cook dismissed a Ministry of Sport by saying: "I think our Government is perfectly right to refuse any such course of action. Sport can only be managed, in my interpretation of it, by the free action of individuals or of the associations they have elected for that purpose."[29] With the reassertion of orthodoxy in political economy and the fading of hope that government action could effect an amateur resurgence in British sport, the noninterventionist creed regained pride of place in the minds of the British upper-middle-class elite.

On August Bank Holiday weekend, 1920, track and field athletes again competed in Glasgow before forty thousand enthusiastic spectators. That year, the men were using the meeting to prepare for the upcoming Olympics, restored after the hiatus of 1916, to be held in Antwerp as a reward for "brave little Belgium." The runners included A. G. Hill, the old Polytechnic Harrier who had helped break the mile-relay world record six years before at the same meet. Another casual glance at the sporting press suggests that competitive and professional sport had not only resumed but had tightened its grip on British culture. Despite typically poor Bank Holiday weather, for example, more than fifty-eight thousand watched the Yorkshire and Lancashire "Roses" cricket match, and paid more than £33,000 to do so. Hobbs, meanwhile was back at the Oval earning his living, as was Woolley at Canterbury.[30] And on training grounds of the professional association football clubs all over Britain, men prepared for the first full season of peacetime football and what would be a record-breaking year for both popularity and profit.

But elite sporting values remained, as well. After flirting with the use of government power to uphold their ideal and then rejecting any attempt to impose outside controls on them, the men who dominated amateur sport had demonstrated their continuing clout. Those who actually comprised the government of sport, through bodies such as the Football Association, the Rugby Football Union, the Amateur Athletics Association, or the Marylebone Cricket Club, were the self-perceived guardians of the nation's sporting life and the collective custodians of British sportsmanship. Intensely practical men in many ways, they had made their adjustments, forged their compromises, and taken their stands in a constant defensive battle against the modern world. Their actions over the previous three decades had made their sports what they were on the eve of the Great War. Hardly anyone among them had wavered in his personal dedication to his peculiarly English and narrowly idealistic view of sport and its value to society. The Great War made little impact upon this dedication—other than to deepen it and sharpen a determination to defend it. And defend it they did, during the war, after the Armistice, and for decades to come. The complaint that the public school–inspired ethos of manliness through amateur sport "largely disappeared, with some of the last vestiges of Victorianism, in the mud of the Somme" is simplistic at best.[31]

The attitudes of elite sports administrators as they faced the future in 1918 and 1919 speak for themselves, though theirs was a losing battle. Significantly, another World War, four more decades, and the dawning of a new, democratic age were to pass before a British government appointed to office anyone historians could describe as a "minister of sport."[32] Not until then did the rearguard action of middle-class sporting ideals at last surrender, after 1960, to changes in finance, popular affluence, and mass communications.

Vanessa's Garden

In the midst of the First World War, Virginia Woolf, who had settled on Sussex as a country alternative to the Cornwall of their childhood, lured her adored artist sister Vanessa Bell to join her in the vicinity of Lewes. The most significant carrot that she dangled in front of Vanessa was that nearby Charleston Farmhouse, available for rent, had a large garden with splendid possibilities. As early as May 1916 she wrote: "I wish you would leave Wissett, and take Charleston. Leonard went over it, and says it's a most delightful house and strongly advises you to take it. . . . It has a charming garden, with a pond, and fruit trees, and vegetables, all now rather run wild, but you could make it lovely."[1] And again in September: "Leonard," she wrote, "says the garden could be made lovely—there are fruit trees, and vegetables, and a most charming walk under trees."[2] It was astute of Virginia to involve her husband, Leonard, in this enterprise, because she knew that Vanessa and Leonard shared a deep love for gardens. No one could forget the wonderful story of Leonard's planting dark iris reticulatas when Virginia "put her head out of the window and called: 'Hitler is making a speech. Do you want to come and hear him?' and Leonard called back: 'No, I'm planting my irises and they'll be flowering long after Hitler is dead.'"[3] And indeed, Olivier Bell, Vanessa's daughter-in-law and the editor of Virginia Woolf's letters, remembers that whenever Leonard came to visit the Bell household or Vanessa arrived at Monk's House, the first thing to be done was to inspect the gardens to see what was new and how the plants were progressing.[4]

The garden has been used as a metaphor ever since biblical times and our vision of the Garden of Eden. Here also, I am thinking not merely of Vanessa's horticultural creation at Charleston, but of her intimate social and familial relationships as well. The latter can be viewed as an intricate example of outward continuity of upper-middle-class tradition which masked the radical lifestyle that has become the hallmark of Bloomsbury and which Vanessa was largely instrumental in initiating. Virginia herself used this metaphor when she wrote to her sister, *à propos* Vanessa's need for male companionship: "You will never succumb to the charms of any of your sex—what an arid garden the world must be for you!"[5] In fact, as I hope to show, Vanessa's metaphorical garden was anything but arid, despite the preponderance of male company, while the planted and landscaped garden became a riot of color and a refuge from a militant world. Both Vanessa's metaphorical and the physical garden illustrate the theme of radical change within a conventional continuity. And one might say that nothing more gently but firmly illustrates this theme in general than the persistent delight the English of all classes take in their gardens. Gardening is an optimistic occupation, an occupation that Vanessa Bell developed both metaphorically and practically in varying degrees throughout her life.

The story of the Bells' move to Charleston Farmhouse at Firle, near Lewes, is well known. Vanessa's husband, Clive, had revived his emotional tie with Mary Hutchinson and spent most of the war at Lady Ottoline Morrell's manor house at Garsington in Oxfordshire. In 1916, with enforced conscription, most young men in the pacifist Bloomsbury circle tried to find work that was considered of national importance in order to avoid combat. Although they knew little of farming, the painter Duncan Grant and his lover, David (Bunny) Garnett, had moved to Wissett Lodge, in the flatlands of Suffolk. This property, then administered by Duncan's father, had belonged to one of his aunts, and, to the horror of the local farmers, these two sophisticated, nonagrarian young men attempted to cultivate it. Bunny's mother, the translator Constance Garnett, came to visit them there, as Vanessa wrote, "full of valuable hints about fowls and vegetables,"[6] and Bunny, of course, had studied botany at Imperial College for four years.[7] Vanessa, herself in love with Duncan, from whom she found it painful to be separated, followed soon afterwards with her two sons, Julian (aged 9) and Quentin (4). "We are so much overcome by the country as compared to London," Vanessa wrote to Lytton Strachey, "that I doubt if I shall ever return to Gordon Sq. . . . The positive delights also of flowers and trees and innumerable unexpected sights and sounds keeps [*sic*] one perpetually happy."[8]

Just one month after Virginia's second letter extolling Charleston, Vanessa had rented and settled her whole extended family in that Sussex farmhouse at Firle: Duncan and Bunny would work for one of the local farmers, thus doing essential war work. Vanessa wrote to her former lover, the artist and art critic Roger Fry, whose friendship she was eager to retain, that he must come to visit her there even though he found it extremely difficult to countenance her love for Duncan Grant. "The pond is most beautiful," she wrote,

> with a willow at one side and a stone or flint wall edging it all round the garden part, and a little lawn sloping down to it, with formal bushes on it. Then there's a small orchard and the walled garden . . . and another lawn or bit of field railed in beyond. There's a wall of trees, one single line of elms all round two sides which shelters us from west winds. We are just below Firle Beacon, which is the highest point on the downs near, . . ."[9]

Firle Beacon and the surrounding sweep of Sussex Downs became the landmark under which Vanessa lived for the next forty-five years, until her death at eighty-one in 1961, and Duncan Grant, who survived her, remained there until his death in 1978 at the age of ninety-three.

The relationship of Vanessa Bell and Duncan Grant is one of the more interesting of the great working and loving partnerships of English history. The key to its longevity may be found in Vanessa's unconventionality and her ability to restrain her passions, in their combined sense of humor, and in Duncan's gentleness and appreciation of her emotional and artistic strength. The story, repeated twice by her biographer Frances Spalding, that, when she first discovered how much she loved Duncan, Vanessa broke down and wept before Virginia, is quite plausible.[10] She remained deeply in love with him throughout her life, writing to him in 1923: "I feel isolated in the world when I can't talk or even write to you."[11] Yet their sexual liaison was brief, lasting only three years, and ended presumably because of Duncan's lack of desire after she had conceived Angelica, a child for whom Vanessa longed, who was born on Christmas Day, 1918. It was clear to Vanessa from the outset, and certainly during their many later years together, that he preferred men as his sexual partners. Throughout her life with him she was always distressingly aware of his innumerable love affairs with a variety of younger men. She wrote at one time to Roger Fry, speaking from her own experience: "One *can* force oneself not to expect or even want much more than is freely given and I think any good relationship depends in the end upon the one person being able to do that. At least I have found that this is what I have to do."[12] And she succeeded in creating friendships with many of Duncan's young men, who often came to stay with both of them at Charleston or at their other homes in Bloomsbury or the Midi, in order that she might retain Duncan's presence. Yet at what cost? Her sister understood her feelings: Virginia had written, "You and Duncan seem to me marmoreally chaste. . . . Ever since Cassis [where she visited them] I have thought of you as a bowl of golden water which brims but never overflows."[13] Vanessa replied, "It is terrible to be thought chaste and dowdy when one would so much like to be neither. . . . My chastity—marmoreal is it?—(*how* it rankles!)."[14] And perhaps even worse, when Duncan was ill and Vanessa feared for his life, Virginia wrote perceptively in her diary: "I think a left handed marriage makes these moments more devastating: a sense remains, I think of hiding one's anguish; of insecurity."[15] Vanessa's insecurity never subsided, as she was always concerned about losing her working artistic and domestic partnership with Duncan whenever he became too emotionally involved with one of his many young lovers.[16] Duncan acknowledged her concern in this regard: "You need not worry about the state of my heart," he wrote on one occasion to let her know that he had begun another such affair.[17] One of the last of Duncan's younger lovers, Paul Roche, moved in with him after Vanessa's death and cared for him until Duncan himself died seventeen years later in 1978. It was to Roche that Duncan explained that his sexual liaison with Vanessa had ended after the birth of their daughter, Angelica.[18]

Vanessa's unconventionality was already an undeniable force when, aged twenty-four, she moved the Stephen household from respectable Kensington to raffish Bloomsbury after their father, Leslie Stephen, had died in 1904. Yet in the many general tributes and analyses of Bloomsbury's individual members' revolutionary ideas in literature, art, and economics, Vanessa's own exemplary achievement as one of the group's essential movers and shakers has not been given its due.[19] Vanessa was a passionate, professional woman who lived an eccentric and productive life. The clearest appreciation of her character comes from Roger Fry, who, in 1917, gave this testimonial:

> You go so straight for the things that are worthwhile—you have done such an extraordinarily difficult thing without any fuss; cut through all the conventions, kept friends with a pernickety creature like Clive, got quit of me and yet kept me your devoted friend, got all the things you need for your own development and yet managed to be a splendid mother. . . . You give one a sense of

security, of something solid and real in a shifting world. . . . Then your marvellous practical power which has, of course, really a quality of great imagination in it because your efficiency comes without worry or effort or fuss.[20]

This seems to have been the view of Vanessa in her circle, with perhaps the exception of Angelica, who was not convinced that Vanessa had been a "splendid mother,"[21] and Vita Sackville-West, whose reservations may have flowed from jealousy of Virginia's close relationship with Vanessa. The lack of fuss, the ability to bestow a sense of security, and her great imagination kept Duncan by Vanessa's side for forty-five years. But their artistic working life was a bond that overrode all potential breaks. They painted together, setting up their easels wherever they went, often working from the same human model, still life, or landscape. It was an essential part of their lives.[22] And it was their mutual passion for art that brought them to the garden that became the physical anchor of their lives.

Vanessa's painterly eye had been beguiled by the wonderful autumnal colors of the Sussex countryside as she traveled toward Firle from Lewes. On an early visit to Virginia, then at Asheham House on the outskirts of Firle, she wrote to Duncan: "One is overcome by the extraordinary peace and beauty of the place. The colour is too amazing now, all very warm, most lovely browns and warm greys and reds with the chalk everywhere giving that odd kind of softness."[23]

It was good that she saw the landscape in September, as neither she nor Duncan was infatuated with green. Sussex is often thought to be one of England's spectacularly verdant counties. Its lush acres of dense trees and the calm, long stretches of the Downs offer a kaleidoscope of various shades of green. When their daughter, Angelica, moved to Yorkshire after her marriage to David Garnett, Vanessa and Duncan were unhappy about visiting her there because, among other problems, they considered Yorkshire "too green." As Vanessa once wrote to Angelica: "Do you really think Yorkshire beautiful and paintable? . . . Isn't it the greenest green all over? . . . It always seems to me it must be a writer's country and not a painter's."[24]

During the half-century in which Charleston was Vanessa Bell's home, the garden became a constantly developing part of both her practical and her emotional life. The ending of Vanessa's letters is intriguing. She often concludes with a few words about the state of the garden, reminiscent of letters that lovers write to each other where the ending coda, in abrupt contrast to what has gone before, is a sentence or two about their feelings for each other. For example, the last line in a letter to Duncan while he was in France: "The peachtree is covered with peaches."[25] To Leonard Woolf she ended a letter in February 1944: "In spite of the cold, a lovely new iris has come out in front and daffodils are in bud."[26] And most dramatic, just six days after the event, at the end of a long letter to Jane Bussy, describing how Virginia's drowned body had been found in April 1941, she wrote succinctly: "The garden is a mass of fruit blossom and things coming up."[27] In this instance, the juxtaposition of Virginia's death and Vanessa's crisp sentence about her spring garden is an example of the optimism that underlies the beauty of all gardens, and particularly in colder climates. In March 1940 Vanessa had written to Ling Su-Hua, the lover of her much-mourned older son, Julian (killed in the Spanish Civil War some three years earlier): "We have had a terribly hard cold long winter. Now at last plants are beginning to shoot and birds to sing and it is difficult not to think how much happiness there could be if the world would allow it."[28]

The splendid secret of continuity and renewal, in Angelica Garnett's words, makes gardens so satisfying and comforting in practice, and as symbols of the regeneration of life.

Angelica also saw the "the secret of continuity and renewal" as the "creative centre" of the Charleston household.[29] And in parallel with their painterly artistic creativity, the garden, often the model for their art, offered constant and pleasurable food for Vanessa and Duncan's canvases. Early in their working life together, in 1927, she wrote to Roger Fry: "Now I am glad to say [Duncan] is taking to [painting] flowers too."[30] As she aged, Vanessa herself gravitated ever more to subjects suggested by the garden. She has often been criticized for abandoning the radical paintings of her earlier years: for example, her mysterious *Studland Beach* (ca. 1912) or *The Tub* (1918), both now in the Tate Gallery. It is said that she lost her nerve, that her palette darkened, "her self-image as an artist faltered,"[31] and that "the sparse intensity [of her work became] somehow lost."[32] But when her son Quentin asked her why she "had turned away from abstraction she replied that she had come to the conclusion that nature was much richer and more interesting than anything one could invent."[33] And equally in life, as in art, she wrote to Jane Bussy: "I find in old age [when she was barely sixty] . . . I like pottering about in the garden and trying to make things grow."[34]

What did she grow? During the First World War, after their arrival at Charleston, most of the walled garden was devoted to vegetables, so that they were more or less self-sufficient. Even later the northwest corner of this part of the garden was reserved for vegetables. Today one can visit the garden restored by Sir Peter Shepheard in the mid-1980's and splendidly brought to life by a young master gardener, Andrew Cavely. Vegetables and fruit trees are still an essential part of both the walled garden and the orchard at the side of the pond. Apart from regular English vegetables, globe artichokes bear witness to Vanessa and Duncan's love of southern climes. Throughout the walled garden and the orchard, apple, pear, and plum trees offer interesting gnarled trunks and lovely spring blossoms. Some of these ancient trees are gradually being replaced by similar young saplings.

Vanessa's craving for color is vividly exemplified in her paintings and in her letters. Descriptions of the garden to friends and visitors who knew it confirm her success in satisfying this craving. She wrote to Julian, when he was teaching in China in 1936: "It has been a really fine—absolutely heavenly summer weather, quite hot and with the corn still in the fields, the most lovely gold, and all the pale colours of this chalk country warm and delicious. . . . The garden is simply a dithering blaze of flowers and butterflies and apples."[35] Or in June 1939, writing to Virginia: "The garden is snowed under by pinks, roses and irises."[36] She once described the walled garden to Roger Fry as "incredibly beautiful. . . . It's full of reds of all kinds, scabious & hollyhocks & mallows & every kind of red from red lead to black. [Red-Hot] Pokers are coming out. . . . I have of course begun by painting some flowers, it seems the inevitable way to begin here."[37]

Eye-catching Red-Hot Pokers not only were a memorable feature in the garden, but they were also often brought into the house for decoration and as part of painted interiors. These vibrant plants, newly arrived in England from South Africa, appealed to Vanessa, who was constantly looking for subjects for her paintings. Virginia Woolf called her "a poet in colour"; Roger Fry wrote that "no English painter equaled her as a colourist"; Duncan Grant thought her "the purest colourist he knew," and the art critic Frances Spalding claimed that she was "the leading colourist of the period."[38]

After they had been at Charleston for ten years, both Vanessa and Duncan began to long for more color and daylight in winter. They had fallen in love with the south of France. Vanessa wrote to Virginia:

> Duncan and I play with the idea of buying a house here. . . . We do seriously
> think of trying to take rooms or studios, or something one could come to at

times, for from our point of view it seems too absurd not to. Painting is a different thing here from what it can be in winter in England. It's never dark, even when the sky is grey. The light . . . is perfect, and even now one could often work out of doors, if one wanted to. It makes so much difference to be sure one won't be suddenly held up in the middle of something by fog or darkness. Also the beauty is a constant delight. . . . It seems more and more ridiculous for painters to spend half their lives in the dark.[39]

Eventually, they rented a house near Cassis, where they usually spent the winter months, and could paint those exotic Mediterranean colors to their hearts' delight. Returning to Charleston in the spring, they often carried masses of French and Italian pottery and tried to recreate their colors both in the house and in the garden.

It is unlikely that Vanessa worked a great deal in the garden herself. She did not, as it were, feel a strong urge to "push her fingers into the soil" as do many dedicated amateur gardeners. She wrote to Virginia in 1926: "Altogether the garden is a picture. What about yours? But of course I can't really compete with Leonard, I know, though I like to pretend I can."[40] And to Helen Anrep she wrote: "My roses though not equal to yours are better than they have ever been and I feel encouraged to go in for a complete rosebed and shall ask your advice about kinds."[41] She employed a series of gardeners, who always proved less than satisfactory. One of them, Walter Higgens, the notoriously lazy husband of Charleston's longtime and devoted cook-housekeeper Grace, figures most unattractively in Bloomsbury correspondence. In order to stir him from his lethargy, Duncan once employed a tough young Irish male painter's model to assist in building a greenhouse.[42] In 1949, however, Vanessa thought she had found the perfect gardener. She wrote to Angelica:

> I seem to have an incredibly easy life now that young Mr. Stevens [roughly 70, son of old Mr. Stevens] has come on the scenes [sic]. . . . He is a charming old man, very kind and gentle and with great character. I have fallen very much in love with him, and have some hopes that it is partially returned, for the other day he told me that coming here exactly suited him and he would make my garden lovely.[43]

She was often concerned about the obstreperousness of the weeds. She wrote to Roger Fry in 1925: "Nature is too much for me altogether, either in the shape of weeds or children, and fills up one's spare time. . . . I very seldom leave the studio except to grapple with weeds in the garden."[44] When she had to go into hospital for an operation in 1944, she wrote to Leonard: "I fear the garden will be weedier than ever."[45] Nevertheless, she had help from the most unlikely sources. Bunny Garnett described how Maynard Keynes[46] (who, in the early years, shared the expenses of renting this house with Vanessa, Duncan, and Clive)

> would often go into the garden carrying a small piece of carpet and spend an hour or two on his hands and knees weeding the gravel path with his pocket knife. He worked slowly and removed every scrap of weed. It would have been easy to tell the length of his visit by the state of the path. If he had stayed for a week there would be four or five yards weeded.[47]

We may imagine his weeding during the summer of 1919 while writing *The Economic Consequences of the Peace* in the bedroom reserved for him.[48]

So Vanessa was not a driven gardener, but rather a painter who loved flowers and colors, and "designed" her garden accordingly. It is interesting to remember that Gertrude Jekyll, who also started life as a painter, and who could not continue this art because of a problem with her eyes, took to gardening and became the most famous promoter of the cottage garden.

Whether it was a cottage garden or a painted picture, the walled garden at Charleston was only one significant aspect of the grounds. A major asset mentioned in every recollection is the Charleston pond. One remembers that it figured strongly in Leonard Woolf's original recommendation of the property, and that Virginia also considered the pond an important selling point. When Vanessa first caught a glimpse of it, she thought of it as a "huge lake" and so described it to her children. And when, as a four-year-old boy, Quentin arrived at Charleston, he was disappointed to find that it was merely a "horse pond."[49] Nevertheless, Vanessa wrote to Roger Fry that "the pond is most beautiful," as indeed it was—and is. It played a major part in the art created there, as Angelica said, "for reflections."[50] It served as an inspiration for paintings, as an amusement for children, and as a farming necessity, because horses and cows did indeed come to drink from it. One of Vanessa's beautiful warm paintings of 1950 shows Charleston Farmhouse, very plain, mostly beige, with a red roof, one leafless tree, and touches of green bushes reflected in the pond.[51]

My own first connection with this garden began when my mother bought a painting of the pond directly from Vanessa at Charleston. It happened because we were friends of the Firle Midwife and District Nurse Afra Leckie, who was one of the well-known Queen's Nurses.[52] In August 1944, Vanessa had a mastectomy, that "rather tiresome piece of news," as she described it to Leonard.[53] After the operation Afra Leckie nursed Vanessa back to health, and thereafter she occasionally dropped by to visit her.

Vanessa then made it a practice to lend her four or five of her paintings, and these were regularly exchanged for others. This exchange of paintings continued until Vanessa's death, some seventeen years after her operation. Ironically, the Queen's Nurse for this part of the county was assigned to live in Little Talland House. This semidetached brick house was rented by Virginia Woolf when she first came to Sussex in 1911, and was named after the beloved St Ives Talland House of her childhood and *To the Lighthouse*. One wonders what she would have thought of the fact that for many years the walls of the house she thought so hideous were embellished by her sister's glowing paintings.

On a visit to Afra, my mother fell in love with one of Vanessa's paintings of Charleston pond seen from an upstairs window. The view ranges over the pond with its famous willow tree, and across a stretch of golden fields beyond. In the foreground is a handsome beehive. Except for Bunny Garnett's beekeeping, which provided the sweetness that rationed sugar denied during the First World War, there had been no bees at Charleston.[54] In 1947, Vanessa, writing one of her grandmotherly letters to the twin daughters of Angelica, mentioned this beehive: "It has been raining cats and dogs here . . . so hard that a lot of water which should have run in a drain underground from the farm has burst out and made a pond near my bee hive—quite a large pond. I expect you would try to get into it if you were here."[55] It has been said that as Vanessa grew older she painted with a "darkened palette,"[56] an appropriate description for the painting of the pond with its beehive, which dates from the late 1940's or early 1950's.

For some reason Nurse Leckie was nervous about asking Vanessa whether my mother could buy the painting, so they went to Charleston together to inquire. Of course, Vanessa was delighted to sell the painting; she immediately framed it herself, and thought of charging the minimal sum of £5. Quentin appeared at just that moment, and remonstrated with her for asking so little. In the end my mother paid the grand sum of £10 for the painting, which still adorns my wall in Vanessa's original mat and frame.

This painting of the pond is clearly one of the later examples of Vanessa's oeuvre. It is almost a sober contrast to the dazzling 1917 post-impressionist apricot-and-cantaloupe pond surrounded by imaginary trees. The apricot pond, seen through a window framed by rosy red curtains with a distinct Bloomsbury or Omega design, was painted soon after Vanessa's arrival at Charleston.[57] Both Vanessa and Duncan often painted garden scenes including the pond, or demonstrating activities in or near it. An important example is Duncan's picture with Vanessa lying in a hammock and Julian on the pond in a boat.[58]

A description of how the children felt about the pond comes from Nicholas Henderson, who (together with Angelica) was a pupil at Marjorie Strachey's small school run at Charleston:

> We also shared the horror of a frequent drama which occurred when cows wandered into the pond, . . . became stuck in the deep mud and had to be extricated by farm-labourers with much heaving and shouting. Not at all the idyllic attribute of many a Charleston painting, the pond was regarded by us as a danger-area, not merely for the cows but for ourselves as Baba Anrep, who was bigger than the rest of us, would entice us to climb along the branch of an over-hanging willow tree and then shake it until we fell off into the water.[59]

At the time when Quentin was fifteen and Julian seventeen, Roger Fry described an amusing episode of clearing the pond of a thick carpet of duckweed. After many attempts with rakes and nets, Vanessa had the idea to tie several ladders end to end to stretch across the pond and to haul these along, thus pushing the duckweed to the edges. Quentin and Julian gradually became interested in this exercise after scoffing at other attempts. As Fry described this incident:

> Fortunately, Quentin fell in accidentally, whereupon there seemed no reason why he shouldn't be used to push the ladders wading. Gradually both boys became naked and under our directions pushed the barrage right across the pond and hauled out the weed by the armful at the side. It led to a great deal of entirely unnecessary swimming in about two feet of muddy water but this only increased the satisfaction and mess and by dinner time the pond was practically clear, the trees and hills all neatly reflected and the banks a mass of smelly and clammy weed, and every one felt exceedingly virtuous and happy.[60]

Whereas Vanessa loved the pond and the natural features of the garden, especially the old trees and flowers, Duncan and her son Quentin seemed to be more interested in exotic plants and in creating garden ornaments. When, occasionally, he found himself alone at Charleston, even Duncan dug and planted and became more interested in the flower garden, "discussing the choice of flowers with Vanessa" by letter.[61] We have glimpses of him "hard at work on his rock garden, which is beginning to look less like earth works."[62] Quentin and Angelica often mentioned Duncan's interest in exotics. Angelica remembers his fantasies, such as "thinking that he had seen an albatross fly past the window when it was in fact a sparrow."[63] He had thought of breeding flamingos on the pond, though, unhappily, this dream never materialized.[64] While in Ravenna Duncan had become intrigued by the famous mosaics.[65] He created the "fish mosaic," embedded in a rectangular stone frame in the little terrace just outside the studio, depicting a large orange fish swimming in blue water. Now restored, as the other, much larger mosaic at the opposite end of the walled garden has also been, this was the first mosaic at Charleston. On the eastern wall, which separates the garden from the orchard and the pond, Duncan mounted plaster heads, discarded sculptures made by students at Brighton Art College, whence he rescued them.[66] These heads are somewhat reminiscent of the Roman emperors around the wall of the Sheldonian Theatre in Oxford. Two new heads were "given by friends to celebrate Quentin's eightieth birthday in 1990 and to commemorate others that are gone," states a small pottery plaque mounted on the flint on the lower part of the wall. Duncan and Vanessa collected plaster casts often discarded by art schools, such as these heads or the still remaining cast of a nude female figure by Giovanni da Bologna now in the walled garden, surrounded by billowy, overgrown box hedges.

Traveling in Spain in the 1930's, Duncan was enchanted by the colored tiles in the Alhambra gardens and dreamed of doing something of that sort at Charleston.[67] When Maynard Keynes presented him with an annuity for life, he wrote to his benefactor that he now had hopes of building "a gazebo by the pond."[68] He enjoyed especially creating his own little, sheltered garden behind the studio, which is known as "Duncan's Folly." It, too, has its own tiny pond with fig trees and garden seats, a very private little corner.

But although Duncan was interested in and responsible for many of the decorative aspects of the garden, it was Vanessa's son Quentin who created most of the notable sculptures and garden ornaments. As Vanessa wrote ironically at one time, "Quentin's idea was to make our garden a second Versailles."[69] On another occasion she recorded her delight that Quentin "has taken to doing all sorts of major works in the garden and orchard by way of exercise. He is making a path, which is going to be brick, round the inside of the walled garden where there are no flowerbeds and which was simply weeds. So one will walk round and pick one's pears and peaches."[70] It was Quentin who first proposed the mosaics in the large northeast corner of the walled garden. They were created out of a mass of pottery shards collected from broken household crockery over the years. The whole family—Vanessa, Duncan, Quentin, Angelica, and Lytton Strachey's niece Jane Bussy—worked on creating this piazza in 1946. In 1958, a few years before Vanessa's death, Quentin added a tiny semicircular pool with an ancient

Egyptian–like head spouting water into its basin, upon which now bloom dark red water lilies. One is able to rest in this sheltered, sunny corner on a comfortable wooden bench and admire the bottom half of a female torso filled with a pink hydrangea.

Several of Quentin's large sculptures enhance interest in the garden. As early as 1930 Quentin produced a female figure made mostly of bricks known as *The Spink*; in 1954 he made a well-endowed concrete female figure, *Pomona*, now standing proudly erect in the orchard with a tall bucket of colored apples on her head; and in 1973 he produced the first of his "levitating" ladies, constructed from molded fiberglass, which is still to be seen levitating horizontally in her draperies as though suspended by a long, twisted braid of hair, about two feet above the ground by the side of the pond.[71]

Fascinatingly, the men and women responsible for this garden had distinctly gendered interests. Frances Spalding states that Duncan and Vanessa planned the garden together, "looking through seed catalogues in the winter months and selecting flowers and plants for their colour."[72] But it was clearly Vanessa who was more concerned with flowers and colors, while Duncan, together with Quentin, created the garden structure and its ornaments. This becomes obvious when one begins to consider their activities and interests as described in their writings, especially Vanessa's letters, and becomes even more pertinent when one compares the work of two other illustrious contemporary gardening couples. The description "a Lutyens House with a Jekyll Garden" sums up the numerous such estates created together by the most distinguished neo-Georgian architect Sir Edwin Lutyens, and Gertrude Jekyll, whose freestyle and impressionist gardens were commissioned by aristocratic and upper-middle-class Britons who could afford them.[73] The other couple, familiar with Charleston, Vita Sackville-West and her husband, Harold Nicolson, created the now famous garden at Sissinghurst Castle in Kent. Vita designed many separate garden "rooms," each featuring special colors and styles (such as the "White Garden" or the "Spring Garden"), while Harold organized the layout of the grounds and sculptured focal points.[74] In both these cases, the women created the overall color schemes, basically concerned with the flowers; the men occupied themselves with architecture and the structure and ornaments of the garden. This gendered pattern in English gardens can be traced back at least to the eighteenth century. Then, women enthusiastically planted flowers, their efforts historically unappreciated, while men rhapsodized about the newly invented, and ever since admired, "landscape gardens" within patriarchal acres heritable only by male descendants.[75]

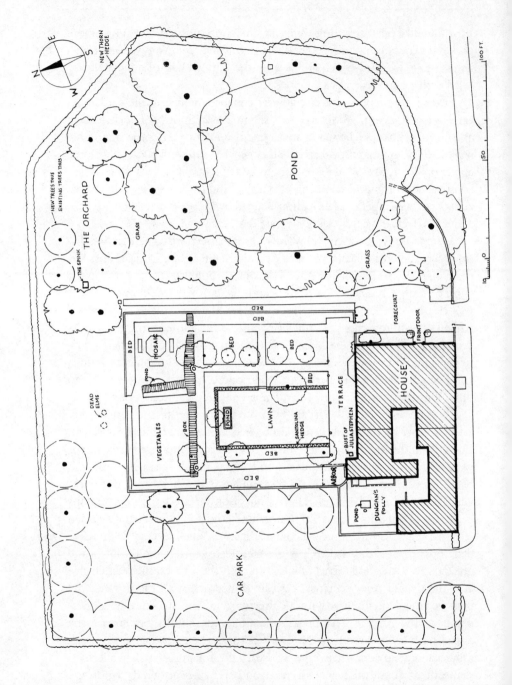

Fig. 1. The Charleston grounds. Reproduced by courtesy of the *Charleston Newsletter*.

Clumps of those striking Red-Hot Pokers had reseeded themselves even half a century later, when the garden was being reconstructed.[76] Sir Peter Shepheard, planning the restoration of the garden in the 1980's, worked from family memories and photograph albums.[77] He used details such as the children's memories of harsh pebbles under their naked bottoms to guide his laying out of paths in the walled garden and elsewhere. These pebbles are brought to life in another way by Vanessa's granddaughter Henrietta Garnett, who described them as "grey-blue, the colour of Vanessa's eyes."[78]

Sir Peter's recollection is that the first design of the actual walled garden was a combination of ideas of Saxon Sydney-Turner and Roger Fry. And while the layout of this part of the garden was a conventional, rectangular design with straight paths, low box hedges, and fruit trees at appropriate corners and distances, the interiors of the flower beds were a mass of flowers grown without any formal pattern or color arrangement. The walled garden is the rectangular part of the grounds to the north of the house and to the west of the large pond and orchard. (See Fig. 1.) Sir Peter considered the walled garden to be the "apotheosis of the traditional English cottage garden."[79] He speaks enthusiastically of his original work at Charleston as being almost like an archaeological dig, and of how he pieced together whatever he could from photographs and memories.[80] However, Andrew Cavely, for the past several years the gardener in charge of the Charleston garden, who plants, weeds, and makes decisions on new plants, comes closer to the reality when he suggests that Charleston was a "painter's garden."[81] Cavely has read extensively in Bloomsbury diaries, letters, and memoirs, and since 1995 has re-created the planting with great sensitivity and imagination. He speaks of his work and the selection of plants and flowers as though he has discussed each item with Vanessa herself. Cavely is convinced that Vanessa looked out her bedroom and studio windows and decided that, just as in a painting, the design of the garden required a swatch of gray or a touch of red or blue in some particular place or corner, then chose whatever flowers would best fill the required color. Having watched Quentin Bell at work, and noticing that he allowed the brush to dribble paint, Cavely also thought Vanessa, possibly working in a similar manner, would also have let self-seeding plants grow in certain places because "nature" willed them to be there. Cavely's sense of what belongs in the garden includes the idea that Vanessa would have chosen certain plants "had she been aware of their existence," but he is also aided by those who wander around the garden pointing to one or another spot and remembering, for example, how when they "were there in 1941 there was a certain rose where now bloom geraniums."[82] The restoration of this garden is an example of subtle changes within a consoling continuity achieved in the most careful and dedicated manner.

By the time Sir Peter Shepheard restored the Charleston garden in the mid-1980's, Sissinghurst had already been a National Trust property for several decades, with thousands of visitors each year. Nigel Nicolson, editor of Virginia Woolf's letters and the son of Harold Nicolson and Vita Sackville-West, who lives at Sissinghurst, was invited to advise on the reconstruction of the Charleston garden. When Sir Peter suggested the need for a car park, Nicolson was incredulous and argued strongly against this plan, as there surely would not be enough visitors to warrant such an expenditure.[83] This attitude is reminiscent of the beginning of the restoration of the decorations of Charleston Farmhouse itself. At that time Quentin Bell thought that it would be optimistic to imagine that a museum would accept Vanessa's and Duncan's paintings lifted off the walls, bedsteads, tables, and windowsills and remounted as artifacts. The restoration of the entire house, with its contents, as well as the garden, was then beyond the wildest hopes of those who cared about preserving the Charleston heritage.[84] In *Bloomsbury Pie: The Making of the Bloomsbury Boom*, Regina Marler cites fifteen thousand visitors a year as of 1995.[85] Two years later, in 1997, Andrew Cavely reported that the figure had already grown to eighteen thousand. He described the difficulties of small gardens as opposed to large estates such as Sissinghurst or some of the extensive National Trust properties, where visitors can lose themselves. A small family house and garden needs entrance fees in order to help pay its expenses, but the fees cannot be raised too high, or students and those whom one wants to attract will not be able to afford the price. Moreover, the number of visitors must be kept down lest the plantings be trampled.[86]

The number of visitors would have astonished—indeed, overwhelmed—the original Bloomsbury tenants of Charleston. Vanessa, especially, was modest about her painting, as the small price she charged my mother indicates, usually deferring to Duncan as the greater artist.[87] And she would have been surprised at the possibility that the garden might be of intrinsic interest to anyone beyond her immediate family, friends, and relations. It is a personal garden; walking around it, one has a feeling as if of intruding on Vanessa Bell's private life. It was to the garden that she retreated like a wounded animal after her son Julian had been killed in Spain, and where Grace, her cook, found her in tears because "no one realised her need to talk about [him]."[88] It was after this event and Virginia's suicide that Vanessa's "silences" became one of her acknowledged characteristics. And it was in the garden that she found not only the physical solace that comforted her in those dark days and throughout her life, but also the inspiration for many of her paintings.

In 1958, three years before her death, Vanessa selected the last three paintings she lent to Afra Leckie from her storeroom.[89] All of them depict the garden in what Vanessa once described to Julian as "a dithering blaze of colour." One of these paintings is a rendering of the corner just outside Duncan's studio on a bright and sunny spring day: the trees beyond the garden wall have not yet sprouted any leaves, but a deck chair stands invitingly over the "fish mosaic." This painting was exhibited in Lewes in 1930. The other two were probably also painted during the 1930's. One shows the garden path leading north through a mass of impressionist blue and light orange flowers to the statue that still stands within the box hedge dividing the flower garden from the crockery-mosaic piazza.[90] The other is Vanessa's painting of the path leading through lighthearted pink, gray, and white borders to the three steps that climb to the rectangular lawn with its narrow ceramic-tiled pond. The feeling in all these paintings is one of light, warmth, tranquillity, and happiness. While the 1917 painting of the apricot pond is a decided flight of post-impressionist fancy, these later paintings of the garden, although more anchored in realism, appear to return to Vanessa's early bursts of delight. They cannot possibly be described as coming from a "dark palette."[91]

I know these paintings well, for their exhilarating color and warmth brightened Afra Leckie's small house for many years, especially on dark or rainy days. They elucidate both Vanessa's feeling about her garden and her appreciation of the people around her. If evidence were still needed of what Vanessa wished for in her garden, it is clearly present in these paintings. The two depictions of garden paths flanked by flower beds (the beds still existing in 1999) are a painter's vision, with artistic license producing colors and shapes almost impossible to achieve in a real—let alone a "cottage"— garden. Impressionist they may be; agrestial they are not. Colors and design are most carefully chosen to produce a picture where hardly a leaf is out of place.

Moreover, these paintings, lent by Vanessa to the nurse who had tended her and others of her extended family for over a decade, were selected with great care, reflecting both the painter's and the nurse's character. They illustrate their concern for people, their love both of gardens and

color, and of humanity. In 1960, when Afra Leckie was offered a position supervising nurses for a larger area of the county, she wrote to Vanessa, who was spending the winter in the south of France in Jane Bussy's house, and asked what should be done with the borrowed paintings of the garden she loved to visit, still in her possession. Vanessa's generous reply offering the paintings to her as a gift has been treasured ever since.[92] While at Firle, Afra Leckie had no idea of the convoluted emotional and sexual relationships forged among the inhabitants of Charleston. Like the rest of the world beyond the walled garden, and despite the fact that she penetrated both the garden and even the bedrooms of the house itself, the nurse took at face value the marriage of Vanessa and Clive (the "husband" cited in Vanessa's letter). Although she knew all these people, she would have been surprised (and at that time possibly shocked) to know that Duncan was Angelica's father and that the father of Vanessa's little granddaughters had been their grandfather's lover many years earlier. Respectability and outward tradition were observed at Charleston.

Innumerable other memories of Charleston, apart from the paintings, are also associated with the garden: Lytton Strachey reading the first parts of his *Eminent Victorians* to Vanessa, Duncan, and David Garnett in the garden room with the French windows wide open; Julian and Quentin, as young boys, sharing secrets with Virginia, "whose clear hoot of laughter could be heard from a corner of the walled garden."[93] David Garnett used the walled garden as the setting for part of his first published story, *Lady into Fox*.[94] A photograph taken during the summer of 1932 shows Vanessa, Julian, Duncan, and Clive at tea on the terrace overlooking the walled garden in full flower. Here she exemplifies the encomiums she has received from her family and friends. She is wearing a long dress reminiscent of medieval draperies, reaching for the teapot, while the whole group is in animated conversation.[95]

The garden had begun as a working refuge for pacifist young men who needed an alternative to conscription in the Great War. And during the Second World War, when many Londoners were evacuated to Sussex, the Charleston garden was a great deal safer than the urban Bloomsbury enclave, where many of the houses of the group were totally destroyed by bombs. Eventually the Charleston garden became not only a pacifist refuge and a provider of unrationed farm produce, but a haven from two World Wars and the turmoil of Bloomsbury emotions.

Vanessa saw her garden as an extension of her house. Her sensuousness, her love of bright colors, red and crimson flowers, her need for light, and her craving to re-create the south of France, are a constant refrain. Light and color were essential both to her painting and to her view of the world. The optimism inherent in gardening, the knowledge that one's labor regenerates annually, offered a particularly comforting "calling" for an atheist like Vanessa, whose relationship with Duncan was fraught with constant anxiety about her potential loss of him. Thus her garden was planted not merely as a physical part of her domain but also as the symbolic world which mirrored her life. Loving Duncan, the father of her youngest child, but also the person with whom she enjoyed above all to work in tandem on their artistic creations, she was determined to accept whatever difficulties in order to preserve the status quo. In the year of her death, Vanessa could still encapsulate a picture of her life as follows: "Yesterday Leonard and Morgan [E. M. Forster] came to lunch & seemed to enjoy themselves—Duncan is painting, I am sitting in my room with the door open between us. The garden is full of Red Admirals, & birds & apples & I hope to return to my studio in a day or two."[96] It was a paradise with strings attached.

It is tempting to equate Vanessa's walled garden with the famous symbol of the *Song of Songs*, the *Hortus conclusus* or enclosed garden. Certainly, the lack of puritanical inhibitions exemplified by Bloomsbury's members and friends might lead to such a connection. Yet I would suggest that the real secret of Vanessa's garden was the exact opposite. It was not "a spring shut up, a fountain sealed," but rather an open paradise, a golden safety net, into which she enticed her husband, two former lovers, and innumerable friends and family members. All of them returned to this refuge as long as they lived, because she offered them the freedom to come and go as they pleased. It was a subversive maneuver on Vanessa's part to keep those she loved and whose company she enjoyed around her. It is significant that while Vanessa's garden was open to everyone, there was a private little garden enclosed by a fig tree hedge that was Duncan's.

As Vanessa herself said, a good relationship depends on expecting no more than is freely given.[97] In a way she personified the garden she had created. It drew her friends like bees to nectar. Virginia had recognized this when she wrote to her sister, while both were still in their twenties, "You have a touch in letter writing that is beyond me. Something unexpected, like coming round a corner in a rose garden and finding it still daylight."[98] And while Vanessa considered the garden an extension of the house, the garden even more than the house offered this freedom, which inspired Duncan on one of his returns to Charleston to write: "The quiet and peace and beauty are unbelievable."[99]

Vanessa's garden, then, symbolically as well as physically, offered much through its regenerative pleasures. It bound together this group of friends, children, and grandchildren, but more significantly, its splendid domestication, centering on artistic creativity, presented a truly radical core within an outwardly traditional extended family.

Whigs and Surrealists: The "Subtle Links" of Humphrey Jennings's *Pandaemonium*

The late nineteenth-century "revolt against positivism" among European intellectuals was particularly harsh when it came to the practice of history.[1] The scientific, materialist approach of Leopold von Ranke, the deterministic preoccupations of Hippolyte Taine, the Whiggish optimism of Lord Acton: all seemed to their critics shallow, a denial of the profundity and passions of life. Friedrich Nietzsche, for example, argued that the nineteenth-century preoccupation with an empirical past was excessive, a "defect and deficiency." The accumulated weight of the past could be vitiating, deflecting spontaneous responses to contemporary existence. "We want to serve history," he admonished, "only to the extent that history serves life."[2] Henrik Ibsen vividly dramatized this view in *Hedda Gabler* (1890), in which the careerist historian Tesman devotes his honeymoon to "collecting and arranging" the notes for his history of "the domestic industries of Brabant in the Middle Ages." His wife, Hedda, does not share his single-minded devotion. She contrasts her antiquarian husband unfavorably with another scholar in her life, Lövberg, a "Dionysian" historian who embodies the vitalist temper of the fin de siècle by writing an impassioned history not of the past, but of the future.[3]

Lövberg's unorthodox approach did not have much of a future itself within the historical profession. But new approaches to the past, pioneered at the turn of the century, attempted to address the alleged deficiencies of positivist history. These new approaches examined the role played by the imagination, the irrational, and the masses in human affairs: new historical "agents" heretofore slighted by most traditional historians. The cultural histories of Jacob Burckhardt and Johan Huizinga, as well as the histories of *mentalité* developed by Marc Bloch and Lucien Febvre, gauged the spirit of an age through indirect interpretive strategies that departed from the positivists' strict reliance on documented "facts" and their emphasis on high politics and diplomacy.

Perhaps the most radical challenge to positivist history (and certainly the least known) was "surrealist history." Although the surrealists wanted to break with most bourgeois conventions, they nevertheless valued history. They accepted Freud's contention that human history continues to affect the present through its shaping influence on the unconscious, and identified the unconscious (or the "imagination") as the primary agent of history. But this agent was not one that operated according to rational logic, and it could not be constrained by a diachronic narrative emphasizing causes and effects. Rather, the surrealists' chronicles of the imagination focused on elements of contingency and chance, using the juxtaposition of seemingly unrelated texts and images as a way to reveal underlying associations, indirect connections, and unexpected relations. Surrealist history did not reject the possibility of attaining "objective" knowledge about the past; for André Breton and many of his followers, what seemed to be arbitrary resulted in actuality from "objective chance." Chaos did cohere, at some unconscious, perhaps even mystical, level. But, following Freud, the surrealists believed reality was "overdetermined" and could be assessed only indirectly.

Indeed, their historical collages did not eschew narrative, although frequent recourse to juxtapositions without authorial comment could make them appear to lack cohesive meaning. Surrealist history attempted to provide an unmediated narrative, in which the diverse sources spoke for themselves, rather than being spoken for by an omniscient author: it intended to protect the polyphony of human experience apart from the univocal constraints of analytic reason. In its desire to encompass the whole of lived experience, surrealist history moved away from focusing on the actions of the elite to examining the expressions of the "collective unconscious." It rejected any narrow focus on the individual strands of traditional historical inquiry—those of politics, economics, or diplomacy—in order to embrace the totality of the "everyday."

Finally, surrealist history was a critical history. Its intention was to jolt its readers out of the analytic mind-set of the bureaucratically administered world widely identified at the time with "modernity." Surrealist history's "profane illuminations," in Walter Benjamin's phrase, were intended to restore to the modern, rational world the passionate myths and holistic dreams that had inspired earlier ages, dormant sparks within the dross of contemporary life that awaited rekindling. The surrealist historians were cultural animists who challenged the well-established view of cultural pessimists like Max Weber that the world was "disenchanted," an "iron cage" of reason.[4] They strove to recover the poetic, imaginative, and spiritual dimensions of everyday life, to illuminate the "subtle links"[5] underlying and uniting the fragmentary character of modernity. Their histories were intended to demonstrate that science, technology, and mass culture need not be understood solely in terms of the triumph—or oppression—of instrumental reason. Modernity, when viewed through their innovative interpretive strategies, could be no less vital, mythic, and magical than so-called premodern cultures and ages.

As a defined genre within historiography, however, "surrealist history" itself might seem only a product of the imagination. The best-known history of modernity influenced by surrealism has been that of the German essayist Walter Benjamin, and even his famous "Arcades Project" (composed during the interwar period) was never completed and exists only in fragments.[6] One unfinished work does not a genre make, but how about two unfinished works? *Pandaemonium*, by the British filmmaker, poet, and painter Humphrey Jennings, raises this question. It shares many similarities with Benjamin's Arcades Project, and I would like to explore these in this essay. Taken separately, each work is rather esoteric, more read about than read; taken together, both circumscribe the possibilities and limitations of a surrealist approach to historical representation, and provide insights into twentieth-century historiography as a whole.

The origins of both can be traced to their authors' involvement with French surrealism in the interwar period. Each history was to consist of juxtaposed quotations or "images" with a minimum of authorial comment; each dealt with the origins of "modernity," and each had the aim of salvaging the collective dreams of humanity buried within the artifacts of mass culture and everyday life. Each sought to present a chronicle of the imaginative experience of modernity through the use of associations and symbols, a history poetic and impassioned rather than analytic and discursive; each tried to do justice to the contingency of history no less than to its causal factors, emphasizing history's heterogeneous elements as well as its more uniform trends. Each focused on the "collective unconscious," the "imagination," or some other, analogous force—invisible yet perceptible—as the primary agent within the historical process; each presented this force as animating the modern no less than the premodern world. Such remarkable similarities between two histories of modernity by two idiosyncratic surrealists who apparently had no knowledge of each other suggest that their works do belong to a category that subsumes both: surrealist history.

I believe that surrealist history expressed one of the boldest attempts to challenge Western conventions of historiography in the twentieth century. Benjamin and Jennings's histories anticipate more recent postmodern experiments in representing the past, as well as postmodernist critiques of historical objectivity, narrative unity, and rational human agency.[7] This is why it is worth comparing these two unfinished and rather fragmentary works, which would otherwise be of interest only to specialists: they address some of the most fundamental dilemmas involved in the writing of history. As we shall see, neither Benjamin nor Jennings resolved these dilemmas—but their attempts are bracing, perhaps even instructive.

Although I will refer to Benjamin's Arcades Project, this essay will focus primarily on Jennings's *Pandaemonium*. In part this is because there has been a tremendous amount of scholarship devoted to Benjamin, and comparatively little to Jennings.[8] But Jennings's *Pandaemonium* also expresses this volume's themes of continuity, tradition, and nostalgia in British history. Surrealist history was certainly a critical history, challenging the bourgeois emphasis on incessant progress through instrumental reason. Jennings's work shared this critical spirit, but it actually had more in common with the Whig tradition of British historiography than he would have wished to acknowledge. Whereas Benjamin's last essay depicted history as an ever-ascending ruin, Jennings continued to invoke the past—particularly the British past—as inspiration for further British glory. Britain's foremost practitioner of surrealist history was also an ardent patriot, and the tensions inherent in this pairing at times became difficult to reconcile. *Pandaemonium* was a work that boldly challenged the canons of traditional history as written in Britain, but in the end it could not escape its own Whiggish veneration of the British past.

Five Sources of 'Pandaemonium'

Humphrey Jennings once asserted that "the chief problem in all times is to fit in all the worlds that exist together."[9] In amassing the material for his history of the imaginative responses to the "coming of the machine," Jennings himself tried to bring together many worlds that he believed had been artificially sundered during the Industrial Revolution: poetry and science, animism and materialism, art and economics. Yet readers confronting the posthumously published version of Jennings's history, condensed from a manuscript draft of over one thousand pages to a volume less than half that length,[10] may still wonder how to bring together all the worlds it contains. *Pandaemonium*, in both its original form and its published incarnation, is a collage of quotes from the late seventeenth through the late nineteenth century, originating from such diverse sources as diaries, letters, official reports, poems, novels, scientific papers, plays, advertisements, travel journals, and so on. Jennings's original manuscript includes several "notes" commenting on a particular passage, but on the whole the quotes (or "Images," as he called them) are allowed to speak for themselves—and among themselves, as Jennings believed a range of meanings would emerge spontaneously from their juxtaposition.

What is a reader to make of a "history" that lacks such basic elements as an explicit thesis or a cohesive narrative supported by analyses of cause and effect? Jennings is not helpful in this regard, maintaining that "as [to] cause and effect—the links of History are subtler than that."[11] Nonsurrealist historians may be forgiven if they turn to Jennings's own history for clues about the possible order to *Pandaemonium*. Here one finds five important influences that contributed to the work's structure and content. These provide the contexts that cast the "subtle links" of his collage account into sharper relief.

The first influence on Jennings's thought was the English arts and crafts movement, in two respects: the way the movement looked to the past for ways of coping with the future, and its romantic belief in the importance of communal solidarity. Jennings's middle-class upbringing was imbued with the aesthetic, social, and nationalist tenets expressed by such founders of the movement as John Ruskin and William Morris. He was born in 1907 in Walberswick, a picturesque village on the coast of Suffolk that could have emerged from an arts and crafts tableau. Both his parents were artists (his father an architect, his mother a painter) as well as adherents of Guild Socialism, which looked to preindustrial corporatist forms of association as a model for future socialist polities. Jennings described his own politics as those of William Cobbett; like his parents and Cobbett, he derived inspiration from romantic conceptions of a preindustrial communal life for his own notions of how industrial Britain might be reshaped in the future. Many of his poems, paintings, and films featured recurring rural images: the plow, the harvest field, the horse, the windmill.[12]

Such nostalgic ruralism, however, was counterbalanced by a genuine enthusiasm for the modern: Jennings hoped to unite past and present in order to forge a more humane future. This was also true for many of the founders of the arts and crafts movement in the late nineteenth and early twentieth century.[13] In much of his art Jennings presented similar connections between the past and the future, the organic and the mechanical. He recalled that as a child he imaginatively associated the horses raced by his grandfather with the train that passed his grandparents' home,[14] and in *Pandaemonium* he demonstrated how writers in the nineteenth century often made similar elisions between the traditional rural world and the new technological one. "Machines," he himself wrote in 1938, "are animals created by man."[15]

The second significant influence on *Pandaemonium* was Jennings's education at Cambridge University in the 1920's. His open-minded attitude toward the arts and sciences of his day may have been fostered during his years at the Perse School in Cambridge, then under the progressive direction of W. H. Rouse. But the issues that come to the fore in *Pandaemonium*—the sharp distinction between the "animism" of the preindustrial world and the "scientific materialism" of modernity; the ways in which art and science, individuals and communities, might be integrated into an organic whole—were certainly fostered by teachers (notably I. A. Richards) and friends at Pembroke College, Cambridge, which he attended between 1926 and 1930.

Like Walter Benjamin, Jennings was a brilliant literary scholar who seemed destined for an academic career. In 1929 he received a Double First with distinction in the English Tripos, as well as a fellowship to pursue postgraduate research in English literature. He was particularly interested in the question of the public role of art, and would always look to Elizabethan England as a golden age in which artists had a social function. Jennings mourned the decline of the public role of art in the modern age, when the artist ceased to provide unifying myths for the people and instead was transformed into a specialized producer of artifacts for the elite.

At Cambridge he began a thesis under the direction of I. A. Richards on the eighteenth-century poet Thomas Gray. Gray represented a sad instance of a poet who could find no social role for his poetry and turned to more formalistic concerns. His dilemma, and Richards's response to the similar dilemma confronted by modern poets, continued to haunt Jennings's later writings after he left Cambridge, his thesis unfinished, to try his hand at art. For Jennings, Gray exemplified the unfortunate hermetic turn poetry had taken since the advent of industrialization, and Richards's theories offered a potential solution to the dissociation of sensibility that disfigured modernity.

Indeed, Richards's ideas about the relation between poetry and modernity might have provided the implicit narrative schema for *Pandaemonium*. He presented them as lectures while Jennings was a student; they were published as *Science and Poetry* in 1928.[16] The similarities between the two books' chronicles of the decline of a poetic, "animistic" view of the cosmos in the wake of the scientific and industrial revolutions are notable.

Richards was deeply concerned about the fate of poetry in the industrial age, and in response formulated a new style of literary criticism that assessed the merits of poetry in terms a scientistic culture would respect. He presented poetry as a mode of cognition, one necessary to keep the personality balanced. Poetry, he argued, united both thought and feeling, thereby integrating the human psyche and assisting the mind to assimilate the chaos of experience in a coherent form. Prior to industrialization, human beings thought poetically or "magically"—they made connections and saw associations among all phenomena; through such subtle links they were able to attain some measure of personal equipoise and harmony with nature. Richards termed this premodern mode of perception the "Magical View" and contrasted it with the dominant mode of thought that emerged as a result of the scientific and industrial revolutions: the "Scientific View." This view rejected any subtle links that could not be measured through the senses; in its emphasis on materialism and rationality it threatened the very existence of poetry, which had emerged as an expression of the Magical View.

Stimulated by contemporary findings in psychology and neurology, Richards developed a method of close critical reading that would enable readers to tease out the subtle links in literature. Through this method he hoped to restore the modern individual's ability to interpret and integrate experience—to make holistic associations. In this manner, psychological (and perhaps social) equilibrium might be restored to an excessively mechanistic and individualistic age.

Jennings was strongly influenced both by his teacher's theories and by his methods of close reading. His handwritten comments in the manuscript of *Pandaemonium* show that he paid obsessive attention to the provenance of the words, metaphors, and phrases used in the passages he selected, as one of his expressed aims was to demonstrate how individuals' imaginative apprehension of the world changed as a result of the modernizing process of industrialization. He also retained Richards's faith in poetry and the imagination as redemptive agents.

However, it is unlikely that Jennings would ever have turned to the composition of history if he had retained a fellowship at Cambridge and remained under Richards's influence. This was because Richards himself rejected history as a source of knowledge or direction. He preferred to stress the contingent in human affairs; his own desire to restore equilibrium to the individual and society was inspired by romantic myths rather than by careful historical scrutiny.[17] It is true that Richards insisted that close readings take into account the historical contexts of literary works, but this was in the service of interpreting passages rather than for the purpose of drawing edifying lessons from the past.[18] Richards would not have encouraged Jennings to become a historian; nor would he have been encouraged in his growing enthusiasm for mass culture. Like many English intellectuals of his generation, Richards scorned mass culture.[19] Jennings, on the other hand, demonstrated a great fondness for mass culture in *Pandaemonium* and many of his other works. His open embrace of history and mass culture in the 1930's resulted from the third major influence on *Pandaemonium*: surrealism.

In the early 1930's Jennings left Cambridge to become a painter, spending much of 1931–32 in France. At this time he may have met some of the French surrealists; what is clear is that after he returned to England he threw himself into the nascent British surrealist movement, serving as one of the organizers of the International Surrealist Exhibition that opened in London in 1936. His continued interest in modern French culture also cemented his friendship with Parisian surrealists like André Breton and Paul Eluard.

The surrealists gave Jennings a greater appreciation of the past than he had received under Richards's tutelage. They were influenced by Freud's explorations of the historical role of the unconscious in everyday life, and they celebrated the invisible agency of the unconscious in even the most seemingly "rational" of human actions. Freud argued that the unconscious had a history: in *Civilization and Its Discontents* (1930) he asserted, "in the realm of mind . . . the primitive type is so commonly preserved alongside the transformations which have developed out of it that it is superfluous to give instances in proof of it."[20] His onetime colleague Carl Jung gave the "collective unconscious" a primary role in human affairs, and he, too, influenced surrealist thought.

By citing Freud and Jung as authorities, surrealists could claim to be "scientific" while undermining reason and logic; they could turn to history for lessons and insights, without having to follow "bourgeois" standards of analysis or causality. These strictures hold true for Jennings's conception of history as it developed in the 1930's and 1940's. His writings contain appreciative references to Freud and Jung, as well as to the collective unconscious (or collective imagination) as agent in history. According to friends, he did not believe in mere "coincidence"[21]—subtle links connected the seemingly arbitrary. Like Walter Benjamin, Jennings wanted his surrealist history to awaken the public from the imposed dreams, or ideologies, of a particular class in order to realize their own utopian dreams retained within the collective unconscious: "The English at present are sleeping. . . . But in their dreams they know very well that they will have to rise and go forth. There are traces of this in their current light writing, in their action, even in their thought."[22]

In addition to directing Jennings's attention to the unconscious as a historical agent and history as a source of collective expression, surrealism encouraged him to appreciate the new mass culture. Modern commodities and entertainments, no less than the expressions of the past, were understood by the surrealists to represent the unconscious dreams and desires of the public. Jennings approached film, newspapers, popular fiction, pop songs, and other cultural artifacts in this light, interpreting them through the method of close reading he had learned at Cambridge.

Further, the surrealists' use of juxtaposition to reveal unexpected associations, and their focus on everyday life to reveal unconscious meanings or "subtle links" invisible to ordinary human reason, proved important to Jennings in his work as both historian and filmmaker. He shared the surrealists' enthusiasm for the poetry of Charles Baudelaire, particularly Baudelaire's "Illuminations" of modernity as expressed in his poems of the city, the crowds, and the commodities of Paris during the Second Empire.[23] Following Baudelaire's conception of modernity as comprising both the transient and the eternal, and his understanding of the poetic image as an "Illumination" of this duality, Jennings insisted that the collective experiences of a people confronting the changes of modernity were best expressed through the juxtaposition of "Images."[24] These Images would reveal the eternal "reality" underlying the transient appearances of everyday life, without the need for analytic exposition, just as Elizabethan Pageants and Triumphs had once expressed the underlying feelings and thoughts of the English.[25]

By capitalizing "Image," Jennings indicated that he attached particular significance to the term. An Image was not just a private symbol or form of representation, but rather an imagined construct, expressing both thought and feeling, that was capable of being realized historically.[26] Images expressed a complex whole, rather than the single strands of reality offered by conventional history. Jennings did not dismiss entirely the "analytic" method of traditional history, but argued that poetic Images were better suited to convey the totality of human experience:

> The analytical historian's business is to disentangle shred by shred like plucking the strand out of a rope. The result is the length of the rope but only one strand's thickness, and although the strand may still be twisted from its position among the other strands it is presented nevertheless alone. The poet might be compared to a man who cuts a short section of the whole rope. The only thing is he must cut it where it will not fall to pieces.[27]

He chose his Images to capture the way individuals experienced imaginatively the onset of modernity, but also to demonstrate that Images were capable of producing the concrete reality they imagined.[28] In one of his manuscript notes, Jennings implied that Marxist historians were right to focus on the "Means of Production" as a motor of historical development, but they were wrong to neglect the "Means of Vision," which also yielded concrete historical effects.[29]

Jennings's mild rebuke to Marxist orthodoxy brings us to the fourth influence on the composition of *Pandaemonium*: historical materialism. Like many artists facing the economic and political crises of the 1930's, Jennings intended his art to have a social function. He was familiar with Marx's *Capital*, and the trajectory of *Pandaemonium*'s images traced the conflict between the "peasants" and the "bourgeoisie." But Jennings, like Benjamin and Breton, was uncomfortable with the orthodox Marxist view that subordinated art to praxis. He insisted that art would always remain more profound than either politics or economics.[30] When he joined the GPO Film Unit in 1934, he spurned the social-realist approach of its head, John Grierson, and the two never got along. Historical materialism made up one half of the history represented in *Pandaemonium*, but the force of the imagination was its equal complement: "Man as we see him today lives by production and by vision. It is doubtful if he can live by one alone."[31]

Jennings began *Pandaemonium* in the late 1930's, probably in 1937.[32] By this time his experiences in film editing only reinforced his earlier exposure to the surrealists' emphasis on the juxtapositions of images. (A friend recalled Jennings telling him that *Pandaemonium* was meant to unfold like a film.)[33] But it was primarily the influences of the arts and crafts movement, the Cambridge of I. A. Richards, surrealism, and historical materialism that shaped the work's structure and content, as they did two other projects that

Jennings was closely involved with in the 1930's: the founding of Mass-Observation in late 1936 and the publication of its first monograph, *May the Twelfth*, in September 1937. Because the beginning of *Pandaemonium* coincided with both the founding of Mass-Observation and the creation of *May the Twelfth*, collectively they can be considered as the fifth important influence on Jennings's gestating history.

Mass-Observation had been founded by Jennings, his friend Charles Madge, and Tom Harrisson, an anthropologist. The three wanted to undertake "an anthropology of our own people" by collating the opinions of the public on subjects as wide-raging as "shouts and gestures of motorists," "anti-Semitism," "bathroom behavior," and the coronation of George VI (which was to be the focus of *May the Twelfth*).[34] Madge, like Jennings, had been involved with the English surrealist movement; their work with Mass-Observation was designed to tap into the collective unconscious of the British people, to let the "people" speak rather than continue to allow the Establishment to speak for them.[35] The collective dreams and aspirations of the people would help to shape the future of Britain—a purpose that itself was similar to Walter Benjamin's aim in the Arcades Project of resurrecting the utopian longings of humanity buried in the detritus of everyday life.

The founders of Mass-Observation insisted that the organization was "scientific"; it developed, as they wrote in 1937, "out of anthropology, psychology, and the sciences which study man."[36] In early pamphlets as well as in *May the Twelfth* they cited Marx, Frazer, Freud, Pavlov, and other scientists to legitimate the rationalist and empirical aspects of their forays into the British collective unconscious, as manifested in dreams and public expressions. Indeed, *May the Twelfth* was as much a work of "surrealist anthropology" as *Pandaemonium* was a work of surrealist history:[37] the former can be seen as a dress rehearsal for the latter. Themes and methods of presentation that recur in *Pandaemonium* first appear in *May the Twelfth*. Statements (elicited by questionnaires; found in newspapers; overheard in conversations; quoted from diaries) are subjected to "close readings"; the unconscious/imagination revealed in these sources is presented as an active agent in history. Such an agent, while immaterial, can nevertheless be traced within everyday expressions, as people are "recording systems" for larger unconscious forces.[38] The ongoing role of the imagination/unconscious links the past with the present, and its ineffable workings are best represented through the technique of juxtaposed quotes, images, and facts. This technique reveals the central tension in human experience between the desires of the imagination and the concrete forces of historical materialism.

May the Twelfth implied that the forces of modernity need not lead to the irrevocable disenchantment of the world. The animistic attitude toward existence of earlier ages, which connected individuals to the earth and to one another, continued to manifest itself under new guises in the present.

In *May the Twelfth* this possibility was only suggested through certain comparisons: the coronation ceremony is compared to ceremonies of "primitive" peoples, linking past and present;[39] "primitive" animistic thought, with its vital, subtle links connecting existence into an organic whole, is retained in the metaphors and similes of modern poetry.[40] *Pandaemonium*, on the other hand, overtly presented "the conflict between animism and materialism" that emerged during the Industrial Revolution, charting its consequences through the late nineteenth century.

The Implicit Narrative of 'Pandaemonium'

By the time of Jennings's death in 1950, his unfinished manuscript had reached over a thousand pages and could be reconstructed in any number of ways. Even if the work had reached publication in the form he intended, it undoubtedly would still require careful interpretation, as it was meant to follow a visual and intuitive, rather than a linear and rational, logic. In 1985 his daughter Mary-Lou Jennings and Charles Madge published a version of the manuscript that was approximately one-third the length of the original, and I will be referring to both this version and to Jennings's original manuscript in the following discussion. Fortunately Jennings, like Walter Benjamin, left notes describing some of his intentions for the work. Whether *Pandaemonium* would ultimately have conformed to these can never be known, but the surviving manuscript and the published version do hew closely to the ideas he sketched in notes interpolated with the Images themselves.

Jennings and Benjamin's surrealist works were meant to "show" rather than "tell" history,[41] and so it is unlikely that they would have included many of these notes in any completed manuscript. Both authors wanted to break with traditional narrative logic, which they believed confined the complexity of experience to a predetermined trajectory extolling reason and progress. By simply juxtaposing passages rather than providing an overt master narrative, they hoped to shock their readers out of a complacent acceptance of history as a rational narrative of ever-ascending achievements. For both, history was as much a chronicle of loss as of gain, and they intended to provide concrete evidence of the ways in which humanity's deepest aspirations and dreams became stunted or lost through the modern embrace of instrumental rationality. These dreams were still buried in history, waiting to be recovered and perhaps actualized in the future. Modernity need not remain disenchanted if earlier dreams and associative habits of thought could be reintegrated with its prevailing emphasis on rational understanding and material progress.

Yet neither Jennings's nor Benjamin's work was as spontaneous, nonrational, or impartial as each wished to believe: both men had a subjective conception of history to which their selection of evidence conformed. This was a fundamental tension in the genre of "surrealist history" that they could not avoid. Benjamin seemed to believe his work was "objective";[42] Jennings acknowledged similar objective forces when he pointed to evidence of the "collective unconscious" affecting historical events.[43] Their histories were meant to exemplify the "objective chance" that the surrealists believed governed life, but the notes they left for their unfinished works reveal more planning than chance, more applied reason than the spontaneous dictates of the unconscious. (Such inconsistency was characteristic of the surrealists: André Breton, for example, could be so dogmatic in the name of freedom and spontaneity that he was dubbed "the pope of surrealism.")

Jennings's notes do provide a useful template on which to affix the chronological sequence of Images he presents. Charles Madge assembled many of these notes together for an "Introduction" to the published version of the manuscript. In this set of remarks Jennings states that he intends to present the "imaginative history of the industrial revolution" through the use of Images: "passages . . . which either in the writing or in the nature of the matter itself or both have revolutionary and symbolic and illuminatory quality. I mean that they contain in little a whole world"; passages which illuminate human historical experience like "the flash time of the photographer or the lightning."[44] Jennings thus established the imagination as a central causal agent in history. *Pandaemonium*, he states, reveals "the place of the imagination in the making of the modern world";[45] in another note, he asserts that such a history is "the real history of Britain for the last three hundred years. That history has never been written."[46]

The series of juxtaposed Images is meant to illustrate two fundamental conflicts: that between the "animist" view of the world and the materialist view, and the "class conflicts" that exacerbated the former.[47] The Industrial Revolution accelerates both these conflicts so that by the late nineteenth century the material, scientific view of the world, and the bourgeoisie who have gained the most from this outlook, have emerged triumphant. Jennings presents this trajectory as a dialectical movement. (He called his method "dialectical Realism.")[48] If, on the whole, a scientific and materialist view seemed to have replaced an earlier "poetic," "magical," "animistic" view, he did not join other cultural pessimists of his time in bemoaning the irreversible disenchantment of the world. Rather, he intimated through the Images he chose for *Pandaemonium* that even the modern industrial world retains animistic or imaginative qualities, albeit in attenuated form. The Crystal Palace of 1851, for example, is one such Image Jennings included late in his history to indicate that the unity of thought and feeling had not been totally lost in the modern world. Its "culmination of the human energy and warmth" of the mid-nineteenth century represented the dialectical union of two earlier Images he had presented: that of St. Paul's, which represented spirituality, "the culmination of the protestantism of the 17th cent.," and that of the Panopticon, which represented instrumental reason, "the culmination of the rationalism of the 18th cent."[49]

Pandaemonium opens with an Image from Book 1 of Milton's *Paradise Lost*. It describes the fallen angels mining the metals in the soils of Hell, whose capital Milton dubbed "Pandaemonium." For Jennings, this particular Image epitomized the onset of the Industrial Revolution as it emerged from the mid-seventeenth-century conflict between the "bourgeoisie" and aristocracy in England. Through the rest of the manuscript he continued to chart a crude Marxist interpretation of the period between the Restoration and the late nineteenth century. The Images, as well as his notes, depict the emerging bourgeoisie "expropriating" the peasants from their lands, rationalizing the processes of production, and replacing the holistic, "animist" outlook of earlier periods with a more mechanistic outlook conducive to the bourgeoisie's own growing power and prosperity under industrial capitalism.

However, Jennings's surrealist belief in the imagination as a central agent of history redeems his historical account from its more economically reductive aspects. Many of the Images represent "The Means of Production" altering social relations and cultural viewpoints. But his expressed aim was to show how such economic forces were themselves associated with "The Means of Vision." In several notes, Jennings presents ideas—Images of the imagination—both preceding and effecting changes in the forces of production.[50] It was through such a complex interplay of the Means of Vision and the Means of Production that a new, instrumental way of envisioning the world arose by the nineteenth century. Jennings accepted that this "modern," rationalist, materialist orientation would continue into the future—"a trend towards the 'mechanisation of thoughts'"[51]—yet he did not believe the modern world would necessarily remain in its bleak state. "Pandaemonium is the Palace of All the Devils. Its building began c. 1660," he stated in a note. But, he added, "it has to be transformed into Jerusalem."[52] The Means of Vision—poetry—might counteract the prevailing instrumentalism fostered by the Means of Production. Jennings's history, like Benjamin's, attempted to reconcile historical materialism with surrealist idealism.

The ongoing conflict between animism/poetry and materialism/science, as well as the potential for their reconciliation, becomes most pronounced in the Images Jennings selected to represent the latter half of the nineteenth century. On the more negative, or "disenchanted" side, he discusses the inability of many artists to confront modernity honestly or effectively. Whereas William Blake had been able to encompass the origins and effects of the Industrial Revolution in a single poem,[53] later poets such as Tennyson and painters such as James Nasmyth glossed over the realities of human oppression and suffering under the bourgeois capitalist order.[54] And impressionist painters like Pissarro and Monet seemed to have delivered the deathblow to an animistic view of the universe, for their scientific emphasis on color and light resulted "in removing the symbolic animistic attributes of objects."[55] In a moving Image drawn from Charles Darwin's writings, Jennings presents Darwin lamenting his inability to enjoy poetry and music after a lifetime devoted to science: "My mind seems to have become a kind of machine for grinding general laws out of a large collection of facts, but why this should have caused the atrophy of that part of the brain alone, on which the higher tastes depend, I cannot conceive."[56]

On the more positive, "animistic" side of the dialectical divide, however, Jennings provides Images that reveal poetry to be alive within the new realist visions of the age. He offers an Image from the writings of George Eliot in which the novelist argues that prose is the modern equivalent of poetry.[57] And if the impressionists challenged the organic holism represented by the animistic viewpoint, post-impressionists such as Seurat and Cézanne were forging a new unity: they, too, were concerned with light and color, but their works brought these atomized flecks of paint together into new syntheses.[58] In Arthur Conan Doyle's tales of Sherlock Holmes, Jennings found a similar emphasis on an underlying holism—"subtle links" conjoining an apparently fractured social polity. Holmes's ability to detect associations that most people would never observe, and his faith in causality rather than chaos, expressed a wider unconscious understanding of, or at least desire for, the sorts of unifying threads that had been taken for granted in the premodern world.[59]

But why did Jennings end his history in the late 1880's? And did he himself genuinely believe that a reconciliation between poetry and science was possible in the future? Jennings stated that his history was not about the place of the imagination in his own time, but rather about the role of the imagination in the formation of modernity.[60] In *Pandaemonium* he did not directly address the early twentieth century, and even his approach to the seventeenth through nineteenth centuries was highly indirect, consisting of subtle rather than explicit links. His unwillingness to draw out the implications of his history for his own time stemmed partly from the nature of the project itself: any overt exegesis of his materials would have run counter to his surrealist method of allowing the collective imagination to speak on its own through juxtaposed Images.[61]

Still, Jennings did articulate his own beliefs about the future of science, poetry, and society in a series of radio lectures for the BBC in 1939. He delivered these as he was in the midst of compiling the Images for *Pandaemonium*, and they offer clues to the sorts of underlying preoccupations and assumptions that appear to have governed his selection of Images. They also suggest why Jennings chose to conclude his history with the late nineteenth century. The BBC lectures make explicit what *Pandaemonium* only implies.

In this series of talks, delivered during one of the darkest years of the 1930's, Jennings was remarkably sanguine about the future of modernity. Unlike the cultural pessimists, he believed there was a role for poets in the age of modern mass media: they could give form to the inchoate emotions expressed over the radio and through film. These new media were already embraced by the modern public but were in need of the balanced and clarifying interpretations of the modern poet.[62] Jennings also insisted that modern poets need not fear adopting the spare prose of scientific reports or newspaper accounts familiar to the public. Novelists such as George Eliot and Arthur Conan Doyle, and poets such as Thomas Hardy and T. S. Eliot, had already demonstrated that everyday speech was capable of being "poetic," marrying thought and feeling, revealing the subtle links within modern existence.[63] By writing in the modern vernacular, rather than the esoteric modes favored by a James Joyce or an Edith Sitwell, contemporary poets could reach a mass audience in the manner of Dante or Shakespeare. Thus, by conforming to the changed modes of mass expression in the new mass age, poetry could be restored to its former social functions.

And a crucial social function was to restore animism to modernity, to reconcile the split between thought and feeling, the individual and nature, charted in *Pandaemonium*. By writing about the everyday life of modernity, poets could counter the excessive rigidities of modern existence; they could restore the habit of associative, holistic thinking threatened by instrumental rationality. Jennings argued that just as the poetry of the Trobriand Island-ers expressed the embracing mysteries of everyday life to the "primitive" mind, modern poets could restore the mystical and mysterious to contem-porary life:

> The poet is the person who corresponds to the [poet] magicians in the Trobri-and Islands. He is the person who's responsible for seeing that this mystery reaches us, that we're aware of it. This is all the more difficult because . . . we're not at all sure that we want to face the mysteries that the poet's discovering . . . . [One] of the poet's functions I want to note is that he can remind us that there are still mysteries—we haven't discovered everything—and these mys-teries reside in the humblest everyday things.[64]

The mystery of the everyday was of course a central theme for the surre-alists, but Jennings also appreciated their emphasis on the importance of "chance" as a way to free oneself from the rigidities of rationalism and the bureaucratic social order.[65] By restoring a sense of mystery to everyday life, poets would remind contemporaries that not everything is amenable to logical interpretation and control. They could thereby undo the harm in-strumental rationality had inflicted on the hearts as well as minds of the community: the poet could instruct modern individuals not to be so proud, and "by pride [I mean] the way in which the industrialization of the world has (so to speak) hardened our hearts."[66]

Poets could also remind the moderns that traditions still had much to offer the "enlightened" present. He cited T. S. Eliot's *Wasteland* as an ex-emplary modernist work in this regard. It both juxtaposed everyday life with the mysterious and showed the inescapable connections between the past and present, a form of "ancestor worship" little different from that of so-called premodern peoples. Eliot's poem demonstrated that "however industrialized we may be, we have ancestors whether we like them or not."[67] By speaking to the community about its contemporary concerns, and by connecting these with the history that helped formulate these con-cerns, the poet is able to show the living associations between past and pre-sent, the quotidian and the mysterious, that continued to exist in the Brit-ish as well as the Trobriand Isles.

Jennings, it seems, chose to end *Pandaemonium* in the late nineteenth century because it was at this point that all the elements of modernity were balanced in a tense equilibrium. Science and poetry were split, and instrumental rationality rather than an animistic outlook was predominant. But, as he emphasized in his BBC lectures, the union of thought and feeling that was "poetry" continued to survive in modern prose forms as well as in more traditional variants, and the advent of new media of communication raised the possibility that poetry could reassume a public role in modern society. As history, *Pandaemonium* highlighted the perils and promises of modernity; as an intervention into the crises of his day, Jennings's BBC lectures articulated how modernity could be reenchanted.

The Ruins of Surrealist History

Much more could be said about the startling congruencies between Humphrey Jennings's and Walter Benjamin's surrealist histories of modernity. Within the limited scope of this essay I have highlighted a few of the most obvious similarities, in order to suggest that each project, long thought to be idiosyncratic, in actuality can be subsumed under the more encompassing category of "surrealist history," one that anticipated contemporary experiments in historical representation at the end of the twentieth century.

Despite their significant similarities, however, there were important differences between Benjamin's and Jennings's surrealist histories. Benjamin was an assimilated German Jew who spent much of his adult life living in Paris; he was as much an "outsider" in the countries in which he resided as Jennings was a comfortable (albeit bohemian) member of the English "intellectual aristocracy." Thus, while both considered their histories universal in scope, with a common "collective unconscious" as protagonist, in *Pandaemonium* the collective unconscious speaks with a pronounced British accent. Jennings's history, like Benjamin's, was highly critical of many of the excesses of modernity, but it also identified the British imagination as the heroic creator of modernity: no mean achievement, that. The Industrial Revolution had brought Pandaemonium to the world, but it could also usher in the New Jerusalem—and the Industrial Revolution, like so many other valuable exports, had been Made in Britain. Jennings was a surrealist, antipathetic to the bourgeoisie; but he was also an upper-class British patriot, and the tensions in these conflicting positions emerge in *Pandaemonium*. (Not everyone condones such peculiarities of the English: when

Jennings accepted the Order of the British Empire for his work with the Crown Film Unit, the surrealists excommunicated him.)[68]

Further, Benjamin became increasingly disillusioned with the emancipatory prospects of surrealism, film, and perhaps even history during the later 1930's, as European fascism grew in strength. His final essay before his suicide in 1940, "Theses on the Philosophy of History," can be read as a despairing lament for the past as well as the future.[69] Jennings, on the other hand, found the war years to be both Britain's finest hour and his most creative period: in these years he completed his best-received films.[70] Even after the war he did not relinquish his faith in his country's role as a historical world power and civilizing force for the Good. While the postwar Labour government was struggling with Britain's change in world status, Jennings was harping on continuity. He argued in 1948 that while "the most important political and economic fact of the day [was] the break-up of the British Empire," the empire must be reestablished in some form or the "English" would "perish":

> There is no middle way. The structure is too tall, too boldly conceived to be dismantled arch by arch and beam after beam. It must stand, or crash. We are watching one small corner cracking—in Palestine; we recognize with horror how great a series of stresses will be opened by the buckling of even a single girder. . . . The English at present are sleeping. . . . But in their dreams they know very well that they will have to rise and go forth. . . . These quick, tremendous, inventive, bold people are to be tested once more.[71]

By 1950 he had accepted Britain's diminished global role, and adopted the view of some within the Labour party that Britain should serve as the mediator between America and Europe.[72] Nevertheless, his ingrained patriotism and ambivalent attitude toward the empire continued to find expression in his last completed film, *Family Portrait*, commissioned for the 1951 Festival of Britain. The film critic Lindsay Anderson observed sadly that "the symbol at the end of the film is the mace of Authority, and its last image is a preposterous procession of ancient and bewigged dignitaries. The Past is no longer an inspiration: it is a refuge."[73] Jennings could never escape from the celebratory version of English history. In *Pandaemonium* modernity may have been found wanting, but it was also a British invention full of promise, just as after the war Jennings may have found the British Empire wanting but still envisioned it as central to the mystical continuity of England itself.

While surrealist history could not live up to all its promises, its own failed aspirations—like the failed or forgotten aspirations of the past it sought to recover—are instructive. In its rejection of an unreflective positivism or the privileging of elites in historical narratives, its questioning of the notion of historical "objectivity" and progress, and its imaginative attempt to find new rhetorical means for expressing all facets of human experience, surrealist history speaks to many contemporary debates within the academy.

But if Jennings's *Pandaemonium* was a work that challenged contemporary historians to change their methods, it was also a work that could not entirely liberate itself from the Whiggish presuppositions of its own time and place. In this respect, Jennings's surrealist history exemplifies this volume's theme of the striking tenacity of continuity, tradition, and nostalgia in modern British culture. Both Benjamin and Jennings intended to remember a past that had been forgotten by other historians. But in the case of Jennings, his own culture's pride in its tradition proved overwhelming: remembering the past condemned him to repeat it.

The Long Nineteenth Century of Conservative Thought

The defeated Labour party was reviving, Harold Laski reported in the fall of 1931, because it was learning the "great lesson that it is ideas and not men which build the spirit of life."[1] Even before 1931 and certainly thereafter, theorists on the left mounted an aggressive ideological offensive while their counterparts on the right complained that conservative ideals were neglected and shunned by their "stupid party." Almost a generation later, the Conservative party was routed in the 1945 general election. Did the defeat depend, at least in part, on the deliberately anti-intellectual stance of conservatives in the first half of the twentieth century?[2] The writings of conservative theorists from Hugh Cecil through the present argue rather that the right, just like the left and the liberal center, justified its existence through systematic thought.[3] That impulse was encouraged by the increasing pressure of unprecedented circumstances. Unlike any preceding period of time, the twentieth century introduced a multiplicity of overwhelming and irreconcilable events, including two World Wars; a worldwide depression; systematic genocide; an explosion of knowledge and technology culminating in nuclear terrors as well as in the extension of life, health, and well-being; and radical changes in the nature of education, work, family, gender, and religion. Very few of these interconnecting events could be reduced for conservatives to essentially materialistic or deterministic explanations. Individual or crowd psychology, or economic need, or social status might partially explain choices made by electors, but the essentially religious context for most conservatives emphasized free will operating in a world moved by ideologies—including those that deny that there are any ideologies. Independent conservatives as well as influential party strategists such as Cecil, Harold Macmillan, Anthony Eden, R. A. Butler, Quintin Hogg, and Iain Macleod believed that mind mattered in the public world, and they made a sustained effort to present conservatism as a continuous set of principles given their modern form after the 1860's.

Among conservative theorists, the writing of historians is an especially limpid window into ideology, because conservatives relied upon history to display the forging and testing of ideas and material events. In the overwhelmingly liberal nineteenth century, there were few conservative theoreticians and even fewer conservative historians. When confronted by the French Revolution and utilitarianism, conservatism had emerged in defense of valued historical traditions. Those traditions, again threatened for conservatives by the activist social-reform policies of the Liberal government elected in 1906 and by the establishment of a socialist regime in post–First World War Russia, led them to redefine their beliefs. There were many different varieties of conservatism, but all of them agreed that history provided immediately applicable object lessons to solve current political, economic, and social problems, and to prevent them from occurring again. Conservative historians extracted from the past those enduring ideas that demonstrated to them the validity of conservatism for the future.

It was more logical for historians, from the First World War through at least the 1960's, to be conservative than either liberal or socialist. While the liberal historian was increasingly confronted by events that he could not explain historically, and the socialist historian castigated the past as a manipulation of people and events by powerful classes achieving and justifying power, the conservative historian celebrated national continuity. Although not necessarily an apologist for any social, political, or economic group, the conservative historian belonged to an established order of influential position, comfortable income, and recognized status. His finding that the historical world was the only world possible allowed those who were ascendant a better conscience than they might otherwise have had. While liberals and socialists were unable to promise that the future would fulfill their expectations, historical evolution assured conservatives that the world shaped by the past would survive.

Three conservative historians, all born before the twentieth century began, were especially conspicuous in their persistent and committed combination of scholarship and polemics. Although they tended to support the same broadly conservative principles, they represented different positions on the spectrum of conservative ideas. F. J. C. Hearnshaw stood nearly in the middle, although he veered periodically to the right; Keith Feiling was the most liberal; and Arthur Bryant ventured the farthest to the right. In spite of fundamental disagreements among intellectuals and among party leaders about what conservative principles ought to be, there was, from the early twentieth century, a growing rhetorical and intellectual currency used by conservatives and their captains to describe a theoretical conservatism. The historians made this currency more solvent by setting consistent conservative doctrines within a broad historical context that reached out to a much wider audience than conservative intellectuals speaking mostly to each other.

The oldest of the three historians, Hearnshaw (1869–1946), when an undergraduate at King's College, Cambridge, in the late 1880's, was deeply influenced by Sir John Seeley's lectures on history as past politics with lessons for the present and future.[4] A youthful flirtation with Fabian socialism and then a brief attraction to free-trade liberalism was followed by his lifelong allegiance to conservatism. During the First World War, Hearnshaw loyally drilled and marched as honorary secretary to the King's College Volunteer Section, but unlike the other conservative historians, he never advocated force as an instrument of national policy, and he condemned Germany as "the aggressor throughout the ages."[5] Professor of medieval history at King's College, London, Hearnshaw was an energetic writer, editor, and intellectual impresario who organized wide-ranging public lecture series in intellectual history and then edited them for publication. He also traveled through Britain giving blistering speeches, later published as books of essays, about contemporary political issues.

Nearly a generation younger than Hearnshaw, Feiling (1884–1977) entered conservative intellectual life with a manifesto on Toryism in 1913 and continued writing as a Tory democrat for the rest of his life. An Oxford fixture for most of his career, Feiling went from Marlborough to Balliol, where he received first-class honors in modern history in 1906 and won a prize fellowship at All Souls. It is telling that the *Essays in British History* presented to him in 1964 were all written by Oxford men. A lecturer in history at the University of Toronto from 1907 to 1909, he returned to Oxford as lecturer and tutor in modern history at Christ Church and won a studentship there in 1911. Entering the army in 1914, he was posted to India in 1916 and from 1917 to 1919 served as secretary to the Central Recruiting Board of India, a post that earned him an OBE in 1918. From 1947 until his retirement in 1950, he was Chichele Professor of Modern History and in 1952 was elected to an honorary studentship at Christ Church.

The youngest, Bryant (1899–1985), a journalist and popular historical author, joined the Royal Flying Corps at the age of eighteen and served in

France during the First World War. Then, he obtained a distinction in the shortened course for ex-servicemen at Queen's College, Oxford, in 1920, taught at a London County Council school, and was called to the bar. Instead, although only twenty-four, he accepted an appointment as principal of what later would be called the Cambridge Technical College. Producing over forty books that sold more than two million copies, he also wrote "Our Note Book" for fifty years for the *Illustrated London News*, succeeding G. K. Chesterton. In 1927 he became educational adviser, later a governor, and, from 1946 to 1949, chairman of the council for the Bonar Law College, Ashridge, founded to disseminate conservative ideas. Bryant's first book, *The Spirit of Conservatism* (1929), was written mainly for the students at the college, where Hearnshaw and Feiling lectured occasionally. Bryant also taught Oxford University Extension classes from 1925 to 1936; lectured tirelessly to Conservative groups all over Britain, and to the troops during the Second World War on military history and strategy, political science, and sociology; and wrote Conservative party tracts and newspaper articles throughout his life. Of the three, only Bryant was a Conservative party spokesman closely tied to Conservative leaders, beginning with Stanley Baldwin, for over four decades. In a largely unsuccessful effort to create a conservative readership that would rival the fifty thousand subscribers to Victor Gollancz's Left Book Club, Bryant edited and produced books for the National Book Association, with a subscription never exceeding three thousand, from 1936 to 1939. He also took great pleasure in the historical pageants that he produced throughout England with thousands of costumed volunteers portraying dramatic pieces of British history. Appointed CBE in 1949, he was knighted in 1954 and became a Companion of Honour in 1967.[6] Feiling and Hearnshaw took nineteenth-century conservative principles and adapted them to a rapidly changing industrial world. Their appeal was directed to those with the greatest demonstrated ability, ambition, and sense of national obligation. Bryant dismissed Hearnshaw's and Feiling's enthusiasm for industrial capitalism and their elitism to praise ordinary country people. A romantic and nostalgic view of the past evoked, for Bryant, a sunny landscape of English gardens, stalwart men, and loving dogs.

To the educated and even semieducated reading public, especially in the interwar and post–Second World War years, the study of history carried the same patina of truth telling that was to shift to the hard sciences by the 1960's. Even within the academic professions, historians were understood as purveyors of disinterested truth who presented the given, inescapable facts. Although Hearnshaw, Feiling, and Bryant wrote about different subjects and times, and used various methods of dealing with evidence, their historical studies and their expositions of conservatism were governed equally by their particular assumptions about human nature, society, the state, and religion. They were not the only conservatives writing about the meaning of conservatism, but as prolific, influential historians they drew upon what appeared to be expert knowledge for their pronouncements, whether historical or political. Each of these conservative historians turned to different kinds of evidence to prove his conservative interpretations of history. Hearnshaw concentrated on intellectual history, a subject little known before the Second World War anywhere in Britain. Beginning with the political theory he had learned as part of the History Honors Tripos at King's College, Cambridge, Hearnshaw pushed it toward greater contextual analysis. Feiling followed his university's emphasis upon traditional political history as the best means of displaying the character of great men and the superiority of the English nation. Bryant, essentially a military historian, saluted virtue and valor. Both Feiling and Bryant endorsed the Disraelian content of nineteenth-century conservatism with little change, while Hearnshaw tried to modify it by the authority of newly emerging disciplines such as psychology, sociology, and biology. In great part, they all distrusted change from a fear of clumsily interfering with God's greater design. Religious faith, an essential element in all human achievement for the three men, taught them about human limitations and powerlessness.

Were these historians deliberate propagandists for their political convictions? Hearnshaw and Feiling tried to believe that they separated their explicitly conservative writing from their historical work. But when writing about the years 1931 to 1936, Hearnshaw admitted that a medievalist writing about contemporary history was "oppressed by the consciousness that, however he may strive to be impartial, he cannot escape from his political prepossessions."[7] Feiling never expressed any doubts about his objectivity in his writing, and he left no private papers where that kind of introspection might have occurred. Bryant, in everything he did, followed his passionate conservative convictions. All three saw themselves as extracting those absolute moral, as well as political, lessons from the past necessary to the present and future. While each of these historians lived a long and productive time, the texts they produced, whether historical or polemical, reveal a remarkable consistency in emphasis and argument. Their responses to new events such as the appearance of a Labour party, communism, fascism, economic decline, social and political unrest, and the consequences of war are substantially the same from their first to their last publications. Only Bryant attempted, after the Second World War, to alter his own personal history. Although he concealed and denied his extremist activities as a pre-war appeaser, he never deviated from his basic attitudes toward conservatism or its justification through the history that he wrote.[8] Bryant and Hearnshaw successfully reached both popular and academic audiences. Feiling, who addressed his own fairly consistent constituency of academic historians and students, was more circumscribed by university walls than the other conservative historians. When he occasionally ventured out, especially as a lecturer at Ashridge in the interwar years, he tended to preach to friendly believers.

The historians' common and unchanging themes illuminate broad areas of agreement within twentieth-century conservative thinking before the Thatcher era, while the ways in which they differed expose the fault lines. All three began with the assumption that most people were not so much evil as weak, lazy, listless, undisciplined, irrational, and selfish. But history demonstrated that a few individuals had greater merit and virtue than others. This conviction led all three to write about the hardworking, energetic, strong, and dependable who were models of what could be done with poor human material. Unlike the socialist or the liberal, the conservative attributed social evils primarily to human weaknesses—far more difficult to alter than the environment.

Hearnshaw and Feiling subscribed to two themes that appeared to be antithetical. The first was a new emphasis upon capitalism as an essential means to national prosperity because it developed capacities for hard work and competence; and the second was the older conviction that only higher, nonmaterialistic aspirations, resting upon religion and divinely created morality, cultivated the kind of life that mattered. The resolution of this antithesis between economics and ethics rested on the inherently redeeming nature of work. People rarely rose to meet God's expectations, but they could aspire to a more noble life through energetic efforts to improve themselves. The reconciliation of material ambitions, necessary to economic growth, with moral law was satisfied by a third theme—an ordered society necessarily based on class and authority. Although Bryant distrusted the avarice driving industrialism, he agreed with Hearnshaw and Feiling that society, intrinsically imperfect, could be improved incrementally because the latently subversive forces in human nature could be redirected to productive ends within an organic and unified nation. All three historians wanted a structured national community to provide limited social mobility in which everyone would receive the well-being appropriate to their particular station in life.

The historians' fourth theme, which made critics suspect conservatives of being anti-intellectual, was opposition to "ideals," understood as incorrect or dangerous abstractions, overarching principles, or utopian fantasies. Instead, they attempted to promote practical, applicable, minimalist, or realistic concepts.[9] Any theory not derived from practice was, for them, an arbitrary and self-serving rationalization of instinctive, usually destructive, tendencies in which the highest ideals often became excuses for the lowest desires. Theories such as socialism and communism had to be denied and destroyed because social and economic problems could not be solved by any grand scheme that ignored the facts of life. The liberal proposition that all ideas should compete freely in the intellectual arena seemed chimerical to the conservatives, who found ideas, like people, unequal. Those ideas that passed the test of history were safeguarded in habits and laws that promised constancy. Conservative purposes were inclusive enough, they were convinced, to subsume pseudoantitheses between freedom and order, continuity and progress, and individualism and community within a greater national interest. Disraeli's idea of "one nation," which condemned the division of Britain into a country of rich and poor, had greater influence in the twentieth century than any other conservative idea. It was stressed by the conservative historians from the early part of the century and was adopted by the Conservative party as an identifying motto from the post–Second World War period until the Thatcher years.[10]

Hearnshaw understood a united nation to depend upon a meritocratic elite, that small number who, because they were effective and responsible, were capable of leading the weaker majority. It was through Hobbes rather than Rousseau that conservatives understood man and the state. In contrast to Rousseau's naive trust in human goodness, social questions were always matters of generally dubious "personal character, and the patent defects of society were the accumulated consequences of the defects of human nature."[11] Hearnshaw's lectures on "Europe in the Middle Ages," delivered at Kings College, London, from 1913 to 1925, have as a running motif the essential role of character, discipline, and authority in the making of civilization. The Roman Empire declined, Hearnshaw taught, as a result of internal decay when the Romans lost their "ancient virtue and valour."[12] In the spring of 1946, Anthony Eden used rhetoric very similar to Hearnshaw's to explain that progress depended on "better men and women," and in 1947 Quintin Hogg stressed the inherent limitations of policy when dealing with imperfect man and the "streak of evil as well as good in his inmost nature."[13] Before the Second World War brought human wickedness into much sharper relief, Hearnshaw believed that the most able and energetic could be guided at least toward greater well-being, if not necessarily moral improvement, through higher wages, greater productivity, and increased profits. Hearnshaw urged conservatives to promote "a property-owning democracy," a slogan introduced by the Macmillan Conservatives in the 1920's, emphasized by Hearnshaw in 1933, and adopted by Eden in his speech to the Conservative Party Conference in 1946.[14] The laudable human instinct for property and its corollary of self-development was violated, for Hearnshaw, by socialism's unnatural elevation of the "underman" and his "cult of incompetence." "Equality" and "merit," the socialist's standards for distributing wealth, were inadequate, because people were not equal.[15] If the proletarian had sufficient merit, he would no longer be a proletarian, just as the socialist, if he understood the world better, would not be a socialist.

Socialism was to their disadvantage, Hearnshaw tried to explain to trades unionists in 1928, on historical, psychological, economic, logical, religious, moral, sociological, political, and genetic grounds. In trying "to extinguish private enterprise and to eradicate competition," socialists dealt mortal "blows to those creative, combative, and acquisitive instincts which—however much they have been abused when unrestrained by conscience—are the very mainsprings of man's most effective economic activities." "Conscience," a pivotal conservative concept, was the invisible hand promoting social and economic justice by propelling individuals, especially with superior qualifications and capacities, to contribute to a larger national good. While socialism, because it was utilitarian, opportunistic, and materialistic, failed the test of the higher imperatives of truth and right, conservative ethics subordinated capitalism to the constraining realm of moral law. Socialism was a system which "creates and fosters, pampers and propagates, a decadent and demoralized proletariat" unwilling "to work in subordination to any sort of authority." Socialism, and worse still communism, were "wrong" because they did not recognize that a stratified social order was the only means for checking unreliable human behavior. Within a hierarchical society, those who knew the most, knew the best, and consequently should be in positions of authority, while everyone else should recognize the rectitude of that order.[16] If Hearnshaw had himself been at the bottom of the ranks, would he have held this position so strongly?

Hearnshaw did believe that, if society became sufficiently prosperous, there could be state support for greater leisure and the opportunity for self-development by the lower classes—that is, the lower classes would come to enjoy those cultural advantages that gave so much pleasure to Hearnshaw. But he expected that as a result of mechanization and scientific attempts to reduce costs of production, unemployment would become the principal problem of the future, and the mass of the unemployed would never again be absorbed into the workforce, because they could not meet "rapidly rising and complex demands for skill and intelligence."[17] Hearnshaw had three solutions to this impending social crisis. The most visionary, occurring to him in 1938, was for the government to treat the unemployed as members of a national family and provide them with the "necessities of a moderately comfortable existence." If they wanted more, then they would have to perform a useful service to the community.[18] Although he never published this solution, the model of a harmonious domestic life (now called "family values"), accepted by both Tories and Liberals since at least 1870,[19] became crucial to conservative discourse in the late 1930's. Another alternative that he considered repeatedly was segregation or even sterilization, in order that the national stock would be preserved. How these "genetically unfit" would be identified did not seem to trouble him, and throughout his writings he treated extreme poverty as the severest of moral failings. Although all three conservative historians blamed deficiencies in individual character for social problems, eugenic remedies were peculiar to Hearnshaw. A third remedy was to "establish new industries in depressed areas" or to transplant those out of work to "new regions of activity and hope." What made him uncomfortable about such interventionist measures was that no amount of public money could help the economy unless it revived "individual energy and initiative" instead of teaching "passive submission to adversity" and an expectation of support by other people's money.[20]

If there were so many incompetent people in contemporary life, how could democracy continue? Hearnshaw's conservatism assumed a people wise enough to accept the advice of a governing elite governed themselves by tradition, institutions, and Christianity. The harmonious society that Hearnshaw wanted all groups to enjoy was, he believed, the product of the best minds. When the sixteenth-century jurist Hugo Grotius described the ways in which the sovereign law of nature was known, his standard was his own mind, Hearnshaw tells us, against which he measured other minds to arrive at criteria for civilized behavior. Hearnshaw's cure for the anticivilized tendencies of socialism and the vagaries of democracy was Disraelian

Tory Democracy. For all three historians and for most conservatives, Disraeli exemplified the qualities of a genuine leader: intellect, character, and national responsibility. When Hearnshaw compared Disraeli to the liberal Gladstone, he found that:

> Gladstone was emotional and confused in mind; Disraeli was clear in intellect and superbly self-controlled. Gladstone was a crowd-interpreter; Disraeli a crowd-compeller. Gladstone was a man of enormous talent; Disraeli one of incontestable genius. Gladstone was an opportunist; Disraeli an idealist. Gladstone was highly ecclesiastical; Disraeli was deeply religious. Gladstone's horizon was small and easily visible to the naked eye; Disraeli lived in a universe of wide expanses and large vistas.

Disraeli created Tory Democracy in 1846 by transforming conservatism from a "class confederacy into a national organisation" that welcomed the workingman and directed the power of the state to the "interest of the community as a whole." For conservative historians, all the social classes either prospered or declined together, but they worried that government intervention in social and economic life would diminish the "personal freedom" necessary for cultivating moral capacity. Conservatives had to undertake the improvement of the condition of the people rather through "intelligent self-help, cultivated ability, enhanced skill, increased specialisation, bettered physique, elevated character, enlarged faith." Those goals were all within reach of the autonomous individual. When Hearnshaw recognized in 1936 the impending conflict in Europe between dictatorship and democracy, he argued that democracy could survive only by "imposing upon itself the discipline that has given such success to its rivals."[21]

Tory Democracy was additionally attractive to the conservative historians for its pragmatism. The Conservative party that Hearnshaw admired concentrated on "affairs rather than theories" and was the party of "strong and efficient administration rather than of incessant and ill-digested legislation; the party which adopts policy to circumstances instead of attempting (like the bolsheviks) to fit circumstances into the procrustean bed of fixed obsessions."[22] Although skeptical of an uncritical acceptance of the contents of ideas, Hearnshaw always considered the mentality of an age when explaining historical events. When considering the causes of the French Revolution, he emphasized the importance of both intellectual discontent and spurious ideas. Hearnshaw admired the conservative Burke's wise repudiation of French radical thought and his reliance upon experience as the fount of his ideas. Burke's appreciation of reality led him to discover the founding and sustaining principles of conservatism: an avoidance of abstract political speculation; insistence on the empirical nature of government; administration rooted in history and experience; an emphasis on expediency, rather than on rights, in decisions about policy; and essentially moderate opinions, even when expressed passionately. Liberals and utopian radicals had engaging dreams. Conservatives like Burke were much duller, because they lived within the restrictions of the working world. Disraelian conservatism also rejected empty abstractions to affirm "principles," or "*operative* ideas; ideas in action; intellectual conceptions applied continuously to practical affairs; thoughts impelled by emotion, will, and even conscience."[23] The dependence of conservative ideology on practicality, evident still in the title and contents of R. A. Butler's autobiography, *The Art of the Possible* (1971), was a recurring message in conservative apologetics from the 1920's.

Hearnshaw thought of the empire as a triumph of Disraelian pragmatism. The interwar conservatives turned to that empire to provide expanding markets for British goods and to supply "inexhaustible stores of raw materials for home industries, fields for emigration and enterprise, invaluable aid in days of difficulty and danger." Conservatives, Hearnshaw urged, must preserve the imperial community from threats, whether "by a fanatical minority in India or by a handful of republican conspirators in Ireland." India, like Egypt, lacked proper leaders and was aware of its lack. What the "inarticulate multitudes of both countries" really wanted was not "a constitutional apparatus which they have as yet neither the mental nor the moral capacity to work, but rather the continued maintenance of the just and ordered rule of the British administrators beneath which they can enjoy peace, prosperity, and opportunities of self-culture."[24] Both dependent countries, Hearnshaw reckoned, preferred to be governed by a superior British elite until they, too, became competent to enjoy "individualism" and "personal freedom."[25]

Conservatives, including Hearnshaw, characteristically tried to settle conflicts whether of ideas or interests, including the clashes between imperial subjects and the mother country, by defining them as false antitheses rather than as irreconcilable opposites. William Pitt's "new Conservative party" had allied freedom and order, while Burke, the great reconciler, combined "devotion to liberty with respect for authority; hope for the future with reverence for the past; support of party with service of the nation; profound patriotism with sincere goodwill to all the 'vicinage of mankind'; essential moderation with zealous enthusiasm; a sane conservatism with a cautious reform." The conservative national institutions of Britain, including the Church of England, were also means of balancing authority and freedom, orthodoxy and toleration, to create harmony domestically and internationally. At the beginning of the Second World War, Hearnshaw had no doubts about Germany's "war guilt," but he looked ahead to a permanent peace maintained by a League of Nations with a strong international police force as the means of imposing order on imminent conflicts. To continue and strengthen the distinctive conciliatory essence of modern conservatism, Hearnshaw wanted to purge his party of reactionaries and install instead the "young, the energetic, the far-sighted, the men of intellectual eminence" who were most likely to find new common grounds for conservatism.[26]

Feiling was young and energetic when his *Toryism: A Political Dialogue* (1913) promoted conservative doctrines that would appear in Hearnshaw, Bryant, and other contemporary writers: a religious basis for the state; principled politics derived from enduring values; the rejection of abstract and a priori thought because of the limitations of reason; the propriety of a hierarchical society based on authority and order in which rights and duties were correlated; and the need for conservatism to concentrate upon improving the condition of the people. Thirty-four years later, in his inaugural lecture as Chichele Professor of Modern History, traditionally an opportunity for the new professor to discuss historical study and methodology, Feiling's description of the "working code of the historian" set the historian's task squarely within the limits of Feiling's own Tory sensibilities: virtue was rarely rewarded, but "vice and weakness" were eventually punished; politics was inseparable from religion; the inheritance of traditions was not necessarily understood by the heirs; the political process was not always rational; and intellect was governed by moral habit. His nineteenth-century optimism continued to triumph, in spite of the Second World War, and he argued still that history taught that it was possible to achieve high-minded goals.[27]

Feiling, in common with the other Tory historians, wanted conservatism to provide opportunities for the formation of character. Throughout his career as a historian he wrote about men who had qualities either to emulate or to avoid. In the book that made his reputation as a historian, *A History of the Tory Party, 1640–1714* (1924), Feiling argued that in the seventeenth century it was not economics or geography that determined politics so much as the views of the local magnates. Feiling singled out the "high-souled idealists" among the Cavaliers as the forerunners of the Tory party.[28]

Throughout history, great men—such as the Earl of Clarendon, the founder of the first Tory party, who in the early 1660's passed on an ideal of government in church and state, or nineteenth-century figures such as George Canning, Coleridge, and even Newman—were progressive or transitional conservatives, able to prevail over both intellectual and political revolutions.

While Hearnshaw and Bryant believed that conservatism had triumphed over other forms of political commitment, Feiling argued additionally that conservatism had absorbed liberal thinking. Even in the seventeenth century, Feiling found, Tories and Whigs were more alike in the ideas and interests they represented than they were distinguished by the issues temporarily separating them. During the late eighteenth and early nineteenth century, Canning, the "liberalizer of Toryism," deliberately adopted liberal principles by acting on the "golden mean between freedom and order which empowers ancient institutions to maximize national energy and happiness." The conservatism appropriate to Britain's interwar years of difficult passage Feiling associated with Canning, who stood apart from reactionary figures such as Clarendon, Blackstone, Eldon, and Peel in his willingness to change with the times. Toryism was not the justifier of the status quo, but in the tradition of Burke, it stood rather for "the proved interest of the whole." Coleridge, too, sought to weave liberal values into a conservative fabric by arguing against the "anarchists of intellect" that some things must be fixed and unquestionable, and against reactionaries that "not only progress, but permanence also, was best safeguarded by allowing the development of a nation's mind."[29]

Far more important to Feiling than political convictions was the certainty provided by belief in the divine, in history, and in ethical obligations. Feiling learned from Coleridge that the only way to move large numbers of people was by appealing to first principles "rooted in religion or morals." A study of biography taught that while expediency was "a useful empirical guide in the prudential sphere of politics," it could not supersede the "inner light, which formed man at his beginning and pointed his goal." The "core of Toryism" was a "faith (so far as it is consciously held) based not on present prejudices so much as on the entire history of the realm." This history demonstrated that institutions ought to endure even when those in charge of them make mistakes about their direction. Newman was also part of Feiling's conservative pantheon, because the cardinal understood that reform was not always a good. Newman accepted the Catholic Church's doctrine of infallibility in 1870 for sound conservative reasons: because he did not want to destroy an "institution or body of teaching, on the whole be-neficent, by tearing apart its connected strands." Instead he saw percep-tively the "general advance in spite of partial retreat—the steady flood tide, in spite of the tired waves breaking." Moreover, as an authoritarian thinker, Newman was rightly skeptical of "unaided reason, and of facile chatter about progress." He knew that man's intrinsic nature did not change greatly with time and found that forms of government had little effect upon that nature. He argued, rather, that there were "tangible realities—God and nature, good and evil—on which rested the living, lasting, systems of law and theology which outlived and transcended individual Popes and parliaments."[30] Feiling also recognized the reality of evil, but he chose from 1913, throughout his writing, to emphasize social and economic change that could promote some measure of goodness.

All the conservatives stressed social reform as a means of containing evil, if not necessarily of promoting good, but they interpreted it differ-ently. Feiling wanted to give scholarships to local schools and trades unions to provide genuine educational opportunity. "Make your nets so wide," he urged, "that all classes, all interests, all districts come into it." Of the three historians, he was the one most concerned with social opportunity, and he sought guarantees such as the assurance of "a minimum, an even chance," a redemption "from foul housing" or the arming "of a child with the educa-tion that any citizen should have." More than a century earlier, Canning had made clear the importance of "intelligence working old institutions" and "showed to posterity how much social reform may be advanced within the bounds of an ancient fabric." Prosperity was a necessary condition for Feiling's social benefits, and he advised capitalists to "make every worker, in some degree, a capitalist," still another formulation of the "property-owning democracy" that conservatism embraced after the Second World War. But the ownership of property did not imply social and economic equality. The hierarchical structure of society, which he endorsed, rested on class. Feiling's case for an unequal, ranked society assumed, as did Hearn-shaw's, differences in intellect and character, determined by both nurture and nature. For both men, the ascendancy of responsible people in the highest classes began with their inheritance of superior values and endow-ments. Conservatism failed for Feiling only because it had not yet concen-trated on either equal opportunities or restrictions of antisocial or wholly unearned wealth. Feiling worried further that the "idle class of great wealth and no felt responsibilities" was "offset by a parasitic half-employed class of unceasing poverty and no possible public obligations." To remedy the predicament of working people who were not a dependent part of this emerging underclass, Feiling recommended that "the National Service should be accompanied by the minimum wage."[31] But except for his discussion of marginal wages and greater access to education, Feiling's prescriptions were vague and rhetorical.

Whenever Feiling was faced with definitions, he retreated to the "moral law" and invoked higher standards. He had considerable difficulty in explaining the meaning of Toryism and argued that a philosophical defense could be found only in history. Much as he appreciated principles, he conceded that Toryism could not have an intellectual base but depended rather on "a concreteness in history, and a prerogative in time. . . . Toryism is thus dogmatic, and claims its dogma as *ex cathedra*: infallible, not as voicing one party or one age, but as the deposit of a long life, a tested revelation, a living society." Every few generations, traditions were reinterpreted; the sharp divergence among Tories was due to the absence of an agreed-upon program and the acceptance only of "a temper or a spirit." That spirit was clear in the seventeenth and eighteenth centuries, when there were "Tories" with very little relation to party. But there were certain indispensable ideas such as liberty, which Feiling understood in a religious sense as the ability to make moral judgments. The Tory party that ended in 1714 developed the lasting ideas of English politics: "the divinity of the state, the natural sanctity of order, the organic unity of sovereign and people, and the indisputable authority attaching to the work of time."[32] In Harley, Bolingbroke, Pitt, Canning, Coleridge, Young England, and Disraeli, Feiling found "true" Toryism, which adapted to radical changes to perpetuate the conservative frame.

Feiling was willing to support any person in any party who had the national interest at heart. In 1931, he endorsed the liberal John Simon as a National candidate because of his services "to the whole state." Simon's view of a National government as the best antidote to socialism was probably a factor in drawing Feiling's support. Even controversial figures such as George Curzon had merit for Feiling, especially in their energy and ability to get things done. For all the conservative historians, character, capacity for work, and moral engagement were the most vital of human qualities. Even when conservatives erred, as did Curzon in his judgments about India, they were usually inspired by the right motives. Curzon was moved by a "sense of the ordained fate and duty laid upon great peoples and ruling classes to inherit the earth."[33] Another problematic Tory leader was Neville Chamberlain. The year after the Second World War ended, Feiling was asked by the Chamberlain family to write a biography. The result was laudatory. Feiling had approved Chamberlain's stand at Munich and in 1938 had congratulated Geoffrey Dawson, the editor in chief of *The Times*, for his "superb lead" in supporting Conservative attempts to achieve peace. In Chamberlain's biography, Feiling explains that the Conservative leader tried to avoid heavier national burdens by buying time for Britain and its allies to arm while trying to persuade the Italian and German peoples to abandon war. While Chamberlain's judgments, like those of Curzon, may have been too inelastic, he tried to do what was right for the nation.[34]

For Bryant, right was defined by patriotic ends, in which personal sacrifice testified to conservative virtues. National crises had traditionally stimulated the renunciation of purely selfish ends, but modern life provided few opportunities for people to devote themselves to higher ideals. The deviation from Britain's historic direction, as he saw it, came in the 1840's when industrialization deprived ordinary people of their rural heritage, the source of their strength and character. Bryant recognized the realities of an industrial age and urged employee involvement in the governing of large companies as a means of avoiding industrial conflict. For Bryant, as for Feiling and Hearnshaw, the capitalist proper was not a consumer but a creator of wealth that benefited great numbers of people. But no matter how the industrial worker or his employer might aspire to be virtuous, Bryant idealized the plain, sensible countryman as sounder than and morally superior to other social and economic groups, including the aristocracy of birth, wealth, or brains. Bryant distrusted "intellectuals" (whom he equated with socialists) and thinkers in general. In Bryant's biographical "tribute" to Stanley Baldwin in 1937, the Conservative leader emerged as a man of the land and people who triumphed over the "clever men who sneered at him" and who restored "character in public life." Following in the tradition of Bolingbroke, Pitt, and Disraeli, Baldwin taught his party to devote itself to "the general body of the nation" rather than to "its own privileged supporters."[35] Hearnshaw and Feiling, too, put the unity of the nation above the selfish interests of wealth. Feiling and Bryant came from comfortable backgrounds: Feiling's father was a stockbroker, and Bryant grew up next door to Buckingham Palace, where his father was chief clerk to the Prince of Wales. None of the three historians gave special privilege any place in their ideal of a just and stable society, permeated by conservative values.

Bryant's view of himself as a historian was supported by the large public which bought his books—and allowed him to live very well—but he was fundamentally a journalist. At Harrow, George Townsend Warner, the senior history master, had taught Bryant and G. M. Trevelyan, the last, perhaps, of the popular historians taken seriously by the academic profession. Of the three conservative historians, only Bryant lived through most of the twentieth century. Paradoxically, he wrote the most conventional of nineteenth-century narrative history. In his first genuinely popular work, *King Charles II* (1931), he told readers that they would find no explanation or arguments in the text because "a simple narrative is the historical method best suited to the English genius."[36] But Bryant's narratives were always larded with romantic Tory patriotism set within a Coleridgean structured society governed by Disraelian Tory Democracy.

When the Second World War began, *Unfinished Victory* (1940) appeared. Andrew Roberts claims that this book, in conjunction with Bryant's private papers, proves that the patriot historian was a fascist sympathizer traveling much farther with Hitler than the other appeasers and changing direction only when faced with arrest in 1940. *Unfinished Victory*, instead of telling Bryant's signature story of British greatness, sets out to explain, very sympathetically, why the defeated Germany of 1918 became the ordered Nazi Germany. Bryant believed that the Third Reich, "despite many revolting cruelties and the unjustified sufferings of the persecuted minority in exile and concentration camps," might produce "a newer and happier Germany in the future." He also supported Franco; in April 1936 he warned Baldwin against joining France in opposing Germany; and as late as 1939 he was personally involved in negotiations, via intermediaries, with Hitler about peace. But by 1940, when he wrote that under Hitler's "forceful leadership Germany was no doubt regaining a just confidence in her old powers," he added that Germany was also regaining "her old arrogant and brutal manner towards her neighbors." There is less ambiguity about charges against Bryant of egregious anti-Semitism, from which Disraeli was excluded because he was a patriot more than a Jew. Bryant described asset-gathering Jews benefiting from Germany's economic crisis in the interwar years and, although less than 1 percent of the population, controlling national wealth, power, and the artistic and learned professions to the detriment of German values and well-being.[37]

Immediately after the cool reception given to *Unfinished Victory*, Bryant returned to his forte in the *English Saga, 1840–1940* (1941), a paean to social and economic values that he wanted restored in a postwar England envisioned as more pastoral than industrial. The best teacher for Bryant was always the land, which "disciplines to duty and virtue all her servants." In his later years, although attached to London life, Bryant bought into his own mythology and became a farmer interested in forestry. The farmer was the embodiment of integrity because of his responsibility for the care of helpless and dependent animals. Bryant apparently had never heard of murderers who loved their dogs. Bryant's sturdy countryman was, for all his "muddy boots and rough, stained hands"—or, better yet, because of these visible marks of virtue—"a man of honour." When soldiers returned from the First World War, instead of being integrated into a restorative land made fit for heroes, they found a "world designed for stockholders and *rentiers* and civil servants." Instead of fulfilling "the image" of the veteran's "apocalyptic dream," the reality was "the utilitarian labyrinth of the money-changers from which they had gone forth in 1914." The shunting aside of the soldiers violated Bryant's sense of justice, because these patriots had made what he considered the supreme sacrifice for their country while the politicians who decided their postwar lives had selfishly stayed at home. In the rebuilding of the post–Great War world, the old standard, Bryant complained, remained exclusively the multiplication of the wealthy. The only just criteria for policy was a plan of action that would "make better men and women."[38]

No matter what the subject, Bryant's purpose consistently was to appeal to those national sentiments which revered an organic society based upon robust national character. His historical writing, his columns and leaders in newspapers and journals all over Britain, and his columns in the *Illustrated London News* presented a chronicle of selflessness in which war was an instrument of national unity that rejuvenated all that was best in the British temperament. When in 1666 the French and Dutch appeared to be winning their war with England, a "confident" country rallied, and the enemy was defeated.[39] While Dunkirk drew an avalanche of justifiably patriotic purple prose, Bryant's version in 1943, the heart of his conservative vision, bears quoting: "The miracle of Dunkirk . . . revived the nation's soul. It made the islanders realise themselves, to know, under God, of what they were capable, and to resolve to do it." Although facing death, "doubts, divisions and sloth, blindness and fear, fell away from them at that hour like the mists of morning at the rising sun. Britain was herself again. The England of the Peace Pledge Union and the dole queue had been changed in a flash of summer lightning into the England of Nelson and Alfred." Patriotism, war, disasters, and the empire inspired Britons to unite altruistically. But Bryant warned that devotion to higher ends during ordinary times depended on some degree of social ballast. In 1929, he had made social justice an integral part of the "conservative creed." The "poor man's health and recreation are held to be forms of property," he wrote, "as sacred as the rich man's dividends." After the Second World War, he concentrated on children and pleaded for the state to fulfill the needs of "every child for the stability of home, education, medical care and nutrition, without which it cannot easily become a good citizen." Adult opportunities for a satisfactory life depended rather on individual energy. The state could only encourage "men to abolish want by their own voluntary efforts," but everyone ought to have "status" and be "recognized for what he is at his best."[40]

Bryant was hardly arguing for social mobility, let alone social improvement, but rather for restoring the kind of secure social place communities had allegedly enjoyed in the Middle Ages and lost after industrialization. Unlike Hearnshaw, who feared special interests as a threat to national unity, Bryant and Feiling wanted greater local government and a dispersion of central power through various intermediary groups that would encourage participation by local people.[41] When Bryant produced his pageants, he was struck by the "pathetic eagerness with which unemployed men and women, who, in the eyes of the State, were only dole-drawers and economic encumbrances," assumed self-respect and dignity because of their small part in the pageant. "It has convinced me," he said, "that the ideal State is one in which the largest possible numbers enjoy some special importance and responsibility."[42] People needed to be assigned those obligations that would bring out the noblest in them. They also needed a meaningful system of education to reinforce the essential concept of role within society by teaching everyone those skills necessary to their security in a fixed place. For all three conservative historians the imperatives of duty, based upon Christian virtues, were of a higher order than claims for rights. But for Bryant the most powerful need was not the alleviation of material want so much as the elimination of spiritual malaise. In 1982, the eighty-three-year-old Bryant reaffirmed his prewar conservative creed to conclude that England had evolved more successfully than other countries because it was a Christian country.[43]

What is so remarkable about the thinking of Hearnshaw, Feiling, and Bryant—and this is largely true of twentieth-century conservative thought until the Thatcher turning—is that no matter how unprecedented and unsettling were the events impinging upon their world, the nineteenth-century inspiration for their conservatism persisted unchanged. The very instability and unpredictability of their times made an organic doctrine, pliable and anchored securely to a successful national and imperial past, a historical gift difficult to refuse. Even after Thatcherism reinvigorated laissez-faire liberalism and adopted a policy that encouraged "Two Nations," the passionate ideology expressed by the conservative historians continued to echo in the rhetoric of the faithful. Hearnshaw's eugenics has long disappeared from any political discourse, and the historians' insistence on the merits of inequality have been modified by newer conservative ideas about social and economic opportunity. But many conservatives still hold that change, based upon practical criteria which respond to altered circumstances, must be subordinated to a historic structure of traditions and institutions. Many of these conservatives think, too, that fundamental political conflicts such as those between freedom and order, society and the individual, continuity and reform, are misunderstandings about the nature of society with its historical mechanisms for conciliation. Ian Gilmour and Mark Garnett argued recently that Conservative governments succeeded when they "pursued 'One Nation' policies until 1979." When those unifying policies were abandoned, the Conservatives began their "Wilderness Years."[44] It remains to be seen whether Conservatives, responding to the Blair phenomenon, will resurrect the long nineteenth century of conservative thought.

FRED M. LEVENTHAL

Essential Democracy: The 1939 Royal Visit to the United States

In 1932 Sir Stephen Tallents, the secretary of the Empire Marketing Board and a redoubtable publicist, warned his fellow countrymen that more effective projection of national personality abroad was essential if Britain, no longer the dominant economic power, was to continue to play a significant role internationally. In identifying those British institutions still of interest to the outside world, Tallents cited the monarchy and the navy, as well as such cultural icons as the English Bible, Shakespeare, and Dickens.[1] It was in part to remedy deficiencies in overseas publicity that the British Council was launched in 1934 to promote a wider appreciation of British civilization in other countries. In view of a widespread perception of American backlash against First World War propaganda, the Foreign Office prohibited official publicity in America, limiting its cultural operations to an innocuous British Library of Information in New York that disseminated press reports and periodicals.

Five years after Tallents's plea, Sir Ronald Lindsay, longtime British ambassador in Washington and astute observer of American opinion,[2] reaffirmed the Foreign Office ban on overt propaganda,[3] but he urged a psychological initiative as an alternative strategy to stimulate American good will:

> I hold that East and West and South and even the middle can be worked on through their emotions. The late King George broadcasting to his Empire, Mr. Baldwin's speech in the House on the abdication crisis, the Stratford Shakespeare Company, *Goodbye, Mr. Chips* by [James] Hilton, Noel Coward's film *Cavalcade*, the successes of Great Britain, the calmness and dignity of her people, these are the things that move America.[4]

Lindsay recognized the delicacy of Anglo-American relations, strained by postwar American disenchantment with Europe, repudiated war-debt payments, and resurgent isolationism, especially in the hinterland. It was therefore advisable to couch an appeal to Americans in traditional imagery designed to evoke nostalgic responses. Even here it was necessary to tread warily. Although Anglophilia pervaded the Eastern academic and social establishment, anti-British sentiment was rampant among Irish-Americans, Jews hostile to restrictive immigration policy in Palestine, and liberals distrustful of a hidebound, imperialistic Britain. Even internationalists, usually sympathetic to British interests, wavered in their loyalty because of Neville Chamberlain's appeasement of Hitler.[5]

Not even the monarchy, invariably and paradoxically an object of fascination for republicans, was immune from transatlantic criticism. As Prince of Wales, Edward garnered media attention and popularity during two highly publicized visits to the United States, whereas his abdication in order to marry his American mistress merely enhanced his romantic aura. If Wallis Simpson's two divorces rendered her unacceptable as queen to the dominions, many Americans perceived her rejection as further evidence of British snobbery. Some of them continued to regard the newly created Duke of Windsor as the legitimate monarch, denied his inheritance by a conspiracy of clerics and politicians suspicious of his purported populist leanings.

No one was more skeptical about being suitable to wear the crown than George VI himself. Growing up in the shadow of his glamorous elder brother, hampered by frail health and a speech impediment he struggled manfully, if not entirely successfully, to combat, totally uncharismatic, he viewed his succession with trepidation bordering on terror. Yet, emulating his father, rather than his brother, he was determined to overcome his innate deficiencies by self-discipline, commitment to duty, and the support of a personable consort.

Following an initial approach by the Canadian governor-general, Lord Tweedsmuir (the writer John Buchan), Prime Minister W. L. Mackenzie King used the occasion of the coronation to extend an invitation to the king and queen to visit Canada, the senior dominion, still reeling from the abdication and riven by religious and ethnic strife. The new monarch was largely unknown in Canada, where the Prince of Wales had enjoyed wide popularity, especially after acquiring his own—though seldom used—ranch in Alberta.

Informed of Mackenzie King's overture, Roosevelt instructed his personal envoy at the coronation, ex-diplomat James Gerard, to broach the subject of an unofficial royal visit to the United States.[6] What Roosevelt envisaged was an informal detour to his family home at Hyde Park to complement the official journey through Canada. Such a casual encounter would not only deflect the suspicions of isolationists, hostile to further entanglements with Britain, but also allow the president to exercise his potent charm removed from the constraints of official protocol. In view of his projected trip to India—subsequently canceled as too expensive and politically risky—and an anticipated general election, the king's response was initially noncommittal.[7]

Having consulted Lindsay, who declared that a "visit to the United States would have the most excellent effect," Foreign Secretary Anthony Eden sought authorization to give Gerard a "temporising but not disencouraging reply." Eden's own opinion was that, while the idea of a visit might then be premature, it would have "important results for Anglo-American relations" at a more opportune moment.[8] The ambassador's opinions influenced the Foreign Office, apprehensive about embarking on the first voyage by reigning monarchs to North America and only the second state visit by the inexperienced king. Lindsay indicated that should the king and queen travel to Canada, the pressure on them to visit the president would be irresistible, but he doubted that such a visit could be restricted to an interlude at Roosevelt's country estate. At the very least, there would be mounting sentiment to include New York City.[9]

So uncertain were the prospects for the visit during the Czech crisis that it took Tweedsmuir's special pleas to elicit a guarantee that it would not be canceled unless the international situation rapidly deteriorated.[10] As he reported to his sister: "I pressed it with the persistence of a horse-leech. As soon as I got Neville on my side I knew it would be all right, for the King was most sympathetic."[11] At the dedication of the International Bridge in August 1938, Mackenzie King was able to reassure Roosevelt that the visit would likely go ahead.

The president, acting very much on his own initiative, sought to keep arrangements "out of diplomatic channels," relying on private communications and relations between Lindsay and the White House. His ingratiating letter aimed to personalize the invitation, noting that "it would give my wife and me the greatest pleasure to see you," but adding that "it would be an excellent thing for Anglo-American relations if you could visit the

United States." Although he mentioned the New York World's Fair, he also intimated that the king might prefer to forgo the "heat of Washington" and travel directly to Hyde Park:

> It occurs to me that a Canadian trip would be crowded with formalities and that you both might like three or four days of very simple country life at Hyde Park—with no formal entertainments and an opportunity to get a bit of rest and relaxation.

Of course, in the event that the king felt impelled to come to Washington, he would be expected to stay at the White House and—a more daunting prospect—be received by Congress. Speaking in avuncular fashion, the president advised him to "do very much as you personally want to do" irrespective of the "demands of the Protocol people."[12] Without committing himself, the king responded that the pleasure the visit would give him personally "would be greatly enhanced by the thought that it was contributing in any way to the cordiality of the relations between our two countries."[13]

From the start, then, the projected trip was marked by a tension between its political and social aspects. Roosevelt's notion of a purely private occasion, with the monarchs shielded from the glare of publicity and queries about diplomatic ramifications, was illusory. The embassy also feared that if the visit were co-opted by the president, it might incur the wrath of neglected American interests—political and regional—which contended for their share of royal attention. The Canadians doubted that an American diversion would dampen enthusiasm for the royal tour of the dominion, provided it did not encroach on the time allocated to Canada.[14]

As plans evolved, the visit was transformed into an official but very brief one—four days, as the king specified when formally accepting the president's invitation in November 1938.[15] Lindsay perceived advantages in its brevity, a way to discourage speculation that the trip was politically motivated. Had the American segment been the principal purpose of the journey, it would have "given rise to every possible misunderstanding." But once the voyage to Canada was scheduled, its extension to the United States was "not only entirely inevitable but also entirely desirable, advantageous, and safe." To accept the invitation would be a compliment to Americans; to refuse, a discourtesy. Even though a royal visit would not engender political negotiations, it was important to reinforce "favorable emotional factors" whose benefit would be found in the "warm feelings of the people" and the improvement in Anglo-American relations.[16]

How the king and queen were to be entertained proved more contentious. Grover Whalen, the brash impresario, wrote to the president proposing that they be issued an official invitation to the New York World's Fair, in view of the prominence of the British Pavilion.[17] But the Palace initially opposed including the World's Fair "for fear that it [would] change the complexion of the visit from an official one to a commercial one."[18] Lindsay countered Roosevelt's preference for Hyde Park over steamy Washington by arguing that, since the president's enemies were prone to accuse him of self-aggrandizement, to make Hyde Park the main focus of a royal visit would incur adverse criticism by emphasizing its "personal nature."[19] A stopover while in New York would be appropriate, but Washington—so Lindsay maintained, ensconced in his Lutyens ambassadorial mansion—was "the place where most time should be spent." A congressional reception would be obligatory, and the king would have to make a short address. Secondary in importance to Washington, New York nonetheless required adroit management because of the rivalry of competing politicians and the fact that the familiar ticker-tape parade had now been "too much cheapened to be suitable" for reigning monarchs. Despite royal misgivings, Lindsay thought that the World's Fair did warrant a short visit: though likely to become "an immense popular attraction, it is being rather vulgarized by over-advertisement" and should not be emphasized. There was much to commend incorporating Chicago, hub of "the most isolationist part of America," into their agenda as well. If there were enough time to allow such a stopover, Their Majesties would be making a contribution to the cause of Anglo-American friendship "at the point where it is most needed."[20]

After conferring with Lindsay, Roosevelt conceded that a visit to the capital was imperative, but refused to regard it, as did the embassy, as "the principal part of the plan." The president was annoyed by Lindsay's failure to mention Hyde Park in his memorandum on their discussion. Appealing over the ambassador's head, Roosevelt told the king that "to the American people the essential democracy of yourself and the Queen makes the greatest appeal of all." Were they able to remain at Hyde Park for two or three days, "the simplicity and naturalness of such a visit would produce a most excellent effect." As for Chicago, the president was "not in the least bit insistent on it" should the king's schedule preclude a stop there. While it might be sensible for the royal party to grace some "New York institution of cultural importance"—he suggested a housing project or a medical center—he did not think the king should be driven "through the narrow, crowded streets of either New York or Chicago."[21] Lindsay persisted in the face of the president's blandishments, warning that Roosevelt wanted to increase "as much as possible the time Their Majesties will spend at his house at Hyde Park, and this at the expense of time given to New York City." As far as he was concerned, "New York ought to be made secondary to Washington; but Hyde Park . . . secondary or even incidental to New York."[22]

At first the Palace seemed less concerned about acceding to Roosevelt's wishes than with doing "all they can to show good feeling towards the United States." Alec Hardinge, the king's private secretary, sounded out J. P. Morgan about the plausibility of a "short visit to Washington, stopping nowhere else in the United States."[23] Hardinge also urged Lindsay to encourage the president to "make clear to his people that the visit had no particular political significance but was simply a natural friendly meeting."[24] Although Lord Halifax, Eden's successor as foreign secretary, was eager to accompany the king, he recognized that this might be misconstrued as foreshadowing secret negotiations. Lindsay broached the subject with Undersecretary of State Sumner Welles and then with the president himself, who agreed that the foreign secretary's presence would "excite a lot of talk about an alliance" and divert attention from the king.[25] The Foreign Office, admitting that a cabinet member in attendance "might lead Americans to think we were trying to angle for political favours and mar the good will aspect of the visit," reluctantly acceded to Roosevelt's suggestion that Mackenzie King assume the role of minister-in-attendance throughout the North American trip.[26]

The official announcement that the king and queen had accepted the president's invitation was favorably reported in the American press, assuring a cordial welcome "despite the fact that the American people feel convinced their own government and nation must travel its own way." Lindsay informed his superiors that some commentators had suggested that the royal itinerary should include the Midwest and the Far West, which have been "the most isolationist and the least impressed with the foreign aspects of American policy."[27] Yet press response was by no means universally enthusiastic: the Hearst papers were cool, and the *Chicago Tribune* was decidedly hostile. The Palace was disturbed by an article in *Scribner's Magazine* entitled "Selling George VI to the U.S.," which claimed that a large part of the country "still believes that Edward, Duke of Windsor, is the rightful owner of the British throne, and that King George VI is a colorless, weak personality largely on probation in the public mind of Great Britain, as well as of the United States." It also drew attention to his speech impediment

and reiterated baseless allegations that he was susceptible to epileptic sei-
zures. The article went on to suggest that Queen Elizabeth was "too plump
of figure, too dowdy in dress" to satisfy American expectations of a reigning queen.[28] A *Saturday Evening Post* profile that detailed the lifestyle,
tastes, and expenses of the monarchy, and offered American readers titil-
lating tidbits ranging from what their friends called them ("Bert and
Betty") to what they preferred to eat ("beef and mashed potatoes"), their
preference for London water for brewing tea, what they liked to read (the
queen, biographies and novels; the king, detective stories and mysteries),
and what they spent on horse feed, could hardly have been much more welcome in court circles.[29] The Foreign Office, hoping to mollify the Palace,
noted that the *Post* article was intended to be "both friendly and compli-
mentary," even though it did "in many respects offend against the canons
of good taste as we understand them." While conceding that the British
must be prepared for "this kind of attitude towards Their Majesties," officials hoped that the vacuous press coverage could be improved.[30]

Less problematic in terms of public relations were the private missives
addressed to the State Department and the Foreign Office by individuals
who sought to wield influence behind the scenes. A New York politician,
on first learning of the rumored visit, derided it as a "publicity stunt for the
New York World's Fair" but feared that it would be exploited by "the tire-
less and powerful people who are perpetually seeking to get us into an alliance with England." He warned that "at the very moment these monarchs
walk into the White House, possibly a million, maybe more, Democrats of
Irish origin will stop voting the Democratic ticket."[31] When his complaint
was accorded cursory acknowledgment by the protocol officer, he demanded that it be brought to the attention of Secretary of State Hull, adding, "We have enough troubles now without having it appear to the world,
as it inevitably will, that we are becoming entangled with the harassed and
probably sinking British Empire."[32] The Foreign Office was sometimes targeted by socially prominent Americans hostile to Roosevelt, employing
well-placed British contacts as intermediaries. One such correspondent declared that "all New York is against the visit, and that to Hyde Park is considered preposterous." Raising the specter of security, she insisted that no
city except Washington would invite them because of fears over public
safety. State Department files testify to the absurdity of such a claim, as a
host of municipalities from coast to coast vied for the honor of extending
hospitality. The letter went on to assert that "Hyde Park is totally inadequate. There is no proper arrangement for secret service men and police.

The House has no proper suites and rooms and the service represents a scratch lot of negro [sic] and whites, English, and Irish."[33] Even Stella Reading, who, as the wife of a former ambassador, claimed to be one of the few English travelers who had actually stayed at Hyde Park, found it "a dismal small house, extremely badly run and most uncomfortable."[34] Lord Cromer transmitted an American letter which speculated that the motive for the royal visit was an "attempt by Great Britain to obtain a more definite international engagement, which the USA will refuse."[35] At the Foreign Office, Victor Perowne bristled at the persistence of what he termed "this whispering campaign" ascribing the visit to some nefarious "ulterior economic and political motive." He faulted his American counterparts for slowness in reaffirming that "the one and only occasion for their visit is the invitation issued by the President."[36]

Over the following months details were hammered out in letters between Roosevelt and the king, in meetings between Lindsay and Welles—the American ambassador in London, Joseph Kennedy, having been marginalized in the planning—and in exchanges between the Foreign Office and Buckingham Palace. Considering the brevity of the tour—8–11 June—the extensive consultation and the meticulous preparations were extraordinary, involving not just faceless bureaucrats, but senior officials in three countries. While British functionaries, schooled in traditional protocol, were anxious to maximize favorable publicity, their innate caution militated against any arrangements deemed either vulgar or compromising to royal dignity. As host, President Roosevelt participated directly through meetings with the British ambassador and personal letters to the Canadian prime minister and the king, whereas George VI tended to rely more on his private secretary to negotiate on his behalf. In the course of deliberations the proposed stop in Chicago was jettisoned as logistically unfeasible, but not without misgivings. Lady Reading relayed a letter she had received from an American friend, urging the royal party to tour the Midwest, where "isolationists and the anti-Europeans are strongly entrenched" and where "the opposition to rearmament etc. will develop." Her correspondent went on to underscore "the inestimable advantage of making the Middle Westerners feel they had had a share in the visit. After which they would rally enthusiastically behind any cause represented by the King and Queen."[37] Lord Halifax admitted that "there was some force in these representations."[38] But other pressures were more compelling. Hardinge told the Foreign Office that Chicago was eventually "dropped by the President himself" and that Mackenzie King was "much opposed to it," presumably because it might impinge on the Canadian segment of the journey.[39]

Even after the itinerary was settled, controversial issues remained. The Colonial Office passed along a suggestion that Their Majesties tour the West Indian community in New York to assuage feelings of neglect among a loyal, if disadvantaged group of subjects.[40] Lindsay demurred, responding that "not all West Indians in New York are nice. Some have tendencies which are unwisely political and almost disloyal." Echoing the president's strictures, he pronounced that "a descent on Harlem is out of the question."[41] The consul general in New York concurred that "a visit to Harlem [was] inadvisable," because "Blacks are an element held in the lowest estimation, for very good reasons." Moreover, it might appear awkward if a visit were paid to the West Indian community while at the same time organizations like the English-Speaking Union and the Pilgrims were being ignored.[42] Nothing more was heard of the proposal, although in the end a motorcade did take the royal party, accompanied by Mayor LaGuardia and Governor Lehman, from the Battery, up the West Side Highway, along the edge of Central Park, across the Triborough Bridge, to the World's Fair grounds on Long Island.

The personal inclinations of the main participants could not be discounted either. The king was keen to entertain the president at a dinner in the British Embassy to reciprocate the state dinner planned at the White House, but Roosevelt expressed reluctance to dine out because of the burden of wearing his leg braces two days in succession.[43] In the end he consented, and then scrapped the plan to accompany the king and queen to New York City, traveling instead directly to Hyde Park to rest while awaiting their arrival. George VI intervened further to modify the preliminary Washington schedule. He was averse to addressing Congress, ostensibly because it would set a precedent for addressing legislatures during subsequent state visits, but in reality because nervousness over his stammer made him shun such occasions. Instead it was agreed that members of Congress would be introduced informally in the Capitol rotunda.[44]

Even after arrangements for the trip were concluded, both the State Department and the White House were inundated with mail from individuals seeking autographs or audiences with the British monarchs; from entertainers—ranging from black dance teams to high-school bands— volunteering their services; from businesses or individuals offering speech therapy for the king, spiritualist readings, photographs, tapestries, commemorative scrolls, dolls for the absent princesses, and food catering;[45] and from a host of private and public institutions proffering invitations to the royal couple. These included such disparate bodies as the International Poultry Conference, the Brooklyn Sunday School Union, the International Peace Garden, the North Dakota legislature, and the Warrior's Shrine in Hoboken. After the royal couple's itinerary was announced, there were numerous requests for their route to be altered or for their train or limousine to slow down when passing through a particular community, so that local spectators could catch a glimpse of the guests.[46]

In the end the success of the royals' visit exceeded all expectations. Effusive coverage by American newspapers of their progress through Canada prepared the way for an enthusiastic welcome south of the border. After greetings at Niagara Falls by the secretary of state during the evening of 7 June and by the president and Mrs. Roosevelt when the royal train arrived in the capital the following morning, the king and queen pursued a grueling schedule in Washington and New York before enjoying a frenetically relaxed twenty-eight hours as guests of the Roosevelts at Hyde Park. On their first day in Washington they received the cabinet and the diplomatic corps, went sightseeing in the sweltering capital, and attended a garden party for 1,500 carefully chosen guests at the British Embassy and a state dinner at the White House, the latter featuring a program of American music selected by Eleanor Roosevelt that encompassed spirituals, cowboy ballads, a square-dance group, and songs by Marian Anderson, Lawrence Tibbett, Kate Smith, and the Coon Creek Girls from Kentucky. The next morning they received members of the British community in Washington, including ex-servicemen, greeted hundreds of congressmen and senators, visited Mount Vernon, a Civilian Conservation Corps camp—a special request of the king's[47]—and placed the obligatory wreaths at Arlington National Cemetery, ending the day by hosting a comparatively small embassy dinner for the Roosevelts.

After another night on the royal train, they embarked from Fort Hancock, New Jersey, on an American navy destroyer to the Battery, at the foot of Manhattan, and then proceeded slowly by motorcade for a brief tour of the British and empire exhibits at the World's Fair, followed by a fifteen-minute reception at Columbia University, finally reaching Hyde Park in the early evening. In the course of a little more than a day at Hyde Park they survived two dinners with Roosevelt family and friends, an Episcopal church service, an informal picnic where the king consumed his celebrated first hotdog.⁴⁸ The king also enjoyed a private swim and car ride with the president, much to the consternation of Mackenzie King, who, having declined an invitation to join the august pair, subsequently regretted having "missed one of the great events of my life."⁴⁹ Photographs of the royal couple in country attire enjoying a cookout with America's first family, emblazoned on front pages of newspapers throughout the United States, struck a more responsive chord than the uniforms and tiaras and formal toasts at the state dinner.⁵⁰

What did the visitors accomplish? In both Washington and New York, where the streets were thronged with cheering crowds, they scored a striking personal triumph, signaling newfound popularity. Newspaper headlines proclaimed the American infatuation with the royal visitors. The first glimpse of reigning monarchs may have dispelled some of their magical aura, but observers were dazzled by the queen's personal style and gracious demeanor, unfazed by the oppressive heat, the crowds, or fatigue. The Foreign Office was delighted that the visit had dispelled any lingering notion that the British monarchy was "in any way stuffed shirt." The simplicity and geniality of the visitors evoked a desire among both press and public to demonstrate "America's sympathy towards the democratic ideals represented by the British monarchy."⁵¹ The elaborate security arrangements coordinated by British, Canadian, and American police were probably superfluous, the entire proceedings taking place without incident or signs of political disaffection.⁵² The consul general in New York surmised that these precautions had been excessive, since "the size, the orderliness and enthusiasm of the crowds lining the route surprised all the prophets." This popularity he attributed to the "natural, friendly yet dignified bearing" of the guests, who revealed

> British royalty in a guise which has surprised and delighted the man in the New York street. That there is a brain underneath Her Majesty's becoming hats, and genuine feeling behind His Majesty's handshake is a discovery that is going to promote a better understanding of Britain's system of government and Britain's problems, and help to consign to limbo legends current since the Abdication.⁵³

Naturally, not all Americans were equally ecstatic about the royal couple or the entertainment provided during their stay. Culling reports from consulates in Los Angeles and San Francisco, a Foreign Office minute acknowledged that "the attitude of the press was noticeably cooler" in the West than in the East.⁵⁴ As First Hostess, Mrs. Roosevelt was subjected to a barrage of letters critical of her arrangements. The president of the Miami Acacia Club declared it "an insult to the British king and queen to present a negro singer for their entertainment,"[55] while anonymous, and sometimes barely literate, correspondents resorted to racist epithets in describing Marian Anderson or White House footmen. Matters of etiquette aroused the ire of others, several correspondents protesting to the State Department— which hastened to dispel such rumors—that Americans might be obliged to bow and curtsy to British royalty.[56] The head of the Enlisted Veterans of the World War, objecting even to standing at attention when the king and queen passed by, demanded instead that Britain repay its war debt, which "will help but never compensate the maimed and mentally ill American veterans."[57]

The singular achievement of the visit was to overcome Yankee republican ambivalence by stripping the monarchy of the visible trappings of majesty. While Americans were certainly fascinated by immemorial traditions and pageantry, so alien to their own national culture, they could openly countenance only a monarch who represented kindred political institutions, thereby reinforcing mutual Anglo-American values. As it became a ceremonial figurehead for parliamentary democracy, the monarchy enhanced its appeal to Americans, whose own statesmen usually seemed— and often deliberately so—unglamorous. In that sense the royal visit did let in daylight upon magic, exhibiting the king and queen not as Olympian figures, but—within limits—as approachable, even ordinary, mortals with familiar concerns and domestic responsibilities. The president may have been correct to identify the "essential democracy" of his guests as the most significant aspect for the American public, perhaps because it effaced lingering, if outmoded, images of royalty.

If it was no longer tactically appropriate to project Britain as steeped in archaic traditions, it was equally evident that American Anglophilia was enmeshed in nostalgia for a bygone age, a sentiment unabashedly exploited in the royal visit. It was necessary to reinforce a view of Britain as adaptable and to show that constitutional monarchy was not an anachronism. At the same time it would have been a travesty to imply that British political culture had become identical to that of the United States. In the face of the Nazi menace, British traditions were rendered all the more potent as symbols of a distinctive Anglo-Saxon civilization. What made the royal visit so resounding a success was that it reflected both continuity and change, a linkage calculated to reassure Americans that their imagined Britain would not vanish in the inevitable process of modernization.

At the same time the "packaging" of the royal couple for an American audience concealed much of their lifestyle from view. While diplomatic etiquette dictated the wearing of uniforms and formal clothes on public occasions—only Hyde Park offered a more informal respite—the press focused little attention on the ritualized entourage of the king and queen, which included two dressers and a hairdresser for her, two valets and a page for him, and five footmen, in addition to the king's acting private secretary, a lord- and two ladies-in-waiting (with accompanying servants), two equerries to the king, the lord chamberlain to the queen—not to mention two police officers, a physician, and other attendants. Much of this staff could not be accommodated either at the White House or at Hyde Park, Their Majesties making do with nine attendants at the White House while others were housed at the British Embassy or remained on the royal train.[58] Several months before their arrival William C. Bullitt, the American ambassador in Paris, regaled Roosevelt with stories about the efforts of the French president to satisfy domestic requirements during the recent royal visit to France, including respective bed ("very soft eiderdown quilt, which can be accordion-pleated at the foot of the bed" for the king) and bath furnishings (toweled bathrobe for the king, but not for the queen) and breakfast preferences ("made separately, on trays, prepared by the private servants"). Bullitt informed the president that "whenever Their Majesties come home, tea should always be kept ready for them" and that everything necessary for the preparation of cocktails should be supplied, even though the king generally brought his own liquor.[59] The acerbic Harold Ickes, less royalist than many Washington insiders, confided to his diary:

> Some of the things that the King and Queen apparently expect seemed to be ludicrous. Great detail was given. The sheets had to be of such a sort and the coverings of the King's bed had to have a reef in them at the foot of the bed. . . . I came to one conclusion, however, and that was that if the King and Queen of England think they are slumming when they come to visit the President and Mrs. Roosevelt at the White House and at Hyde Park, they ought to stay at home.[60]

Although he subsequently modified his views, noting that the king and queen made "an excellent impression on people" and "accomplished some good," he remained doubtful that there would be "any relaxation of our wariness" about foreign entanglements.[61]

If the visit was initiated without political overtones, by the time it occurred, less than two months before Germany invaded Poland, wider implications were inescapable. Although neither party would dare to hint openly at a renewed alliance, the press was notably vigilant in watching for telltale signs. The *Washington Post*, stressing that the purpose of the visit was "the furtherance of Anglo-American goodwill," cautioned that any effort in the direction of an alliance "would arouse more mistrust than it would remove."[62] The *Baltimore Sun* assured readers that the king's object was not to forge a military alliance, but to combine "the good faith and good will of two strong nations."[63] The *Washington Star* was even more sanguine when it proclaimed:

> Our isolationists can sleep just as soundly at night this week as they are accustomed to do when British crowned heads are not in our midst spinning imaginary webs of entanglement. The King and Queen are come to us purely and simply bearing the olive branch of a comradeship that has endured unbroken for nearly a century and a half.[64]

Arthur Krock, in the *New York Times*, claimed that the royal visitors had shown "how democratic and wholesome are the symbols of the constitutional monarchy that is Britain's."[65] Only the isolationist *Chicago Tribune* demurred, insisting that the real motive for the visit was to inveigle the United States out of isolation. Still, Cordell Hull pointedly noted in his welcoming remarks that "it was particularly timely for nations that held common views on matters of freedom to exchange visits."[66] Both at the White House and, more especially, at Hyde Park the king and the president talked seriously about politics. George VI, fully primed by a detailed report that the embassy had prepared on New Deal programs and on American foreign policy,[67] impressed his host as well informed about issues and personalities. He left with the conviction that the British had a reliable friend in the White House, Roosevelt confiding—mistakenly, as it transpired—"if London was bombed U.S.A. would come in."[68]

While the royal visit produced no immediate concrete results and had little impact on American isolationism, it did evoke the psychological effects that Ambassador Lindsay had anticipated. Warning that it would be dangerous to imagine that the British government "had America politically 'in the bag,'" he was nonetheless confident that the emotions of the American public "have been stirred to their very roots."[69] Even if it did little to alter the views of those senators who opposed abrogation of the neutrality law, it seemed to justify his conviction that "our hidden reserves have been immensely strengthened."[70]

Reflecting on Lindsay's sanguine assessment, David Scott, head of the

Foreign Office's American Department, summed up the Whitehall perspective: "Emotions which have been so stirred will for a long time to come be more susceptible to those influences which in a time of real crisis determine the course of public opinion and would tip the balance in our favour."[71] What neither Lindsay nor Foreign Office commentators foresaw was that it would take more than two years and a Japanese surprise attack on Pearl Harbor before Roosevelt's confident predictions of American intervention materialized.

Autobiography, Nostalgia, and the Changing Practices of Working-Class Selfhood

In the first of their two volumes charting the rise to fame of George Orwell, Peter Stansky and William Abrahams comment perceptively on Orwell's somewhat awkward relationship with the working class. They argue that *Down and Out in Paris and London* (1933), his lightly fictionalized factual account of working-class poverty, was a success insofar as it persuaded its readers that it reported events that actually happened. But they also suggest that there was something evasive and inauthentic about the book, that "no matter how sincerely he participated in the experience at the time, or how convincingly he later presented it on the page, his friends and acquaintances could not help noticing the pretence it entailed."[1] Nobody knew this better than the would-be working-class writers whom Orwell befriended and encouraged. When Jack Common, the young worker-writer from Newcastle, first met Orwell in 1930, he was wary: although a genuine friendship developed between the two authors, Common initially viewed Orwell as a public-school man, who, because of his background, was unable to experience the life of the tramp. In short, Orwell was judged and found wanting because he lacked authentic working-class experience and could therefore not speak from *inside* the working class.[2]

The claim that "experience" authenticates the voice of the dispossessed, coupled with the suspicion that those who do not share particular experiences cannot adequately convey them to others, has often been used to validate working-class writing in Britain. In the nineteenth century, one of many workers who struggled to tell the story of his life, and gain for it a degree of legitimacy and respect, argued in his autobiography, *One of the Multitude*, that "the public will recognize that experiences LIVED, and written down however poorly are of more real value and interest than imaginary fictions beautifully disguised."[3] If such appeals to the authority of experience were widespread among worker-writers in the nineteenth century, they have become even more ubiquitous since the end of the Second World War. As a result, those who wish to extol the virtues of working-class experience continue to denigrate as "imaginary fictions beautifully disguised" many novels of working-class life that purport to capture the essence of it. For example, despite the fact that Pat Barker's novel *Union Street* (1982) won the Fawcett Prize—in part because it challenged many previous male-centered stories of the working class—it has been suggested that her work is very much *about* the working class, rather than *of* it; like so much nineteenth-century fiction, and like Orwell's *Down and Out*, it has been attacked for representing working-class experience from the outside.[4]

Barker's novel was published in the midst of a period that witnessed a flowering of working-class autobiographical writing in Britain, writing that staked its authority on the evidence of the experience in which it was grounded. Beginning in the late 1960's, and more often in the 1970's and 1980's, workers were encouraged through a number of local history projects to record their memories, to recount their experiences, and to offer the "truth" of the working-class past in ways that would challenge (or at least supplement) academic histories—and would be much more authentic than the fictional representations of working-class life encountered in novels such as those by Orwell and Barker. To some extent there was nothing new in this: workers had struggled to tell their own stories long before the 1970's, and one can trace many continuities in the tradition of working-class autobiographical writing, a tradition that is now some two centuries old.[5] Nevertheless, the stories told in the 1970's and after differed radically from those told by nineteenth-century worker-writers in terms of their emphasis, content, style, and, more crucially, in terms of the conditions of their production. This essay briefly explores the reasons for the proliferation of working-class autobiographical writing in postwar Britain. In addition, it examines the structure, form, and content of a few of the narratives of the working-class past produced in the "golden years" of the 1970's. In so doing, it attempts to shed some light on patterns of change and continuity in the practices of working-class selfhood since the nineteenth century.

Social Change and Working-Class Selfhood
in Postwar Britain

Hundreds of working-class autobiographical reminiscences were collected, edited, printed, and disseminated by community publishers in the 1970's and 1980's. The majority of them, as we will see, offered a glimpse into a way of life that had vanished; in many, that life was portrayed in nostalgic terms. The publication of these autobiographies, along with the valorization of the memories that gave rise to them, needs to be understood in the context of a number of changes that took place in British society during the two decades following the Second World War. Of these, two are particularly important. First, and more important, were those changes that resulted in an extensive rebuilding of the nation after the war, leading to the demise of the so-called traditional working-class community. Second was a series of related cultural shifts that led to the emergence and consolidation of new forms of reflexively organized selfhood and informed a number of new beliefs about the importance of cultivating and managing the self.

Looking back from the vantage point of the early 1970's, Louis Heren, born in the slums of Shadwell, in London's East End, and ending his working life as deputy editor of *The Times*, reflected bitterly that "nothing was done to commemorate Cockney courage in the blitz. Instead, so-called planners set out to destroy what had survived the bombing. In their arrogant ignorance they destroyed the conditions of Cockney culture, the tight little neighbourhoods, the street markets, the intimate pubs and the corner shops."[6] His was a belief that had come to be widely shared by the 1970's, and while planners may have received too much of the blame for the changes that that had taken place, it was indeed the case that in little more than a quarter of a century Britain's built environment had been profoundly transformed. The need to repair houses damaged in the war, and to reinstate slum-clearance policies halted by the war, occupied Labour and Conservative governments thereafter. While 245,000 houses were demolished in Britain between the wars, 1.3 million more were razed between 1945 and 1975, a remarkable era of urban redevelopment that has no parallel in British history and that displaced approximately three million people.[7] Moreover, as critics have been keen to point out, not only were buildings destroyed in the process of reconstruction, but so was the very fabric of the traditional working-class community. Coupled with the growth of women's employment outside the home and the effects of affluence on many traditional working-class values, urban redevelopment gradually undermined a way of life that had been in existence for close to a century. As the editors of one collection of popular reminiscences aptly noted in 1979: "The destruction of old neighbourhoods and their replacement by estates of flats is, perhaps, the biggest single change in working class life since the last war."[8]

The story of the demise of the traditional working-class community has yet to be told in all its complexity. But one of the most important, and least understood, products of that demise was the advent of nostalgia for the world of mills and cobbled streets, and for the communities and community spirit that sustained them. In short, parallel with the rise of the tower block was an intensification of nostalgia for the built environment the tower block replaced. Richard Hoggart's classic study of the topography of that rapidly vanishing world, *The Uses of Literacy* (1957), is certainly the best-known of the many laments for the working-class past that appeared in the 1950's, offering an affirmation of the values and strengths of a way of life that appeared to be in rapid decline. But his was by no means a voice in the wilderness. As "Wanderer" wrote sadly in the *South London Press* on April 5, 1956:

> Why is local life so impersonal now? . . . We have lost so many street markets, music halls, and small picture palaces, and the pubs don't teem with life now. You won't see people dancing on the streets on Bank Holiday now. They're off in coaches to the coast. . . . What I think we need is some new social life to take the place of the comradeship of the old days, when everyone knew everyone else in the street.[9]

More often than not, these laments were expressed by Hoggart's "scholarship boys," by those whose own mobility through education rendered problematic their relationship to the community they left behind. In the 1970's such individuals continued to lament the loss of the past, largely in terms that had been established by individuals such as Hoggart and "Wanderer" two decades earlier. As Jeremy Seabrook argued, "our sense of home-place has been destroyed," and the working class had been detached "from any sense of continuity with the past."[10] By the time Seabrook contributed his own stories of loss, an extensive discourse of nostalgia had emerged. Moreover, it was a discourse that, as we shall see, informed and shaped those working-class autobiographical practices that also emerged in the 1970's.

If the rebuilding of Britain after the war led to nostalgia for traditional working-class culture and for the old working-class communities, it also fueled attempts to codify the unique practices and ways of life that defined those communities. Although historians have argued that it was in the late nineteenth century that a recognizably distinct working-class culture emerged in Britain, it is no accident that it was not until the 1950's, at the moment of its demise, that the term "working-class culture" was used to any appreciable extent. Raymond Williams was among the first to give shape to the term and explore its possible meanings.[11] Others followed, and by the late 1960's working-class communities had been studied exhaustively by sociologists, traced historically, enacted on the stage, appropriated as background for the fictions of the Angry Young Men, and, perhaps most important, become the subject of the immensely popular television serial *Coronation Street*.[12] By the time working-class writers were encouraged to publish their own stories of life in traditional working-class communities en masse in the 1970's, they lived in a world that was saturated with images of working-class culture, images that shaped their own understanding of the proletarian past.

By the 1970's, then, many representations of the old working-class communities circulated widely throughout British society; so, too, did a series of nostalgic laments for the structure of daily life in those communities. In addition, the 1970's also witnessed a growing emphasis on the importance of working-class testimony, a new insistence that members of the working class could and should speak about their experience of life in the old communities. In general, this valorization of the "authentic" working-class voice is related to a series of broader changes in the structures of selfhood in twentieth-century Britain, to the ways in which the self is ordered and experienced.[13] More specifically, it is related to the ways in which the postwar state stressed the importance of working-class selfhood and encouraged its development and articulation. James Griffiths, who piloted Britain's welfare legislation onto the statute book after 1945, spoke in the Commons on the Beveridge Report in 1943: "Our people have memories of what happened at the end of the last war, memories of the period of depression, memories of the unemployment, frustration, poverty and distress into which large masses of our people were thrown."[14] For Griffiths, not only were working-class memories important to the arguments made on behalf of the new welfare legislation, but so too was the need for legislation that would encourage a sense of dignity and self-worth among the recipients of the new benefits. Looking back on the promises of that more optimistic moment, Carolyn Steedman has spoken about the relationship between welfare politics and working-class selfhood: "I would be a very different person now if orange juice and milk and dinners at school hadn't told me, in a covert way, that I had a right to exist, was worth something."[15]

If the welfare policies of the postwar years served in part to confer on members of the working class a new sense of self-worth, so also did many of the educational practices implemented in the 1950's and 1960's. These crucial years witnessed the development of an extensive program of teaching self-expression in British schools, of using creative writing as a means of fostering ethical self-cultivation. For the first time, working-class children were being asked en masse to draw on the resources of their own experience in order to tell the story of the self, a self that was now deemed not only to be valuable but to be worth narrating. It is no accident that one of the earliest postwar reminiscences we have of change in the traditional working-class community, Valerie Avery's *London Morning*, first published in 1955, was written when the author was fifteen, in school, at the instigation of her English teacher. The book's importance rests on the assumption that the dispossessed were able to tell their own stories and come into consciousness of their selves through the practice of writing. Moreover, Avery's story was made available to many other children so that they might likewise come into and develop a sense of self.[16]

These changes in the practices of the self as taught in the schools were linked to a series of broader changes in academic history writing and in the political commitments of a new generation of social historians. As is well known, in the 1960's Edward Thompson became the champion of popular experience, rescuing the voices of the dispossessed, of those who had been silenced by history. In the 1970's, he defended the epistemological importance of the category of experience—in a decade when early History Workshop enthusiasts were collecting experience and encouraging individuals to recall and share their own stories of the working-class past.[17] It is in this context that the practice of oral history, the cultivation of worker-writers, and the development of community publishing need to be understood. The obsession with the decline of the traditional working-class community, coupled with the regard for working-class selfhood and the enthusiasms of an increasingly ascendant cohort of social historians, served as the backdrop against which the proliferation of working-class autobiographical writing took place.

Narrating the Working-Class Past

In 1971, two teachers in Stepney published a collection of poems written by the children they taught, leading to a debate about whether or not such writing ought to be objectified in published form. That same year, Centerprise, a small community center and bookshop, opened in Hackney. In 1972, Centerprise published a reader set in Hackney for local schoolchildren, along with a collection of local history materials, also for use in the schools. Around the same time, several tutors in the Hackney branch of the Workers' Education Association (WEA) attended a History Workshop conference at Ruskin College and returned to London even more convinced of the need to make history a mass activity, to write popular history based on the experiences and memories of ordinary working people. "The scales fell away from our eyes; we were converted," wrote Ken Worpole, one of those who attended the Ruskin conference and soon organized the community publishing program at Centerprise.[18] Thus began one of the larger ventures in community publishing in the 1970's. The local WEA offered a class, "A People's History of Hackney," which further encouraged the recording and the subsequent publication of local reminiscences. Moreover, what was taking place in the early 1970's in Hackney was also taking place in other parts of London—in Peckham and Stepney in particular—and around the country, giving rise to groups that included the Aberdeen People's Press, Bristol Broadsides, Commonword (Manchester), and QueenSpark (Brighton). The process culminated in 1976 when the Federation of Worker Writers & Community Publishers was established.[19]

The aim of these projects was twofold: to give voice to working-class experience and to capture traces of the everyday life of the rapidly vanishing working-class past. The emphasis placed on these goals was made explicit in the books and pamphlets published by the community projects. In terms of the importance of experience, for example, a flyer advertising the community histories published by Brighton's QueenSpark asserted that "we would like people to believe that our own lives and experiences are as important as those who find their way into print with apparent ease." Likewise, the declared mission of Stepney Books was "to encourage the writing and publishing of local working people's experience."[20] Moreover, it was often the very ordinariness of the experience recounted in these works that gave it special importance: as the frontispiece to one of the booklets published by Bristol Broadsides stressed, the experiences recorded therein were "nothing

out of the ordinary. . . . They are the experiences of the great maj
us."[21] Not only were they shared, but they usually pertained to
world of the old working-class community—lost experiences in the
of being rescued. One community-arts officer who helped a local
group near Manchester record its experiences stressed the importance of
such rescue work in his introduction to the group's study: they "voiced
their fears that all traces of their history were vanishing and would soon
disappear, going unrecognised and unrecorded."[22] Such fears were expressed again and again: "Now that the bulldozers destroy the rows of ter-
raced houses, I feel this story must be told, otherwise the memory will go
into oblivion."[23] It was, as Joanna Bornat has noted, at the end of a period
of massive change that such anxieties about the need to capture the past
were most often expressed, "a time when urban decay and reconstruction as
well as industrial change had altered a physical and spatial environment familiar to many older people."[74]

In terms of their emphasis on the importance of personal experience,
working-class autobiographies published in the 1970's and 1980's were not
unlike those published in the nineteenth century. In terms of their attempts
to rescue, organize, and give meaning to a rapidly vanishing past, however,
they differed radically from most reminiscences penned by their Victorian
forebears. In an impressive analysis of Victorian working-class autobiographical writing, Regenia Gagnier has suggested that the nostalgic memoir that commemorated a lost, or dying, past was only one of several genres
evident in such work. Others included the therapeutically organized self-
examination, the personal confession, and the narrative that charted the
author's educational and political progress.[25] Much has been written about
the latter genre, about works that focused on the struggle for "bread,
knowledge, and freedom," to borrow from the title of William Lovett's
autobiography. Such works charted the progress of the autodidact, a life in
motion that moved from the world of work to an enlightened world of literature, politics, and writing. They were resolutely whiggish in their stories
of improvement, mapping the lives of their authors as they moved from
workshop to war cabinet, from pit to Parliament, from stonemason's bench
to Treasury Bench.[26] While the theme of personal advance and achievement
was a staple of much Victorian working-class autobiographical writing, it
has, however, been virtually absent in such writing in the postwar period.
Whereas the Victorian autodidact narrative recounted a story of progress,
in which past and present were linked, the former leading to the latter,

more recent works tend to sever past and present; they constitute a "be-fore" and an "after" and focus almost exclusively on the former. These works posit a breakage with the past, a world frozen in time that can now be recuperated only through writing. In short, unlike those Victorian working-class writers who celebrated their moment of arrival in the pres-ent, more recent writers can seem to celebrate only a world already lost.

Almost entirely absent in recent working-class autobiographical narra-tives is an explicit sense of politics. Unlike the Victorian autodidact, most writers in the 1970's and 1980's did not chart a progress in politics; few were involved in any formal way in the world of politics, and few offered a cri-tique of their experiences rooted in a political understanding of them. If politics was mentioned at all, it was often little more than one of many as-pects of a lost past, fondly remembered. Jack Cummins, for example, view-ing himself as "a scholarly type," recalled reading Robert Blatchford's *Mer-rie England* and poems by William Morris. He recounted his involvement with the Independent Labour party, his membership in various anarchist groups, his friendship with suffragettes, and his role as secretary of the Cen-tral London branch of the *Daily Herald* League when it was chaired by George Lansbury.[27] And yet despite the fact that Cummins offers a vivid account of his political activities in the 1910's and 1920's, he makes no at-tempt to interpret those activities—or to connect them to any subsequent experiences in his life—rather, he merely resurrects and presents a series of isolated moments from past times. In so doing he was certainly not alone. Les Moss, another worker-writer who, like Cummins, was published by QueenSpark in Brighton, commented on the tendency for such memoirs to overlook political engagement. He hoped that subsequent reminiscences published by the group might be more "politically minded" than they had been, especially because he, for one, "did not just want to reminisce."[28]

Most worker-writers of the 1970's and 1980's, unlike Moss, were con-tent merely to reminisce. The stories they told about the working-class past are all exercises in "thick description," to borrow from Clifford Geertz, ac-counts of the minutiae of a vanished way of life. Their focus is always on the concrete, the mundane, the ordinary—neighborhood ties, street life, school days, the corner shop, laundry day, local entertainments, shopping, and the like. They are, in short, archaeologies of the particular and excavations of the densities of everyday life in the traditional working-class community. Wallace Brereton, for example, described in detail the rhythms of daily life in the Salford community where he grew up between the wars: the rituals of wash day, childhood street games, school adventures, going to the corner shop, trips away to Blackpool, and the visits of tradesmen, who added "colour and character to the scene."[29] Chapter titles in these works reflect their emphasis on the ordinary and everyday: Arthur Potts, in his recollections of life in the industrial suburbs of Manchester, entitled two of his chapters "Everyday Life" and "Local Characters"; Alice Cordelia Davis included in her account of life in Peckham reflections on "Everyday Life at Home"; likewise, Albert Paul's study included sections on "Our Spare Time" and "Street Life."[30] So important was the focus on the local neighborhood in these works that, after a short digression on Sunday outings, Richard Heaton, in his account of life in interwar Salford, felt the need to "get back to everyday happenings" in the vicinity of home.[31]

All these studies detail the physical and spatial fabric of traditional working-class communities and stress the importance of place in conferring meaning on the lives that were once lived in them. Indeed, they are organized entirely around a sense of place; for their authors, place had become a vital container of memories, and it is, consequently, the experience of living in a particular place—a street, a small neighborhood—that is remembered and described. By contrast, very little attention is paid to the experience of work. Although Centerprise published a two-volume collection of reminiscences entitled *Working Lives: A People's Autobiography of Hackney* (1976–77), in which individuals recounted their occupational experiences, the focus in virtually all the autobiographies published by such organizations in the 1970's and 1980's was a "topology of community" rather than of work.[32]

Most of the communities that are the focus of these topological writings in the 1970's and 1980's are frozen in time and studied synchronically, not diachronically. While the classic nineteenth-century autodidact narrative charts the author's movement through time, there is little sense of time as an organizing principle in any of these works. Instead, incidents in the past are often recounted randomly, incidents that point to the texture of everyday life in a now distant past in which chronological change seemed wholly absent. In his reflections, for example, Albert Paul has no way of connecting his anecdotes and thus simply lets his readers know when he wants to move from one story to the next: "I'll tell you a little interesting story about my young brother . . ."; "Here are two more family stories . . ."; "Here are two of the games we used to play . . ."; "And now to a different subject. . . ."[33] Other writers find different ways of moving from one story to another, but the result is always the same—the addition of one incident to another in such a way that the resulting study ends up offering "a slice of a very full life," as QueenSpark described one of its volumes.[34] One consequence of such anecdotal stockpiling is the abruptness with which these autobiographical reminiscences often end. Marriage, entry into the workforce, movement away from the old neighborhood, the advent of war—these events bring change to life as experienced in the community and are always the excuse to stop the flow of reminiscences. Change comes; anecdotes cease. Paul ends his narrative with the advent of the First World War, writing, "I now come to the end of the ten years of excitement and poverty, having done my best to put into words the happenings and the life our parents and us children endured"; A. S. Jasper closes his account with his own marriage and his father's death, concluding, "At this point in my life, I end the present narrative"; Bert Healey abruptly stops with the outbreak of the Second World War: "I really was very happy and had some wonderful times until the war started and I signed up. Ah well, that's another story."[35]

For many worker-writers in the 1970's and 1980's the Second World War was indeed "another story," and a good number of them end their reminiscences suddenly in the 1940's. The war often became the divide that severed the past from the present and allowed them to isolate a world temporally distinct from the one in which they now lived, a world remembered through writing. Sometimes they merely described the lost world of the interwar working-class community, recounting in detail incidents from their own lives and experiences that took place in those communities. More often than not, however, they did so nostalgically, evoking a past that was not only lost but mourned. Past and present were contrasted, the latter found wanting: "There are now no small communities with local churches but soul-less high rise flats and plastic shopping centres. We are the losers," wrote Barbara Vaughan; "Neighbours now live in a world of pills, tranquillised and double glazed, insulated from the ever present roar of traffic," complained Jo Barnes. "How can we say we have advanced . . . ?" asked Bert Healey, comparing the "bad old days" with today; "I'd willingly go back to them today if it were possible."[36] This sense of loss was conveyed in moving terms by the individuals who were brought together by Centerprise in the mid-1970's to reminisce about their former lives on what they called "the Island," a small neighborhood of five streets, covering some seven acres, in Clapton, in the London borough of Hackney. This was the traditional working-class community par excellence, and its ex-residents lamented its demise. "The Island was marvellous," recalled one of them fondly: "Life will never be the same again. We all used to help one another. We were all like a family concern."[37] Despite the fact that "the Island" was demolished to make way for a new housing estate as late as 1970—and that many of those interviewed lived there until they were evicted—those who spoke nostalgically about the past focused almost entirely on the interwar years: of the fifteen whose reminiscences were published, only three spoke to any extent about life on "the Island" after 1945.

Tacitly organized around a positive evaluation of the past—even to the point of mythologizing that past—these works romanticized life in the traditional working-class community and lamented the loss of those forms of sociability that supposedly existed in the old neighborhoods.[38] In this they were very much unlike the majority of working-class autobiographies published in the nineteenth century. According to David Vincent, the prevailing tone of these earlier works was considerably more optimistic: they were "founded on a sense of progress," and their authors attacked "any tendency to romanticize the past."[39] This is not to say, however, that nostalgia is a characteristic only of recent working-class autobiographical writing. As Regenia Gagnier has noted, many nineteenth- and early twentieth-century rural laborers, itinerant entertainers, and vagrants—along with domestic servants between the wars—lamented the changes they witnessed taking place around them and wrote in order to preserve memories of a way of life that was changing or had already ceased to be. Their writing—like so much of that discussed in this essay—was often "unstructured, thematically arbitrary," and full of "disconnected anecdotes" about the past.[40] Nevertheless, nostalgia was characteristic of only one of many strands of working-class autobiographical writing in the nineteenth century; by contrast, it was ubiquitous in the accounts of the past narrated by worker-writers in the 1970's and 1980's.

Nostalgia for the nation's preindustrial past, for its pastoral qualities and for a way of life supposedly undermined by the coming of industry, has been a major feature of British writing since at least the late eighteenth century. The classic examples of rural nostalgia include William Cobbett's *Rural Rides* (1830) and Flora Thompson's "Lark Rise" trilogy, published just over a century later. Coupled with those important mid-twentieth century tributes to the nation's so-called organic community—*Culture and Environment* by F. R. Leavis and Denys Thompson, and *Pandaemonium* by Humphrey Jennings, among others—these works locate the enduring qualities of the nation in a series of values that are always to be found else-where, in an increasingly distant past.[41] So, too, do the working-class auto-biographies discussed here, studies that discover in the traditional commu-nities a way of life that is lost but not forgotten. Historians have often dis-cussed the prevalence of rural nostalgia in Britain, but these texts exhibit a form of "industrial nostalgia" that is equally as powerful and evocative of a sense of loss as are those texts associated with the decline of rural ways of life. As we have seen, they were written during a period of massive social and economic dislocation; indeed, most of them were written in the 1970's and early 1980's, a period characterized by high unemployment, unprece-dented rates of inflation, the so-called Winter of Discontent (1978–79), and the decline of the nation's traditional industries. Small wonder, then, that such works contrast the past favorably with the present. But those contrasts could not be made by members of a younger generation who bore the full brunt of the economic malaise of the period and had no personal experience of the "good old days." In 1980, Bristol Broadsides set out to record the lives of local working-class youths. A picture of unmitigated despair was the result.[42] For an older generation, the industrial past had become an asset against which subsequent loss could be measured; for a younger genera-tion, "dole queue rock" was a protest against the present, a belligerent as-sertion of support for the Sex Pistols' cry of "No Future!" and a prophylac-tic against the sugar-coated pill of parental nostalgia.

Experience, Memory, and Heritage

Working-class autobiographies published in the 1970's and 1980's of-fered their readers stories of the past—often nostalgic in nature—and en-gaged in reconstructing the traditional working-class community. But they were complicated products of the present, embedded in a system of pro-duction and circulation that made them very different from much of the testimony of nineteenth-century worker-writers. First and foremost, they differed insofar as they were published—and often written to be published. By contrast, many of the autobiographical fragments we have from workers in the nineteenth century were not. In addition, they circulated widely in the communities where they were written. Some 3,500 to 13,000 copies of Centerprise's early titles were printed, many of which were used in schools.[43] They also found an enthusiastic readership among older people, "for whom the authors conjure up vivid memories," as one of the flyers for QueenSpark put it. As a consequence, they often elicited other reminiscences of the working-class past and helped give expressive form to those reminiscences. As A. S. Jasper noted in *A Hoxton Childhood*, when he initially published some of his reflections about the local past, he received many letters from readers that told "of similar memories and similar experiences."[44] Memories begat other memories, the result being a collective staging of the working-class past by individuals who rediscovered their identity in that past.

These reminiscences also differed from their nineteenth-century counterparts in that they were seldom the product of one individual's solitary writing. While nineteenth-century autobiographies were usually written alone, by candlelight, in time snatched from the job, these works were often highly collaborative ventures, the result of the interaction of worker-writers and middle-class activists and intellectuals. Although Stephen Yeo, a historian at the University of Sussex and a founding member of QueenSpark in Brighton, argued that local history projects should reclaim "lived experience" and "let people speak for themselves," what appeared in print was rarely the unmediated voice of the people.[45] Take, for example, the reminiscences recounted in *The Island*. The project began when members of the local community took their story to Centerprise. The community center then mounted a small exhibition of photographs of the neighborhood and placed a call for further information in the *Hackney Gazette*. The circle of contacts widened, discussions were held with ex-residents of "the Island," reminiscences were taped, and a book was produced that was the work of many hands. The QueenSpark collective that produced *Live and Learn*, by Les Moss, described a similar process. First, eight people asked Moss a series of questions about his life and taped his responses; the tapes were transcribed (by another group); a group of ten people (including the author) then edited the transcripts; finally, the author was read the resulting manuscript and made final changes to it. The collective responsible for Moss's book argued that it was "his" book, insofar as it was an account of his experiences, and "our" book, insofar as "we" put his words in an order that made them flow.[46]

Such complexities of production raise the question of *whose* stories, exactly, we are reading when we read the stories of the working-class past published by local projects such as QueenSpark and Centerprise. Richard Gray addressed this issue in recounting his role at the Peckham Publishing Project in South London. Employed by this collective, Gray helped to establish the local People's History group and served as its "convenor"—a role, he suggested, usually played by "a middle-class intellectual like me."

Gray noted the inherent tensions in such a position. He said that his interest in local history came both from a desire to discover his roots in the class from which his family originated and from his socialist commitments. But he then said that he was an outsider, set apart from those with whom he worked because of his education and skills. This, he added, "makes for an apparent contradiction" and, for some people, "undermines the credibility of our achievement."[47] Few community-publishing workers were as self-reflective as this in print. But it is abundantly clear that working-class autobiographies published by local history projects were shaped by the enthusiasms, concerns, and nostalgic investments of the officers who assisted local worker-writers. Most of them, like Gray, were part of a particular intellectual and social formation—working-class or lower-middle-class in origin and politically on the left—that was crucial to the development of cultural studies in the 1960's and 1970's. One of them suggested that published reminiscences should reflect the lives of "ordinary" people, adding that the best works were those in "which a particular individual's experience could clarify, express with precision, stand for and carry the weight of the typical and common experiences of a much larger group of people."[48] His concern with the "ordinary," the "typical," and the "common" was real enough, but his specific understanding of these terms informed what he believed was worth noting.

In the early 1980's a debate raged about the nature of this relationship between the conveners of local history projects and the individuals whose stories they elicited and helped to produce. It was part of a debate with an older history on the left, concerning how one connected serious intellectual analysis and socialist understanding with the more commonsensical and spontaneous ideas of workers themselves. In the 1980's what was at stake was the very meaning of these autobiographical projects. For their enthusiasts, they empowered people to share their personal experiences of the past, emphasized the crucial importance of experience as a form of historical knowledge, and offered valuable lessons in the practices of cultural production.[49] For their critics, by contrast, such projects were limiting, because they rarely encouraged any analysis of the experience captured. Instead, they made a fetish of inconsequential detail and operated on the naive assumption that working-class experience would somehow lead to socialist, or protosocialist, forms of understanding.[50] Ultimately, the entire debate revolved around the value of working-class experience—the importance, to return to Jack Common's critique of George Orwell, of working-class representations of working-class life. But in focusing on the value of such experience, this debate seldom addressed the ways in which it was actually constituted through the various local history projects and community-publishing ventures. It is not enough to say that the facilitators who worked for the local history projects merely authorized the reminiscences of others; we must think of them as "speaking through the workers' testimony, ventriloquising a discourse which is not theirs."[51]

It is now commonplace to suggest that oral histories "draw on general cultural repertoires . . . which help to determine what may be said, how and to what effect."[52] This is certainly apparent in the published stories of the working-class past written (largely) by worker-writers in the 1970's and 1980's. If those stories can best be characterized by their emphasis on experience, this is in part because so many others made a point at the time of extolling the virtues of experience. If they focused on the daily rituals of street life in the traditional working-class community, this is in part because such a focus was the central feature of the most popular representation of that community available at the time they were written, *Coronation Street*. If they are saturated by nostalgia for the social life of a vanishing world, this is in part because so many scholarship boys and girls—some of whom helped to produce these stories—had, from the 1950's to the 1970's, from Richard Hoggart to Jeremy Seabrook, already cast the traditional working-class community in nostalgic terms.

This last point cannot be overemphasized. These stories were written at a time when a series of settled images of the working-class past had already been consolidated, images that were often the work of those individuals who were most eager to champion authentic working-class experience. Moreover, those who encouraged worker-writers to reminisce were themselves emotionally invested in the values of community life that were now being resurrected in writing.[53] When Orwell wrote about hop picking in Kent, he focused less on community than on the ways in which hop pickers were exploited by their employers. When, in 1991, by contrast, London women and their families reminisced about their work in the fields of Kent in *Our Lovely Hops*, they concentrated, often in detail and with much emotional investment, on the important sense of community they had once shared.[54] The decline of community—and the nostalgia for community—had become central to the ways in which the working-class past was narrated in such works. It was, in short, an organizing principle of remembrance that united worker-writers with those who both encouraged them in their reminiscences and urged them to contrast their experiences with the story of hop picking told more than fifty years earlier by Orwell.

In recent years, community publishers and local history projects have focused less on recording the experience of life in the traditional working-class community than they once did. In part, their very success has led them into new territory. For example, the Ethnic Communities Oral History Project has helped foster a growing multiculturalism in community publishing, resulting in works that include *The Motherland Calls: African-Caribbean Experiences* (1989) and *Chinese Liverpudlians* (1989). In 1992, QueenSpark published *Daring Hearts: Lesbian and Gay Lives of '50s and '60s Brighton*, in part hoping to introduce issues of sexuality and gender into the popular reminiscences that remain a staple of community publishing. These more recent works still focus on the importance of experience, but the experience is often that of very different groups of people, whose lives, by necessity, are recounted through very different narrative conventions. Immigrant stories are cast not as tales of loss and subsequent nostalgia, but as accounts of struggle, of attempts to survive in a cold and often hostile climate. Likewise, the lesbians and gay men who recall the past in *Daring Hearts* do so ambivalently; the traditional working-class community recalled with warmth elsewhere is portrayed here in less glowing terms.

The extent to which community publishers now encourage individuals who were barely recognized twenty-five years ago to recount their pasts tells us a good deal about the dwindling fortunes of "old" labor in Tony Blair's "new" Britain. Meanwhile, white working-class experience, of the kind discussed in this essay, has found a new home in the heritage industry. From the Blists Hill Open Air Museum in Shropshire, to the North of England Open Air Museum at Beamish, in County Durham, to the Wigan Pier Heritage Centre in Lancashire, the experience of the working-class past has been packaged anew.[55] Those images of the past conjured up by worker-writers in the 1970's and 1980's—images that built upon and contributed to the way we understand the "truth" of the traditional working-class community—have shaped the way the past is presented in these heritage centers. Once again, it is nostalgia for the ordinary and the everyday that characterizes the memory work being carried out, suggesting the continuing hold of the story of loss told about the working-class past. It is a story of loss in which reconnection to the past is once again sought, this time not through writing but through the assembled objects from a vanished way of life. As one enthusiast for the new heritage centers put it, discussing the Woodhorn Colliery Museum, the exhibits displayed there "stir memories. . . . These few surviving objects, once ordinary and everyday, sit all neat and tidy in the typical kitchen and the pit settings keep us in touch with the past."[56] Keeping us in touch with the past was also what those reminiscences discussed here were all about. For many it seemed a necessary pursuit, because, as Robert Roberts put it in his own account of Edwardian working-class life, a "kind of culture unlikely to rise again had gone in the rubble," and many lamented its loss.[57]

HOWARD L. MALCHOW

Nostalgia, "Heritage," and the London Antiques Trade: Selling the Past in Thatcher's Britain

The 1970's and early 1980's saw a keen and widespread interest among the British in tangible artifacts of their past. In antique shops, fairs, arcades, and street markets, period furniture, precious bijouterie and *objets de vertu* commanded a lively interest, as did common "collectibles" (especially Victoriana) of seemingly little inherent value. Indeed, the most ordinary domestic objects—horse brasses and blue-glass medicine bottles, toasting forks and pot lids[1]—apparently became talismanic objects of desire by their "heritage" associations. In an era of anxiety and social disconnection, it has been argued, almost anything could serve this need, "from the great collective features of the environment to the most trifling of souvenirs." The phenomenon was, some claim, but one aspect of a widespread "cult of nostalgia," not unique to Britain but very pronounced there, that was much commented upon (and criticized) at the time.[2]

"Heritage," as the late Raphael Samuel has reminded us, is a vague and fluid, heterogeneous concept, a "nomadic term" capable of accommodating "wildly discrepant meanings" and subject, in the 1970's and 1980's, to a kind of inflation of reference. It has also been politically pluralist.[3] A nostalgic sense of the people's or the nation's heritage (as an endangered inheritance of defining and empowering tradition or material culture) has in the past served to mobilize both radicalism and establishment, both the left and the right, and can embrace and idealize either cottage or stately home. A polymorphous thing of continuity and change, it demands an historical reading that searches for critical shifts in time and specific social locations.

"Heritage" surfaced as an overtly political issue in 1974 when Labour's proposed tax on wealth (targeting personal property) inspired Hugh Legatt, a London fine-art dealer, to found the lobby "Heritage in Danger."

For Legatt and many of his friends the threat was to their trade: it was a matter of *"Collecting* in Danger," as a supportive editorial in the trade journal *Antique Collector*, as well as a trade memorandum to the Parliamentary Committee on the Wealth Tax, made explicit.[4] Nevertheless, the movement quickly found allies beyond the commercial-arts world. The year 1975 was designated European Architectural Heritage Year. This, and Roy Strong's "polemical" exhibition at the Victoria and Albert Museum,[5] "The Destruction of the Country House 1875–1975," helped focus the threat on the most visible locus of "heritage" collections, the stately homes still in private hands. (Labour also proposed to close inheritance-tax loopholes with a new capital-transfer tax.) By late 1975 the arts-trade interest was largely submerged into a broader but politically more partisan lobby, "SAVE Our Heritage," with a one-nation, country-Tory message. Though the wealth tax faltered in committee, predictions of pending losses to the nation seemed confirmed by the sale of Mentmore Towers and its manifold "treasures" in 1977.

If the "heritage preservation" movement of the 1970's had its origins as a concern of the commercial-arts trade, the metropolitan arts institutions, architectural antiquarians, a defensive traditional elite, and backbench anti-socialists, its message appealed strongly to a substantial part of the middle-class, country-house-visiting public. A million signatures to an anti–wealth tax petition were gathered in country houses open to the public in 1975.[6] Throughout the 1970's, National Trust visiting (and membership) surged dramatically.[7] In the early 1980's English Heritage, the Department of the Environment's quango to run public monuments, and—down-market—the more commercial theme parks and popular "family entertainment" centers, such as that created at Warwick Castle in 1981 by its new owners, Madame Tussaud's, explored this popular market for what came to be called, usually derisively, the "heritage industry." They, and the older, established institutions as well—from the V&A to the British Museum, or, with its on-site souvenir shops, the National Trust—also began to offer, as did the upper end of the high-street department stores, a host of replica items to a public wanting to acquire simulacra of a (highly selective) past aesthetic.

The cult of nostalgia from the 1960's to the 1980's and the "heritage industry" that is associated with it have been the subjects of close and usually critical examination. Indeed, by the early 1990's, when the discipline of cultural studies took up the core issue of the representation and reproduction of the past embedded in the heritage movement, one could speak of an academic "heritage-*baiting* industry."[8] Raphael Samuel devoted much of his last work to attacking with surprising acerbity what he believed to be the inherent snobbery (even envy and misogyny) of this (usually left-wing) journalistic and academic assault on a significant part of contemporary popular culture. While his apparent animus against postmodern theory and cultural studies may vitiate some of the force of his attack, Samuel did expose major weaknesses of the antiheritage critique—its emotive and partisan 1980's engagement with Thatcherism, its crude generalizations and ready theorizing, the lack, indeed, of a workable definition for "heritage" itself, a dubious sociology about the manipulation of popular culture by elites, and a lack of interest in authentic, popular sources for the "energies and strength" of the heritage movement.[9] This essay will attempt to refocus the debate by moving away from the issue that has preoccupied much antiheritage criticism—the *interpretation* of history as a crude right-wing project or strategy offered by heritage centers and theme parks—toward an exploration of the "popular roots" of one sector of the heritage industry that nevertheless suggests a significant relationship with the political and economic gospel of the new right.

The past as commodity had long been available to collectors in the West End shops of the London antiques trade. Stefan Methusias has located the origins of the modern antiques market, aimed at the modest collector and bourgeois home decorator rather than the wealthy connoisseur, in the late nineteenth century.[10] But if potential middle-class demand continued to expand thereafter, changing taste—beginning perhaps with an elite reaction against Victorianism and Ruskinian arts and crafts in the interwar years and aggressive modernism in interior design after the Second World War—served to limit the popular attractions of "antiques." This trend, however, was dramatically reversed in Britain from the late 1960's, and the antiques market expanded explosively in the 1970's and 1980's. A closer look at this sector of enterprise culture will allow us to probe the idea of heritage nostalgia more deeply, at both its consumption and its production ends, and further to explore at a popular level the odd interconnectedness of past and future, of heritage and enterprise, in the era of Thatcherite reconstruction.[11]

The London antiques trade occupies a peculiar position. On the one hand, it often seems to have promoted a snob aesthetic that by the early 1980's was, ironically perhaps, attractive to the newly prosperous, socially mobile, self-consciously meritocratic, and often Thatcherite salaried class with new homes to decorate[12]—if not with costly genuine antiques, then with reproduction furniture and "antiqued" artifacts, "a curious phenomenon" especially of this era.[13] But the country-gentry style (with its Aga ranges and Laura Ashley fabrics) or the gauzy-curtained Raj-rattan look would seem to enshrine just what Thatcher herself derisively condemned and dismissed as the "museum society," the "piled up lumber from Britain's past" that kept the country down.[14] On the other hand, the antiques trade, largely unregulated, marked by an extreme entrepreneurial individualism, and responding to a striking opportunity provided not only by the expanding domestic market but by wildly burgeoning jet tourism, was a model of the sort of service-sector enterprise that the new right embraced and encouraged. This was as true of the ethics as it was of the structure of a trade that, at least at the lower, small-shop and street-market end, celebrated a make-a-buck-quick mentality in an environment where the "Victorian value" of caveat emptor ruled. The fact that the trade appeared to be often in the hands of a new breed of young dealer with a looser sense of professional ethics, eager to ship off "heritage" items en masse to American buyers,[15] seems to have a parallel in other growth sectors (in, say, finance and insurance) and to highlight inherent ambiguities within Thatcherism itself—which endorsed patriotism and a return to national greatness while pursuing policies that made Britain more vulnerable to multinational corporatism and denigrated "social" values, Victorian or otherwise.

A Tory Nostalgia?

Driven, in part, by exploding demand, the 1970's "antiques" market redefined just what the commerce in past commodities might legitimately entail. It did this by abandoning the trade's "hundred-year" rule, offering even very recent styles as collectible, and by extending the definition of chic from objects of elegance, rarity, craftsmanship, and precious material to the commonest mass-produced goods, to evocative kitsch. But evocative of what?

It can be argued that the anxious and entropic climate of the mid-1970's, the "Ice Age" of Margaret Drabble's 1976 novel, compelled a nostalgic reading of artifacts of the past, a reading that was powerfully coded as a particularly *Tory* form of nostalgia—a flight from modernism-read-as-socialism. In fact, of course, the mainstream antiques market had long before this depended upon a degree of nostalgic sentimentality. For the modestly well-off, salaried middle class, this was, however, complicatedly entwined with a sensible view that good antiques might be "better value" than shoddy modern goods, as well as with whatever satisfaction the collecting of status objects—especially if they were "bargains"—might hold. This was the audience from the late 1960's for Arthur Negus, the avuncular antiques expert of BBC-1's "Going for a Song" (1968–73, 1976), an audience that grew in the early Thatcher years to over thirteen million viewers for the follow-up "Antiques Roadshow" (from 1979).[16] A question is not whether there was a popular sense of nostalgic identity and national heritage involved in the trade—clearly there was—but how this might newly relate to both traditional and new-right conservatism.[17] There can be, of course, no simple relationship between popular culture and emerging or ascendant political ideology. Those antiheritage commentators of the 1980's who saw in the heritage industry merely an attempt to *impose* either traditional or Thatcherite values and interpretations were admittedly insensitive to the quite complicated dialogue—an often mutual process of transforming and enabling—that exists between "everyday life" and political ideology.[18]

When the Conservatives came to power in 1979, the heritage-preservation lobby, which owed much of its initiative and support to backbench and constituency Tory activists, looked to reap its reward. Labour's proposed wealth tax was dead. An early measure of the new government was in fact the National Heritage Act (1980), which established the Memorial Fund to help save future Mentmores for the nation. In 1983 a second National Heritage Act allowed Michael Heseltine's Department of the Environment to turn the keeping of state-owned heritage properties over to an Historic Buildings and Ancient Monuments Commission ("English Heritage"), with the National Trust as its model. And the next year the new chancellor, Nigel Lawson, allowed the Memorial Fund to be used to help the National Trust dramatically "save" Calke Abbey.

This record conceals, however, a considerable tension within Tory circles over the fundamental understanding of "heritage" and how best to preserve whatever it might be for the nation. This was a microcosm of the more general struggle between the traditional one-nation Toryism of those whom Thatcher derisively labeled the "wets" and the new right's free-enterprise ideologues chiefly intent on dismantling socialism. From the beginning there was little chance that the Memorial Fund would be supported with really substantial revenues, or that public museums and galleries would find any relief from the economies imposed by Denis Healey's regime. Quite the reverse.

The government was committed to private, not public, ownership. And Heseltine, at this time still "one of us," was more interested in privatizing state properties than in preserving them as perpetual objects of stewardship. English Heritage, if it could not be shunted into the private sector, was expected to begin to pay its way, to impose admission charges, promote its leisure amenities, and "move into the tourist business."[19] Nor was Calke Abbey, the most tangible victory for the preservationists in the early 1980's, anything like a Mentmore Towers. Significantly, as Patrick Wright has argued,[20] it was not a building of historical or architectural importance or full of precious paintings and fine antiques, but "a little piece of England," essentially a private house full of domestic "junk"—just, of course, the kind of everyday objects that in the 1970's had begun to command increasing interest in the lower end of the London antiques trade.[21] This may, of course, be seen as a democratization of the idea of heritage—ordinary things from the past lives of ordinary people rather than rare museum pieces. But as a receptacle of private property, of mere common *commodities* (advertising labels intact), Calke Abbey—like Brodsworth Hall, another "mothballed" repository more recently acquired by English Heritage—can also be seen as symbolizing a particularly Thatcherite idea of democracy. It was not so much a "document of social history" as a shrine to commodity culture, symbolic of a political-economic egalitarianism—Everyman as consumer—that was entirely appropriate to the credit boom of the early 1980's. A logical extension of this sense of heritage-as-commodity was oddly articulated a few years later by the new "marketing manager" of the most important museum in the country when he declared that the V&A should be seen "as the Harrods of the museum world."[22]

What of the prime minister herself? Early in 1983, the year of the second National Heritage Act, and a year after she had mobilized the rhetoric of history and nostalgia in the Falklands War, Thatcher adopted and reiterated the phrase "Victorian values" as a leitmotif of that year's election campaign. This reflects, inevitably, a highly selective, at times contradictory, invocation of history and tradition. It raises the question—one that both Peter Mandler and Raphael Samuel have touched upon—of the extent to which the New Tory gestures toward heritage preservation, as well as Thatcher's own rhetorical invocation of historic national virtues, may have been a *politique* accommodation of the demotic nostalgia "that had spread deep and wide in the culture . . . well beyond public policy" in the 1970's.[23]

In fact, Thatcher was able to use history and nostalgia as weapons against both the "socialist" opposition and the grandees of her own party—just as Baldwin (perhaps more her model than has been appreciated) had done in the 1920's and 1930's—by emphasizing a particular middle-class historical reading of "national" virtues, those of hard work, thrift, independence, patriotism, and family values. This counterpoised an image of a traditional Britain of self-discipline and personal morality to one of miners' strikes, football hooliganism, and rioting in the streets.[24]

Some have seen such rhetoric as a kind of "double-coding" that allowed the new right to sound traditionalist while concealing the deep disjunction with the past that their American-style enterprise ideology entailed, of disguising a program for the future as a narrative of the past.[25] Rather than simple strategies to obscure and disguise, however, Thatcherism's historical glosses in fact reflect a sense of the past that can be said to have grown very widely in popular culture from at least the late 1960's. Like the collectible past frozen in posed Victorian family photographs, it is a kind of history that relates directly to the commodities found in the antiques markets of the 1970's or in BBC prop rooms — that is, it is a history fixed as *things*, shorn of dynamic process, ready to be picked over for illustrating heritage myths and heritage morality. This is history seen from the antiques marketplace, where the past *is* its physical detritus — commodities stripped of social relations in their production or use.

For the traditional right, "heritage" was necessarily an ambiguous and highly selective concept. Its utility (for, say, those who lived in country houses and enjoyed their "national" treasures) lay in a fluidity and intangibility that served to justify, through the ideas of "stewardship" and (perhaps) public access, an historically "British" hierarchy of taste and, not incidentally, class distinction. For the *new* right however, heritage, like Britain itself, was more literally a property, a tangible asset, a sum of things, like the wealth John Major saw "cascading down the generations," to be possessed (or, as with the Falkland Islands, repossessed). As Thatcher said, looking back from 1992: "We *reclaimed* our heritage."[26]

Selling Heritage: The London Antiques Trade

The compelling populist ideal of the ascendant new right was that of a property-owning (house-owning, share-owning) democracy. If, in the world of antiques, "heritage" is reduced to collectible objects, then the antiques trade was a perfect Thatcherite enterprise — promising a democracy of heritage ownership. When David Coombs, editor of the trade's oldest and most established journal, *Antique Collector*, lent his support to the heritage-preservation, anti–wealth tax lobby in the mid- and late 1970's, he was at pains to justify *private* collecting of fine art and antiques as beneficial to the nation: "Every antique we buy and cherish . . . makes a contribution to the maintenance and improvement of the nation's total heritage. This is not yet properly recognized."[27] In fact, however, antiques dealers (as opposed to taxpaying antiques collectors) were likely to be of two minds about the anti–wealth tax campaign: on the one hand they did not want potential buyers deterred from collecting, or the market swamped with goods put up for sale to pay tax; on the other, they naturally looked forward to a market made lively by the increased circulation of goods otherwise locked up in private collections. Nor did many of them share much concern for the "threat" posed by the "loss" of Britain's heritage to the United States—a trade in which they looked to do quite well.[28]

The rhetoric of Coombs's monthly editorials in the decade after 1975 offers ample evidence of other contradictions. His own sentiments were clearly traditionalist and hierarchic—"art is not and never can be, democratic. By definition its creation and appreciation at the higher levels are elitist."[29] He struggled in the pages of his journal to maintain an image of the refined, educated, heritage-loving, aesthetic, and essentially upper-class collector (a characterization no doubt flattering to his readership), but it was an image that seems increasingly out of touch with the reality of the antiques market. In his effort to attach the world of the collector to that of the country house, in the stewardship of heritage, he was driven to deny, then attack and bemoan what was patently undeniable by the late 1970's—that, at one end, the collecting passion of the suburban classes might say more about acquisitiveness and status than about heritage and taste, and, at the other, among the rich, collecting was increasingly motivated by attempts to avoid tax, beat inflation, and score a speculative profit. It was this wealthy but often art-illiterate buyer who drew Coombs's particular ire: the "creative role of the collector has been obscured by the ridiculous 'art as investment' craze of recent years"; "As a matter of definite policy this magazine does not support the idea of art as an investment."[30] The fine-arts salesrooms, he thought, had within the recent past been transformed "from the preserve of professional dealers and a few dedicated collectors into a kind of huge lottery for everyman," inadvertently attracting "the malign attention of the taxman to the genuine collector."[31]

Though others, like the art-and-antiques columnist in the *Sunday Telegraph* Deborah Stratton, might occasionally echo these sentiments ("Greed affects every aspect of the art and antiques market"),[32] the fact was that such motives—fright at high inflation and uncertainty about the stock and property markets—did play some role in driving the antiques trade to ever higher levels of volume and profit. In the depth of a recession, in 1974–75,

Christie's total sales for "antiques" rose sevenfold (to £1,780,000),[33] and in the following years, just when it seemed that the collecting mania had peaked, that "the euphoria was over,"[34] trade activity would climb to ever new heights. In 1979, in the midst of that "winter of discontent," Coombs himself could write that "the antiques and art market has seldom if ever been so prosperous: money is rapidly becoming the market."[35]

There were dangers of course both for the dealer and for the investor in a trade that was highly volatile. Indeed, there were sharp reverses in the 1980's, when the upward spiral of prices and volume was checked, but there proved to be an underlying strength. Many in the trade and its press organs would have found Coombs's head-shaking in the midst of such prosperity oddly out of step with the interests of "the industry." *Antique Collector*'s junior rival, the weekly *Art and Antiques*, endorsed collecting as an investment and recommended a new publication like *Alternative Investment Report* as filling "a need in the antiques world."[36]

Most of the general trade magazines (there were twenty or so in the field, and many more specialist journals) did attempt to reach out to what they and their advertisers identified as the most significant new readership, not the wealthy investor but the new acquisitive democracy, relatively well-off suburban bargain hunters galvanized by television and radio antiques shows and motivated by a combination of status seeking, cupidity, and heritage nostalgia. This was the market for a host of publications like the price manuals prepared by the Antiques Collectors' Club or Lyle's pocket guides. As early as 1970 *The Listener* had added a regular column on antiques by Arthur Negus, and most of the broadsheets included columns on collecting from time to time during the 1970's. In 1975 *Antique Collector* began the "startling innovation" of including prices for items it illustrated. Subsequently it ran regular columns on where to find "good buys." In the late 1970's and early 1980's it offered an advice column on home decoration, another on how new collectors could spot fakes and forgeries, special offers (at special prices) of "fine reproduction" ware, antiques holidays where the uninitiated could be lectured in the arcane science of identifying bargains, and (by the early 1980's) credit schemes which (at high interest rates) could provide up to £1,000 to those who had not quite put enough by for that great find:

> You might browse for months looking for a particular print, a jug, a piece of silver or a Chippendale chair and then suddenly see it—just as you've paid the school bills or come back from holiday. Now you can buy it at once—and pay through the Antique Collector Credit Plan, without worry. . . . No longer need you wait until you have saved up the cash.[37]

If the consumer-credit boom of the early 1980's—an unintended by-product of Thatcher's deregulationist policies—did contribute to a surge in the demand for antiques (though it is difficult to distinguish domestic from foreign buying), the antiques trade was a service-sector economy that had been rapidly expanding with only minor hiccups for more than a decade, and in the face of the deepest postwar recession. Speculation about the growth of the antiques market has usually centered on demand factors, especially the increases in tourism and a suburban class motivated by television and radio shows that demystified the arts and antiques market. But there were also changes in the structure of the trade that pushed along demand, besides responding to it. Most notable was the rapid development in London, from the mid-1960's, of selling beyond the traditional shops. At the top end, there was the increased volume of business done by the great auction houses like Christie's and Sotheby's and the growing importance of the annual antiques "fairs" in prestigious locations like Burlington House or the Grosvenor House Hotel. At the other end, and perhaps more significant for the demotic increase in the trade, was the swift growth of arcades like Antiquarius and Camden Passage and street markets like those at Bermondsey and, far more important, Portobello Road.

The fashionable, expensively organized, slickly advertised fairs, with their royal or aristocratic patronage, catered to the wealthy buyer—often from overseas—and to those who responded to their considerable "snob element."[38] By the late 1970's the London season for these extravaganzas extended from early spring to autumn. Of the major fairs (Burlington House, Chelsea, Olympia, and Grosvenor House), that at the Grosvenor House Hotel, one of the oldest (from 1934), was arguably the most prestigious and often commanded the largest turnover. (Sales of over £10 million were reported for the 1983 season.)[39]

The apparent success of the fairs in drawing international buyers to London, as a minor if expanding export sector that boomed while others faltered, helped fuel growing claims that this aspect of the heritage industry was integral to the future economic health of a trading nation—a way of neatly turning a liability ("the museum society") into an asset. The fairs were the most visible, respectable, and successful face of antiques entrepreneurship (though dealers often complained that the storied profits at Burlington House or Grosvenor House were very unequally enjoyed or greatly exaggerated). Early Thatcherism embraced them, oddly perhaps, given the traditional, mandarin feel of these well-patroned occasions. The libertarian new right responded positively, however, to the unregulated entrepreneurship of this particular export sector, while to many the idea of the state blocking export of important heritage goods as a matter of course in order to enable public institutions to pick them up at knockdown prices seemed difficult to defend. And in the summer of 1979, just weeks after the formation of the first Thatcher government, the new right had further ground to sympathize. The Grosvenor House Antiques Fair, due to be opened by Prince Philip, was canceled at short notice because of "union action." Chambermaids at the hotel had gone on strike; the workers setting up the exhibition refused to cross their picket line and walked out in sympathy. Coombs railed in the next edition of *Antique Collector* against "intimidation" directed "against society as a whole" and urged the need to "hold firm, stand guard" in the face of a "common enemy."[40]

Though the Grosvenor House Fair remained closed for two years, its prestigious counterpart at Burlington House thrived with prime-ministerial support. In 1980, because of remaining difficulties, the two fairs were combined at the Royal Academy and opened by Margaret Thatcher, who held forth on the need people felt to "live with something whose beauty exceeds its utilitarian value" as an antidote to "the silicon chip age." She then proceeded through the fair, asking "sharp questions" of dealers specializing in the porcelain she herself collected. Subsequently her husband, Denis, opened the Chelsea Antiques Fair in September, though less assertively: "I like everything my wife likes."[41]

What Margaret Thatcher liked, in particular, were objects that were, she said, "reminders of the achievements of past ages." As in her highly selective reading of history in general, the antiques she enjoyed most were heritage with a message—the Worcester pieces she owned represented a particularly *British* (*sic*) creativity. Free-trade Cobden (a Staffordshire piece with pink trousers)[42] held pride of place on her mantle, and figures of Nelson and Wellington were appropriate to the years of the South Atlantic task force and her assault on the Brussels bureaucrats. What drew the prime minister's interest, unsurprisingly in this most lecturing of politicians since Gladstone, was the *commemorative* (justifying) object. In March 1983 she insisted on buying the first of a limited edition of expensive bone-china figurines showing the Royal Marines raising the Union Flag in the Falklands.[43]

If the art and antiques fairs were the trade at its most elegantly posed, at that juncture of high aestheticism, heritage, and conspicuous consumption, the down-market end of arcades and street stalls represented the business at its most democratic, and it was here where the real revolution occurred from the late 1960's. The New Caledonian Market at Bermondsey was not new, but it had evolved away from its character as a typical secondhand goods fair into an important venue for specialist dealers; Camden Passage was created in the mid-1960's as "London's antique village"; by the late 1960's Antiquarius in Chelsea also offered indoor places for traders that were a step up from the street markets but much cheaper than a high-street shop; and Portobello Road was transformed by the influx of "hippie crafts," vegetarian food stalls, cannabis, and a general carnivalesque atmosphere of street entertainers and flaneurs—to the dismay, often, of the "legitimate" shop owners in the Westbourne Grove area. By the mid-1970's Portobello Road Market was twice the size it had been a decade earlier, with an indoor "Antiques Supermarket" at its central junction, and more than two thousand stallholders and shop owners.[44]

This rapid emergence of the small dealer has been seen as an inevitable response to the opportunity of rising demand, and in particular to the great growth in the tourist trade. But it also may reflect the economic difficulties facing those in the more traditional shops—with their high overhead, especially rising rents and rates.[45] A stall in an arcade or street market was relatively cheap—in 1974 as little as £8 per week for a street-stand license in the Portobello Road—and it did provide access to a larger, if less discriminating, clientele.[46] If, however, the explosion of demand evident in the crowds of buyers surging through these markets by the late 1970's was as much a result as a cause of the structural change in the London trade, it is likely that the structural change itself was less a result of traditional shop owners' being forced down-market than of the emergence of a new kind of antiques dealer, a robust, often young trader on the make, with little capital and only a small range of stock, eager for a quick turnover, with a lighter regard for "professional" ethics. Contrasting with this is the traditional image of the antiques dealer as a fond collector himself, in love with his objects, a pottering, middle-aged or elderly eccentric, rather like the stereotypical small-bookshop owner, reluctant to part with his best pieces and happy to carry on so long as he could make ends meet. This has always enshrined elements of both myth and truth, but by the 1980's perhaps more myth than truth. A successful dealer and picture-gallery owner like Gavin Graham had no such modesty when, in 1982, he told Deborah Stratton: "I'd like to be rich and have a house in Campden Hill Square."[47]

Graham himself, however, deplored what he saw as a disturbingly prevalent tendency to fraud and tax evasion among some dealers. Stories of rogues and hucksters, get-rich-quick artists, and dealers in stolen goods reach of course back into the nineteenth century—though this was commonly a complaint about the very bottom of the market, the "knockers" and "runners" and the smallest, most ephemeral shop owners. The perennial problem of rogue dealers, or more exactly of the public's suspicion that all dealers may be rogues, lay behind efforts to professionalize the trade through organizations like the prestigious British Antique Dealers' Association (BADA, founded in 1918 during a previous scare over a proposed "luxury tax") or the London and Provincial Antique Dealers' Association (LAPADA, founded in 1974, itself a product of the great expansion of the trade after the late 1960's). Both insist on a code of integrity, though the boundary between merely sharp and "unethical" practice is in fact very hazy. But they have never directly represented more than the top of the pyramid. The explosion of trade in the 1970's and 1980's at the street-market and arcade level has left most traders outside such bodies—which have, in any case, been more active in ensuring good public relations than in actually policing the market. Indeed, when, in the mid-1980's, one insider wrote a humorous exposé of illegal practices like dealers' "rings" at auctions, he was dropped from LAPADA for bringing the trade into disrepute.[48]

It has been estimated that by the mid-1980's there were something like ten thousand antiques traders in Britain, with perhaps four thousand dealers in London alone—almost certainly an underestimate.[49] Beyond these were an uncountable number who dealt from home via FAX and telephone. The large majority (perhaps 80–90%) were not members of BADA or LAPADA, or registered for Value-Added Tax (VAT). It remains to look at how this extremely diverse body can be seen to have responded to the market opportunities and "enterprise culture" of the 1970's and 1980's.

Though some could employ family money and connections to start at the top—like the ill-starred fine-art dealer Robert Fraser in the 1960's—most dealers served a period of apprenticeship to learn the trade, and even among the grand West End shops there could be found a wide spectrum of social origins. At the lower end, where little start-up capital was needed for stock (often borrowed and sold on commission or acquired on credit), selling antiques had particular attraction for young men on the make with few resources or useful connections.[50] Even before the great expansion of the trade after the late 1960's there are many examples of success from obscure backgrounds. Ronald Pearsall cites a leading dealer who was once a chauffeur in Birmingham and another who began as a dentist, while a third had been a merchant seaman.[51] Arthur Negus, who started as a modest provincial dealer in the 1920's and 1930's before moving to a large auction house and, in old age, a remarkable career on television, told the story of Ben Nyman, a prewar specialist in porcelain and objets d'art who rose from a very poor East End family to an elegant shop in Camden High Street and considerable wealth, flamboyantly displayed.[52] Or there was William Tillman, a builder's son who bred rabbits to help support his family before leaving home for London at age sixteen in 1946. Beginning in an antique shop as an untrained "restorer," he moved up into his own business, became the largest furniture restorer in the country, and by the 1960's was positioned to dominate the West End trade in the newly expanding reproduction-furniture market. In the late 1960's he switched his workshops entirely to reproductions and was, by the time *Antique Collector* interviewed him in 1983, a self-professed "self-made millionaire."[53]

With such earlier diversity of background, can one really speak of a significant change in the social world of antiques dealing in the 1970's and 1980's? The answer seems to be a cautious yes. At least there was a wide perception in the trade that a particular kind of "new blood" came in with the great explosion of numbers. For one thing, the market was much more volatile, and success (or perhaps failure) seemed to come earlier in life. *Antique Collector*'s interview pages are full of success stories about very young dealers. There is, for example, the case of Geoffrey Munn, who began in the early 1970's, aged nineteen, as a shop assistant, anticipated the booming late-1970's market in "largely unexplored" Victorian jewelry, and by 1984, at age thirty, had become a director of Wartski's, the established West End firm specializing in very expensive jewelry, Fabergé, and eighteenth-century gold boxes. Jack Ogden left school at sixteen in the mid-1960's to go into the relatively modest family jewelry trade, discovered the market for "ancient" antique jewelry, and by his early thirties had his own fashionable West End shop selling Egyptian pieces to "the intelligent rich." Or there was Francis Raeymaekers, who began in 1979 with a stall in Antiquarius dealing, at age twenty-three, in silver. He found that Americans were less diffident than the British about buying Sheffield plate, expanded a "telephone trade" with American clientele (one way of surviving the Thatcher recession of the early 1980's), and was able, still in his mid-twenties, to go "up-market"—moving to the Knightsbridge Pavilion as "A. D. C. Heritage."[54]

Beyond the youth (and sometimes prodigal lifestyle) of dealers in the late 1970's and early 1980's, there is the question of a change in the culture of dealing, especially at the lower end of the trade, where the expansion had been greatest. Again, there is a general perception of an increasing speculative, entrepreneurial element, widely commented upon by (usually older) traders themselves and those who have studied the industry. Pearsall in 1974 noted: "A type of entrepreneur has joined in, a person who is not really interested in antiques but knows the prices down to the last five pence." Chamberlin, in 1979, observed that there seemed to be a very high entry and mortality rate among contemporary dealers. In 1981, Frank Taylor, in the *Sunday Times*, echoed the complaint that "a new type of antique dealer had appeared in the last decade," one who was motivated, he suggested, by quick profit rather than a love of the objects themselves: "He knows what he likes when he's sold it." And in 1984 a dealer who had been trading for more than thirty years claimed that what had once been "a rare occupation" now attracted "instant antique dealers" with their cheaply rented "antique centre" stalls: "Now everyone wants to get into the act."[55] Such impressions are inevitably difficult to substantiate. There had always been a speculative, opportunistic side to the trade in antiques, though it is reasonable to assume that this did grow more pronounced as demand mushroomed. Inevitably, charges that there was a new kind of dealer also implied a lifestyle consistent with the increasing youthfulness especially of the lower end of the trade in an era of disco, recreational drugs, and ostentatious display.

A trade that had always had its critics came—at least a visible minority of it did—to reflect some of the worst excesses and insubstantiality of the new entrepreneurism of the Thatcher boom. In 1985 Jeremy Cooper, familiar with the arts and antiques market from the inside, painted a picture (perhaps only marginally exaggerated) of "easy money," quick turnover, buccaneers, insider dealing, and a host of shady practices—a secretive business comparable to the drug traffic, where collector-clients were hooked on goods the value of which was artificially inflated by stock-hungry dealers in a frenzy of buying and selling back and forth among themselves until the next recession, when the bubble burst: a trade where "over-valued, over-restored and over-the-top objects," luxuries no one (except the clandestine "restorer") had been paid to produce, were sold by "parasites feeding off the remains of past generations."[56]

While most established dealers would be offended by such a representation, there undoubtedly was some change in the ethical culture at the stall and small-shop level (though not only there), a shift that parallels the easier, speculative business morality of the early Thatcher years generally—though the evidence is inevitably anecdotal. There also seems to be a resonance between charges of shady practices (misrepresentation of goods, overrestoration, etc.) and a sense that, like many of the things they sold, the young dealers themselves were often not what they seemed. While many were of very modest East or South London background, affectation and a "camp" snobbery were common among them. (It helped to sell.) The most favored accent in the trade, it has been observed, was a kind of "subcounty."[57] Many dealers in fact were gay, an important subculture in the trade. Some of the younger of them embraced the liberated hedonism of the late 1970's,[58] and saw in the trade itself an entertaining theatricality ("resting" actors and overage dancers have long been drawn to the profession), enjoying perhaps the "art" of a little deception in selling over-the-top goods of doubtful provenance.

Straight or gay, this was a somewhat shadowy world,[59] with just that element of risk taking and quasi legality that some young entrepreneurs found exciting—and not just in the antiques trade, but in the most respectable City merchant banks and insurance firms of the 1980's boom years. David Coombs, unintentionally perhaps, suggested just this connection: "Whatever our other commercial weaknesses, we remain good at trading: how else could you describe banking, stock-broking or antique dealing?"[60] Even the most respectable antiques firms traditionally dealt on the unregulated margins of a particularly laissez-faire economy, where overrestoration and misrepresentation may not have been illegal per se. At the base of the pyramid, among the smallest shop owners and stallholders, whose (declared) turnover was too little, perhaps, to require registration for VAT, business was very fluid, with small-scale enterprises mushrooming and going bust season to season, a world of undeclared cash sales or trades, and one where overinsurance against theft or fire offered a convenient way out of incompetent or unlucky management.

Dealers in secondhand goods have always been suspected of (knowingly or without wanting to know) trading in stolen property. In the 1970's and 1980's the great demand for Georgian and Victorian features in home decoration did in fact create a very profitable market in such items—wood paneling, fireplaces, brass lighting and bath fixtures—spawning both a legitimate trade in furnishings ripped from demolished or renovated properties and an illegitimate one in stolen pieces. In the late 1970's, old paving stones began to disappear overnight from public and private properties; brass fittings were prized off Victorian drinking fountains—indeed the fountains themselves might vanish, along with ornamental park furniture or the carved-stone cemetery monuments admired by Betjeman. Even stone slates from Cotswold churches and barns attracted Cockney "wideboys" who could expect easy and quick disposal to less than scrupulous dealers or homeowners. Beyond the building trade, there was a vigorous economy in fakes and forgeries, from netsuke to art-nouveau glass, in unscrupulously "married" furniture, in "antique" horse brasses newly cast or porcelain with altered maker's marks, while skills in "distressing" pieces transferred easily from the legitimate "repro" trade to the antique-shop back rooms. In March 1986, a twenty-one-year-old dealer specializing in Steiff bears was fined over £1,000 by a York magistrate's court for selling counterfeit teddies.[61]

Finally, loss of respect for the customer—in an era when the faceless tourist or suburban shopper may be seen to be an ignorant nouveau-riche with more money than sense—clearly played a part in defining the 1980's morality of the "cowboy" end of the antiques trade. The distinction was between dealing with a knowledgeable collector, the canny buyer who came early to the markets and who knew the dealers, and selling to the uninformed who only wanted something to decorate a mantle and who, passport in hand, would never walk into the shop again, who would dumbly overpay for shoddy goods if they were cheap but balk at a fair price for an expensive item. Fair game, many thought.

The antiques trade did undergo a transformation of culture in the late 1970's and early 1980's. It was a fringe economy rife with misrepresentation, overrestoration, and insurance fraud, with a high rate of bankruptcy (and bankruptcy fraud). For a significant minority of dealers these were roller-coaster years of exuberance and high living on the edge. Caught out by a changing whim of fashion, the skyrocketing rents of the Thatcher property boom, or bad judgment in their buying, some turned to even less legitimate areas of the street economy—fencing stolen goods or dealing in the London cocaine and hashish market. Temptation was great, especially among those who were young and new to the game (and remarkably unnostalgic about the goods they shoveled in bulk to the United States), who came to it as a speculative venture, and who were caught in the volatile trade or fashion cycles of the period. Comparative statistics are not available, but oral evidence drawn from dealers and their associates who were young when they began to trade in the late 1970's and early 1980's suggests a widespread erosion of ethical standards among at least these urban, commercial "stewards of heritage."[62]

Whose Heritage Is It, Anyway?

When David Coombs posed the preceding question to the readers of *Antique Collector* in that fraught December of 1978, it was in the narrow context of the ongoing debate about the export of cultural property to the United States. But it begs much larger questions of definition and ownership. In the period we have considered, there was clearly a shift—especially among the core market for heritage sentiment, the middle-class, suburban, homeowning professionals—from what might legitimately be called "Brideshead nostalgia" to a quite different sense and use of the past that is not a form of longing at all but a celebration of possession. The first is located specifically (though by no means exclusively) in the dystopian 1970's and can be summed up as a fear of loss and a search for refuge, sentiments made exactly clear in a passage from Roy Strong's diary for 1973: "London is such *Hell* these days. . . . So one creates one's place in the country, plants one's flowers and trees, watches over the kitchen-garden, cooks honest country dishes on the Aga and writes, looking towards the hills of an England which is disappearing."[63] This is the nostalgia that sociologist Fred Davis identified—a reaction inspired by "present fears, discontents, anxieties, or uncertainties."[64]

"Heritage" in the 1980's often has quite a different timbre, and Hewison's ironic insistence that the "heritage industry" should be read chiefly as a characteristic of a climate of decline now seems inadequate, just as it is also inadequate to assess its message as merely reactionary propaganda in the sense employed by Patrick Wright or Neal Ascherson.[65] It is clear that "heritage" will be regarded differently by different social groups. Different classes, ages, "races," genders, even sexualities may "read" the past at some level in their own way, investing it with a sense of ownership (or alienation) peculiar to their own condition and memory. And it is also true that none of these readings is fixed across time; as people's conditions change, so may their understanding of "their" heritage. In Britain there was a quite rapid movement in the 1980's, particularly after 1982 with the successful resolution of the Falklands War and the apparent retreat of economic recession, away from a sense of entropy and nostalgia—especially among those spending classes (a majority perhaps in the southeast) which at least felt themselves to be prospering. Heritage-as-refuge often became, in Thatcher's Britain, heritage-for-consumption—a privatization of the past. This involved an implicit redefinition (and reification) of culture itself as, on the one hand, objects that were bought to satisfy more directly the needs of interior decoration and status than feelings of nostalgic longing. On the other hand, it became an ephemeral entertainment—in arts and costume-drama television programming, to be consumed privately, or in trips to heritage centers and fee-charging museums, no longer public spaces but amenities for paying customers.

In this shift, the greatly expanded antiques trade played the role of handmaiden by encouraging, through its structural changes, the democratization of the market for heritage objects, but also by asserting the primacy of "market" generally, by destroying much of the mystique of the dealer and his goods, and with it much of the aura of "stewardship." The antiques market, at the popular level, no longer functioned as a special, intimate community of dealers and collectors. It was merely a commercial agora, and it is in this context that the increase in sharp and unethical practices—the misrepresentation, overrestoration, faking, and forgery that drew so much comment in the 1970's and 1980's—can be seen. It is also true that these practices, while hardly new,[66] sharply parallel in the 1980's a more general erosion of the distinction between the authentic and the simulated past at craft centers and "living" museums, as well as in the "reproduction" industry. By the 1990's the repro market itself had spread into every high street and shopping center, with chain stores like "Days Gone By" (pine furniture) or "Past Times" (candles and teddy bears).

If the antiques trade suffered in the recession of the late 1980's and early 1990's, its driving force, a popular desire (resonant with Thatcherism) privately to possess the past, seems to have endured. In the summer of 1998 the table around which Ramsay MacDonald, Keir Hardie, and others sat in 1900 to found a socialist Labour party came to auction. The "New Labour" sports minister, Tony Banks, expressed an interest: "I like to be able to hold and touch things of the past—they have a magic to them." His interest did not, however, imply a desire that this particular heritage object be preserved for the nation: "I want everybody to be interested in it . . . but not so much that *I* end up not being able *to buy it*."[67]

NOTES

Notes

Behlmer: Introduction

1. *The Sunday Times*, Apr. 5, 1998.
2. *The Scotsman*, Aug. 29, 1997; Blair, as quoted on CBS News, "60 Minutes," Nov. 15, 1998.
3. Raphael Samuel, *Theatres of Memory*, vol. 1, *Past and Present in Contemporary Culture* (London, 1994), part 4.
4. *The Guardian*, May 5, 1998.
5. John Lloyd, "Cool Britannia Warms Up," *New Statesman*, Mar. 13, 1998: 10–11.
6. *The Independent*, Sept. 8, 1997; Mark Leonard, *Britain™: Renewing Our Identity* (London, 1997), p. 12.
7. Leonard, "It's Not Just Ice-Cream," *New Statesman*, July 3, 1998: 15–16; *The Guardian*, Apr. 11, 1998; *The Economist* (U.S. edition), Dec. 19, 1998: 73–74.
8. Raymond Williams, *The Country and the City* (New York, 1973), p. 254.
9. Thatcher's speech to a Conservative party meeting, July 3, 1982, as quoted in John Taylor, *A Dream of England: Landscape, Photography and the Tourist's Imagination* (Manchester, 1994), pp. 217–18.
10. Martin Wiener, *English Culture and the Decline of the Industrial Spirit 1850–1980* (New York, 1982), pp. 43–44.
11. *Ibid.*, pp. 165–66.
12. Samuel, *Theatres of Memory*, p. 259.
13. Reba N. Soffer, *Discipline and Power: The University, History, and the Making of an English Elite, 1870–1930* (Stanford, 1994), pp. 198–203. See also Peter Mandler, *The Fall and Rise of the Stately Home* (New Haven, 1997), pp. 109, 113–14.
14. C. J. Simon and C. Nardinelli, "The Talk of the Town: Human Capital, Information, and the Growth of English Cities, 1861 to 1961," *Explorations in Economic History*, 33 (July 1996): 384–413; Martin Daunton, "Ancient and Modern: Culture and Capitalism in Victorian Britain," unpublished plenary address delivered to the North American Conference on British Studies, Colorado Springs, Oct. 1998, pp. 15–18.

15. Michael Hunter, "Introduction: The Fitful Rise of British Preservation," in *idem*, ed., *Preserving the Past: The Rise of Heritage in Modern Britain* (Stroud, Gloucestershire, 1996), pp. 7–8.

16. Patrick Wright, *On Living in an Old Country* (London, 1985), pp. 82–83, 87, 70–71.

17. Kevin Walsh, *The Representation of the Past: Museums and Heritage in the Post-Modern World* (London, 1992), pp. 1–4, 138–39.

18. Robert Hewison, *The Heritage Industry: Britain in a Climate of Decline* (London, 1987), pp. 9, 86–89. For the case that "history" and "heritage" should be uncoupled, see David Lowenthal, *Possessed by the Past: The Heritage Crusade and the Spoils of History* (New York, 1996), pp. 128–30.

19. Hewison, *Heritage Industry*, pp. 16–21. Orwell never saw the "pier" for which Wigan had earned a measure of music-hall fame. Both the elevated tramway originally dubbed a "pier" and the small iron frame used to tip coal into barges that inherited this name were long gone when the journalist reached Wigan in the autumn of 1936. Yet in 1984, students from the Wigan College of Technology dutifully installed another iron frame beside the canal. Orwell's three-week stay in Wigan and its impact on the book that followed receives careful comment in Peter Stansky and William Abrahams, *Orwell: The Transformation* (London, 1979), pp. 129–33, 148–62.

20. Peter Mandler, "Nationalizing the Country House," in Hunter, ed., *Preserving the Past*, pp. 99, 105, 112–14.

21. Richard Sykes et al., "Steam Attraction: Railways in Britain's National Heritage," *Journal of Transport History*, 3d ser., 18 (Sept. 1997): 157. I thank Dr. Norris Pope for directing me to this source.

22. Samuel, *Theatres of Memory*, pp. 184–85.

23. *Ibid.*, pp. 295, 139–40, 274–76.

24. Taylor, *Dream of England*, p. 239.

25. Adrian Mellor, "Enterprise and Heritage in the Dock," in John Corner and Sylvia Harvey, eds., *Enterprise and Heritage* (London, 1991), pp. 93–94.

26. For a bold assertion of this view, see Janice Doane and Devon Hodges, *Nostalgia and Sexual Difference: The Resistance to Contemporary Feminism* (New York, 1987). A more nuanced treatment of the relationship between gender and reconstructions of national identity will be found in Alison Light's *Forever England: Femininity, Literature and Conservatism Between the Wars* (London, 1991).

27. Fred Davis, *Yearning for Yesterday: A Sociology of Nostalgia* (New York, 1979), pp. 1–5.

28. *Ibid.*, pp. 36–37.

29. Terence Ranger, "The Invention of Tradition Revisited: The Case of Colonial Africa," in *idem* and Olufemi Vaughan, eds., *Legitimacy and the State in Twentieth-Century Africa* (Basingstoke, Hampshire, 1993), pp. 79–82. Ranger credits Benedict Anderson's work with stimulating this shift in perspective.

30. Stefan Collini, "The Heritage and the Truth," *Times Literary Supplement*, Mar. 10, 1995: 3.

31. George Orwell, "The Lion and the Unicorn," in Sonia Orwell and Ian An-

gus, eds., *The Collected Essays, Journalism and Letters of George Orwell*, vol. 2 (New York, 1968 [1941]), p. 78. For a very different gloss on Orwell's words, see Andrew Sullivan, "The End of Britain," *New York Times Magazine*, Feb. 21, 1999: 78–79.

Seleski: Identity, Immigration, and the State

1. *Proceedings on the King's Commission of the Peace, Oyer and Terminer, and Gaol Delivery of Newgate, Held for the City of London and County of Middlesex at Justice Hall in the Old Bailey* (London, 1813 [hereafter *OBSP*]), pp. 440–50; *The Times*, 27 July 1813. The case was also covered extensively in the *Morning Chronicle* and the *Morning Post*.

2. *OBSP*, pp. 440–50.

3. Andrew Knapp and Willam Baldwin, *The New Newgate Calendar: Comprising interesting memoirs of notorious characters who have been convicted of outrages on the Laws of England*, vol. 6 (London, 1828), pp. 48–60.

4. M. Dorothy George, *London Life in the Eighteenth Century* (reprint.: London, 1979 [1925]), p. 125.

5. M. A. G. O Tuathaigh, "The Irish in Nineteenth-Century Britain: Problems of Integration," *Transactions of the Royal Historical Society*, 5th ser., 31 (1980): 161; Sheridan Gilley, "English Attitudes to the Irish in Britain, 1780–1900," in *Immigrants and Minorities in British Society*, ed. Colin Holmes (Boston, 1978), p. 99.

6. Linda Colley, *Britons: Forging the Nation 1707–1837* (New Haven, 1992), pp. 321–64; Mary Poovey, "Curing the 'Social Body' in 1832: James Phillips Kay and the Irish in Manchester," *Gender and History*, 5 (1993): 196–211.

7. Poovey, "Curing the 'Social Body,'" p. 209.

8. See Pierre Bourdieu, *Outline of a Theory of Practice*, trans. Richard Nice (New York, 1977), pp. 14–30. For an idea of how such an approach might operate in regard to the construction of identity, see Laura Tabili, "The Construction of Racial Difference in Twentieth-Century Britain: The Special Restriction (Colored Alien Seaman) Order, 1925," *Journal of British Studies*, 33 (1994): 54–98. My thinking about the functional importance of the various ingredients that make up identities has been stimulated by Philip D. Morgan, "British Encounters with Africans and African-Americans, circa 1600–1780," in *Strangers Within the Realm: Cultural Margins of the First British Empire*, ed. Bernard Bailyn and Philip D. Morgan (Chapel Hill, 1991), pp. 157–219.

9. Martin Daunton, "London and the World," in *London—World City, 1800–1840*, ed. Celina Fox (New Haven, 1992), pp. 21–38; Peter Linebaugh, *The London Hanged: Crime and Civil Society in the Eighteenth Century* (New York, 1992), pp. 409–22.

10. Gearoid O Tuathaigh, *Ireland Before the Famine, 1798–1848* (Dublin, 1990), p. 141.

11. "Report on the State of the Irish Poor in Great Britain," *Parliamentary Papers*, 34 (1836): 429–30.

12. Anthony D. King, "'The World Economy Is Everywhere': Urban History and the World System," in *Urban History Yearbook* (Leicester, 1983), p. 7.

13. John Friedmann, "The World City Hypothesis," in *World Cities in a World-*

System, ed. Paul L. Knox and Peter J. Taylor (New York, 1995), pp. 317–31; Anthony D. King, *Global Cities: Post-Imperialism and the Internationalization of London* (New York, 1990), pp. 24–32.

14. [James Grant,] *The Great Metropolis*, vol. 1 (London, 1838), pp. 13, 15.

15. George, *London Life*, pp. 116–57; *Third Report of the Society Established for the Suppression of Mendicity* (London, 1821), pp. 1–3.

16. Colley (*Britons*, p. 329) suggests that the figure may have been as low as 40,000 in the 1780's.

17. Linebaugh, *London Hanged*, p. 349; Colin Holmes, *John Bull's Island: Immigration and British Society, 1871–1971* (London, 1988), p. 10; Lynn Hollen Lees, *Exiles of Erin: Irish Migrants in Victorian London* (Ithaca, 1979), p. 36; Ruth-Ann M. Harris, *The Nearest Place That Wasn't Ireland: Early Nineteenth-Century Labor Migration* (Ames, 1994), pp. 134–35.

18. Arthur Redford, *Labour Migration in England*, 2d ed. (London, 1964), pp. 131–33. The most complete account of the Irish in seventeenth-century London is Kathleen Maurice Noonan, "Brethren Only to a Degree: Irish Immigration in the Mid-Seventeenth Century, 1640–1660" (Ph.D. diss., University of California, Santa Barbara, 1989). Ruth-Ann Harris (*Nearest Place*, pp. 27–102) argues that the changes outlined below, especially the pressing need of Irish tenants to earn cash to pay rents, increased the numbers of temporary, seasonal migrants in the period under discussion in this essay.

19. Linebaugh, *London Hanged*, pp. 94–97, 297–300; Lees, *Exiles*, p. 36.

20. Barbara M. Kerr, "Irish Seasonal Migration to Great Britain," *Irish Historical Studies*, 3 (1942/43), pp. 365–80.

21. *Hansard's Parliamentary Debates*, 2d ser., 23 (11 Mar. 1830): 210.

22. Harris, *Nearest Place*, pp. 27–73; Cormac O Grada, "Poverty, Population, and Agriculture, 1801–45," in *A New History of Ireland*, ed. W. E. Vaughan, vol. 5 (Oxford, 1989), pp. 108–9, 112; Brenda Collins, "Proto-Industrialization and Pre-Famine Emigration," *Social History*, 7 (1982): 146.

23. Harris, *Nearest Place*, pp. 131–83; Collins, "Proto-Industrialization," pp. 127–46; Cormac O Grada, "Some Aspects of Nineteenth-Century Irish Emigration," in *Comparative Aspects of Scottish and Irish Economic and Social History, 1600–1900*, ed. L. M. Cullen and T. C. Smout (Edinburgh, 1977), pp. 65–73; Cormac O Grada, "Across the Briny Ocean: Some Thoughts on Irish Emigration to America, 1800–1850," in *Ireland and Scotland, 1600–1850*, ed. T. M. Devine and David Dickson (Edinburgh, 1983), pp. 118–30; William J. Symth, "Irish Emigration 1700–1920," in *European Expansion and Migration: Essays on the Intercontinental Migration from Africa, Asia and Europe*, ed. P. C. Emmer and M. Moerner (New York, 1992), pp. 49–78; S. H. Cousens, "The Regional Variations in Emigration from Ireland between 1821 and 1841," *Transactions of the Institute of British Geographers*, 37 (1965): 15–30.

24. "Report on the State of the Irish Poor in Great Britain," p. 495; Brenda Collins, "Irish Emigration to Dundee and Paisley During the First Half of the Nineteenth Century," in *Irish Population, Economy and Society: Essays in Honor of the Late K. H. Connell*, ed. J. M. Goldstrom and L. A. Clarkson (Oxford, 1981), pp. 195–212.

25. Matthew Martin, *Substance of a Letter . . . to the Right Honorable Lord Pelham on the State of Mendicity in the Metropolis* (London, 1811), pp. 22–24.

26. *Third Report of the Society Established for the Suppression of Mendicity*, pp. 31–32; emphasis added.

27. Anon., *Visit to the Irish Poor in the Borough, Addressed to the Marquess of Lansdowne and the Proprietors of the Irish Soil Resident in London* (London, 1832), p. 5; Lynn Hollen Lees, *The Solidarities of Strangers: The English Poor Laws and the People, 1700–1948* (New York, 1998), pp. 22–41; James Stephen Taylor, *Poverty, Migration and Settlement in the Industrial Revolution: Sojourners' Narratives* (Palo Alto, 1989), pp. 169–70.

28. Sheridan Gilley ("English Attitudes," pp. 84–85) notes the absence of evidence documenting sustained anti-Irish attitudes in England prior to the mid-nineteenth century. He argues that anti-Irish rhetoric and actions emerged in "fits and starts" over the centuries. For example, Noonan ("Brethren," pp. 232–53) finds very little such rhetoric in seventeenth-century London. O Tuathaigh ("The Irish," pp. 159–61) agrees and sees the mid-1840's as the crucial period. On the timing of anti-Irish "racism" see L. P. Curtis, *Anglo-Saxons and Celts* (Bridgeport, 1968), and *idem*, *Apes and Angels: The Irishman in Victorian Caricature* (Washington, D.C., 1971).

29. "Report on the State of Mendicity in the Metropolis," *Parliamentary Papers*, 3 (1814–15): 271.

30. James Stephen Taylor, "The Impact of Pauper Settlement," *Past and Present*, 73 (1976): 69–70.

31. St. Giles's reputation as a haven for both the poor and the Irish was long-standing, dating back to the sixteenth century. See John Parton, *Some Account of the Hospital and Parish of St. Giles-in-the-Fields, Middlesex* (London, 1822), pp. 298–302.

32. Joint Vestry of the United Parishes of St. Giles-in-the-Fields and St. George, Bloomsbury, *An Abstract of some important parts of a Bill now depending in Parliament, intitled, 'A Bill for the better support and maintenance of the poor'; with some practical observations on the effects that would probably be experienced . . . if the said Bill is passed into a Law* (London, 1797), pp. 22–24.

33. *First Report of the Society Established in London for the Suppression of Mendicity* (London, 1819), pp. 9, 21.

34. *The Times*, 26 Mar. 1819. Sturges Bourne was a member of the Mendicity Society's governing board. For more on this group, see Peter Mandler, "Tories and Paupers: Christian Political Economy and the Making of the New Poor Law," *Historical Journal*, 33 (1990): 81–104.

35. St. Giles-in-the-Fields, Vestry Minutes, 12 Apr. 1819, Holborn Local History Library, London.

36. "Report on the State of Mendicity in the Metropolis," pp. 281–84. In his testimony, Sampson Stevenson claimed that the parish used £20,000 (out of a £32,000 budget) to support the Irish.

37. St. Giles Vestry Minutes, 21 Apr. 1818, 4 Feb. 1819.

38. *Hansard's*, 2d ser., 1 (7 June 1820): 885.

39. *Fourth Report of the Society Established in London for the Suppression of Mendicity* (London, 1822), pp. 14–15.

40. "Report from the Select Committee on the Laws Relating to Irish and Scotch Vagrants," *Parliamentary Papers*, 4 (1828): 221. 59 Geo. III, cap. 12, also applied to Scottish vagrants. Redford (*Labour Migration*, pp. 138–41) shows, however, that the Scots were less affected, because the numbers of poor Scots emigrating south remained relatively small. Moreover, while Scotland had less liberal Poor Laws and settlement regulations than England, it did have them, making Scots' legal relationship to the English Poor Law quite different from that of the Irish.

41. *Ninth Report of the Society for the Suppression of Mendicity*, pp. 18–21; *Tenth Report of the Society*, p. 16; *Thirteenth Report of the Society*, p. 15; *Fifteenth Report of the Society*, pp. 15, 18. The Mendicity Society had ambivalent feelings about the 1819 act, although it supported the legislation. Society officials recognized that because of the act a large portion of the Irish poor were "suddenly deprived of a species of assistance which, up to that time, had been uniformly afforded, and to which by long custom they had been induced to consider themselves legally entitled." But they also granted the act its salutary effects: "Many of the Irish poor, resident in London, who were in the constant habit of receiving parochial relief, have been supported without it, ever since they were forced on their own resources by the passing of the Act" (*Third Report of the Society*, pp. 5–7).

42. "Report from the Select Committee on Irish Vagrants," *Parliamentary Papers*, 16 (1833): 327–33; St. Giles Local District Society, *A Short Account of the Wretched State of the Poor, in a Populous District, in the Parish of St. Giles-in-the-Fields* (London, 1828), pp. 14–15, 46–47; Redford, *Labour Migration*, pp. 140–41.

43. "Report on the State of the Irish Poor," pp. 411–12.

44. *Ibid.*, p. 411.

45. *Hansard's*, 2d ser., 23 (11 Mar. 1830): 194, 221.

46. *Hansard's*, 3d ser., 17 (7 May 1833): 1023.

47. *Hansard's*, 3d ser., 18 (30 May 1833): 109.

48. On the making of the Irish Poor Law, see Helen Burke, *The People and the Poor Law in 19th-Century Ireland* (Littlehampton, Sussex, 1987), pp. 17–49; and Oliver MacDonagh, "The Economy and Society," in *Ireland Under the Union, 1801–1870*, ed. W. E. Vaughan, in *A New History of Ireland*, vol. 5 (Oxford, 1989), pp. 225–27.

49. Knapp and Baldwin, *New Newgate Calendar*, p. 50.

50. Parish officials actually dealt quite gently with Mary Burke. Though she was confined to the House of Corrections during the investigation of Clifford's murder and her newborn child was declared chargeable to St. Giles's, the gentlemen and gentlewomen who took an interest in the case raised a subscription to support her other children. The magistrates did, however, make sure to write to Ireland to see if Burke's first husband, whom she deserted, was still alive, since legally he was responsible for Burke and his children's support. (*Morning Chronicle*, 18 Sept. 1813; *Morning Post*, 3–5 Aug. 1813.) Yet Knapp and Baldwin insist that Burke defrauded both the charitable citizenry who came to her aid and the parish, and they assert that she was unworthy of any support—an attitude not in evidence in 1813.

Bronstein: Rethinking the "Readmission"

1. *Jewish Chronicle*, Apr. 1, 1887: 8.

2. *Jewish Chronicle*, Apr. 8, 1887: exhibition supplement.

3. See *Jewish Chronicle*, Mar. 18, 1887: 6; Apr. 1, 1887: 11–12.

4. Although David Cesarani has discussed the emergence of Anglo-Jewish history in connection with antialienism, he does not analyze the emergence of the readmission narrative in detail. See "Dual Heritage or Duel of Heritages? Englishness and Jewishness in the Heritage Industry," in Tony Kushner, ed., *The Jewish Heritage in English History: Englishness and Jewishness* (London, 1992), pp. 29–41. See also Tony Kushner, "The End of the 'Anglo-Jewish Progress Show': Representations of the Jewish East End, 1887–1987," in Kushner, ed., *Jewish Heritage in English History*, pp. 78–105.

5. John A. Garrard, *The English and Immigration* (London, 1971), pp. 15–16.

6. Bill Williams, "The Anti-Semitism of Toleration," in Alan J. Kiss and K. W. Roberts, eds., *City, Class and Culture* (Manchester, 1985), p. 92.

7. David Katz, *Philosemitism and the Readmission of the Jews* (Oxford, 1982).

8. Lucien Wolf, *Menasseh ben Israel's Mission to Oliver Cromwell* (London, 1901), p. liii.

9. Henry Jessey, *A Narrative of the Late Proceedings at Whitehall (1656)* (London, 1656), p. 9.

10. See Ismar Schorsch, "From Messianism to Realpolitik: Menasseh ben Israel and the Readmission of the Jews to England," *Proceedings of the American Academy for Jewish Research*, 45 (1978): 187–208.

11. Capt. Fraser Willoughby to Robert Blackborne, Dec. 15, 1655, in Mary Anne Green, ed., *Calendar of State Papers, Domestic, Interregnum*, 9 (London, 1879–86), p. 57; Jessey, *A Narrative*, p. 9.

12. *Calendar of State Papers, Domestic, Interregnum*, 9, p. 16.

13. The petition is reprinted in Wolf, *Menasseh ben Israel's Mission*, p. lxxxvi.

14. Capt. Fraser Willoughby to Robert Blackborne, Dec. 17, 1655: *Calendar of State Papers, Domestic, Interregnum*, 9, p. 58.

15. Some credible evidence does exist that London's Jews practiced some religious observances secretly during the Interregnum, although the first detailed description of their practices by an English observer was set down in 1662. See Cecil Roth, *Anglo-Jewish Letters* (London, 1938), pp. 55–65.

16. For contemporary "philo-Semitic" proponents of Jewish conversion, see John Dury, *An Information Concerning the Present State of the Jewish Nation in Europe* (London, 1658); idem, *A Case of Conscience: Whether It Be Lawful to Admit Jews into a Christian Commonwealth* (London, 1656); Thomas Thorowgood, *Jewes in America, or Probabilities That Americans Are of That Race* (London, 1650); and Moses Wall, *Considerations upon the Point of the Conversion of the Jews* (London, 1652). Modern reevaluation of the events of 1656 has shown that Menasseh ben Israel was out of step with the constituency he purported to represent. See David Katz, "Anonymous Advocates of the Readmission of the Jews to England," *Michael*, 10 (1986): 117–42; David Katz, "The Abendana Brothers and the Chris-

tian Hebraists of Seventeenth-Century England," *Journal of Ecclesiastical History*, 40 (1989): 28–52; David Katz, *Jews in the History of England* (Oxford, 1994), pp. 107–44; and Bernard Glassman, *Anti-Semitic Stereotypes Without Jews* (Detroit, 1975), p. 36.

17. Some examples include W[illiam] H[ughes], *Anglo-Judaeus, or the History of the Jews Whilst Here in England* (London, 1656); William Prynne, *A Short Demurrer to the Jewes Long Discontinued Remitter into England* (London, 1656); Thomas Fuller, *A Pisgah-sight of Palestine* (London, 1650); James Howell, *The Wonderful and Deplorable History of the Latter Times of the Jews* (London, 1652); and Eleazar Bargishai, *A Brief Compendium of the Vain Hopes of the Jewish Messias* (London, 1652). As Frank Felsenstein has pointed out, in his petition to Oliver Cromwell, Menasseh ben Israel was compelled by harsh feelings against the Jews to try to dispel various stereotypes about his people, including the famous "blood libel" and the allegation that Jews intended to convert Christians to Judaism. See Frank Felsenstein, *Anti-Semitic Stereotypes: A Paradigm of Otherness in English Popular Culture, 1660–1860* (Baltimore, 1995), pp. 32, 34.

18. For one contemporary statement of the official history, see the review of S. R. Gardiner's *History of the Commonwealth and the Protectorate*, in the *Jewish Chronicle*, Mar. 1, 1901: 24.

19. Cecil Roth, "The Resettlement of the Jews in England in 1656," in V. D. Lipman, ed., *Three Centuries of Anglo-Jewry* (London, 1961), pp. 1–21. For the most extreme formulation of the readmission as English democracy at work, see Cecil Roth, *England in Jewish History*, Lucien Wolf Memorial Lecture for 1948 (London, 1949).

20. On this question in general, see Edward Said, *Orientalism* (New York, 1978).

21. On the discourse surrounding the Gypsies, the other cultural group accused of being a wandering race, see George K. Behlmer, "The Gypsy Problem in Victorian England," *Victorian Studies*, 28 (Winter 1985): 231–53.

22. William Gregory, who traveled around the Middle East with Benjamin in 1830, described one typical attention-getting costume: "a shirt entirely red, with silver studs as large as sixpences, green pantaloons with a velvet stripe down the sides, and a silk Albanian shawl with a long fringe of divers colours round the waist, red Turkish slippers, and to complete all his Spanish majo jacket covered with embroidery and ribbons" (B. R. Jerman, *The Young Disraeli* [London, 1960], p. 125).

23. Gigliola Sacerdoti Mariani, "An Aspect of Disraeli's Parliamentarian Rhetoric," *Il Politico*, 49 (1984): 593–606.

24. *Ibid.*, p. 601.

25. Isaiah Berlin, "Benjamin Disraeli, Karl Marx, and the Search for Identity," in Henry Hardy, ed., *Against the Current: Essays in the History of Ideas* (New York, 1979), pp. 252–86.

26. Lord Beaconsfield to Queen Victoria, Sept. 10, 1876: *The Oriental Question*, Royal Archives at Windsor, vol. H.9.

27. William Ewart Gladstone, "Bulgarian Horrors and the Question of the East," in Bernard Tauchnitz, ed., *Bulgarian Horrors and Russia in Turkistan* (Leipzig, 1876), pp. 11–69.

28. R. W. Seton-Watson, *Disraeli, Gladstone and the Eastern Question* (New York, 1979 [1935]), p. 78.

29. *Ibid.*, p. 113. See also Charles A. Moser, "The April Uprising, the American Journalist, and the Statesmen of Europe," *Eastern European Quarterly*, 25 (Mar. 1987): 29.

30. Anne Pottinger Saab, "Disraeli, Judaism and the Eastern Question," *International History Review*, 10 (Nov. 1988): 558–78.

31. Anthony S. Wohl, "'Dizzi-Ben-Dizzi': Disraeli as Alien," *Journal of British Studies*, 34 (1995): 375–411; Cesarani, "Dual Heritage," p. 31.

32. David Feldman, *Englishmen and Jews: Social Relations and Political Culture, 1840–1914* (New Haven, 1994).

33. Garrard, *The English*, pp. 25–26.

34. David Feldman, "The Importance of Being English: Jewish Immigration and the Decay of Liberal England," in D. Feldman and G. Stedman Jones, eds., *Metropolis: Histories and Representations of London After 1800* (New York, 1989), p. 78. It was easier, perhaps, for English men to indict the Jews as their competitors rather than indict destitute English women workers, but see Charles Booth, *Life and Labour of the People in London*, 1st ser., 4 (London, 1902): 37–68.

35. Garrard, *The English*, pp. 27–28.

36. Wolf's first exposition of his views on the readmission was his paper "The Resettlement of the Jews in England," given at the Jews' College Literary Society and reprinted in the *Jewish Chronicle*, Dec. 2, 1887: 8–11; and Dec. 23, 1887: 4.

37. Wolf, *Menasseh ben Israel's Mission*, p. lxxvii.

38. Cecil Roth, "Lucien Wolf: A Memoir," in *Essays in Jewish History* (London, 1934), p. 18.

39. For Wolf's *Dictionary*, see *Jewish Chronicle*, Nov. 11, 1887: 16–17. Wolf listed Menasseh ben Israel as "Founder of the Anglo-Jewish Community." On Wolf's social role, see Eugene C. Black, *The Social Politics of Anglo-Jewry, 1880–1920* (New York, 1988), pp. 33–35.

40. Roth, "Lucien Wolf: A Memoir," p. 18. Wolf was not alone. The prestigious Jewish Board of Guardians, claiming sole right to determine the fate of incoming Jews, deported 31,000 prospective immigrants between 1881 and 1906. See Feldman, "The Importance of Being English," p. 66.

41. *Jewish Chronicle*, June 17, 1887: 10–11.

42. *Jewish Chronicle*, May 13, 1887: 9.

43. On Wolf's and Abrahams's opposition to Zionism, see Stuart A. Cohen, *English Zionists and British Jews: The Communal Politics of Anglo-Jewry, 1895–1920* (Princeton, 1982), pp. 163–68; and David Cesarani, *The Jewish Chronicle and Anglo-Jewry, 1841–1991* (Cambridge, 1994), p. 86.

44. Cohen, *English Zionists*, p. 176.

45. Felsenstein, *Anti-Semitic Stereotypes*, p. 205.

46. Wolf, *Menasseh ben Israel's Mission*, p. lxx. See also Lucien Wolf, "American Elements in the Re-settlement," *Transactions of the Jewish Historical Society of England*, 2 (1899): 78–100.

47. Wolf, *Menasseh ben Israel's Mission*, p. lxxv. Wolf's characterization of the Ashkenazim during the readmission era influenced modern scholarship; see A. S. Diamond, "The Community of the Resettlement, 1656–1684: A Social Survey," *Transactions of the Jewish Historical Society of England*, 24 (1975): 150.

48. Cesarani, *Jewish Chronicle and Anglo-Jewry*, p. 57.

49. Wohl, "Dizzi-Ben-Dizzi," p. 397.

50. Todd Endelman, *Radical Assimilation in English Jewish History* (Bloomington, 1990), pp. 13, 22. Wolf knew very well the distance between "New Christians" and Jews, as his work to redeem the Portuguese Marranos of his own time indicates. Many contemporary Marranos were completely ignorant of Jewish tradition, or considered their own rough version of secret practice the "true" Judaism. See Lucien Wolf, *Report on the "Marannos" or Crypto-Jews of Portugal* (London, 1926).

51. Wolf, "The Resettlement of the Jews in England," *Jewish Chronicle*, Dec. 23, 1887: 8. See also *idem*, "The First English Jew: Notes on Antonio Fernandez Carvajal," *Transactions of the Jewish Historical Society of England*, 2 (1895): 14–45; and "Crypto-Jews Under the Commonwealth," *ibid.*, 1 (1893): 55–88.

52. *Jewish Chronicle*, Apr. 15, 1887: exhibition supplement.

53. Black, *Social Politics*, pp. 153–54.

54. See Endelman, "Writing English Jewish History," *Albion*, 27 (1995): 623–36.

55. Lucien Wolf, "A Plea for Anglo-Jewish History," *Transactions of the Jewish Historical Society of England*, 1 (1893): 4.

56. Anglo-Jews were normally Orthodox and generally resistant to the Enlightenment movements to reform Jewish practice. Todd Endelman has argued that this was due less to spirituality than to the Anglo-Jews' veneration of Orthodoxy's conservative, established nature, and to similarities between the hierarchy of the Orthodox rabbinate and of the Anglican Church. See Endelman, "The Englishness of Jewish Modernity in England," in Jacob Katz, ed., *Toward Modernity: The European Jewish Model* (New Brunswick, 1987), p. 235.

57. Charles Booth, *Life and Labour of the People in London*, 1st ser., 3 (London, 1902): 191.

58. *Jewish Chronicle*, Jan. 4, 1901.

59. Cesarani, *Jewish Chronicle and Anglo-Jewry*, p. 75; *idem*, "Dual Heritage," p. 34.

60. John P. Fox, "British Attitudes to Jewish Refugees from Central and Eastern Europe in the Nineteenth and Twentieth Centuries," in Werner Mosse, ed., *Second Chance* (Tübingen, 1991), pp. 466–84.

61. Garrard, *The English*, pp. 33–41.

62. Moses Gaster, "Leaves from the History of the Sephardim in England," *Jewish Chronicle*, May 31, 1901: 10–11; June 21, 1901: 20–21; June 28, 1901: vi–viii; July 12, 1901: 30–32; July 26, 1901: 18–19.

63. *Jewish Chronicle*, Apr. 19, 1901: 24. See Moses Gaster, *History of the Ancient*

Synagogue of Spanish and Portuguese Jews (London, 1901), p. 3; *Jewish Chronicle*, May 24, 1901: 21.

64. As the *Jewish Chronicle* (Jan. 25, 1901: 17) noted upon the death of Queen Victoria: "Under the benign sway of Queen Victoria England has grown to be the great exemplar in matters of religious toleration. Here, in this thrice-blessed realm, every creed may raise its head, and every race breathe the pure air of liberty. As the reign of the late Sovereign progressed, the last rags and tatters of intolerance were cast off till now it is in England almost alone from which the law of freedom goes forth."

65. In contrast, perusal of the *Jewish Chronicle* for 1855–56 revealed no evidence either of celebration or even awareness about the fact that it was the two-hundredth anniversary of the Whitehall Conference—the drive for emancipation absorbed much of the Jewish community's collective energies.

66. N. Adler, "A Homage to Menasseh ben Israel," *Transactions of the Jewish Historical Society of England*, 1 (1893): 25–54.

67. "The Whitehall Conference: Celebration of the 250th Anniversary," *Transactions of the Jewish Historical Society of England*, 5 (1902–5): 276–98.

68. *Ibid.*

69. This should not be construed as an argument that the Jewish community did nothing to modify the legislation against aliens; as John Garrard (*The English*, p. 45) points out, the legislation which eventually did pass had been modified, by militant Jewish opposition, to provide safeguards protecting religious refugees.

70. See Redcliffe N. Salaman, *Whither Lucien Wolf's Anglo-Jewish Community?* Lucien Wolf Memorial Lecture for 1953 (London, 1954).

71. Cecil Roth ("England in Jewish History," pp. 10–12) went out of his way to congratulate the English for their liberality, noting that the informal readmission of the Jews had made possible a residence in England free from the ghetto system that blighted other countries. The resettlement of the Jews had been accompanied, furthermore, by the granting of all fundamental human rights; the late (1858) political emancipation of the Jews was therefore of very little moment.

72. Cecil Roth, "Jewish History for Our Own Needs," *Writings*, no. 32, quoted in Lloyd P. Gartner, "Cecil Roth, Historian of Anglo-Jewry," in Dov Noy and Issachar Ben-Ami, eds., *Studies in the Cultural Life of the Jews of England* (Jerusalem, 1975), p. 82.

73. Roth, "The Resettlement of the Jews," p. 1.

74. "Tercentenary Celebrations," *Jewish Chronicle*, June 1, 1956: 17.

75. Todd Endelman shows that Jews had made major, assimilationist changes in the Jewish lifestyle before 1770; yet he considers the fact that anti-Semitism in England was fairly limited to have been the work of Englishmen rather than Jews. See Endelman, "Englishness of Jewish Modernity," p. 242.

76. Anglo-Jewish historians gradually became aware of the biases inherent in the traditional history and expanded their focus to include the Jews from Eastern Europe, along with radicalism, criminality, women, and a host of other topics once thought unimportant or embarrassing. See Kushner, "The End of the 'Anglo-Jewish Progress Show,'" pp. 79–105.

Weaver: The Pro-Boers

1. *Sunday Times*, Aug. 17, 1902; *The Times*, Aug. 18, 1902; L. Botha to J. C. Smuts, Sept. 25, 1902, in W. K. Hancock and J. van der Poel, eds., *Selections from the Smuts Papers*, vol. 2 (Cambridge, 1966), p. 35.

2. Hancock and van der Poel, eds., *Selections from the Smuts Papers*, vol. 2, p. 35, n. 1.

3. See Stephen Koss, ed., *The Pro-Boers: The Anatomy of an Antiwar Movement* (Chicago, 1973), pp. xiii–xxxviii; J. W. Auld, "The Liberal Pro-Boers," *Journal of British Studies*, 14: 2 (May 1975): 78–101; Arthur Davey, *The British Pro-Boers, 1877–1902* (Cape Town, 1978).

4. Barbara Hammond to Ellen Bradby, Aug. 17, 1902 (courtesy of Anne Ridler).

5. Thomas Metcalf, *Ideologies of the Raj* (Cambridge, 1995), p. 63; *The Nation*, Mar. 30, 1907.

6. G. K. Chesterton, *The Autobiography of G. K. Chesterton* (New York, 1936), p. 112.

7. Peter Warwick, ed., *The South African War* (London, 1980), p. 14; A. N. Porter, *The Origins of the South African War* (Manchester, 1980); John Cell, *The Highest Stage of White Supremacy: The Origins of Segregation in South Africa and the American South* (Cambridge, 1982), p. 61; Preben Kaarsholm, "Pro-Boers," in Raphael Samuel, ed., *Patriotism: The Making and Unmaking of British National Identity*, vol. 1 (London, 1989), p. 122, n. 10; Iain R. Smith, *The Origins of the South African War, 1899–1902* (London, 1996), p. 170.

8. Sir William Molesworth, minute of 1854, quoted in Cell, *Highest Stage of White Supremacy*, p. 59.

9. See J. S. Galbraith, *Reluctant Empire* (Berkeley and Los Angeles, 1963), pp. 37, 74; and Davey, *British Pro-Boers*, p. 7.

10. Martin J. Wiener, *English Culture and the Decline of the Industrial Spirit* (Cambridge, 1981), p. 5.

11. The literature on the pastoral impulse in Victorian England is vast. See, for a start, Jan Marsh, *Back to the Land* (London, 1982); Jeffrey Spear, *Dreams of an English Eden* (New York, 1984); and, classically, Raymond Williams, *The Country and the City* (London, 1973).

12. Herbert Paul, *The Life of Froude* (New York, 1906), p. 268.

13. W. H. Dunn, *James Anthony Froude*, vol. 2 (Oxford, 1963), p. 407.

14. J. W. Burrow, *A Liberal Descent: Victorian Historians and the English Past* (Cambridge, 1981), p. 242.

15. J. A. Froude, *Short Studies on Great Subjects*, 3d ser. (New York, 1877), pp. 290–91; J. A. Froude, *Oceana, or England and Her Colonies* (New York, 1886), p. 17.

16. Froude, *Oceana*, pp. 42–44; *idem, Short Studies*, p. 357.

17. Davey, *British Pro-Boers*, p. 15; *Hansard's Parliamentary Debates*, 3d ser., 242 (Aug. 15, 1878): c. 2068; *ibid.*, 244 (Mar. 25, 1879): c. 1693; *ibid.*, 245 (Mar. 31, 1879): c. 24; G. P. Gooch, *Life of Lord Courtney* (London, 1920), p. 160.

18. J. A. Froude, "South Africa Once More," *Fortnightly Review*, n.s., 44 (Oct. 1, 1879): 457; Davey, *British Pro-Boers*, p. 23.

19. Davey, *British Pro-Boers*, pp. 24–27, 31, 192–93; *Hansard's*, 3d ser., vol. 263 (July 25, 1881): cols. 1850–51.

20. See Francis Wilson, "Farming, 1866–1966," in Monica Wilson and Leonard Thompson, eds., *The Oxford History of South Africa*, vol. 2 (Oxford, 1971), pp. 126–36.

21. Imperial South African Association, *The Question of Right Between England the Transvaal* (London, 1900), as quoted in John S. Galbraith, "The Pamphlet Campaign on the Boer War," *Journal of Modern History*, 24 (June 1952): 122.

22. Olive Schreiner, *Thoughts on South Africa* (New York, 1923), p. 15; Olive Schreiner, *The Story of an African Farm* (London, 1883).

23. Olive Schreiner, *Thoughts on South Africa*, pp. 151, 245, and *passim*; Ruth First and Ann Scott, *Olive Schreiner* (New York, 1980), p. 195.

24. For a full bibliographic history of the essays, see First and Scott, *Olive Schreiner*, p. 374.

25. F. R. Statham, *South Africa As It Is* (London, 1897), pp. 187–98; James Bryce, *Impressions of South Africa* (New York, 1897), pp. 422–23.

26. Edward Carpenter, *Boer and Briton* (Manchester, 1900), p. 3; First and Scott, *Olive Schreiner*, p. 241; *Labour Leader*, Jan. 6, 1900.

27. J. A. Hobson, *The War in South Africa* (London, 1900), pp. 12, 14, 25, 44.

28. Elie Halévy, *Imperialism and the Rise of Labour* (New York, 1951), p. 93.

29. See Alfred F. Havighurst, *Radical Journalist: H. W. Massingham (1860–1924)* (London, 1974), pp. 100–108.

30. See David Ayerst, *The Manchester "Guardian": Biography of a Newspaper* (Ithaca, 1971), pp. 275–86.

31. *Speaker*, Dec. 9, 1899; *Reynolds News*, Jan. 12, 1896; Bernard Porter, "The Pro-Boers in Britain," in Peter Warwick, ed., *The South African War* (London, 1980), p. 239.

32. *Speaker*, Nov. 18, 1899.

33. Beatrice Webb, *Our Partnership* (Cambridge, 1948), p. 194.

34. Stephen Koss, *Fleet Street Radical: A. G. Gardiner and the "Daily News"* (London, 1973), p. 39. For Lloyd George's takeover of the *Daily News*, see also W. T. Stead, "The Reconversion of the *Daily News*," *Review of Reviews*, 23 (Feb. 15, 1901): 147–53; and Stephen Koss, *The Rise and Fall of the Political Press in Britain*, vol. 1 (Chapel Hill, 1984), pp. 396–99. For Emily Hobhouse's crusade on behalf of Boer women and children, see Ruth Fry, *Emily Hobhouse: A Memoir* (London, 1929); and Rykie van Reenen, ed., *Emily Hobhouse: Boer War Letters* (Cape Town, 1984). For J. L. and Barbara Hammond's opposition to the Boer War, see my own *The Hammonds: A Marriage in History* (Stanford, 1997), pp. 44–75.

35. Hobson, *War in South Africa*, p. 197.

36. Chesterton, *Autobiography*, p. 112.

37. John Morley to Lord Curzon, Nov. 26, 1900, as quoted in Koss, ed., *Pro-Boers*, p. xxi.

38. A. M. S. Methuen, *Peace or War in South Africa* (London, 1901), p. 44; J. Morley to L. T. Hobhouse, Sept. 18, 1899, as quoted in Peter Clarke, *Liberals and Social Democrats* (Cambridge, 1978), p. 69.

39. Davey, *Pro-Boers*, p. 55. The Orange Free State, relatively untouched as yet by the corrupting influences of mineral wealth, had long held a special place in the ata-vistic imagination of British radicals. See Hobson, *War in South Africa*, pp. 136–45.

40. Kaarsholm, "Pro-Boers," p. 113.

41. G. B. Shaw to John Burns, Sept. 11, 1903, in Dan H. Laurence, ed., *Bernard Shaw: Collected Letters*, vol. 2 (New York, 1972), p. 369.

42. C. Tsuzuki, *H. M. Hyndman and British Socialism* (London, 1961), p. 126.

43. Hobson, *War in South Africa*, pp. 233, 285; F. W. Hirst, Gilbert Murray, and J. L. Hammond, *Liberalism and the Empire* (London, 1900), pp. 182–83.

44. For the standard works, see H. V. Emy, *Liberals, Radicals, and Social Politics, 1892–1914* (Cambridge, 1973); Clarke, *Liberals and Social Democrats*; and Michael Freeden, *The New Liberalism: An Ideology of Social Reform* (Oxford, 1986).

45. Sir Henry Campbell-Bannerman to Winston Churchill, Sept. 9, 1907, as quoted in Koss, ed., *Pro-Boers*, p. 268.

46. Davey, *British Pro-Boers*, p. 157.

47. R. C. K. Ensor, *England, 1870–1914* (Oxford, 1936), p. 255, n. 1.

Behlmer: Character Building and the English Family

I wish to thank Jane Cater, Fred Leventhal, and Michael J. Moore for their com-ments on earlier drafts of this essay.

1. Octavia Hill, "Our Dealings with the Poor," *Nineteenth Century*, 174 (Aug. 1891): 161.

2. See, for example, George K. Behlmer, *Friends of the Family: The English Home and Its Guardians, 1850–1940* (Stanford, 1998), pp. 31–46.

3. The role of "character" in Victorian and Edwardian social discourse has drawn much scholarly attention. Perhaps the most lucid analysis appears in Stefan Collini, *Public Moralists: Political Thought and Intellectual Life in Britain, 1850–1930* (Oxford, 1991), chap. 3.

4. Edward Bulwer Lytton, *England and the English*, vol. 1 (New York, 1833), p. 141.

5. Charles Dickens, *American Notes* (London, 1985 [1842]), p. 25.

6. Credit for fielding England's first paid social workers probably should go to Ellen Ranyard's "Biblewomen" charity. See F. K. Prochaska, "Body and Soul: Bible Nurses and the Poor in Victorian London," *Historical Research*, 60 (1987): 338.

7. Charles Trevelyan, *Address on the Systematic Visitation of the Poor in Their Own Homes* . . . (London, 1870), p. 15; Helen Bosanquet, *Social Work in London, 1869–1912* (London, 1914), pp. 53–54.

8. Charles Trevelyan, *Seven Articles on London Pauperism* . . . (London, 1870), p. 6.

9. *Idem, Three Letters on London Pauperism to the Times* (1870), as quoted in Ga-reth Stedman Jones, *Outcast London*, 2d ed. (London, 1984), p. 253. Stedman Jones's discussion of the "deformation of the gift" remains the best account of early COS psychology.

10. Charles Loch Mowat, *The Charity Organisation Society 1869–1913* (London, 1961), pp. 22–23; *House-to-House Visitation* (London, 1871), pp. 6–7; Charles Bosan-

quet, *A Handy-Book for Visitors of the Poor in London* (London, 1874), pp. 4–6; Octavia Hill, *District Visiting* (London, 1877), pp. 7–8.

11. Anthony S. Wohl, "Octavia Hill and the Homes of the London Poor," *Journal of British Studies*, 10 (May 1971): 108–9.

12. Octavia Hill to Florence Davenport Hill, Feb. 17, 1867, in C. Edmund Maurice, ed., *Life of Octavia Hill As Told in Her Letters* (London, 1914), pp. 227–28.

13. Octavia Hill, *Homes of the London Poor*, 2d ed. (London, 1883), pp. 20–22, 42.

14. *Eadem*, "Letters to Fellow Workers," as quoted in Standish Meacham, *Toynbee Hall and Social Reform 1880–1914* (New Haven, 1987), p. 6; Hill, *Homes*, pp. 29–30, 52.

15. On the subject of housing reform in Victorian England, see especially Anthony Wohl, *The Eternal Slum* (Montreal, 1977); and J. N. Tarn, *Five Per Cent Philanthropy* (Cambridge, 1973).

16. Hill, *Homes*, p. 42; *Justice*, Mar. 29, 1884: 1.

17. Martha Vicinus, *Independent Women: Work and Community for Single Women 1850–1920* (Chicago, 1985), pp. 216–18; Patricia Hollis, *Ladies Elect: Women in English Local Government 1865–1914* (Oxford, 1987), pp. 13–14. On the costs of professionalized social work for English women, see Seth Koven, "The Dangers of Castle Building—Surveying the Social Survey," in Martin Bulmer et al., eds., *The Social Survey in Historical Perspective 1880–1940* (Cambridge, 1991), p. 373; and more broadly for American women, Daniel J. Walkowitz, "The Making of a Feminine Professional Identity: Social Workers in the 1920s," *American Historical Review*, 95 (Oct. 1990): 1051–75.

18. Jane Lewis, *Women and Social Action in Victorian and Edwardian England* (Stanford, 1991), pp. 42–43, 51, 65–66; U. M. Cormack, "Developments in Case-Work," in A. F. C. Bourdillon, ed., *Voluntary Social Services* (London, 1945), pp. 98–99; Mary E. Richmond, *Friendly Visiting Among the Poor* (New York, 1914 [1899]), pp. 180–81.

19. A. F. Young and E. T. Ashton, *British Social Work in the Nineteenth Century* (London, 1956), pp. 107–8; Ronald G. Walton, *Women in Social Work* (London, 1975), p. 29; Roy Lubove, *The Professional Altruist* (Cambridge, Mass., 1965), p. 2.

20. Jane Lewis, *The Voluntary Sector, the State and Social Work in Britain* (Aldershot, 1995), p. 8.

21. Beatrice Webb, *My Apprenticeship* (New York, 1926), pp. 189, 196–97.

22. George Lansbury, *My Life* (London, 1928), p. 129; Barnett, as quoted in Asa Briggs and Ann Macartney, *Toynbee Hall: The First Hundred Years* (London, 1984), p. 36.

23. Robert D. Storch, "The Problem of Working-Class Leisure: Some Roots of Middle-Class Moral Reform in the Industrial North, 1825–1850," in A. P. Donajgrodzki, ed., *Social Control in Nineteenth-Century Britain* (London, 1977), p. 139; Kathleen Woodroofe, *From Charity to Social Work in England and the United States* (Toronto, 1962), pp. 50–51; Derek Fraser, *The Evolution of the British Welfare State* (New York, 1973), p. 119; T. H. Marshall, *Social Policy* (London, 1965), p. 168.

24. Stedman Jones, *Outcast London*, pp. 156–57, 269–70.

25. H. Bosanquet, *Social Work*, pp. 190, 192–95; José Harris, *Unemployment and*

Politics: A Study in English Social Policy 1886–1914 (Oxford, 1972), pp. 108–9; A. W. Vincent, "The Poor Law Reports of 1909 and the Social Theory of the Charity Organisation Society," *Victorian Studies*, 27 (Spring 1984): 343–46.

26. Stephen Yeo, *Religion and Voluntary Organisations in Crisis* (London, 1976), pp. 219–20; Alan J. Kidd, "Charity Organization and the Unemployed in Manchester c. 1870–1914," *Social History*, 9 (Jan. 1984): 45–46; Geoffrey Finlayson, *Citizen, State, and Social Welfare in Britain 1830–1990* (Oxford, 1994), pp. 148–50.

27. David Garland, *Punishment and Welfare: A History of Penal Strategies* (Aldershot, 1985), p. 119.

28. H. Bosanquet, *Social Work*, pp. 55–56.

29. *Eadem, The Family* (New York, 1923 [1906]), pp. 325–26.

30. *Eadem, The Strength of the People* (London, 1902), p. 227.

31. Helen Dendy [later Bosanquet], "Thorough Charity," *Charity Organisation Review*, June 1893, pp. 206–12.

32. Bernard Bosanquet, "The Meaning of Social Work," *International Journal of Ethics*, 11 (Apr. 1901): 296; *idem*, "The Principles and Chief Dangers of the Administration of Charity," in *Philanthropy and Social Progress* (New York, 1893), pp. 249–50.

33. *Idem*, "Character in Its Bearing on Social Causation," in *idem*, ed., *Aspects of the Social Problem* (New York, 1968 [1895]), p. 112.

34. *Ibid.*, p. 117; *Dwellings of the Poor: Report of Dwellings Committee of the Charity Organisation Society* (London, 1881), pp. 7, 39–40.

35. COS form no. 28, as quoted in Woodroofe, *From Charity to Social Work*, p. 41.

36. C. Bosanquet, *Handy-Book*, pp. 12–13; Helen Bosanquet, *Rich and Poor* (London, 1896), p. 6.

37. Lewis, *Women and Social Action*, p. 151; Mowat, *Charity Organisation Society*, p. 37; C. S. Loch, *Charity and Social Life* (London, 1910), p. 400.

38. Young and Ashton, *British Social Work*, pp. 102–4; C. R. Attlee, *The Social Worker* (London, 1920), pp. 64–65; Judith Fido, "The Charity Organisation Society and Social Casework in London 1869–1900," in Donajgrodzki, ed., *Social Control*, p. 218.

39. Fido, "Charity Organisation Society," p. 217. It is unclear from COS records how many visitors patrolled London during the mid-1880's. A decade later, according to Helen Bosanquet (*Social Work*, pp. 79–80), metropolitan district committees claimed about twelve hundred members, of whom perhaps eight or nine hundred "took a constant part in the Society's weekly work."

40. *Charity Organisation Reporter*, 11 (Mar. 2, 1882): 60–61.

41. Webb, *My Apprenticeship*, p. 197.

42. For a useful study of COS work in the provinces, see Robert Humphreys, *Sin, Organized Charity and the Poor Law in Victorian England* (New York, 1995).

43. "A Morning with a Charity Organisation Society," *The Standard* (Mar. 1889), in Leamington COS Newspaper Cutting Book, 1877–1913, p. 55: Warwick County Record Office, CR51/1883.

44. T. B. Dudley, *A Complete History of Royal Leamington Spa* (Leamington,

1896), p. 11; David C. Ward, "The Deformation of the Gift: The Charity Organisation Society in Leamington Spa," unpublished M.A. thesis (University of Warwick, 1975), pp. 15, 17, 19.

45. Ward, "Deformation of the Gift," pp. 29, 31–32; Woodroofe, *From Charity to Social Work*, p. 38.

46. One of the few examples of loans to solvent working-class applicants involved Mrs. Elizabeth Clarke, twenty-seven, the wife of a plasterer, who received £2 to expand the stock in her "little green grocer's shop" (Leamington COS Case Record Book: Warwick County R. O., CR51/1878, case no. 524).

47. *Ibid.*, CR51/1880, case no. 1288.

48. Loch, *Charity and Social Life*, p. 402; Una Cormack and Kay McDougall, "Case-Work in Social Service," in Cherry Morris, ed., *Social Case-Work in Great Britain*, 2d ed. (New York, 1955), p. 29; Walton, *Women in Social Work*, p. 61; Elizabeth Macadam, *The Equipment of the Social Worker* (New York, 1925), pp. 33–35. Between 1903 and 1912, the School of Sociology operated as an independent body committed to teaching social-work methods. In July 1912 it was absorbed by the London School of Economics.

49. Teresa Merz, notes for a lecture "Social Work from the Charity Organization Society's Point of View" (Oct. 27, 1911), Northumberland County Record Office, NRO 2281/14.

50. S. P. Grundy, "The Relations of the Charity Organisation Societies and the Guilds of Help," *Charity Organisation Review*, July 1912, pp. 85–87.

51. W. Milledge, "Guilds of Help," *Charity Organisation Review*, July 1906, p. 50. The London-based Personal Service Association, formed in 1908, echoed the guilds' call for visitation founded on a sense of civic responsibility. Rebecca West, an ardent feminist and socialist, saw nothing new here. Rather uncharitably, one might say, West damned the PSA's "Zoo Spirit"—a spirit of "benevolence that offers buns through the bars on an umbrella-point" (*The Clarion*, Dec. 13, 1912, p. 4).

52. L. V. Shairp, "Guilds of Help," *Charity Organisation Review*, July 1912, pp. 74–75, 78; Michael Cahill and Tony Jowitt, "The New Philanthropy: The Emergence of the Bradford City Guild of Help," *Journal of Social Policy*, 9 (July 1980): 359, 374. On relations between the guild-of-help movement and the "old" philanthropy, see Keith Laybourn, *The Guild of Help and the Changing Face of Edwardian Philanthropy* (Lampeter, Dyfed, 1994).

53. Cahill and Jowitt, "New Philanthropy," p. 375; Hill, "Our Dealings," p. 166.

54. Bradford City Guild of Help [hereafter "BCGH"], "Instructions to Helper," Bradford District Archives.

55. Dorothy C. Keeling, *The Crowded Stairs: Recollections of Social Work in Liverpool* (London, 1961), p. 12.

56. BCGH casebook no. 3536, Bradford District Archives. This file appears among a systematic sample of 100 cases registered between Mar. 20, 1905, and Oct. 18, 1911.

57. BCGH Exec. Comm. Min. Bk., Feb. 21 and Mar. 7, 1905: Bradford District Archives no. 39 D83.

58. BCGH casebook no. 2544.

59. *Ibid.*, casebooks no. 2540 and no. 3537.

60. Attlee, *Social Worker*, p. 79; Michael J. Moore, "Social Work and Social Welfare: The Organization of Philanthropic Resources in Britain, 1900–1914," *Journal of British Studies*, 16 (Spring 1977): 85, 91–93; Yeo, *Religion and Voluntary Organisations*, p. 219; Cahill and Jowitt, "New Philanthropy," p. 382. On Sept. 28, 1905, the Bradford guild's paid secretary, Walter Milledge, complained about delays in reporting cases to headquarters. As a result of these delinquencies, "the Central Office was constantly in the ignominious position of having to confess complete ignorance about cases which had been . . . visited weeks and months before." See BCGH Exec. Comm. Min. Bk., Sept. 28, 1905.

61. Garland, *Punishment and Welfare*, pp. 119–20.

62. Christopher Lasch, *Haven in a Heartless World: The Family Besieged* (New York, 1979), pp. 14–15.

63. Jacques Donzelot, *The Policing of Families*, trans. Robert Hurley (New York, 1979), pp. 96–97.

64. Jean Snelling, "Medical Social Work," in Morris, ed., *Social Case-Work*, pp. 82–102; M. Penelope Hall, *The Social Services of Modern England* (London, 1959), p. 134.

65. Mary E. Richmond, *The Long View: Papers and Addresses*, ed. Joanna Colcord (New York, 1930), pp. 559–60.

66. Lubove, *Professional Altruist*, pp. 7–8, 20; Robert H. Bremner, *American Philanthropy*, 2d ed. (Chicago, 1988), pp. 93–96, 109–10; Cormack and McDougall, "Case-Work in Social Service," p. 29.

67. Mary E. Richmond, *Social Diagnosis* (New York, 1917), pp. 39, 71–72, 115, 130–31.

68. *Eadem, What Is Social Case Work?* (New York, 1922), pp. 78–79.

69. *Eadem, Social Diagnosis*, pp. 40, 55–56. Linda Gordon (*Pitied but Not Entitled: Single Mothers and the History of Welfare, 1890–1935* [New York, 1994], pp. 102–4), commenting on American casework theory, distinguishes between a "nineteenth-century" notion that poverty emerged from character flaws, and a New Deal notion that "poverty damaged the character . . . , and that social work expertise was needed to help people cope with stress and break with bad . . . behavior patterns." In both views, however, character mending remained the core concern.

70. Sibyl Clement Brown, "Social Work in Action 1925–34" (unpubl. ms.), as quoted in Walton, *Women in Social Work*, p. 113. Miss Brown, a tutor in the L.S.E.'s Social Science Department, nonetheless discerned "significant changes in content" between the case records of 1924 and those of 1934. *Eadem,* "The Methods of Social Case Workers," in F. C. Bartlett et al., eds., *The Study of Society: Methods and Problems* (New York, 1939), pp. 384–85.

71. Sidney Webb and Beatrice Webb, *The Prevention of Destitution* (London, 1911), p. 241.

72. Attlee, *Social Worker*, p. 27.

73. Cormack, "Developments in Case-Work," p. 86.

74. Elizabeth Macadam, *The Social Servant in the Making* (London, 1945), p. viii; *eadem, Equipment of the Social Worker*, pp. 16, 188–90.

75. Keeling, *Crowded Stairs*, pp. 137–38; T. S. Simey, "Introduction" to Eric McKie, *Venture in Faith* (Liverpool, 1963), pp. xii–xiv; Jane Rowe, *Parents, Children and Adoption* (London, 1966), pp. 25–26.

76. Harold Perkin, *The Rise of Professional Society: England Since 1880* (London, 1989), pp. 348–49; Ray Lees, "Social Work, 1925–50: The Case for a Reappraisal," *British Journal of Social Work*, 4 (Winter 1971): 371–73; Robert Pinker, *Social Work in an Enterprise Society* (London, 1990), pp. 82–83.

77. Noel Parry and José Parry, "Social Work, Professionalism and the State," in Noel Parry et al., eds., *Social Work, Welfare and the State* (Beverly Hills, 1980), pp. 42–43.

78. Northumberland County Record Office, Northumberland and Tyneside Council of Social Services, casepaper no. 1, NRO 2281/4a.

79. Newton, "Miss Case-Worker Goes Scientific," as quoted in Walkowitz, "Making of a Feminine Professional Identity," p. 1051.

80. Woodroofe, *From Charity to Social Work*; Kenneth E. Reid, *From Character Building to Social Treatment: The History of the Use of Groups in Social Work* (Westport, 1981).

Mayhall: The Making of a Suffragette

My thanks to Mrs. Patricia J. Cowan, for her generosity and hospitality, and for her continued interest in this project. My thanks also to Frances S. Martin, for sharing her family memories and insights with me; to Leah Leneman, for encouragement over the years; and to the editors of this volume, for their comments on earlier drafts. Permission to cite material from Eunice Guthrie Murray's unpublished journals was granted by Mrs. Patricia J. Cowan; permission to cite from *Frances Murray* (1920) was granted by Mrs. Sylvia Butters. This essay owes much to Peter Stansky, from whom I have learned a great deal.

1. Kate Flint, *The Woman Reader, 1837–1914* (Oxford, 1993), p. 42. Flint's concern, like that of many scholars interested in the history of reading, lies largely with communities of readers and representations of the act of reading itself. More recently, attention has become directed at what one collection terms an integration of "the broad narrative of the expansion of readership over the centuries . . . with the actual experience of men and women" (James Raven, Helen Small, and Naomi Tadmore, eds., "Introduction," in *The Practice and Representation of Reading in England* [Cambridge, 1996], p. 15). My study draws upon Andrew Bennett's definition of the reader (after Roger Chartier) as "an individual in a particular historical situation whose responses are available to empirical investigation through written records" ("Introduction," in Bennett, ed., *Readers and Reading* [London, 1995], p. 2). I use the phrase "reading practices" to designate those habits and gestures constituting modes of access to texts, modes argued by Chartier to be "historically and socially differentiated"; see Roger Chartier, "Labourers and Voyagers: From the Text to the Reader," in Bennett, ed., p. 137.

2. Flint, *Woman Reader*, p. 248.

3. Antoinette Burton, *Burdens of History: British Feminists, Indian Women, and Imperial Culture, 1865–1915* (Chapel Hill, 1994), pp. 52–59.

4. Ian Christopher Fletcher, "'A Star Chamber of the Twentieth Century': Suffragettes, Liberals, and the 1908 'Rush the Commons' Case," *Journal of British Studies*, 35, no. 4 (1996): 504–30. Critic Glenda Norquay has described suffragette writings as "a form of public intervention"; see Norquay, ed., "Introduction," in *Voices and Votes: A Literary Anthology of the Women's Suffrage Campaign* (Manchester, 1995), p. 3.

5. On the Women's Freedom League in Scotland, see Leah Leneman, *A Guid Cause: The Women's Suffrage Movement in Scotland* (Edinburgh, 1995).

6. Frances Stoddard Murray published two books: *Painted Wallcloths in Sweden*, reprinted from *Transactions of the Glasgow Archaeological Society* (1900); and *Summer in the Hebrides: Sketches in Colonsay and Oronsay* (Glasgow, 1887). Her lectures are described in Eunice Guthrie Murray, *Frances Murray: A Memoir* (Glasgow, 1920 [hereafter *Frances Murray*]), pp. 148, 168–69.

7. Information on Sylvia Murray comes from the *Girton College Register: 1869–1946*, vol. 1 (Cambridge, 1948), p. 87; on Dorothy, from *Frances Murray*, p. 206.

8. Her publications include: *Prejudices Old and New* (Edinburgh, 1912); *Liberal Cant* (London, 1913); *The Illogical Sex?* (Edinburgh, 1914); *The Hidden Tragedy* (London, 1917); *A Reply to the Bishop of Durham Regarding Women's Place in the Church* (London, n.d.); *Woman's Value in Wartime* (London, 1917); *The Lass He Left Behind* (London, 1918); *Frances Murray: A Memoir* (Glasgow, 1920); *Women in the Ministry* (n.p., 1923); *Scottish Women in Bygone Days* (London, 1930); *Impressions of Palestine and Beyond: To-day, Yesterday and Tomorrow* (London, 1932); *Saint Mochta and the Chapel of Kilmahew: A Chapter in the Early History of the Parish of Cardross* (Dumbarton, 1932); *The Church of Cardross and Its Ministers* (Glasgow, 1935); *A Gallery of Scottish Women* (London, 1935); *Scottish Homespun* (London, 1947); *The Old School of Cardross: A Chapter in Village Life* (Glasgow, 1949).

9. The Eunice Guthrie Murray journals (hereafter "EGM") are held privately, by Mrs. Patricia J. Cowan, widow of Murray's nephew Alan Cowan. On Murray's work for the League of Pity and in settlement houses, see EGM, vol. 1: 2 May 1901, p. 98; 8 Jan. 1902, p. 115; 19 Oct. 1904, pp. 178–79. (Pagination of vol. 1 is Murray's; pagination of vol. 2 is my own.) On her temperance work, see EGM, vol. 2, June 1910, p. 73. Note that dates used by Murray vary: sometimes she recorded the day of the month; other times, merely the month.

10. EGM, vol. 2, Jan. 1909, p. 44.

11. EGM, vol. 1, 31 Oct. 1900, p. 87.

12. See her comments on attending a meeting in London at which James Larkin spoke: EGM, vol. 2, 15 Nov. 1913, p. 153.

13. EGM, vol. 2, Mar. 1910, p. 71; EGM, vol. 1, Aug. 1904, p. 174; EGM, vol. 3, Nov. 1917, p. 172. (Pagination of vol. 3 is my own.)

14. EGM, vol. 2, Jan. 1911, p. 87, suggests that Sylvia was a member of the National Union of Women's Suffrage Societies, while the *Suffrage Annual and Women's Who's Who* (London, 1913) listed Sylvia as a member of the Women's Freedom League (p. 315).

15. Reprinted in *Frances Murray*, p. 76.

16. For Frances Murray's membership in the Women's Freedom League, see

Suffrage Annual and Women's Who's Who (1913). That entry also described her as an occasional lecturer for women's suffrage (p. 315). Eunice Murray recorded marching with her mother in a 1909 WSPU procession for women's suffrage in Edinburgh: EGM, vol. 2, July 1909, p. 80. For Frances Murray's expressions of support, see her letter dated Dec. 1909, reprinted in *Frances Murray*, pp. 234–36.

17. *Frances Murray*, pp. 55, 74, 186–87.

18. EGM, vol. 1, 7 Mar. 1905, pp. 195–96.

19. *Frances Murray*, p. 101.

20. *Frances Murray*, p. 219.

21. Sandra Stanley Holton, "The Suffragist and the Average Woman," *Women's History Review*, 1 (1992): 19; and Lucy Bland, "The Married Woman, the 'New Woman' and the Feminist: Sexual Politics of the 1890s," in Jane Rendall, ed., *Equal or Different? Women's Politics 1800–1914* (Oxford, 1987), pp. 141–64. On the importance of family dynamics in shaping feminist consciousness, see Olive Banks, *Becoming a Feminist: The Social Origins of 'First Wave' Feminism* (Brighton, Sussex, 1986).

22. See Jane Rendall, "Citizenship, Culture and Civilisation: The Languages of British Suffragists, 1866–1874," in Caroline Daley and Melanie Nolan, eds., *Suffrage and Beyond: International Feminist Perspectives* (New York, 1994), pp. 127–50.

23. For a contrast, see John Brewer, "Reconstructing the Reader: Prescriptions, Texts and Strategies in Anna Larpent's Reading," in Raven et al., eds., *Practice and Representation of Reading*, pp. 226–45.

24. EGM, vol. 2, July 1908, p. 15.

25. EGM, vol. 2, Jan. 1909, p. 43; Jan. 1912, p. 93; Feb. 1914, p. 157.

26. EGM, vol. 1, 3 May 1905, p. 198.

27. EGM, vol. 1, 1 Feb. 1903, p. 133. Sandra Holton, "'In Sorrowful Wrath': Suffrage Militancy and the Romantic Feminism of Emmeline Pankhurst," in Harold L. Smith, ed., *British Feminism in the Twentieth Century* (Amherst, 1991), pp. 7–24.

28. EGM, vol. 1, 9 Feb. 1897, p. 31.

29. See the discussion of the Women's Press in Ann Morley and Liz Stanley, *The Life and Death of Emily Wilding Davison* (London, 1988), pp. 81–95.

30. EGM, vol. 2, Jan. 1912, p. 93.

31. EGM, vol. 1, 18 Aug. 1897, p. 38.

32. EGM, vol. 1, 19 Oct. 1904, pp. 179–81.

33. EGM, vol. 2, Mar. 1914, p. 160.

34. See, for example, EGM, vol. 2, pp. 94, 133–35, 143.

35. EGM, vol. 3, 25 July 1918, p. 218.

36. EGM, vol. 1, 13 Dec. 1902, p. 128; 30 Dec. 1901, p. 112; Aug. 1903, p. 149.

37. EGM, vol. 1, 12 July 1896, p. 24.

38. EGM, vol. 2, Sept. 1912, p. 110.

39. For the influence of the Victorian feminist press, see Burton, *Burdens of History*, pp. 98–102; and Philippa Levine, "'The Humanising Influence of Five O'Clock Tea': Victorian Feminist Periodicals," *Victorian Studies*, 33 (1990): 293–306.

40. EGM, vol. 1, 9 Nov. 1896, pp. 27–28.

41. EGM, vol. 1, 1 May 1897, p. 34.

42. Patrick Joyce, *Democratic Subjects: The Self and the Social in Nineteenth-Century England* (Cambridge, 1994), pp. 156, 196. See also Fletcher, "Star Chamber," pp. 520–23.

43. Joyce, *Democratic Subjects*, p. 201.

44. EGM, vol. 2, June 1908, p. 13.

45. Jane Lewis, "Women's Social Action: Possibilities and Limitations," in her *Women and Social Action in Victorian and Edwardian England* (Stanford, 1991), pp. 302–12; and Martha Vicinus, *Independent Women: Work and Community for Single Women, 1850–1920* (Chicago, 1985).

46. EGM, vol. 2, July 1910, p. 79.

47. Martin Pugh, "The Limits of Liberalism: Liberals and Women's Suffrage 1867–1914," in Eugenio Biagini, ed. *Citizenship and Community: Liberals, Radicals and Collective Identities in the British Isles, 1865–1931* (Cambridge, 1996), pp. 45–65.

48. EGM, vol. 1, 2 June 1906, p. 326; vol. 2, Oct. 1908, p. 25; Jan. 1909, p. 47; May 1908, p. 8.

49. David Rubinstein, *Before the Suffragettes: Women's Emancipation in the 1890s* (New York, 1986), p. 141.

50. Vicinus, *Independent Women*, pp. 247–80; Sandra Stanley Holton, *Suffrage Days: Stories from the Women's Suffrage Movement* (London, 1996), p. 29.

51. Andrew Rosen, *Rise Up, Women! The Militant Campaign of the Women's Social and Political Union, 1903–1914* (London, 1974), pp. 49–51.

52. EGM, vol. 1, Oct. 17, 1905, pp. 212–14; 2 June 1906, p. 324.

53. EGM, vol. 1, 30 Dec. 1901, p. 112.

54. EGM, vol. 2, June 1908, p. 10; Nov. 1911, p. 83.

55. EGM, vol. 2, 25 June 1912, p. 107; Apr. 1914, p. 163. Historians have seen the WFL's unwillingness to criticize the WSPU as either its strength or its weakness: see Brian Harrison, *Prudent Revolutionaries: Portraits of British Feminists Between the Wars* (Oxford, 1987), pp. 41, 51; and Les Garner, *A Brave and Beautiful Spirit: Dora Marsden, 1882–1960* (Brookfield, 1990), p. 25.

56. For Eunice Murray's attendance at WSPU meetings, see EGM, vol. 2, Feb. 1913, pp. 132–33. Historians have noted the fluidity between suffrage organizations: see Sandra Stanley Holton, *Feminism and Democracy: Women's Suffrage and Reform Politics in Britain, 1900–1918* (Cambridge, 1986), p. 39; and Morley and Stanley, *Life and Death of Emily Wilding Davison*, p. 152.

57. EGM, vol. 2, Apr. 1914, p. 164.

58. Thomas Holt, *The Problem of Freedom: Race, Labor, and Politics in Jamaica and Britain, 1832–1938* (Baltimore, 1992); Catherine Gallagher, *The Industrial Reformation of English Fiction: Social Discourse and Narrative Form, 1832–1867* (Chicago, 1985).

59. Clare Midgley, *Women Against Slavery: The British Campaigns, 1780–1870* (London, 1992); Moira Ferguson, *Subject to Others: British Women Writers and Colonial Slavery, 1670–1834* (New York, 1992); Antoinette Burton, "States of Injury: Josephine Butler on Slavery, Citizenship, and the Boer War," *Social Politics*, 5 (1998): 338–61.

60. Byron and Mill quoted in EGM, vol. 1, 9 Feb. 1897, p. 31; Shelley quoted in EGM, vol. 2, May 1910, p. 73.

61. Burton, "States of Injury," p. 342.

62. EGM, vol. 1, 25 Apr. 1900, p. 71.

63. Margot Finn, *After Chartism: Class and Nation in English Radical Politics, 1848–1874* (Cambridge, 1993).

64. Fletcher, "Star Chamber," pp. 529–30.

65. EGM, vol. 2, May 1914, pp. 168–69. She reiterated her assessment of the importance of *Jane Eyre* in EGM, vol. 3, 23 Dec. 1915, p. 40.

66. Quoted in Sandra M. Gilbert and Susan Gubar, *The Madwoman in the Attic: The Woman Writer and the Nineteenth-Century Literary Imagination* (New Haven, 1979), p. 337. A useful overview of recent interpretations of the novel is found in Antoinette Burton, "Recapturing Jane Eyre: Reflections on Historicizing the Colonial Encounter in Victorian Britain," *Radical History Review*, 64 (1996): 59–72.

67. Mary Jean Corbett, "Representation and Subjectivity in the Edwardian Suffrage Movement," in her *Representing Femininity: Middle-Class Subjectivity in Victorian and Edwardian Women's Autobiographies* (New York, 1992), pp. 150–79; Barbara Green, *Spectacular Confessions: Autobiography, Performative Activism, and the Sites of Suffrage, 1905–1914* (New York, 1997), pp. 105–41.

68. EGM, vol. 2, Sept. 1910, p. 81.

Osborne: Continuity in British Sport

1. R. J. Q. Adams and Philip P. Poirier, *The Conscription Controversy in Great Britain, 1900–1918* (London, 1987), p. 6; Derek Birley, *Playing the Game: Sport and British Society, 1910–45* (Manchester, 1995), p. 1.

2. *The Newspaper Press Directory and Advertiser's Guide* (London, 1914), pp. 1–4.

3. *Athletic News* (Manchester), Jan. 4, 1915: 4.

4. The reality, of course, was more complicated. In a report to the Foreign Office on the visit of a Royal Naval Squadron to Kiel in June 1914, for instance, the British naval attaché in Berlin noted specifically "the striking progress made by the German Navy in sports and games." He recorded that the German sailors had defeated the British in one of two association football matches held to celebrate the visit, and that "our men were entirely outclassed in all the usual sports." More notable is the fact that he praised the sportsmanship of the German competitors, saying that the German navy had "succeeded in instilling in their players the difference between playing for the game's sake and playing for the cup" (Wilfred Henderson to Sir Horace Rumbold, July 3, 1914, in G. P. Gooch and Howard Temperley, eds., *British Documents on the Origins of the War, 1898–1914*, vol. 11 [London, 1938], pp. 10–11). I am indebted to Professor Timothy Lang of the Department of History, Dickinson College, for this reference.

5. Reproduced in *Sports Times* (Bristol), Mar. 6, 1915: 1. One may note that since travel and hotel "expenses" were to be paid, only amateurs would play in this fantasy war.

6. *Newspaper World* (London), Dec. 15, 1915: 2.

7. Siegfried Sassoon (*Memoirs of a Fox-Hunting Man* [London, 1928], p. 286)

remembers regularly reading the football results aloud to his keenly interested platoon in 1915.

8. The closing lines of "On Receiving News of the War (Cape Town, 1914)," reprinted in I. M. Parsons, ed., *Men Who March Away: Poems of the First World War* (London, 1965), p. 93.

9. Theodore A. Cook, *Character and Sportsmanship* (London, 1927), p. 169.

10. T. A. Cook, "Games and the Citizen," *The Field*, Jan. 25, 1919: 99.

11. F. R., "Future Sport," *Football Mail and Southern Sport* (Portsmouth), Mar. 29, 1919: 3.

12. "When the Boys Come Home," *Sports Trade Journal*, Nov. 1918: 130; F. Davidson Currie, "The Future of Association Football," *Football Mail and Southern Sport* (Portsmouth), Jan. 4, 1919: 3; *The Field*, Nov. 16, 1918: 442.

13. Speech reported in *Football Argus* (Birmingham), Mar. 15, 1919: 7; Lord Kinnaird, "Football of the Future," *The Field*, Nov. 30, 1918: 491; *ibid.*, Nov. 16, 1918: 442.

14. Anonymous leading amateur to V. A. S. Beanland, reported in *Sports Echo* (Leeds), Aug. 30, 1919: 1.

15. Ministry of Reconstruction, *Public Health I—The Present Problem and the Ministry of Health, Reconstruction Problems, no. 23* (HMSO, 1919), p. 29; *Memorandum on Physical Training and Development*, Ministry of Reconstruction, 1918, RECO1, 692/2009, p. 11.

16. Sir George Newman, "An Outline of the Practice of Preventative Medicine," *Parliamentary Papers*, 39 (1919 [Cmd 363]): 92.

17. *Parliamentary Debates*, 5th ser., 92 (Apr. 19, 1917): 1914.

18. Paul Barton Johnson, *Land Fit for Heroes* (Chicago, 1968), p. 245.

19. Tony Mason, *Only a Game? Sport in the Modern World* (Cambridge, 1993), p. 44.

20. George Sullivan, "A Ministry of Sport," *Sports Trader*, June 1916: 1.

21. *Football News* (Nottingham), Nov. 30, 1918: 2.

22. *Football News* (Nottingham), Mar. 8, 1919: 2.

23. *Football Argus* (Bradford), Apr. 12, 1919: 6; *Sports Trader*, Dec. 1918: 8, and Apr. 1919: 2.

24. Perhaps the most realistic comment on the possibility of government assistance in the building of a new sports world came from a sports editor in the south of England who advised after less than three months of peace: "Anyone who expects a revolution in methods and control is going to be somewhat disappointed. Parliament and Corporations will have their hands full in other matters for some time to come" (*Football Mail and Southern Sport* [Portsmouth], Feb. 1, 1919: 1).

25. Arthur Marwick, *The Deluge* (London, 1967), p. 279.

26. *Athletic News*, July 20, 1918: 1.

27. *Athletic News*, June 18, 1918: 1.

28. *Football Mail and Southern Sport* (Portsmouth), Mar. 22, 1919: 2; *Athletic News*, May 12, 1919: 1.

29. Cook, *Character and Sportsmanship*, p. 253.

30. *Athletic News*, Aug. 9, 1920: 1–4.

31. Norman Vance, "The Ideal of Manliness," in Brian Simon and Ian Bradley, eds., *The Victorian Public School* (London, 1975), p. 128. Vance's view is only one of many such oversimplifications that have undervalued the persistence of Edwardian values in society.

32. Successive governments did take notice of both the domestic and the international aspects of sport before this, however. See, for example, Brian Stoddart, "Sport, Cultural Politics and International Relations: England Versus Germany, 1935," in Norbert Muller and Joachim Ruhl, eds., *Sport History: Olympic Scientific Congress 1984, Official Report* (Niederhausen, 1985), pp. 385–412.

Bell: Vanessa's Garden

My greatest debt is to Peter Stansky, one of the first men I knew who was receptive to the possibilities of women's history while not working on the subject himself, who many years ago validated my interest in the Bloomsbury Group. The members of the spring 1998 scholars' seminar at the Institute for Research on Women and Gender provided useful, and here incorporated, suggestions after listening to a previous version of this article. Regina Marler kindly lent me printed and manuscript material on Vanessa Bell. She, Olivier Bell, Sir Peter Shepheard, and Andrew Cavely answered many questions and gave me much of their valuable time. The skill and talent of Carolyn Caddes re-created a splendid photograph of Vanessa's "Pond and Beehive" painting. Finally, Afra Leckie and Bridget Ogden have escorted me to Charleston year after year, in order to soak up the scents and atmosphere of Vanessa's ever regenerating and refreshing garden.

1. Nigel Nicolson and Joanne Trautmann, eds., *The Letters of Virginia Woolf*, vol. 2 (New York, 1976 [hereafter "Virginia Woolf, *Letters*"]), no. 757, p. 94.

2. Virginia Woolf, *Letters*, vol. 2, no. 789, p. 118.

3. Regina Marler, ed., *Selected Letters of Vanessa Bell* (New York, 1993 [hereafter "Marler, *Bell: Letters*"]), p. 518.

4. Olivier Bell, interview at Firle, 27 Aug. 1997.

5. Virginia Woolf, *Letters*, vol. 3, no. 1760, p. 381.

6. Marler, *Bell: Letters*, vol. 4, no. 17, p. 198.

7. David Garnett, *The Flowers of the Forest* (New York, 1956), p. 13; and see the first volume of his autobiography, *The Golden Echo* (New York, 1953).

8. Marler, *Bell: Letters*, vol. 4, no. 15, p. 195.

9. *Ibid.*, no. 19, p. 201.

10. Frances Spalding, *Vanessa Bell* (London, 1983 [hereafter "Spalding, *Bell*"]), p. 133.

11. Letter dated 11 June [1923], cited in Frances Spalding, *Duncan Grant* (London, 1997 [hereafter "Spalding, *Grant*"]), p. 252.

12. Letter dated Aug. 1918, cited in Spalding, *Bell*, pp. 173–74.

13. Virginia Woolf, *Letters*, vol. 3, no. 1743, p. 363.

14. Marler, *Bell: Letters*, vol. 6, no. 10, p. 313.

15. Anne Olivier Bell, ed., *The Diary of Virginia Woolf*, vol. 3 (New York, 1980), p. 124. See also Spalding, *Bell*, p. 215.

16. For the emotional relationship of Vanessa Bell and Duncan Grant, see

Spalding, *Bell*; Mary Ann Caws, *Women of Bloomsbury* (London and New York, 1990); and Spalding, *Grant*.

17. Cited in Spalding, *Grant*, p. 236.

18. *Ibid.*, p. 226.

19. For example, Leon Edel, *Bloomsbury: A House of Lions* (Philadelphia, 1979); S. P. Rosenbaum, ed., *The Bloomsbury Group: A Collection of Memoirs, Commentary and Criticism* (London, 1975); Carolyn G. Heilbrun, *Towards a Recognition of Androgyny* (New York, 1973); and, most recently, Peter Stansky, *On or About December 1910: Early Bloomsbury and Its Intimate World* (Cambridge, Mass., 1996).

20. Denys Sutton, ed., *Letters of Roger Fry*, vol. 2 (New York, 1972 [hereafter "Roger Fry, *Letters*"]), no. 406, pp. 415–16.

21. Angelica Garnett, *Deceived with Kindness: A Bloomsbury Childhood* (New York, 1984); and especially in Alen MacWeeney and Sue Allison, *Bloomsbury Reflections* (New York, 1990), pp. 6–9.

22. Germaine Greer, *The Obstacle Race* (New York, 1980); Lisa Tickner, "The Left-Handed Marriage: Vanessa Bell and Duncan Grant," in Whitney Chadwick and Isabelle de Courtivron, eds., *Significant Others: Creativity and Intimate Partnership* (London, 1993), pp. 65–81.

23. Spalding, *Bell*, p. 155. See also Michael Brundle in a *Charleston Newsletter* (no. 3, Feb. 1983: 13): "One of the reasons the house was selected by its eminent inhabitants was because of its setting. By this I mean the house within the immediate context of the farmyard and garden, which itself lies within the larger context of the fields, hedgerows and Downs beyond. Many paintings by Duncan Grant and Vanessa Bell testify to this. The landscape was to an extent the generator of their art and is fundamental to the appreciation of their work."

24. Marler, *Bell: Letters*, vol. 9, no. 13, p. 526.

25. *Ibid.*, vol. 5, no. 11, p. 254.

26. *Ibid.*, vol. 8, no. 24, p. 482.

27. *Ibid.*, no. 21, p. 478.

28. *Ibid.*, no. 12, p. 462. See also Peter Stansky and William Abrahams, *Journey to the Frontier: Two Roads to the Spanish Civil War* (London and Boston, 1966).

29. Angelica Garnett, "The Earthly Paradise," in *Charleston Past and Present* (London, 1987), pp. 104–52.

30. Marler, *Bell: Letters*, vol. 6, no. 15, p. 323.

31. Simon Watney, *English Post-Impressionism* (London, 1980), p. 134.

32. Tickner, in Chadwick and de Courtivron, eds., *Significant Others*, p. 80.

33. Spalding, *Bell*, p. 163.

34. Marler, *Bell: Letters*, vol. 8, no. 1941, p. 473.

35. *Ibid.*, vol. 7, no. 26, p. 420.

36. *Ibid.*, vol. 8, no. 7, p. 455.

37. Cited in Quentin Bell and Virginia Nicholson, *Charleston: A Bloomsbury House and Garden* (London, 1997), p. 134.

38. Diane Filby Gillespie, *The Sisters' Arts: The Writing and Painting of Virginia Woolf and Vanessa Bell* (Syracuse, 1988), p. 278.

39. Marler, *Bell: Letters*, vol. 6, no. 7, pp. 305–6.

40. *Ibid.*, no. 3, p. 296.

41. *Ibid.*, vol. 7, no. 5, p. 376.

42. Spalding, *Grant*, p. 356.

43. Marler, *Bell: Letters*, vol. 9, no. 9, p. 517.

44. *Ibid.*, vol. 5, no. 31, pp. 285–86.

45. *Ibid.*, vol. 8, no. 25, p. 483.

46. Charleston Farmhouse was part of the estate of Lord Gage, who refused to sell any part of his property. It was not until the 1980's, when the Charleston Trust was founded, that the house and grounds were purchased for the trust. The Bells, Duncan Grant, and Maynard Keynes therefore rented the Charleston house and gardens from 1916 onwards. Clive Bell continued to have his own rooms in the house until his death.

47. D. Garnett, *Flowers*, p. 145.

48. Spalding, *Bell*, p. 184; *eadem, Grant*, p. 221.

49. *Charleston Magazine*, 15 (Spring/Summer 1997): 34.

50. "A Talk by Angelica Garnett Introducing the Film About the Restoration of Charleston," *Charleston Newsletter*, 23 June 1989: 19.

51. Reproduced in *Charleston Newsletter (Annex)*, no. 1, 14 Mar. 1986: 39, and available as a popular postcard in color from the Charleston Shop.

52. State Certified Midwife, State Registered Nurse, Queen's Nurse and Health Visitor (SCM, SRN, QN, HV). For the history and definition of Queen's Nurses, granted a Royal Charter in 1889, see E. J. Merry and I. D. Irven, *District Nursing* (London, 1948).

53. Marler, *Bell: Letters*, vol. 8, no. 25, p. 482.

54. D. Garnett, *Flowers*, chap. 8, pp. 142, 151. Olivier Bell (interview, 27 Sept. 1997) believes that the beehive in this painting may have been one that Vanessa accommodated for one of the local farmers at this time.

55. Marler, *Bell: Letters*, vol. 9, no. 7, p. 514.

56. Caws, *Women of Bloomsbury*, p. 195.

57. This painting, now owned by the Sheffield City Art Galleries, is reproduced in color in Jan Marsh, *Bloomsbury Women: Distinct Figures in Life and Art* (New York, 1996), p. 105; it is also reproduced in Bell and Nicholson, *Charleston*, p. 85.

58. Also reproduced in Marsh, *Bloomsbury Women*, p. 105. This painting now hangs in the Laing Art Gallery, Newcastle-on-Tyne. See also Spalding, *Grant*, p. 249.

59. "Child of Bloomsbury," in *Charleston Magazine*, 13 (Spring/Summer 1996): 23.

60. Roger Fry, *Letters*, no. 566, p. 576 (to Helen Anrep).

61. Letter from Duncan Grant to Vanessa Bell (25 Apr. 1924), quoted in Spalding, *Grant*, p. 257.

62. Marler, *Bell: Letters*, vol. 7, no. 27, p. 425.

63. *Charleston Newsletter*, 23 June 1989: 19.

64. Spalding, *Bell*, p. 159.

65. *Ibid.*, p. 134.

66. Andrew Cavely, interview, 27 Sept. 1997.

67. Spalding, *Grant*, p. 341.

68. *Ibid.*, p. 352.

69. Marler, *Bell: Letters*, vol. 8, no. 15, p. 468.

70. *Ibid.*, vol. 9, no. 9, p. 518.

71. All these sculptures are reproduced in Bell and Nicholson, *Charleston*, pp. 144–45.

72. Spalding, *Grant*, p. 369.

73. See, for examples, Betty Massingham, *Miss Jekyll: Portrait of a Great Gardener* (Newton Abbot, 1973).

74. Anne Scott-James, *Sissinghurst: The Making of a Garden* (London, 1974).

75. See Susan Groag Bell, "Women Create Gardens in Male Landscapes: A Revisionist Approach to Eighteenth-Century English Garden History," *Feminist Studies*, 16 (Fall 1990): 471–91.

76. Interview with Sir Peter Shepheard, 13 Sept. 1997.

77. *Ibid.*; see also Quentin Bell and Angelica Garnett, eds., *Vanessa Bell's Family Album* (London, 1981).

78. *Charleston Past and Present*, p. 154.

79. Bell and Nicholson, *Charleston*, p. 125.

80. Interview with Sir Peter Shepheard, 13 Sept. 1997.

81. Interview with Andrew Cavely, 27 Sept. 1997.

82. *Ibid.*

83. Interview with Sir Peter Shepheard, 13 Sept. 1997.

84. Regina Marler; personal communication.

85. Regina Marler, *Bloomsbury Pie: The Making of the Bloomsbury Boom* (New York, 1997), p. 4.

86. Andrew Cavely, interview, 27 Sept. 1997. It is intriguing to see how much effort is expended on the dangerous trampling of the Charleston lawns and flowers when so little thought seems to have been given to trampling on Bloomsbury's intimate relationships ever since Michael Holroyd published his detailed biography of Lytton Strachey.

87. See Spalding, *Bell*; Marler, *Bell: Letters,* especially her letters to Roger Fry; Caws, *Women of Bloomsbury*, pp. 91–97.

88. Spalding, *Bell*, p. 299.

89. Afra Leckie, personal communication, 13 Feb. 1998.

90. See the illustration of the newly restored garden reproduced in Bell and Nicholson, *Charleston*, p. 146.

91. The three paintings described in this paragraph are now in private collections.

92. The unpublished letter (dated Mar. 6th [1960]) reads as follows: "My dear Nurse. It was very nice of you to write to me—I had only just heard through Mrs. Higgens [the cook] that you were leaving Firle which is of course very sad for us and everyone there. I quite see that you couldn't refuse such a new appointment and I hope you will be as successful there as you have been at Firle. Please keep my little paintings if you still like them—I am only too glad that they should have a home with someone who cares about painting. You did so much for me and for all

of us at different times. My husband seems to be much better and enjoys being in this warm climate where one sees the oranges and lemons growing outside one's window. With best wishes for success in your new work, Yours sincerely, Vanessa Bell."

93. D. Garnett, *Flowers*, p. 161.

94. *Ibid.*, p. 246.

95. Reproduced in A. Garnett, *Deceived with Kindness*, p. 91.

96. To Angelica Garnett, 27 Sept. 1960 (Tate Gallery Archives).

97. Virginia Woolf, *Letters*, vol. 3, no. 1743, p. 363.

98. *Ibid.*, vol. 1, no. 432, p. 349.

99. Spalding, *Grant*, p. 257.

Saler: Whigs and Surrealists

1. For the classic history of the intellectual "revolt against positivism," see H. Stuart Hughes, *Consciousness and Society* (New York, 1958).

2. Friedrich Nietzsche, "On the Uses and Disadvantages of History for Life," trans. R. J. Hollingdale, in *Untimely Meditations*, ed. Daniel Breazeale (Cambridge, 1997), pp. 59–60.

3. Henrik Ibsen, *Hedda Gabler* (New York, 1990 [1890]).

4. Max Weber, *The Protestant Ethic and the Spirit of Capitalism*, trans. Talcott Parsons (New York, 1958 [1921]).

5. A phrase based on Jennings's view, discussed below.

6. Walter Benjamin, *The Arcades Project*, trans. Howard Eiland and Kevin McLaughlin (Cambridge, Mass., 1999).

7. Among many such works, see Simon Schama, *Dead Certainties* (New York, 1992); and Hans Ulrich Gumbrecht, *In 1926* (Cambridge, Mass., 1997).

8. For another examination of *Pandaemonium*, see Kevin Robins and Frank Webster, "Science, Poetry and Utopia," *Science and Culture*, 1:1 (May 1987): 35–80.

9. Humphrey Jennings, letter of 28 July 1942, in Kevin Jackson, ed., *The Humphrey Jennings Film Reader* (Manchester, 1993), p. 60.

10. Humphrey Jennings, *Pandaemonium*, ed. Mary-Lou Jennings and Charles Madge (London, 1995 [1985]). In this essay I will be citing both that published edition (hereafter *Pandaemonium*) and the original manuscript (hereafter "Pms"), which was graciously provided to me by Kevin Jackson and Mary-Lou Legg (née Jennings).

11. Humphrey Jennings, "Day Report," 17 Aug. 1947, in Jackson, ed., *Humphrey Jennings Film Reader*, p. 111.

12. Kathleen Raine, "Humphrey Jennings," in Mary-Lou Jennings, ed., *Humphrey Jennings* (London, 1982), p. 51.

13. Michael Saler, *The Avant-Garde in Interwar England: Medieval Modernism and the London Underground* (New York, 1999). For an exceptional history of the English arts and crafts movement, see Peter Stansky, *Redesigning the World: William Morris, the 1880s, and the Arts and Crafts* (Princeton, 1985).

14. Humphrey Jennings, "Childhood," in M.-L. Jennings, ed., *Humphrey Jennings*, p. 6.

15. Humphrey Jennings, "The Iron Horse," in Jackson, ed., *Humphrey Jennings Film Reader*, p. 226.

16. I. A. Richards, *Science and Poetry* (London, 1935 [1928]).

17. J. P. Russo, *I. A. Richards* (Baltimore, 1989), p. 168.

18. *Ibid.*

19. *Ibid.*, p. 163.

20. Sigmund Freud, *Civilization and Its Discontents*, trans. Joan Riviere (New York, 1994 [1930]), p. 4.

21. Kevin Jackson, "Introduction," in *idem*, ed., *Humphrey Jennings Film Reader*, p. xiii.

22. Humphrey Jennings, "The English," *ibid.*, p. 243.

23. Humphrey Jennings, "Tableaux Parisiens," *ibid.*, p. 21.

24. *Pandaemonium*, p. xxxv.

25. David Mellor, "Sketch for an Historical Portrait of Humphrey Jennings," in M.-L. Jennings, ed., *Humphrey Jennings*, p. 66.

26. Charles Madge, "A Note on Images," *ibid.*, pp. 47–49.

27. *Pandaemonium*, p. xxxvi.

28. *Ibid.*, p. 38.

29. *Ibid.*, pp. xxxviii–xxxix.

30. Humphrey Jennings, letter of 15 June 1941, in Jackson, ed., *Humphrey Jennings Film Reader*, pp. 29–30.

31. *Pandaemonium*, pp. xxxviii–xxxix.

32. Charles Madge, "Editorial Tasks and Methods," *ibid.*, p. xvi.

33. Jacob Bronowski, "Recollections of Humphrey Jennings," *Twentieth Century*, 165:983 (Jan. 1959): 49.

34. M.-L. Jennings, ed., *Humphrey Jennings*, pp. 14–18.

35. Paul C. Ray, *The Surrealist Movement in England* (Ithaca, 1971), pp. 176–78.

36. Letter to *New Statesman*, 30 Jan. 1937, in M.-L. Jennings, ed., *Humphrey Jennings*, pp. 16–17.

37. Jeremy MacClancy, "Brief Encounter: The Meeting, in Mass-Observation, of British Surrealism and Popular Anthropology," *Journal of the Royal Anthropological Institute*, 1:3 (Sept. 1995): 495–512.

38. Humphrey Jennings and Charles Madge, *May the Twelfth* (London, 1937), pp. 14, 325, 337.

39. *Ibid.*, p. 22.

40. *Ibid.*, p. 84.

41. Susan Buck-Morss, *Dialectics of Seeing* (Cambridge, Mass., 1989), p. 73.

42. *Ibid.*

43. One vivid reference to the collective unconscious can be found in *Pandaemonium*, p. 292.

44. *Ibid.*, p. xxxv. The latter phrase calls to mind Walter Benjamin's famous description of surrealist juxtaposition as a "profane illumination."

45. *Ibid.*, p. xxxix.

46. *Ibid.*, p. 5.

47. *Ibid.*, p. xxxvi.
48. Pms, no. 894.
49. Pms, no. 274.
50. See, for example, *Pandaemonium*, pp. 6–7.
51. *Ibid.*, p. 16.
52. *Ibid.*, p. 5.
53. *Ibid.*, p. 107.
54. *Ibid.*, p. 298.
55. *Ibid.*, p. 324.
56. *Ibid.*, p. 344.
57. Pms, no. 653.
58. *Ibid.*, no. 962.
59. *Ibid.*, no. 963; see also Jackson, ed., *Humphrey Jennings Film Reader*, p. 241.
60. *Pandaemonium*, p. xxxix.
61. Humphrey Jennings, "Who Does That Remind You Of?" *ibid.*, pp. 230–31.
62. Humphrey Jennings, "The Poet Laureateship," *ibid.*, pp. 271–76.
63. *Ibid.*, p. 241.
64. *Ibid.*, pp. 279–80.
65. Humphrey Jennings, "Surrealism," *ibid.*, pp. 220–21.
66. *Ibid.*, p. 279.
67. *Ibid.*, p. 281.
68. Kevin Jackson, "Introduction," *ibid.*, p. xii.
69. Walter Benjamin, "Theses on the Philosophy of History," in *Illuminations*, ed. Hannah Arendt, trans. Harry Zohn (New York, 1969), p. 257.
70. Peter Stansky and William Abrahams, *London's Burning* (London and Stanford, 1994), pp. 71–125.
71. Humphrey Jennings, "The English," in Jackson, ed., *Humphrey Jennings Film Reader*, p. 243.
72. Humphrey Jennings, "A Family Portrait," in Jackson, ed., *Humphrey Jennings Film Reader*, p. 177.
73. Lindsay Anderson, "Only Connect: Some Aspects of the Work of Humphrey Jennings," in M.-L. Jennings, ed., *Humphrey Jennings*, p. 59.

Soffer: The Long Nineteenth Century of Conservative Thought

1. Harold Laski, *Daily Herald*, Oct. 24, 1931, quoted in Robert Dare's persuasive "Instinct and Organization: Intellectuals and British Labour After 1931," *Historical Journal*, 26 (1983): 685.

2. John Ramsden has argued convincingly in *The Age of Churchill and Eden, 1940–1957* (London, 1995), pp. 55–92, that the factors responsible for the Conservative party's defeat in 1945 included a deficit of newspaper opinion on the right; Churchill's unwillingness to provide for a postwar Conservative program as well as the misconduct of his campaign; the lack of Conservative responses to successful attacks by books on the left; the effective use of BBC broadcasts by the left; increasing public identification of Conservatives and vested or class interests; public

rejection of the old gang as responsible for wartime mismanagement; the weakness of Conservative party organization; and changed rules of voting that penalized Conservative constituencies.

3. John D. Fair and John A. Hutcheson, Jr., have made this argument very well in "British Conservatism in the Twentieth Century: An Emerging Ideological Tradition," *Albion*, 19 (Winter 1987): 549–78. See, too, Michael Freeden's monumental *Ideologies and Political Theory: A Conceptual Approach* (Oxford, 1998), part 3.

4. For a discussion of Seeley, see Reba N. Soffer, *Discipline and Power: The University, History and the Making of an English Elite, 1870–1930* (Stanford, 1994); and *eadem*, "History and Religion: J. R. Seeley and the Burden of History," in R. W. Davis and R. J. Helmstadter, eds., *Religion and Irreligion in Victorian Society* (London, 1992), pp. 133–50.

5. F. J. C. Hearnshaw, *Germany the Aggressor Throughout the Ages* (London, 1940).

6. See the Arthur Bryant Papers, the Liddell Hart Centre for Military Archives, King's College, London. Pamela Street, Bryant's secretary, further documents the frantic pace of her employer's life in her eulogistic *Arthur Bryant: Portrait of a Historian* (London, 1979).

7. F. J. C. Hearnshaw, *Prelude to 1937: Being a Sketch of the Critical Years A.D. 1931–1936* (London, 1937), p. v.

8. See the Arthur Bryant Papers (above, n. 6).

9. For the continuity of this theme see *Conservative Realism: New Essays in Conservatism*, ed. Kenneth Minogue (London, 1996).

10. Benjamin Disraeli, *Sybil* (1845). Iain Macleod and Angus Maude, eds., *One Nation: A Tory Approach to Social Problems* (London, 1950), with an approving foreword by R. A. Butler, was published by the Conservative Political Centre set up by Cuthbert Alport in 1945. The authors, who became the One Nation Group, included Richard Fort, Edward Heath, and Enoch Powell. The CPC became a major asset to the party in its propagation of Conservative ideas.

11. F. J. C. Hearnshaw, *Conservatism in England: An Analytical, Historical, and Political Survey* (London, 1933), p. 19, was based on lectures given at Ashridge College. See also *idem*, *A Survey of Socialism: Analytical, Historical and Critical* (London, 1928), p. 428.

12. F. J. C. Hearnshaw, "Europe in the Middle Ages," part 1, typescript in Fossy John Cobb Hearnshaw Papers, King's College Library, London, K/PP13/12, p. 25.

13. Anthony Eden, "Free Enterprise and State Power," Mar. 7, 1946, quoted in Peter Goldman, ed., *The New Conservatism: An Anthology of Post-war Thought* (London, 1955), p. 72; and Quintin Hogg, *The Case for Conservatism* (London, 1947), p. 11.

14. Hearnshaw, *Conservatism in England*, p. 304; Anthony Eden, "A Nation-Wide Property-Owning Democracy," speech at Conservative Party Conference, Blackpool, Oct. 3, 1946, in *New Conservativism*, pp. 76–78; Ramsden, *Age of Churchill*, p. 141.

15. Hearnshaw, *Survey of Socialism*, pp. 348, 362–64, 365.

16. *Ibid.*, pp. 392, 396, 399, 403.

17. *Ibid.*, pp. 344, 444.

18. F. J. C. Hearnshaw, "The Paradox of Unemployment: A Utopian Study" (1938), typescript in Hearnshaw Papers, K/PP13/16, pp. 10, 18, 104, 111, 113.

19. See George Behlmer, *Friends of the Family: The English Home and Its Guardians, 1850–1940* (Stanford, 1998), esp. pp. 22, 121.

20. Hearnshaw, *Prelude to 1937*, p. 175.

21. F. J. C. Hearnshaw, "Hugo Grotius," in *idem*, ed., *The Social and Political Ideas of Some Great Thinkers of the Sixteenth and Seventeenth Centuries* (Port Washington, 1967), p. 149; "Benjamin Disraeli, Earl of Beaconsfield," in *idem*, ed., *The Political Principles of Some Notable Prime Ministers of the Nineteenth Century* (London, 1936 [1926]), pp. 208, 228; *Conservatism in England*, p. 303; *Prelude to 1937*, p. 174.

22. Hearnshaw, *Conservatism in England*, p. 33.

23. F. J. C. Hearnshaw, "Edmund Burke," in *idem*, ed., *The Social and Political Ideas of Some Representative Thinkers of the Revolutionary Era* (London, 1931), p. 89; "Benjamin Disraeli," pp. 216–17.

24. Hearnshaw, *Conservatism in England*, p. 305; *idem*, *Democracy and the British Empire* (New York, 1920), p. 150.

25. F. J. C. Hearnshaw, *The Development of Political Ideas* (London, 1927), pp. 78–79.

26. F. J. C. Hearnshaw, *British Prime Ministers of the Eighteenth Century* (London, 1928), p. 76; "Edmund Burke," p. 99; "Benjamin Disraeli," pp. 219, 221; "Pathway to Permanent Peace," (1941?), typescript in Hearnshaw Papers, K/PP13/16, pp. 8, 70–71; *Conservatism in England*, p. 293.

27. Keith Feiling, *The Study of the Modern History of Great Britain, 1862–1946*, Inaugural Lecture as Chichele Professor of Modern History (Oxford, 1947), pp. 16, 19.

28. Keith Feiling, *A History of the Tory Party, 1640–1714* (Oxford, 1924), pp. 18, 61.

29. Feiling, *History*, p. 23; *idem*, *Sketches in Nineteenth-Century Biography* (London, 1930), pp. 48, 62, 104–5. See also *idem*, *The Second Tory Party, 1714–1832* (London, 1938), pp. 318–24.

30. Feiling, *Sketches*, pp. 97–98, 62, 116.

31. Keith Feiling, *Toryism: A Political Dialogue* (London, 1913), pp. 125, 126, 149; *idem*, *What Is Conservatism?* (London, 1930), pp. 19, 23; *Sketches*, p. 51.

32. Feiling, *Sketches*, pp. 176–77; *Second Tory Party*, pp. 2, 9; *History*, p. 493.

33. Keith Feiling, letter to Sir John Simon, 1931. Simon believed that the "*Real* issue of the election is not tariffs: it is national policy v. Socialism" (MS. Simon 68, fols. 142, 160, Bodleian Library, Oxford); Feiling, *Sketches*, p. 162.

34. Keith Feiling, letter to Geoffrey Dawson, Sept. 30, 1938 (MS Dawson 80, fol. 45, Bodleian Library); *idem*, *The Life of Neville Chamberlain* (London, 1970 [1946]), pp. 398–402; *idem*, *A History of England: From the Coming of the English to 1918* (London, 1950), p. 1120.

35. Arthur Bryant, *Stanley Baldwin: A Tribute* (London, 1937), pp. 88–89, 104.

36. Arthur Bryant, *King Charles II* (London, 1931), p. xii. In his preface (p. xi), Bryant acknowledged his great debt to Feiling's "brilliant" work in the period.

37. The full story is told in the Arthur Bryant Papers (above, n. 6). Andrew Roberts's "Patriotism: The Last Refuge of Sir Arthur Bryant," in his *Eminent Churchillians* (London, 1997), pp. 287–322, a searing and witty indictment of Bryant, is often careless in its use of facts and of the fuller text from which quotations are taken. Arthur Bryant, *Unfinished Victory* (London, 1940), pp. xiv, xx, 136–52; R. A. C. Parker, *Chamberlain and Appeasement: British Policy and the Coming of the Second World War* (New York, 1993), pp. 88, 266, 317–18.

38. Arthur Bryant, "The Painful Plough," taken from columns on Nov. 29, 1958, Aug. 19, 1961, and Oct. 3, 1963, in *The Lion and the Unicorn: A Historian's Testament* (New York, 1970), p. 265; *idem, The Pageant of England (1840–1940)* (New York, 1941 [publ. in England as *The English Saga (1840–1940)*]), pp. 311, 329.

39. Bryant, *King Charles II*, p. 144.

40. Arthur Bryant, "The Summer of Dunkirk," *Daily Sketch*, June 3–4, 1943: 72–73; *idem, The Spirit of Conservatism* (London, 1929), p. 7; "The Needs of Social Man" (Oct.–Nov. 1941) and "The Ultimate Evil" (Mar. 1948) in *Lion and the Unicorn*, pp. 115, 250.

41. Bryant, "Needs of Social Man," p. 116. For similar views see Eustace Percy, "The Conservative Attitude and Conservative Social Policy," in Percy et al., eds., *Conservatism and the Future* (London, 1935), pp. 10–15.

42. Bryant, "Needs of Social Man," p. 117.

43. Arthur Bryant, *The Spirit of England* (London, 1982), pp. 221–28.

44. Ian Gilmour and Mark Garnett, *Whatever Happened to the Tories? The Conservative Party Since 1945* (London, 1997), pp. vii, 385.

Leventhal: Essential Democracy

1. Stephen Tallents, *The Projection of Britain* (London, 1932), pp. 11–14.

2. Lindsay served as British ambassador from 1930 to 1939, following two earlier postings in Washington. An initial five-year appointment was extended first to March 1938, then to March 1939, and his retirement was subsequently postponed until after August 1939, when he was succeeded by Philip Kerr, Lord Lothian. Lindsay's American wife was a longtime friend of Eleanor Roosevelt's. The king shared Lord Halifax's concern that Lindsay, with "his long experience and great knowledge," should be on hand in Washington to help ensure the success of the royal visit for the sake of Anglo-American relations (Lord Halifax to Neville Chamberlain, 16 Nov. 1938, PRO FO 794/17/20).

3. It was the British Embassy in Washington rather than the Foreign Office that enforced adherence to this policy. Sir Robert Vansittart noted in February 1939: "The reason that we do not attempt propaganda in the USA is the firm and invincible opposition of the Embassy. This is an old bone of contention between us at the Foreign Office and Sir Ronald Lindsay and his predecessors" (Foreign Office Minute, 16 Feb. 1939, PRO FO 371/22827/A1143).

4. Sir Ronald Lindsay to Anthony Eden, 22 Mar. 1937, PRO FO 371/20651/A2378.

5. Vansittart told his Foreign Office colleagues: "It is a mistake to underestimate the *real* moral consternation and even horror with which the great majority of

Americans greeted Munich" (Foreign Office Minute, 16 Feb. 1939, PRO FO 371/21538/A5092).

6. Eden to Lindsay, 11 May 1937, Avon Papers, PRO FO 954/29/US/37/4; James W. Gerard to Franklin D. Roosevelt, 30 June 1939; FDR to Gerard, 6 July 1939, Franklin D. Roosevelt Library: Roosevelt Papers, President's Secretary's File (PSF): Diplomatic, box 32.

Although the visit was to attract enormous contemporary press coverage, it has been subsequently ignored by most historians. Several popular books have documented the Canadian tour, including G. Gordon Young, *Voyage of State* (London, 1939), and Keith V. Gordon, *North America Sees Our King and Queen* (London, 1939). A more recent retelling is Tom MacDonnell, *Daylight upon Magic: The Royal Tour of Canada, 1939* (Toronto, 1989). The first American article, by Philip L. Cantelon, "Greetin's, Cousin George," appeared in *American Heritage*, 19 (Dec. 1967): 6–11, 108–11. Based exclusively on American sources, primarily contemporary newspaper accounts, it was a nostalgic reconstruction aimed at a general readership. Two more scholarly articles have since been published: Benjamin D. Rhodes, "The British Royal Visit of 1939 and the 'Psychological Approach' to the United States," *Diplomatic History*, 2 (Spring 1978): 197–211; David Reynolds, "FDR's Foreign Policy and the British Royal Visit to the U.S.A., 1939," *The Historian*, 45 (Aug. 1983): 461–72.

7. Alexander Hardinge to F. H. Hoyer Millar, 22 May 1937, Royal Archives (RA) PS/GVI/PS 03400/003/02/02. Material in the Royal Archives has been made available with the gracious permission of Her Majesty Queen Elizabeth II.

8. Hoyer Millar to Hardinge, 20 May 1937, RA PS/GVI/PS 03400/003/02/01.

9. Lindsay to Eden, 11 May 1937, Avon Papers, PRO FO 954/29/US/37/5.

10. The possibility of international conflict continued to overshadow prospects for the visit to the end. According to Ambassador Kennedy, Chamberlain told the king early in May 1939 that "there was little likelihood of acute international trouble developing during his absence but that he would not venture an opinion as to what might happen after the time of the King's return": Joseph Kennedy to Cordell Hull and Sumner Welles, 6 May 1939, National Archives (NA) 841.001/George VI/473.

11. Quoted in Janet Adam Smith, *John Buchan* (London, 1965), p. 451. Also see John W. Wheeler-Bennett, *King George VI: His Life and Reign* (London, 1958), p. 372.

12. FDR to George VI, 17 Sept. 1938, RA PS/GVI/PS 03400/003/01/001.

13. George VI to FDR, 8 Oct. 1938, RA PS/GVI/PS 03400/003/01/004.

14. David Key to Hull, 20 Oct. 1938, NA 841.001/George VI/263. Before the official announcement was made, Hardinge promised to remind Tweedsmuir that "the time required for the visit to the USA is *additional* to the time promised for the Canadian tour and will not be deducted from it" (Hardinge to George VI, 5 Nov. 1938, RA PS/GVI/PS 03400/003/01/037).

15. George VI to FDR, 3 Nov. 1938, RA PS/GVI/PS 03400/03/01/016.

16. Lindsay to Sir Alexander Cadogan, 1 Nov. 1938, PRO FO 371/21548/A8828.

17. Grover Whalen to FDR, 10 Oct. 1938, NA 841.001/George VI/225.

18. Kennedy to Hull, 15 Oct. 1938, NA 841.001/George VI/259. Lindsay had

previously opposed any member of the royal family's opening the British exhibit at the New York World's Fair as politically inadvisable (Foreign Office Minute, 23 June 1938, PRO FO 371/21538/A5092).

19. Lindsay to Foreign Office, 25 Oct. 1938, PRO FO 371/21548/A8061. Also, Lindsay to Sir Launcelot Oliphant, 29 Dec. 1938, PRO FO 372/21548/A9777.

20. Lindsay to Cadogan, 1 Nov. 1938, PRO FO 371/21548/A8828. Cadogan expressed the Foreign Office view that the tour should begin with a visit to Washington, but also deprecated the idea of a drive through New York City. He agreed with Lindsay that a short inspection of the World's Fair could not be avoided (Cadogan to Hardinge, 22 Nov. 1938, RA PS/GVI/PS 03400/003/01/025; also Lindsay to Marvin McIntyre, 26 Oct. 1938, NA 841.001/George VI/267½).

21. FDR to George VI, 2 Nov. 1939, RA PS/GVI/PS 03400/003/01/015.

22. Lindsay to Cadogan, 22 Nov. 1938, PRO FO 371/21548/A9293.

23. Morgan consulted John W. Davis about the advisability of visiting only Washington and whether they could be adequately protected from "intrusion by Press or undesirable parties" (J. P. Morgan to John W. Davis, 2 Nov. 1938, RA PS/GVI/PS 03400/003/02/11). Davis, a Wall Street lawyer and a former ambassador to the Court of St. James's, recommended that the visit "should be brief and with as little hullabaloo along the way as possible" but anticipated great pressure for a stopover in New York (Davis to Morgan, 4 Nov. 1938, RA PS/GVI/PS 03400/003/02/12).

24. Hardinge to George VI, 5 Nov. 1938, RA PS/GVI/PS 03400/003/01/037.

25. Lindsay's memorandum on conversation with President Roosevelt, 6 Mar. 1939, PRO FO 800/324/26. Also see memorandum of conversation between Lindsay and Welles, NA 841.001/George VI/347½.

26. J. Balfour, Foreign Office Minute, 23 Mar. 1939, PRO FO 371/22800/54–56. Mackenzie King irritated the Foreign and Dominions offices by his relentless lobbying to be appointed as minister-in-attendance (W. L. Mackenzie King to Chamberlain, 14 Mar. 1939, PRO DO 121/65; Foreign Office Minute, 22–24 Mar. 1939, PRO FO 371/22800/A2138; Lindsay to Halifax, 10 Mar. 1939, PRO FO 800/324/23–29).

27. Lindsay to Cadogan, 16 Nov. 1938, RA PS/GVI/PS 03400/003/01/024.

28. Josef Israels II, "Selling George VI to the U.S.," *Scribner's Magazine*, 195 (Feb. 1939): 16–21. The king's late younger brother, John, had been an epileptic.

29. Ben Robertson, "King George Strives to Please," *Saturday Evening Post*, 211 (4 Feb. 1939): 5–7, 66–69.

30. Charles Peake to Eric Mieville, 2 Feb. 1939, PRO FO 371/22800/18.

31. John D. Moore to Hull, 22 Oct. 1938, NA 841.001/George VI/265. Moore was a member of the New York State Labor Relations Board.

32. Moore to George T. Summerlin, 28 Oct. 1938, NA 841.001/George VI/270. A New York woman complained to the secretary of state about the purported expenditure to entertain the royal visitors: "We do not respect them or the Government they represent and we object to being taxed that a few may bow the knee to the only enemy America ever had" (Catherine B. Baldwin to Hull, 18 May 1939, NA 841.001/George VI/527).

33. Extract from letter to Oliphant, 24 Mar. 1939, PRO FO 371/22800/209.
34. Lady Reading to Halifax, 16 Feb. 1939, PRO FO 371/22799/232.
35. Lord Cromer to Halifax, 1 Feb. 1939, PRO FO 371/22786/195–98. J. V. Perowne, in the accompanying Foreign Office minute (10 Feb. 1939), observed that it was "a pity that the visit could not have been confined to Washington and Hyde Park but that cannot be altered now" (PRO FO 371/22786/194).
36. Minute by Perowne, 19 May 1939, PRO FO 371/22800/270. Also see minute by Perowne, 10 Feb. 1939, PRO FO 371/22786/194.
37. Helen Woods to Lady Reading, 6 Feb. 1939, PRO FO 371/22799/233. Stella Reading told Halifax that her husband (Rufus Isaacs, Lord Reading) "found the moment one got as far as Chicago the strong feeling against British missions changed in favour of them" (Lady Reading to Halifax, 16 Feb. 1939, PRO FO 371/22799/232).
38. Cadogan to Hardinge, 17 Feb. 1939, PRO FO 371/22799/237. The issue was also raised by M. Phillips Price, who was told that an extension of the trip was impossible and that the Canadians were unwilling to lose more time from days devoted to Canada (R. A. Butler to M. Phillips Price, 19 Mar. 1939, PRO FO 371/22800/21–22).
39. Hardinge to Cadogan, 20 Feb. 1939, PRO FO 371/22799/239.
40. A. Beckett to Balfour, 6 Jan. 1939, PRO FO 371/22799/152.
41. Lindsay to Balfour, 11 Jan. 1939, PRO FO 371/22799/166.
42. Godfrey Haggard to Perowne, 31 Jan. 1939, PRO FO 371/22799/182–84. The king and queen did receive representatives of the English-Speaking Union and other Anglo-American societies at the British Embassy on 9 June.
43. Memorandum by Alan Lascelles, 8 Dec. 1938, RA PS/GVI/PS 03400/003/01/026; George VI to FDR, 8 Feb. 1939, RA PS/GVI/PS 03400/003/01/041; memorandum by Lindsay, 6 Mar. 1939, RA PS/GVI/PS 03400/003/01/044.
44. Memorandum of conversation between Lindsay and Welles, NA 841.001/George VI/339; Lindsay memorandum, 6 Mar. 1939, RA PS/GVI/PS 03400/003/01/044. Since the king could not evade a response to the president's toast at the White House dinner, Lindsay prepared a succinct speech, avoiding polysyllables and using only the simplest language (Lindsay to David Scott, 9 May 1939, PRO FO 371/22800/A3524). Welles was informed by the British Embassy that "because of the slowness with which the King speaks, it will take him about three minutes to deliver this speech" (Welles to FDR, 27 May 1939, NA 841.001/George VI/578A).
45. A Jewish woman from the Bronx offered to prepare gefilte fish, while a black chef who had once catered for Queen Marie of Romania volunteered his services to cook Southern-fried chicken and spoon cornbread (Franklin D. Roosevelt Library: Eleanor Roosevelt Papers, box 987).
46. Most of these requests were handled routinely by George Summerlin, chief of the Division of Protocol at the State Department. He was deputed to inform petitioners that Their Majesties did not accept gifts from private individuals during state visits and were able to meet only persons having official status.
47. Lascelles to Lindsay, 20 Mar. 1939, RA PS/GVI/PS 03400/003/01/046.
48. The humble hotdog, which proved to be the most enduring emblem of the

Hyde Park visit, was surprisingly controversial. Eleanor Roosevelt received a number of letters from meatpackers vying for the right to supply their products, from people who queried whether hotdogs might be indigestible for delicate royal stomachs, and even from some who insisted that the frankfurter was not truly American. One irate Southern woman admonished the First Lady for serving so plebeian a dish, claiming that it would dishonor the American people and cause the Queen Mother (*sic*) to swoon when she learned what her son was being fed. In fact the picnic menu also included roast turkey, perhaps more incontrovertibly patriotic.

49. Mackenzie King to FDR, 1 July 1939, Roosevelt Papers, PSF: Diplomatic, box 38.

50. *State Visit of Their Britannic Majesties*, June 1939, Roosevelt Papers, PSF: Diplomatic, box 38; Lindsay to Halifax, 16 June 1939, PRO FO 414/276/A4437. Also, Nicholas Murray Butler to FDR, 4 Apr. 1939, Roosevelt Papers, PSF: Diplomatic, box 32; Hull to Fiorello LaGuardia, 27 May 1939, NA 841.001/George VI/415.

51. Foreign Office Minute, 3 July 1939, PRO FO 371/22801/A4443.

52. Security concerns were paramount during the months before the royal visit. The commissioner of the Royal Canadian Mounted Police sought particulars from police throughout Canada about suspected troublemakers or mentally unstable individuals. In addition the head of Special Branch at Scotland Yard visited New York to confer with police officials as well as with J. Edgar Hoover. Particular attention was paid to the threat of Irish terrorist activity. John Garratt, a former IRA member, was interrogated by the NYPD and the Secret Service, and Sean Russell, reputed IRA chief of staff, was arrested in Detroit. A letter warning that "a desperat [*sic*] attempt will be made by the IRA to eliminate . . . the representative of tyranny [and that] bombs and machine guns will be directed from windows on the route of the march" may have been a hoax (PRO FO 371/22800/83–86; NA 841.001/George VI/308, 408½, 410½, 588). In addition, Alan Lomax, singer and collector of American folk songs, who was scheduled to perform cowboy ballads at the White House dinner, was denounced by his aunt to the FBI as "a radical communist" who might "do something violent during the visit" (J. Edgar Hoover to Hull, 9 June 1939, NA 841.001/George VI/677).

53. Haggard to Lindsay, 14 June 1939, RA PS/GVI/PS 03400/003/45/2.

54. Foreign Office Minute, 5 July 1939, PRO FO 371/22801/83. Lindsay furnished the foreign secretary with a comprehensive summary of American press reaction to the visit (Lindsay to Halifax, 20 June 1939, PRO FO 371/22801/A4441).

55. Frank S. Griffin to Eleanor Roosevelt, 24 May 1939, Eleanor Roosevelt Papers, box 987.

56. See, for example, Helen D. Fuhrmeister to Hull, 11 May 1939, NA 841.001/George VI/490.

57. George A. Hurley to FDR, 9 June 1939, NA 841.001/George VI/659.

58. Hoyer Millar to Summerlin, 10 Apr. 1939, NA 841.001/George VI/458. Royal servants were accommodated on the third floor of the White House, customarily occupied by Roosevelt grandchildren.

59. William C. Bullitt to FDR, 23 Mar. 1939, Roosevelt Papers, PSF: Diplomatic, box 38. Mrs. Roosevelt explained in her "My Day" column written on 8 June that the White House was expected to provide early morning tea, bread and butter, and water "which must be cooled but must not have ice in it."

60. Entry for 15 Apr. 1939, Harold L. Ickes, *The Secret Diary of Harold L. Ickes*, vol. 2 (New York, 1954), pp. 617–18. Ickes's informant seems to have been Eleanor Roosevelt.

61. Entry for 11 June 1939, *ibid.*, p. 650.

62. *Washington Post*, 10 June 1939.

63. *Baltimore Sun*, 8 June 1939.

64. *Washington Star*, 8 June 1939.

65. *New York Times*, 9 June 1939.

66. *Toronto Globe and Mail*, 8 June 1939. Hull's remarks were delivered at a 7 June press conference at which he declined to answer the question whether the visit indicated a definite pro-British attitude on the part of the administration.

67. This lengthy document, supplied by embassy officials at the request of the king, dealt with the achievements of the New Deal and flaws in the president's character, besides providing a twenty-page analysis of American foreign policy. Somewhat implausibly, the document suggested that Roosevelt was unlikely to seek a third term in office. The king particularly wished to know of any "special pitfalls to be avoided" (Foreign Office to Lindsay, 5 May 1939, PRO FO 371/22800/217; also minute and notes prepared for use and guidance of the king, 23 May 1939, PRO FO 371/2280/A3880).

68. George VI's notes, quoted in Wheeler-Bennett, *King George VI*, p. 391. Lascelles told Hardinge that the king was "particularly pleased with personal contact with President" (Lascelles to Hardinge, 12 June 1939, RA PS/GVI/PS 03400/003/01/053). Mackenzie King, gilding the lily, reported to Roosevelt that the king "found it easier to carry on a conversation with you than with almost any one" (Mackenzie King to Roosevelt, 1 July 1939, Roosevelt Papers, PSF: Diplomatic, box 38).

69. Lindsay to Halifax, 20 June 1939, PRO FO 371/22801/A4443.

70. Lindsay to Halifax, 12 June 1939, PRO FO 414/276/A4139.

71. Scott, Foreign Office Minute, 4 July 1939, PRO FO 371/22801/A4443.

Waters: Autobiography, Nostalgia, and Working-Class Selfhood

1. Peter Stansky and William Abrahams, *The Unknown Orwell* (London, 1981 [1972]), p. 244.

2. *Ibid.*, p. 247. See also Michael Pickering and Kevin Robins, "'A Revolutionary Materialist with a Leg Free': The Autobiographical Novels of Jack Common," in *The British Working-Class Novel in the Twentieth Century*, ed. Jeremy Hawthorn (London, 1984), pp. 77–92.

3. Quoted in Regenia Gagnier, *Subjectivities: A History of Self-Representation in Britain, 1832–1920* (New York, 1991), p. 145.

4. Kathryn Dodd and Philip Dodd, "From the East End to *EastEnders*: Repre-

sentations of the Working Class, 1890–1990," in *Come On Down? Popular Media Culture in Post-War Britain*, ed. Dominic Strinati and Stephen Wagg (London, 1992), pp. 122–25.

5. The classic study is David Vincent, *Bread, Knowledge and Freedom: A Study of Nineteenth-Century Working-Class Autobiography* (London, 1981).

6. Louis Heren, *Growing Up Poor in London*, introduction by Peter Hennessy (London, 1996 [1973]), p. 207.

7. Patrick Dunleavy, *The Politics of Mass Housing in Britain, 1945–1975* (Oxford, 1981), p. 1; John English, Ruth Madigan, and Peter Norman, *Slum Clearance: The Social and Administrative Context in England and Wales* (London, 1976), pp. 38–40.

8. *The Island: The Life and Death of an East London Community 1870–1970* (London, 1979), p. 4. For a good summary of these changes, see Joanna Bourke, *Working-Class Cultures in Britain 1890–1960: Gender, Class and Ethnicity* (London, 1994), chap. 5.

9. Quoted in Sheila Patterson, *Dark Strangers: A Sociological Study of the Absorption of a Recent West Indian Migrant Group in Brixton, South London* (London, 1963), p. 251. On nostalgia for the working-class past in these years, see Chris Waters, "Representations of Everyday Life: L. S. Lowry and the Landscape of Memory in Postwar Britain," *Representations*, 65 (Winter 1999): 121–50.

10. Jeremy Seabrook, *What Went Wrong? Why Hasn't Having More Made People Happier?* (New York, 1978), p. 226. On Seabrook's laments, see Huw Beynon, "Jeremy Seabrook and the British Working Class," *Socialist Register*, 1982: 285–301; Carolyn Steedman, *Landscape for a Good Woman: A Story of Two Lives* (London, 1986), pp. 5–16.

11. Raymond Williams, "Working-Class Culture," *Universities and Left Review*, 1 (Summer 1957): 29–32. For historical work on the origins of that culture, see Eric Hobsbawm, "The Formation of British Working-Class Culture," in his *Worlds of Labour: Further Studies in the History of Labour* (London, 1984), chap. 10; Gareth Stedman Jones, "Working-Class Culture and Working-Class Politics in London, 1870–1900: Notes on the Remaking of a Working Class," in his *Languages of Class: Studies in English Working-Class History 1832–1982* (Cambridge, 1983), chap. 4.

12. For a survey of these developments, see Stuart Laing, *Representations of Working-Class Life 1957–1964* (London, 1986). See also Richard Dyer et al., *Coronation Street* (London, 1981). The best of the sociological studies is Brian Jackson, *Working-Class Community* (Harmondsworth, 1968).

13. For an elaboration of these ideas, see Anthony Giddens, *Modernity and Self-Identity: Self and Society in the Late Modern Age* (London, 1991); Nikolas Rose, "Assembling the Modern Self," in *Rewriting the Self: Histories from the Renaissance to the Present*, ed. Roy Porter (London, 1997), chap. 14. For their importance in early postwar Britain, see Becky Conekin, Frank Mort, and Chris Waters, eds., "Introduction," in *Moments of Modernity: Reconstructing Britain 1945–1964* (London and New York, 1999), pp. 10–14.

14. Quoted in David Vincent, *Poor Citizens: The State and the Poor in Twentieth-Century Britain* (London, 1991), p. 111.

15. Steedman, *Landscape for a Good Woman*, p. 122.

16. These points are developed further by Carolyn Steedman, "State-Sponsored Autobiography," in Conekin et al., eds., *Moments of Modernity*, pp. 41–54.

17. For an elaboration, see Dennis Dworkin, *Cultural Marxism in Postwar Britain: History, the New Left, and the Origins of Cultural Studies* (Durham and London, 1997), esp. chap. 6; Raphael Samuel, "History Workshop, 1966–80," in *People's History and Socialist Theory*, ed. Samuel (London, 1981), pp. 410–17.

18. Ken Worpole, *Local Publishing and Local Culture: An Account of the Work of the Centerprise Publishing Project 1972–1977* (London, 1977), p. 9.

19. For the Peckham project, see Richard Gray, "'History Is What You Want to Say . . .': Publishing People's History—The Experience of Peckham People's History Group," *Oral History*, 12 (Autumn 1984): 38–39; for community publishing in general, see Dave Morley and Ken Worpole, eds., *The Republic of Letters: Working-Class Writing and Local Publishing* (London, 1982), pp. 2–7, 12–17; for an extensive bibliography of working-class reminiscences published in these years, see Bourke, *Working-Class Cultures*, pp. 244–49.

20. Doris M. Bailey, *Children of the Green* (London, 1981), p. 127.

21. Jo Barnes, *Arthur and Me: Docker's Children* (Bristol, 1979).

22. *Bridging the Years: A History of Trafford Park and Salford Docks As Remembered by Those Who Lived and Worked in the Area* (Salford, 1992), p. vii.

23. Edward Williams and Elizabeth Cass Williams, *Within a Mile of Dockland It Started* (Gibraltar, 1988), p. 1.

24. Joanna Bornat, "The Communities of Community Publishing," *Oral History*, 20 (Autumn 1992): 26.

25. Gagnier, *Subjectivities*, chap. 4.

26. For examples, see George N. Barnes, *From Workshop to War Cabinet* (New York, 1924); David Lowe, *From Pit to Parliament: The Story of the Early Life of James Keir Hardie* (London, 1923); *Henry Broadhurst, M.P.: The Story of His Life from a Stonemason's Bench to the Treasury Bench, Told by Himself*, 2d ed. (London, 1901). For a more recent study, see F. M. Leventhal, *Respectable Radical: George Howell and Victorian Working-Class Politics* (London and Cambridge, Mass., 1971).

27. Jack Cummins, *The Landlord Cometh* (Brighton, 1981), pp. 15–24.

28. Les Moss, *Live and Learn: A Life and Struggle for Progress* (Brighton, 1979), p. 117.

29. Wallace Brereton, *Salford Boy* (Salford, 1977), p. 28.

30. Arthur Potts, *Whitsters Lane: Recollections of Pendleton and the Manchester Cotton Trade* (Swinton, Manchester, 1985); Alice Cordelia Davis, *The Times of Our Lives* (London, 1983); Albert Paul, *Poverty-Hardship but Happiness: Those Were the Days 1903–1917* (Brighton, 1974).

31. Richard Heaton, *Salford, My Home Town* (Swinton, Manchester, 1982), p. 4.

32. The phrase is Bornat's: "Communities of Community Publishing," p. 26.

33. Paul, *Poverty-Hardship*, pp. 12, 13, 30, 63.

34. Cummins, *The Landlord Cometh*, inside back cover.

35. Paul, *Poverty-Hardship*, pp. 65–66; A. S. Jasper, *A Hoxton Childhood* (London, 1969), p. 126; Bert Healey, *Hard Times and Easy Terms* (Brighton, 1980), p. 153.

36. Barbara Vaughan, *Growing Up in Salford 1919–1928* (Swinton, Manchester, 1983), p. 3; Barnes, *Arthur and Me*, p. 35; Healey, *Hard Times*, p. 20.

37. *The Island*, p. 32.

38. For an elaboration of these themes, see Bornat, "Communities of Community Publishing," pp. 136–37; S. Dentith, "Contemporary Working-Class Autobiography: Politics of Form, Politics of Content," *Prose Studies*, 8 (Sept. 1985): 67–68.

39. Vincent, *Bread, Knowledge, and Freedom*, p. 197.

40. Gagnier, *Subjectivities*, p. 156.

41. Flora Thompson's three autobiographical novels have been published together as *Lark Rise to Candleford* (Harmondsworth, 1973 [1945]). The classic study of this tradition is Raymond Williams, *The Country and the City* (New York, 1973).

42. *Fred's People: Young Bristolians Speak Out* (Bristol, 1980).

43. Worpole, *Local Publishing*, pp. 21–22.

44. Jasper, *Hoxton Childhood*, p. 127.

45. Stephen Yeo, "The Politics of Community Publications," in *People's History*, ed. Samuel, pp. 45–46.

46. Moss, "Introduction" (n.p.).

47. Gray, "History Is What You Want to Say," p. 42.

48. Worpole, *Local Publishing*, p. 6.

49. See Ken Worpole, "A Ghostly Pavement: The Political Implications of Local Working-Class History," in *People's History*, ed. Samuel, esp. pp. 29–31.

50. Popular Memory Group, "Popular Memory: Theory, Politics, Method," in *Making Histories: Studies in History-Writing and Politics*, ed. Centre for Contemporary Cultural Studies (London, 1982), p. 227; Jerry White, "Beyond Autobiography," in *People's History*, ed. Samuel, pp. 33–37. For a discussion of these debates, see Dentith, "Contemporary Working-Class Autobiography," pp. 61–65; Alistair Thomson, Michael Frisch, and Paula Hamilton, "The Memory and History Debates: Some International Perspectives," *Oral History*, 22 (Autumn 1994): 33–34.

51. Alessandro Portelli, "The Peculiarities of Oral History," *History Workshop Journal*, 12 (Autumn 1981): 105; see also Marianne Debouzy, "In Search of Working-Class Memory: Some Questions and a Tentative Assessment," *History and Anthropology*, 2 (Oct. 1986): 277. On the epistemological status of experience, see Joan Scott, "The Evidence of Experience," *Critical Inquiry*, 17 (Summer 1991): 777.

52. Popular Memory Group, "Popular Memory," p. 229.

53. See Bourke, *Working-Class Cultures*, pp. 137–38.

54. Tom Woodin, "Recent British Community Histories," *Oral History*, 20 (Autumn 1992): 68.

55. For Blists Hill and Beamish, see, respectively, Bob West, "The Making of the English Working Past: A Critical View of the Ironbridge Gorge Museum," and Tony Bennett, "Museums and 'the People,'" both in *The Museum Time Machine: Putting Cultures on Display*, ed. Robert Lumley (London, 1988), pp. 36–85. For the Wigan Heritage Center, see Robert Hewison, *The Heritage Industry: Britain in a Climate of Decline* (London, 1987), pp. 15–24, 28.

56. William Feaver, *Catalogue of the Ashington Group: Paintings at Woodhorn Colliery Museum* (Ashington, 1991), p. 7.

57. Robert Roberts, *The Classic Slum: Salford Life in the First Quarter of the Century* (Harmondsworth, 1971), p. 10. Roberts's work is interesting insofar as it is half academic history, half popular reminiscence, written early in the period under consideration here. Unlike most of the popular autobiographies I discuss, it does not sentimentalize the past, even though in its preface it refers to a sense of loss shared by many workers.

Malchow: Nostalgia, "Heritage," and the London Antiques Trade

My thanks to James Smith Allen and Melanie Hall for their helpful comments on earlier drafts of this essay.

1. In 1980 the Antique Collectors' Club published the second edition of A. Ball's *Price Guide to Pot-Lids* (which first appeared in 1970).

2. David Lowenthal and Marcus Binney, eds., *Our Past Before Us: Why Do We Save It?* (London, 1981), pp. 13, 17. For contemporary critique see, for example, Michael Wood, "Nostalgia or Never: You Can't Go Home Again," *New Society*, 7 Nov. 1974: 343–46; Douglas Johnson, "Not What It Used to Be," *Vole*, 5 (1978): 42–43; Roy Strong's letter to *The Times*, 24 Sept. 1983, "Taking the Age out of Heritage"; or Peter Conrad, "Don't Look Back," *The Tatler*, Apr. 1986: 98–105, 148. E. R. Chamberlin's *Preserving the Past* (London, 1979) is the first sustained consideration of "one of the odder phenomena of our times—the current almost obsessional desire to preserve the past" (p. ix). In 1979 there was a symposium held in London on preservationism (see Lowenthal and Binney, eds., *Our Past Before Us*), and, drawing in part on British evidence, the American academic Fred Davis published his relevant study *Yearning for Yesterday: A Sociology of Nostalgia* (New York, 1979).

3. Raphael Samuel, *Theatres of Memory*, vol. 1, *Past and Present in Contemporary Culture* (London, 1994), pp. 205, 208, 281; Adrian Mellor, "Enterprise and Heritage in the Dock," in John Corner and Sylvia Harvey, eds., *Enterprise and Heritage: Crosscurrents of National Culture* (London, 1991), pp. 99–100.

4. *Antique Collector*, June 1975: 2; "Minutes of Evidence Taken Before the Select Committee on the Wealth Tax," *Reports, Accounts and Papers,* 1974/75, vol. 37, appendix 44, pp. 1392–98.

5. In Strong's own words, the exhibition was "an exercise in polemic" (*The Roy Strong Diaries 1967–1987* [London, 1997], p. 139).

6. Robert Hewison, *The Heritage Industry: Britain in a Climate of Decline* (London, 1987), p. 67.

7. Peter Mandler, "Nationalising the Country House," in Michael Hunter, ed., *Preserving the Past: The Rise of Heritage in Modern Britain* (Stroud, 1996), p. 113; Chamberlin, *Preserving the Past* (above, n. 2), p. 57.

8. See, especially, Patrick Wright, *On Living in an Old Country: The National Past in Contemporary Britain* (London, 1985); Hewison, *Heritage Industry*; and Corner and Harvey, eds., *Enterprise and Heritage*. See also David Lowenthal, *The Past Is a Foreign Country* (Cambridge, 1985) and *Possessed by the Past: The Heritage Crusade and the Spoils of History* (New York, 1996).

9. Samuel, *Theatres of Memory*, esp. pp. 242–73.

10. Stefan Methusias, "Why Do We Buy Old Furniture? Aspects of the Authentic Antique in Britain 1870–1910," *Art History*, 11:2 (June 1988): 233.

11. For general speculation about some aspects of this interconnectedness, see John Corner and Sylvia Harvey, "Mediating Tradition and Modernity: The Heritage/Enterprise Couplet," in *idem*, eds., *Enterprise and Heritage*, pp. 45–75.

12. Homeownership increased significantly in this period, from 43% of households in 1961 to 53% in 1971, 55% in 1979, and 62% in 1985 (Andrew Adonis and Steve Pollard, *A Class Act: The Myth of Britain's Classless Society* [London, 1998], p. 193).

13. Roy Strong, "Making Things As Good As Old," *The Times*, 16 Feb. 1985. See the pages of a late 1970's trade magazine like *Art and Antiques* (e.g., 27 Oct. 1979) for the plethora of advertisements by firms such as John Hancock Reproductions of Wimbledon, which offered a range of over a thousand imitation antiques—including Staffordshire pottery, horse brasses, toasting forks, warming pans, candlesticks, coal buckets, etc., etc.

14. Roy Strong, *Diaries*, p. 231.

15. In the late 1970's a number of London firms began to specialize in arranging bulk shipment to America. See, for example, an advertisement in *Art and Antiques* in 1979 for Stephen Morris shipping, Specialist Packers & Shippers of Antiques and Bric-A-Brac, "a young company well experienced. . . . We offer a special 'All-in' rate for full containers [up to 40 cubic feet]" (8 Sept. 1979).

16. John A. Walker, *Arts TV: A History of Arts Television in Britain* (London, 1993), p. 63.

17. This is not to deny, of course, that nostalgia has long played an important role on the left, and particularly among the late 1960's–early 1970's back-to-the-earth, small-is-beautiful counterculture.

18. For a recent example of scholarship that focuses on "how concrete and mundane actions in the everyday may themselves transform the abstract structures of polity and economy" (p. 4), see Leora Auslander, *Taste and Power: Furnishing Modern France* (Berkeley and Los Angeles, 1996).

19. Hewison, *Heritage Industry*, p. 101. Also see Wright, *On Living in an Old Country*, pp. 148–50. There were, of course, separate institutions (not within Heseltine's remit) for Scotland, Wales, and Northern Ireland, and these seem to have been less driven by consumer-market ideology in their operation.

20. Wright, *On Living in an Old Country*, pp. 39–42.

21. Though there was one fine piece—a state bed of ca. 1700 with Chinese embroidered hangings in pristine condition. Even this, as a "mothballed" item still in its packaging, was less a social document than a simple commodity.

22. Quoted by Robert Hewison, "Commerce and Culture," in Corner and Harvey, eds., *Enterprise and Heritage*, pp. 162–77.

23. Peter Mandler, *The Fall and Rise of the Stately Home* (New Haven, 1997), p. 411; Raphael Samuel, "Mrs. Thatcher's Return to Victorian Values," in *Proceedings of the British Academy*, 78 (1992): 14.

24. Samuel, "Mrs. Thatcher's Return," p. 18. Also see Davis, *Yearning for Yesterday*, pp. 11–15. For the suggestion that Thatcherism is best located in the interwar

era, see Stephen Evans, "Thatcher and the Victorians: A Suitable Case for Comparison?" *History*, 82 (1997): 601–20. On Thatcher's reading of Victorian values as middle-class values see Bernard Porter, "'Though Not an Historian Myself . . .': Margaret Thatcher and the Historians," *Twentieth-Century British History*, 5:2 (1994): 246–56.

25. Samuel, "Mrs. Thatcher's Return," p. 24.

26. Quoted in *Newsweek*, 27 Apr. 1992, p. 14 (and cited in Porter, "Though Not an Historian," p. 252); emphasis added.

27. *Antique Collector*, Feb. 1976: i.

28. One dealer claimed that by 1984 he had shipped 600 containers of antiques (each 40' x 8' x 8') to America ("Alec Simpson" [John H. Collins], *Smarty! The Lid off the Antique Trade* [Winscombe, 1984], pp. 79–80).

29. *Antique Collector*, Dec. 1976: i.

30. *Ibid.*, Dec. 1976: i; and June 1977: 1.

31. *Ibid.*, Sept. 1975: i.

32. Deborah Stratton, *Collecting in the 1970s* (London, 1975), pp. 5, 117. Stratton would subsequently (1982–83) also write a column, "Inside the Trade," for *Antique Collector*.

33. Chamberlin, *Preserving the Past* (above, n. 2), p. 70.

34. Stratton, *Collecting in the 1970s*, p. 7.

35. *Antique Collector*, Mar. 1979: 1.

36. *Art and Antiques*, 15 Dec. 1979: 3.

37. *Antique Collector*, Nov. 1981: advertisement.

38. Ronald Pearsall and Graham Webb, *Inside the Antique Trade* (Shaldon, Devon, 1974), p. 53.

39. *Sunday Times*, 12 June 1983: front page. At the 1985 Grosvenor House fair it was estimated that the value of goods on view exceeded £100 million (*ibid.*, 16 June 1985: 43).

40. *Antique Collector*, Aug. 1979: 1.

41. *The Times*, 10 Sept. 1980.

42. Julian Critchley, "Confessions of an Antique Collector," *Sunday Times*, 19 Feb. 1984: 10.

43. *Antique Collector*, Mar. 1983: 51.

44. Jeremy Cooper, *The Complete Guide to London's Antique Street Markets* (London, 1974), pp. 23, 81; Ronald Pearsall, *The Joy of Antiques* (Newton Abbot, 1988), p. 9.

45. Anna Shaw, "Off to Market," *Antique Collector*, July 1982: 8, 12.

46. Pearsall and Webb, *Inside the Antique Trade*, p. 28.

47. *Antique Collector*, Feb. 1982: 96.

48. *The Times*, 11 Feb. 1985. John H. Collins published *Smarty!* in 1984 under the pseudonym "Alec Simpson."

49. Noel Riley and Godfrey Golzen, *Running Your Own Antiques Business*, 2d ed. (London, 1986), p. 10. Methusias ("Why Do We Buy Old Furniture?" p. 243) estimates that, after the first great growth in the trade before the First World War, there were about two hundred London dealers.

50. While the trade was certainly not entirely a male preserve, men dominated the market—especially among the younger high-flyers. Older women were common as stallholders in some sections, like bijouterie.

51. Pearsall and Webb, *Inside the Antique Trade*, p. 31.

52. Arthur Negus, *A Life Among Antiques* (London, 1982), pp. 25–29.

53. *Antique Collector*, Mar. 1983: 95.

54. *Ibid.*, Jan. 1984: 67; July 1983: 83; Apr. 1982: 120.

55. Pearsall and Webb, *Inside the Antique Trade*, p. 113; Chamberlin, *Preserving the Past* (above, n. 2), p. 72; *Sunday Times*, 29 Nov. 1981: 18; "Alec Simpson" [John H. Collins] *Smarty!* p. 94.

56. Jeremy Cooper, *Dealing with Dealers: The Ins and Outs of the London Antiques Trade* (London, 1985), pp. 26, 38, 55, 60, 62, 127, 131, and *passim*.

57. Pearsall and Webb, *Inside the Antique Trade*, p. 115.

58. One interviewed dealer, himself gay, claimed that an exuberantly homosexual presence was most notable at the sociable fairs and markets; he thought the profession at the shop level, however, was "staid and unflamboyant, and though many dealers are gay, there is no especially sexual network."

59. John FitzMaurice Mills, in one of a series of articles for *Antique Collector* on how to spot unscrupulous misrepresentation and forgery, wrote of "the shadow world of antiques" (Feb. 1980: 43).

60. *Antique Collector*, Nov. 1982: 58.

61. *The Guardian*, 19 Mar. 1986: 19.

62. I have interviewed a number of dealers who, naturally, wish to remain anonymous. The picture drawn here is taken largely from their testimony, and especially confirms the prevalence of insurance and bankruptcy fraud in the early 1980's.

63. Strong, *Diaries*, p. 124.

64. Davis, *Yearning for Yesterday*, pp. 29, 34–35.

65. John Corner and Sylvia Harvey ("Mediating Tradition and Modernity," p. 57) question the association of the heritage movement with a sense of decline, a point reiterated by Kevin Walsh (*The Representation of the Past: Museums and Heritage in the Post-Modern World* [London, 1992], p. 4). For Ascherson's views, see his articles in *The Observer*, "Why 'Heritage' Is Right Wing" (8 Nov. 1987: 9), and "'Heritage' as Vulgar English Nationalism" (27 Nov. 1987: 9).

66. Methusias ("Why Do We Buy Old Furniture?" p. 244) discusses the substantial problem of fakes in the market before the First World War.

67. *The Independent on Sunday*, 5 July 1998: 10; emphasis added.

Index